ALSO BY PETER DALE SCOTT

The Politics of Escalation in Vietnam (1966, with Franz Schurmann and Reginald Zelnik)

The War Conspiracy (1972, 2008)

The Assassinations: Dallas and Beyond (1976, with Paul Hoch and Russell Stetler)

Crime and Cover-Up: The CIA, the Mafia, and the Dallas-Watergate Connection (1977)

The Iran-Contra Connection: Secret Teams and Covert Operations in the Reagan Era (1987, with Jonathan Marshall and Jane Hunter)

Coming to Jakarta: A Poem about Terror (1988, 1989, poetry)

Cocaine Politics: Drugs, Armies, and the CIA in Central America (1991, 1992, 1998, with Jonathan Marshall)

Listening to the Candle: A Poem on Impulse (1992, poetry)

Deep Politics and the Death of JFK (1993, 1996)

Crossing Borders (1994, poetry)

Deep Politics II: The New Revelations in Government Files, 1994–1995 (1994, 2007)

Minding the Darkness: A Poem for the Year 2000 (2000, poetry)

Drugs, Oil, and War: The United States in Afghanistan, Colombia, and Indochina (2003)

The Road to 9/11: Wealth, Empire, and the Future of America (2007)

The War Conspiracy: JFK, 9/11 and the Deep Politics of War (2008)

Mosaic Orpheus (2009, poetry)

American War Machine: Deep Politics, the CIA Global Drug Connection, and the Road to Afghanistan (2010, 2014)

Tilting Point (2012, poetry)

Oswald, Mexico, and Deep Politics (2013, formerly *Deep Politics II*)

The American Deep State

The American Deep State

*Wall Street, Big Oil, and
the Attack on U.S. Democracy*

PETER DALE SCOTT

ROWMAN & LITTLEFIELD

Lanham • Boulder • New York • London

Published by Rowman & Littlefield
A wholly owned subsidiary of The Rowman & Littlefield Publishing Group, Inc.
4501 Forbes Boulevard, Suite 200, Lanham, Maryland 20706
www.rowman.com

16 Carlisle Street, London W1D 3BT, United Kingdom

Copyright © 2015 by Peter Dale Scott

British Library Cataloguing in Publication Information Available

Library of Congress Cataloging-in-Publication Data

Scott, Peter Dale.
 The American deep state : Wall Street, big oil, and the attack on U.S. democracy / Peter Dale Scott.
    pages cm
 Includes bibliographical references and index.
  ISBN 978-1-4422-1424-8 (cloth : alk. paper) — ISBN 978-1-4422-1426-2 (electronic) 1. Elite (Social sciences)—United States. 2. Power (Social sciences)—United States. 3. Interest groups—United States. 4. Wall Street (New York, N.Y.) 5. Conspiracy—United States. 6. Democracy—United States. I. Title.
 HN90.E4S43 2015
 305.5'20973—dc23

                                                          2014029231

∞™ The paper used in this publication meets the minimum requirements of American National Standard for Information Sciences—Permanence of Paper for Printed Library Materials, ANSI/NISO Z39.48-1992.

Printed in the United States of America

Contents

Acknowledgments

I could never have finished this book without the generous assistance of three skilled editors: Mark Selden at Japan Focus, my French translator Maxime Chaix, and my wife Ronna Kabatznick. I also owe a great debt to the guidance and patience of my editors, Susan McEachern and Jehanne Schweitzer at Rowman & Littlefield, and to the many people who have offered me support, advice and criticism over the last few years. Among these I would particularly like to thank Daniel Ellsberg, Jonathan Marshall, Gary Aguilar, Paul Hoch, Brian Kabatznick, Rex Bradford, Jefferson Morley, David Talbot, and Karen Croft. For my thinking about the deep state in particular, I would like once again to acknowledge my general debt to Ola Tunander and Eric Wilson.

My thanks to Freeman Ng for his generous assistance and perseverance with the cover of this book. And my thanks to the copyeditor Naomi Mindlin who devoted so much labor to these pages, to my indexer PJ Heim, and to my longtime agent, Victoria Shoemaker.

My thanks and love to all my family and close friends who have suffered with me through these last four years.

My greatest debt of all can never be acknowledged enough or too often: to my wife Ronna Kabatznick, who has sustained me now for a quarter century, and given me the life I so cherish. I wish to say to her here, in the words of Hermann Hesse, "If I know what love is, it is because of you."

Note about the Cover Image

MANY PEOPLE ARE UNAWARE THAT ON THE MORNING OF 9/11, DURING THE attack on the Pentagon, the so-called "Doomsday plane," the E-4B, appeared briefly in the forbidden air space over the White House and the Capitol. (For CNN's account, which CNN soon took off the Internet, go to https://www.youtube.com/watch?v=4upVtXLJ3Ps.) The E-4B, a product of Continuity of Government (COG) planning, is a survivable mobile command post, based at Offutt AFB in Nebraska, for the National Command Authority (the President and Secretary of Defense, though neither were in it that day). Its purpose, to quote CNN, is "to keep the government running no matter what, even in the event of a nuclear war, the reason it was nicknamed the 'Doomsday plane' during the Cold War." Its presence on 9/11 has never been officially acknowledged or explained; unofficially it has been attributed to a war game scheduled for the same day. Metaphorically the E-4B flyover of the White House on 9/11 symbolizes the way COG plans (the so-called "Doomsday Project") on that day preempted constitutional authority, sending the President against his will to the E-4B's base at Offutt.

CHAPTER 1

The Doomsday Project, Deep Events, and the Shrinking of American Democracy

I know the capacity that is there to make tyranny total in America, and we must see to it that this agency [the National Security Agency] and all agencies that possess this technology operate within the law and under proper supervision, so that we never cross over that abyss. That is the abyss from which there is no return.

—Senator Frank Church (1975)

IN RECENT YEARS I HAVE BECOME MORE AND MORE CONCERNED WITH THE interactions between three important and alarming trends in recent American history. The first is America's increasing militarization, and above all its inclination, even obsession, to involve itself in needless and pernicious wars. (As former President Jimmy Carter has rightly noted, "The rest of the world, almost unanimously, looks at America as the No. 1 warmonger."[1]) The second, closely related, is the progressive shrinking of public politics and the rule of law as they are subordinated, even domestically, to the requirements of covert U.S. operations abroad.

The third, also closely related, is the important and increasingly deleterious impact on American history of what I have called deep events: events, like the JFK assassination, the Watergate break-in, or 9/11, which repeatedly involve lawbreaking or violence, are mysterious to begin with, are embedded in ongoing covert processes, have consequences that enlarge covert government, and are subsequently covered up by systematic falsifications in media and internal government records.

One factor linking Dallas, Watergate, the 1980 "October Surprise" plot to prevent Carter's reelection, Iran-Contra, and 9/11 has been the background involvement in all these deep events of personnel from America's highest-level emergency planning, that is, Continuity of Government (COG) planning, known inside the Pentagon as "the Doomsday Project." The implementation of COG plans on 9/11 was the culmination of decades of such planning, and has resulted in the permanent militarization of the domestic United States,

1

and the imposition at home of institutions and processes designed for domination abroad.

Writing about these deep events as they occurred over the decades, I have been interested in the interrelations among them. It is now possible to show how each was related both to those preceding it, and those which followed.

In this chapter, I would like to go still further, and propose a framework to analyze the ongoing forces underlying all of the most important deep events, and how they have contributed to the political ascendance of what used to be called the "military-industrial complex." I hope to describe certain impersonal governing laws that determine the sociodynamics of all large-scale societies (often called empires) that deploy their surplus of power to expand beyond their own borders and force their will on other peoples. This process of expansion generates predictable trends of behavior in the institutions of all such societies, and also in the individuals competing for advancement in those institutions. In America it has converted the military-industrial complex from a threat at the margins of the established civil order, to a pervasive force dominating that order.

With this framework I hope to persuade readers that in some respects our recent history is simpler than it appears on the surface and in the media. Our society, by its very economic successes and consequent expansion, has been breeding impersonal forces both outside and within itself that are changing it from a bottom-up elective democracy into a top-down empire. And among these forces are those that produce deep events.

I am far from alone in seeing this degradation of America's policies and political processes. A similar pattern, reflecting the degradation of earlier empires, was described at length by the late Chalmers Johnson:

> The evidence is building up that in the decade following the end of the Cold War, the United States largely abandoned a reliance on diplomacy, economic aid, international law, and multilateral institutions in carrying out its foreign policies and resorted much of the time to bluster, military force, and financial manipulation.[2]

But my analysis goes beyond that of Johnson, Kevin Phillips, Andrew Bacevich, and other analysts, in proposing that three major deep events—Dallas, Watergate, and 9/11—were not just part of this degradation of American democracy, but played a significant role in shaping it.

As authors like Michael Lind have observed, for a long time there have been two prevailing and different political cultures in America, underlying political differences in the American public, and even dividing different sectors of the American government.[3] One culture is predominantly egalitarian and democratic, working for the legal consolidation of human rights both at home and abroad. The other, less recognized but with deep historical roots, prioritizes and teaches the use of repressive violence against both domestic and Third World populations to maintain "order."

To some extent these two mindsets are found in all societies. They correspond to two different and opposing modes of power and governance that were defined by Hannah Arendt as "persuasion through arguments" versus "coercion by force." Arendt, following Thucydides, traced these to "the common Greek way of handling domestic affairs, which was persuasion (πείθειν), as well as the common way of handling foreign affairs, which was force and violence (βία)."[4] In another essay, she wrote that "violence and power [i.e., persuasive power] are not the same. . . . Power and violence are opposites; where the one rules absolutely, the other is absent."[5]

Arendt's defense of persuasive power as the norm for an open constitutional society can be contrasted with the defense by Harvard Professor Samuel P. Huntington of top-down, coercive, or dark power as a prerequisite for social cohesion. The coercive power extolled by Huntington was antithetical to that of persuasion and openness: in his words, "Power remains strong when it remains in the dark; exposed to the sunlight it begins to evaporate."[6]

Arendt admired the American Revolution for having created a constitution to ensure the rule of politics by openness and persuasion. Huntington in contrast advised the Botha government of white South Africa on how to set up a powerful state security apparatus outside public control. We can say that Arendt was a theorist of constitutional power, and Huntington, of nonconstitutional power. Power "in the dark" is the essence of what I, borrowing in 2007 a term from Turkey, meant by the deep state: a power not derived from the constitution but outside and above it, "more powerful than the public state."[7] In 2013 the return of the military to power in Egypt, together with the revelations about NSA surveillance by Edward Snowden, gave currency to the notion of a deep state, which a *New York Times* op-ed article defined as "a hard-to-perceive level of government or super-control that exists regardless of elections and that may thwart popular movements or radical change."[8] Starting in chapter 2, I intend to expand on this definition.

Writing amid the protests and riots of the 1960s, both Huntington and Arendt feared that traditional authority was at risk, threatened (in Arendt's eyes) by the contemporary "loss of tradition and of religion." A half century later, I would argue that a far greater danger to social equilibrium comes now from the deep state, allied with those on the right who invoke authority in the name of security, tradition, and religion. With America's huge expansion into the enterprise of covertly dominating and exploiting the rest of the world, the open processes of persuasion, which have been America's traditional ideal for handling domestic affairs, have been increasingly subordinated to top-down violence.

In terms of this book, the bottom-upward processes of democracy have been increasingly supplanted by the top-downward processes of the deep state. The deeper strain in history, I would like to believe, is in the opposite direction: the ultimate diminution of violence by the forces of persuasion. Tsarist Russia became an anachronism waiting to collapse from its lack of popular roots. I would wish a better future for America.[9]

The current tilt toward top-down violent or repressive power is defended rhetorically as a means to preserve security and social stability, but in fact it threatens it. As Kevin Phillips and others have demonstrated, empires built on violent or repressive power tend to rise and then fall, often with surprising rapidity.[10] Underlying the discussion in this chapter is the thesis that repressive power is unstable, creating dialectical forces both within and outside its system. Externally, repressive power helps create its own enemies, as happened with Britain (in India), France (in Indochina), and Russia (in Eastern Europe).

THE SOCIODYNAMICS OF REPRESSIVE POWER IN LARGE-SCALE SOCIETIES

But more dangerous and destabilizing has been the conversion of those empires themselves into hubristic mechanisms of war. The fall of Periclean Athens, which inspired Thucydides's reflections, is a case in point. Thucydides described how Athens was undone by the overreaching greed (*pleonexia*) of its unnecessary Sicilian expedition, a folly presaging America's follies in Vietnam and Iraq. Thucydides attributed the rise of this folly to the rapid change in Athens after the death of Pericles, and in particular to the rise of a rapacious oligarchy.[11] Paul Kennedy, Kevin Phillips, and Chalmers Johnson have described the recreation of this process in the Roman, Spanish, Portuguese, Dutch, and British empires.[12] Its recurrence again in recent American history corroborates that there is a self-propelling dynamic of power that becomes repressive.

It is useful to be reminded of the historical division between two cultures in America, which both underlay and predated the Civil War.[13] But these two cultures have evolved and been reinforced by many factors. For example urbanization in America's South and West worked for most of the twentieth century to meld the two cultures, but after about 1980 the increasing disparity of wealth in America tended to separate them to an extent recalling the Gilded Age of the nineteenth century.

More importantly, postwar U.S. history has seen the institutions of domestic self-government steadily displaced by an array of new institutions, like the CIA and Pentagon, adapted first to the repressive dominance and control of foreign populations abroad, and now increasingly to dominance domestically. The manipulative ethos of this repressive bureaucracy promotes and corrupts those who, in order to be promoted, internalize the culture of repressive dominance into a mindset.

The egalitarian mindset is widely shared among Americans. But Washington today is securely in the hands of the global repressive dominance mindset, and a deepening of the military-industrial complex into what in my most recent book I call the "American war machine." This transformation of America represents a major change in our society. When Eisenhower warned against the military-industrial complex in 1961, it was still a minority element in our political economy. Today it finances and dominates both parties, and indeed is now also financing threats to both parties from the right, as well as dominating our international policy. As a result, liberal Republicans are as scarce in the Republican Party today as Goldwater Republicans were scarce in that party back in 1960.

That change has been achieved partly by money, but partly as a result of deep events like the JFK assassination, the Watergate break-in, and 9/11. As a rule, each of these deep events is attributed by our government and media to marginal outsiders, like Lee Harvey Oswald, or the nineteen alleged plane hijackers.

I have long been skeptical of these "lone nut" explanations, but recently my skepticism has advanced to another level. My research over four decades points to the conclusion that each of these deep events

1. was carried out, at least in part, by individuals in and out of government who shared and sought to promote this repressive mindset;
2. enhanced (at least in the long run) the power of the repressive mindset within the U.S. government; and
3. formed another stage in a continuous narrative whose result has been a transformation of America into a social system dominated from above, rather than governed from below.

Please note that here I am talking about the *result* of this continuous narrative, not about its *purpose*. In saying that these deep events have contributed collectively to a major change in American society, I am not attributing them all to a single manipulative "secret team." Rather I see them as flowing from the workings of repressive power itself, which (as history has shown many times) transforms both societies with surplus power and also the individuals exercising that surplus power.

We are conditioned to think that the open institutions of American governance could not possibly provide a milieu for plots like 9/11 against public order. But since World War II covert U.S. agencies like the CIA have helped create an alternative world where power is exercised with minimal oversight, often at odds with public agencies' proclaimed policy objectives of law and order, and often in conjunction with lawless and even criminal foreign and domestic elements.

The expansion of this covert world has occurred principally in Asia. There covert U.S. decisions were made to build up drug-financed armies in Burma, Thailand, and Laos, in a series of aggressive actions that by the 1960s involved America in a hot Indochina War. This war, like the related wars that ensued later in Kuwait, Iraq, and Afghanistan, was initiated by America for a mix of geostrategic and economic reasons—above all the desire to establish a dominant U.S. presence in an important region of petroleum reserves.

One country affected by all these Asian wars has been the United States itself. Its expansive forces, backed by powerful interest groups, are now out of control, as our managers, like other empire managers before them, have "come to believe that there is nowhere within their domain—in our case, nowhere on earth—in which their presence is not crucial."[14]

To illustrate this loss of control, let us look for a moment at a milieu that I believe to have been an important factor in at least some of America's major domestic deep events: the CIA's ongoing interactions with the global drug connection.

UNACCOUNTABLE POWER: THE CIA AND THE RETURN OF THE GLOBAL DRUG CONNECTION

Since World War II the CIA has made systematic use of drug trafficking forces to increase its covert influence—first in Thailand and Burma, then in Laos and Vietnam, and most recently in Afghanistan.[15] With America's expansion overseas, we have seen more and more covert programs and agencies, all using drug traffickers to different and opposing ends.

In 2004 *Time* and *USA Today* ran major stories about two of the chief Afghan drug traffickers, Haji Juma Khan and Haji Bashir Noorzai, alleging that each was supporting al-Qaeda, and that Khan in particular "has helped al-Qaeda establish a smuggling network that is peddling Afghan heroin to buyers across the Middle East, Asia and Europe."[16] Later it was revealed that both traffickers were simultaneously CIA assets, and that Khan in particular was "paid a large amount of cash by the United States," even while he was reportedly helping al-Qaeda to establish smuggling networks.[17]

There is no longer anything surprising in the news that large U.S. payments were made to a drug trafficker who was himself funding the Taliban and al-Qaeda. The arrangement is no more bizarre than the CIA's performance during the U.S. "war on drugs" in Venezuela in the 1990s, when the CIA first set up an anti-drug unit in Venezuela, and then helped its chief, Gen. Ramon Guillén Davila, smuggle at least one ton of pure cocaine into Miami International Airport.[18]

It would be easy to conclude from these reports that the CIA and Pentagon intentionally use drugs to help finance the enemy networks that justify their overseas operations. Yet I doubt that such a cynical Machiavellian objective is ever consciously voiced by those responsible in Washington.

More likely, it is an inevitable consequence of the U.S. repressive style of conducting covert operations. Great emphasis is put on recruiting covert assets; and in unstable areas with weak governance, drug traffickers with their own ample funds and repressive networks are the most obvious candidates for recruitment by the CIA. The traffickers in turn are happy to become U.S. assets, because this status affords them at least a temporary immunity from U.S. prosecution.[19]

In a nutshell: I am describing a development that is not so much intentional, as a consequence of repressive dynamics. A related example would be the CIA's recurring use of double agents, again for the reason just suggested. In the 1998 bombing of the U.S. Embassy in Kenya, we shall see that the chief planner was a double agent, Ali Mohamed, who surveyed the Embassy and reported to Osama bin Laden in 1993, just months after the FBI had told the Royal Canadian Mounted Police (RCMP) to release him from detention.[20] In the Mumbai terrorist attack of 2008, the scene was initially surveyed for the attackers by a DEA double agent, David Headley (alias Daood Sayed Gilani) whom "U.S. authorities sent . . . to work for them in Pakistan . . . despite a warning that he sympathized with radical Islamic groups."[21]

The central point is that expansion beyond a nation's borders engenders a pattern of repressive power with predictable results—results that transcend the conscious intentions of anyone within that repressive power system. Newly formed and ill-supervised agencies spawn contradictory policies abroad, the net effect of which is usually both expansive and deleterious—not just to the targeted nation but also to America.

This is especially true of covert agencies, whose practice of secrecy means that controversial policies proliferate without either coordination or review. Since 1945, Asia in particular has been the chief area where the CIA has ignored or overridden the policy directives of the State Department. As I document in *American War Machine*, CIA interventions in Asia, especially those that escalated into the Laotian, Vietnam, and Afghan wars, fostered an ongoing global CIA drug connection, or what I have called elsewhere a "dark quadrant of unaccountable power."

This drug connection, richly endowed with huge resources and its own resources of illegal violence, has a major stake in both American interventions and, above all, unwinnable wars to aggravate the conditions of regional lawlessness that are needed for drug trafficking. Thus it makes perfect sense that the global drug connection has been an ongoing factor in the creation of an overseas American empire that most U.S. citizens never asked for. More specifically, the dark quadrant has contributed to all the major deep events—including Dallas, Watergate, and 9/11, that have helped militarize America and overshadow its public institutions.[22]

"CONTINUITY OF GOVERNMENT" (COG)
AND THE MILITARY OCCUPATION OF AMERICA

I have said that, underlying the surface of America's major deep events, there has been a pattern of conflict between two mindsets—that of openness and that of repressive dominance—dating back to the Civil War and the Indian wars of the mid-nineteenth century (and before that to the American Revolution).[23] But it would be wrong to conclude from this ongoing pattern of conflict that there is nothing new in our current situation. On the contrary, America is in the midst of a new crisis arising from this very old antagonism.

Since World War II, secrecy has been used to accumulate new covert bureaucratic powers under the guise of emergency planning for disasters, planning known inside and outside the government as the "Doomsday Project." Known more recently (and misleadingly) as "Continuity of Government" (COG) planning, the Doomsday Project, under the guiding hands in the 1980s of Oliver North, Donald Rumsfeld, Dick Cheney, and others, on 9/11 became the vehicle for a significant change of government. The extreme repressive powers accumulated under the guise of the Doomsday Project were first developed to control the rest of the world. Now, to an unprecedented extent, America itself is being treated as an occupied territory.

These plans, originally concerned with decapitation of the U.S. government after a nuclear attack, were progressively reshaped to deal with the problem of civil disobedience generally, and specifically American public opinion's resistance to foreign wars. Indeed COG plans were adapted in the Reagan era to treat the American people as a kind of enemy. As Oliver North told the Iran-Contra Select Committees, "We didn't lose the war in Vietnam, we lost the war right here in this city."[24] Thus the Doomsday Project picked up and expanded the Army's Operation Garden Plot plans to deal with anti-war demonstrations and urban rioting, which had resulted after the Martin Luther King, Jr. assassination in the creation of the Pentagon's so-called "domestic war room," the Directorate of Civil Disturbance and Planning Operations. The COG planners also incorporated earlier Justice Department plans for a system of detention centers to house the thousands of known dissidents it had listed to be picked up immediately in an emergency.[25]

The result of this COG planning was the package of repressive mechanisms (which I will discuss in chapter 3 under their official name of "continuity of government" or COG plans), that was prepared over two decades by an elite

COG planning group, and then implemented on 9/11. The package included 1) warrantless surveillance (as has since been confirmed by the Snowden revelations), 2) warrantless detention (including unprecedented abridgments of the right to *habeas corpus*), and 3) unprecedented steps toward the militarization of domestic security enforcement and shrinking of the *posse comitatus* acts.

One recent development, for example, has been the permanent deployment in the United States since 2008 of a U.S. Army Brigade Combat Team. Part of its dedicated assignment is to be "called upon to help with civil unrest and crowd control."[26] Many people seem to be unaware that Americans, together with this Brigade, have lived since 2002 under a U.S. Army Command called NORTHCOM.[27]

The brigade is likely to remain, as a symbol of our militarized homeland security, until Congress fulfills its obligations under the National Emergencies Act, and hopefully terminates our thirteen-year national emergency.

POSTSCRIPT

The following chapters represent successive efforts to define a system that is essentially as inchoate and yet powerful as a weather system—the American deep state. From diverse perspectives, and with occasional corroborative repetitions, I shall try to describe the presence of a transnational dark hole at the center of our present diverse political predicaments.

It is clear that from time to time dark forces intervene to redirect American policies, such as Kennedy's announced decision in 1963 to start withdrawing troops from Vietnam, or 9/11, which launched the global terror war.[28] What is much more difficult to establish is that these interventions have anything in common. To investigate this possibility, one must look outside the publicly available archival records we are trained in universities to work with.

I shall argue that underlying the accessible institutions and records of the public state is a deeper, only partially acknowledged and recorded system, the deep state. Central to the latter are various agencies that have been established outside the scrutiny of Congress and the public, such as the CIA, the NSA, and since 1980 the Joint Special Operations Command (JSOC). On paper the CIA was created in 1947 by a Congressional statute, but in reality it was designed and pressed into being on a reluctant president by bankers and lawyers like Allen Dulles on Wall Street. I show in chapter 2, where I describe the deep state system in the context of Wall Street and big oil.

In chapter 3 I report how the under-reported Doomsday Project, COG plans that were implemented on 9/11, helped subordinate the U.S. Constitution to the various emergency procedures just described in chapter 1—procedures that in 2014 are still in place.

Chapters 4 to 7 look at falsifications in authorized accounts of the so-called "war on terror"—a campaign that has been invoked to justify these emergency COG procedures. I discuss how the "war" has masked the protection provided by key figures in the U.S., Saudi, and Qatari governments to key members of al-Qaeda, from 1990 until even after 9/11. More specifically, chapter 7 looks at hidden motives for the U.S. Terror War waged since 9/11.

Chapter 8 shows how deep powers took their toll of successive American Presidents since 1961, leading to the case—developed in chapter 9—that deep events like 9/11, and before it the Kennedy assassination and Watergate, are only apparently external intrusions on to American history. As shown in chapter 9, on a deeper level they can be seen as a central and structural part of the American deep state's history, linked, for example, because of the recurring role in each event of the emergency communications network set up by what the Pentagon called the Doomsday Project.

In Chapter 10 we return to the deep state itself, reprising old material in the light of the Saudi and other connections described in chapters 4 to 9. This leads to a major new claim, that funds from kickbacks on major long-term arms sales to Saudi Arabia "are the common denominator in all of the major structural deep events (SDEs) that have afflicted America since . . . 1976." These deep events include both Iran-Contra and 9/11.

To better understand the current attack on American democracy, chapters 11 and 12 describe the earliest origins of COG planning, from the Red Scare of 1919, the sometimes illegal surveillance by J. Edgar Hoover, the state of emergency proclaimed by Truman in the Korean War, to the short-lived Huston Plan of 1970 that was rejected as unconstitutional by Nixon's Attorney-General John Mitchell.

Finally I join with those who assess the decay of the so-called Pax Americana into ever widening arms build-ups and military violence, in the light of the very similar decay a century ago of the so-called Pax Britannica. We need to rescind policies that are as visibly detrimental to America and the world today as they were to Britain then. The problem is that American institutions are again in the grip of a collective mania, as they were in the Palmer raids of 1919 and the McCarthy persecutions of the early 1950s. People outside government must work for a redirection of the U.S. government away from mania and illegality, like the awakening that ended the McCarthy era. But to regain control of their politics, Americans must learn to understand and cope with the dark forces of the deep state.

America, I try to suggest at the end, has like Britain far more to contribute to the world than violent power.

CHAPTER 2

The Deep State, the Wall Street Overworld, and Big Oil

I hate to say that big oil is bigger than the United States Government; but its favored treatment at the hands of our government certainly leads to that conclusion.

—Connecticut Attorney General Robert. K. Killian[1]

In some of the faraway countries where it did business . . . Exxon's sway over local politics and security was greater than that of the United States embassy.[2]

IN THE LAST DECADE IT HAS BECOME MORE AND MORE OBVIOUS THAT WE have in America today what the journalists Dana Priest and William Arkin have called

two governments: the one its citizens were familiar with, operated more or less in the open: the other a parallel top secret government whose parts had mushroomed in less than a decade into a gigantic, sprawling universe of its own, visible to only a carefully vetted cadre—and its entirety . . . visible only to God.[3]

And in 2013, particularly after the military return to power in Egypt, more and more authors referred to this second level as America's "deep state."[4] Here for example is the Republican analyst Mike Lofgren:

There is the visible government situated around the Mall in Washington, and then there is another, more shadowy, more indefinable government that is not explained in Civics 101 or observable to tourists at the White House or the Capitol. The former is traditional Washington partisan politics: the tip of the iceberg that a public watching C-SPAN sees daily and which is theoretically controllable via elections. The subsurface part of the iceberg I shall call the Deep State, which operates according to its own compass heading regardless of who is formally in power.[5]

The political activities of the deep state are the chief source and milieu of what I have elsewhere called "deep politics": "all those political practices and arrangements, deliberate or not, which are usually repressed rather than acknowledged."[6] Others, like Tom Hayden, call the deep state a "state within the state," and suggest it may be responsible for the failure of the Obama administration to follow the policy guidelines of the President's speeches.[7]

We can see an antecedent to the notion of a deep state in Henry Fairlie's definition of a prevailing establishment in Great Britain: "the whole matrix of official and social relations within which power is exercised."[8] A more relevant antecedent was Wright Mills's notion of a tripartite American power elite, composed of corporate executives, the military establishment, and a "political directorate."[9] Both concepts are relevant, but Fairlie's establishment was more of a restraining than an enabling force; while Mills's power elite (combining both state and deep state elements), was focused conversely on those with more open and active managerial roles. Mills himself believed, as he wrote in 1958, that "much of what was once called 'the invisible government' is now part of the quite visible government."[10] This was just six years before the first major exposure of how powerful the invisible government of the CIA had become.[11]

This expansion of a two-level or dual state has been paralleled by two other dualities: the increasing resolution of American society into two classes—the "one percent" and the "ninety-nine percent"—and the bifurcation of the U.S. economy into two aspects: the domestic, still subject to some governmental regulation and taxation, and the international, relatively free from governmental controls.[12] All three developments have affected and intensified each other—particularly since the Reagan Revolution of 1980, which saw American inequality of wealth cease to diminish and begin to increase.[13] Thus for example I shall describe how Wall Street—the incarnation of the "one percent"—played a significant role in creating the CIA after World War II, and how three decades later the CIA and big oil played a significant role in realigning American politics for the Reagan Revolution.

In earlier books I have given versions of this America-centered account of America's shift into empire and a deep state. But another factor to be mentioned is the shift of global history toward an increasingly global society dominated by a few emergent superpowers. This trend was accelerated after the Industrial Revolution by new technologies of transport, from the railroad in the nineteenth century to the jet plane and space travel in the twentieth.[14]

In the fallout from this rearrangement we must include two world wars, as a result of which Britain ceased to act as the dominant superpower it had been since Napoleon. Not surprisingly, the Soviet Union and the United States subsequently competed in a Cold War to fill the gap. It was not however pre-determined that the Cold War would be as thuggish and covertly violent as for decades it continued to be. For that we should look to more contingent causes on both sides of the Iron Curtain—starting with the character of Stalin and his party but also including the partly responsive development of the Dulles brothers and more generally of the American deep state, which has become by far the bigger threat to U.S. democracy today.

THE DEEP STATE, THE SHADOW GOVERNMENT
AND THE WALL STREET OVERWORLD

The "deep state" was defined by the U.K. newsletter *On Religion* as "the em-bedded anti-democratic power structures within a government, something very few democracies can claim to be free from."[15] The term originated in Tur-key in 1996, to refer to United States–backed elements, primarily in the intelli-gence services and military, who had repeatedly used violence to interfere with and realign Turkey's democratic political process. Sometimes the definition is restricted to elements *within* the government (or "a state-within-the-state"), but more often in Turkey the term is expanded, for historical reasons, to in-clude "members of the Turkish underworld."[16] In this chapter I shall use "deep state" in the larger sense, to include both the second level of secret govern-ment inside Washington and those outsiders powerful enough, in either the underworld or overworld, to give it direction. In short I shall equate the term "deep state" with what in 1993 I termed a "deep political system": "one which habitually resorts to decision-making and enforcement procedures outside as well as inside those publicly sanctioned by law and society."[17]

Like myself, Mike Lofgren suggests an ambiguous symbiosis between two aspects of the American deep state:

1. the Beltway agencies of the shadow government, like the CIA and NSA, which have been instituted by the public state and now overshadow it, and
2. the much older power of Wall Street, referring to the powerful banks and law firms located there.

Top-level Treasury officials, CIA officers, and Wall Street bankers and lawyers think much alike because of the "revolving door" by which they pass easily from private to public service and back. In Lofgren's words,

> It is not too much to say that Wall Street may be the ultimate owner of the Deep State and its strategies, if for no other reason than that it has the money to reward government operatives with a second career that is lucrative beyond the dreams of avarice—certainly beyond the dreams of a salaried government employee.[18]

I shall argue that in the 1950s Wall Street was a dominating complex. It included not just banks and law firms but also the oil majors whose cartel arrangements were successfully defended against the U.S. government by the Wall Street law firm Sullivan and Cromwell, home to the Dulles brothers. This larger complex is what I mean by the Wall Street overworld.

By recognizing this power reach of Wall Street, we can see that Tom Hayden's notion of a "state within a state" is too restricted: those with that inner power (such as the higher echelons of the CIA) exercise it not by their seclusion, but by their interactions with an outside overworld. And Lofgren's metaphor of the deep state as an iceberg, though useful, risks suggesting a too solid or structural relationship to that overworld. Unlike the state, the deep state is not a structure but a system, as difficult to define, but also as real and powerful, as a weather system.

An important thesis of this chapter and this book is that in the uncharted and virtually unregulated milieu of the overworld deep state we encounter not just dominating influence but also antisocial lawbreaking and sometimes murderous malfeasance.

THE LONG HISTORY OF THE WALL STREET OVERWORLD

Lofgren's inclusion of Wall Street in his definition of the deep state reinforces Franklin Roosevelt's observation in 1933 to his friend Col. E. M. House that "The real truth . . . is, as you and I know, that a financial element in the larger centers has owned the Government ever since the days of Andrew Jackson."[19]

FDR's insight is well illustrated by the efficiency with which a group of Wall Street bankers (including Nelson Rockefeller's grandfather Nelson Aldrich and Paul Warburg) were able in a 1910 highly secret meeting to establish the Federal Reserve System—a system that in effect reserved oversight of the nation's currency supply and of all America's banks in the not impartial hands of its largest.[20] The political clout of the quasi-governmental Federal Reserve Board (where the federal Treasury is represented but does not dominate) was clearly demonstrated in 2008, when Fed leadership secured instant support from the successive administrations of a Texan Republican president, followed by a Midwest Democratic one, for public money to rescue the reckless management of Wall Street banks: banks "Too Big to Fail," and of course far "Too Big to Jail," but not "Too Big to Bail."[21]

In 1946 General Vandenberg, as Director of Central Intelligence (DCI), recruited Allen Dulles, then a Republican lawyer at Sullivan and Cromwell in New York, "to draft proposals for the shape and organization of what was to become the Central Intelligence Agency in 1947." Dulles promptly formed an advisory group of six men, all but one of whom were Wall Street investment bankers or lawyers.[22] Dulles and two of the six (William H. Jackson and Frank

Wisner) later joined the agency, where Dulles proceeded to orchestrate policies, such as the overthrow of the Arbenz regime in Guatemala, that he had previously discussed in New York at the Council on Foreign Relations.[23]

There seems to be little difference in Allen Dulles's influence whether he was a Wall Street lawyer or a CIA director. Although he did not formally join the CIA until November 1950, he was in Berlin before the start of the 1948 Berlin Blockade, "supervising the unleashing of anti-Soviet propaganda across Europe."[24] In the early summer of 1948 he set up the American Committee for a United Europe (ACUE), in support of what became, by the early 1950s, "the largest CIA operation in Western Europe."[25]

THE DEEP STATE AND FUNDS FOR CIA COVERT OPERATIONS

Wall Street was also the inspiration for what eventually became the CIA's first covert operation: the use of "over $10 million in captured Axis funds to influence the [Italian] election [of 1948]."[26] (The fundraising had begun at the wealthy Brook Club in New York; but Allen Dulles, still a Wall Street lawyer, persuaded Washington, which at first had preferred a private funding campaign, to authorize the operation through the National Security Council and the CIA.)[27]

Dulles's friend Frank Wisner then left Wall Street to oversee an enlarged covert operations program through the newly created Office of Policy Coordination (OPC). Dulles, still a lawyer, campaigned successfully to reconstruct Western Europe through what became known as the Marshall Plan.[28] Together with George Kennan and James Forrestal, Dulles also "helped devise a secret codicil [to the Marshall Plan] that gave the CIA the capability to conduct political warfare. It let the agency skim millions of dollars from the plan."[29]

This created one of the earlier occasions when the CIA, directly or indirectly, recruited local assets involved in drug trafficking. American Federation of Labor (AFL) organizer Irving Brown, the assistant of AFL official Jay Lovestone (a CIA asset), was implicated in drug smuggling activities in Europe, at the same time that he used funds diverted from the Marshall Plan to establish a "'compatible left' labor union in Marseilles with Pierre Ferri-Pisani. On behalf of Brown and the CIA, Ferri-Pisani (a drug smuggler connected with Marseilles crime lord Antoine Guerini), hired goons to shellack striking Communist dock workers."[30]

An analogous funding source for the CIA developed in the Far East: the so-called

"M-Fund," a secret fund of money of enormous size that has existed in Japan [in 1991] for more than forty years. The Fund was established by the United States in the immediate postwar era for essentially the same reasons that later gave rise to the Marshall Plan of assistance by the U.S. to Western Europe, including the Federal Republic of Germany. . . . The M-Fund was used not only for the building of a democratic political system in Japan but, in addition, for all of the purposes for which Marshall Plan funds were used in Europe.[31]

For at least two decades the CIA lavishly subsidized right-wing parties in countries including Japan and Indonesia, again using captured Axis funds.[32] (According to Chalmers Johnson, "The M-Fund . . . was initially created from sales of confiscated Japanese military stockpiles of industrial diamonds, platinum, gold, and silver that had been plundered in occupied countries."[33])

As a general rule the CIA, rather than assimilating these funds into its own budget, appears to have left them off the books in the hands of cooperative allied powers—ranging from other U.S. agencies like the Economic Cooperation Administration (ECA, set up in 1948 to administer the Marshall Plan) to oil companies, to powerful drug kingpins.[34]

The CIA never abandoned its dependency on funds from outside its official budget to conduct its clandestine operations. In Southeast Asia in particular, its proprietary firm Sea Supply Inc. supplied an infrastructure for a drug traffic supporting a CIA-led paramilitary force, PARU.[35] The CIA appears also to have acted in coordination with slush funds from various U.S. government contracts, ranging from the Howard Hughes organization to the foreign arms sales of U.S. defense corporations like Lockheed and Northrop.[36]

LOCKHEED PAYOFFS AND CIA CLIENTS: THE NETHERLANDS, JAPAN, ITALY, INDONESIA, AND SAUDI ARABIA

Through the 1950s, payouts from the M-Fund were administered by Kodama Yoshio, "probably the CIA's chief asset in Japan"; while "All accounts say that after the end of the occupation, the fund's American managers came from the CIA."[37] Kodama also received and distributed millions of funds from Lockheed to secure military contracts, in which a percentage was kicked back to local agents who time after time were also, like Kodama, assets of the CIA.[38] The CIA knew about this operation but has never admitted involvement in it, even after it was revealed that the U.S. Air Force also had a hand in a Lockheed payoff program, code-named "Operation Buttercup."[39] Lockheed's system of payoffs was worldwide; and there was CIA involvement with it in at least four other countries: the Netherlands, Italy, Indonesia, and Saudi Arabia. (Lockheed, the builder of the U-2, was a major CIA-cleared contractor.)[40]

The beneficiary in the Netherlands was Prince Bernhard (a close friend of CIA directors Walter Bedell Smith and Allen Dulles) and the organizer of the Bilderberg Group along with Joseph Retinger of the CIA-funded American Committee for a United Europe and C. D. Jackson in Eisenhower's White House.[41] In the case of Italy, payments were handled through a contact ("Antelope Cobbler") who turned out to be whoever was the Italian Prime Minister of the moment (always from one of the parties subsidized earlier by the CIA).[42]

In the revealing instance of Indonesia, Lockheed payments were shifted in May 1965, over the legal objections of Lockheed's counsel, to a new contract with a company set up by the firm's longtime local agent or middleman, August Munir Dasaad.[43] This was just six months after a secret U.S. decision to have the CIA covertly assist "'individuals and organizations prepared to take obstructive action against the PKI [Indonesian Communist Party].' Over the longer term this meant identifying and keeping tabs on "anti-regime elements" and other potential leaders of a post-Sukarno regime."[44]

Although Dasaad had been a longtime supporter of Sukarno, by May 1965 he was already building connections with Sukarno's eventual successor, General Suharto, via a family relative, General Alamsjah, who knew Suharto and was the beneficiary of the new Lockheed account.[45] After Suharto replaced Sukarno, Alamsjah, who controlled certain considerable funds, at once made funds available to Suharto, earning him the gratitude of the new president.[46]

In July 1965, furthermore, at the alleged nadir of U.S.-Indonesian aid relations, Rockwell-Standard had a contractual agreement to deliver two hundred light aircraft (Aero-Commanders) to the Indonesian Army (not the Air Force) in the next two months. Once again the commission agent on the deal, Bob Hasan or Hassan, was a political associate (and eventual *cukong* or business partner) of Suharto. More specifically, Suharto and Bob Hasan established two shipping companies to be operated by the Central Java army division, Diponegoro. This division, as has long been noticed, supplied the bulk of the personnel on both sides of the Gestapu coup drama in September 1965—both those staging the coup attempt, and those putting it down.[47]

While this was happening, Stanvac (a joint venture of the Standard companies known later as Exxon and Mobil) increased payments to the army's oil company, Permina, headed by an eventual political ally of Suharto, General Ibnu Sutowo. Alamsjah (along with a well-connected Japanese oilman, Nishijima Shigetada) is said to have been allied with Ibnu Sutowo in plotting against Sukarno.[48] After Suharto's overthrow of Sukarno, *Fortune* wrote that "Sutowo's still small company played a key part in bankrolling those crucial operations, and the army has never forgotten it."[49]

We shall deal later with the special case of Lockheed kickbacks to Saudi Arabia, which were far greater than those to Japan. It is important to note, however, the linkage between Middle East oil and arms sales: as U.S. imports of Middle East oil increased, the pressure on the U.S. balance of payments was offset by increased U.S. arms sales to the region. "In the period 1963–1974, arms sales to the Middle East went from 10 per cent of global arms imports to 36 per cent, half of which was supplied by the United States."[50]

The result was to create a vital triangle at the heart of the American deep state, in which oil companies paid Saudi Arabia for oil; Saudi Arabia paid the U.S. arms industry for planes and weapons, and the resulting huge arms contracts (as we shall see in chapter 10) paid for off-the-books U.S. covert operations like Iran-Contra.

IRAN IN 1953: HOW AN OIL CARTEL OPERATION BECAME A JOB FOR THE CIA

The international lawyers of Wall Street did not hide from each other their shared belief that they understood better than Washington the requirements for running the world. As John Foster Dulles wrote in the 1930s to a British colleague,

> The word "cartel" has here assumed the stigma of a bogeyman which the politi-
> cians are constantly attacking. The fact of the matter is that most of these politi-
> cians are highly insular and nationalistic and because the political organization
> of the world has under such influence been so backward, business people who
> have had to cope realistically with international problems have had to find ways
> for getting through and around stupid political barriers.[51]

This same mentality also explains why Allen Dulles as an Office of Strategic Services (OSS) officer in 1945 simply evaded orders from Washington forbidding him to negotiate with SS General Karl Wolff about a conditional surrender of German forces in Italy—an important breach of Roosevelt's agreement with Stalin at Yalta for unconditional surrender, a breach that is regarded by many as helping lead to the Cold War.[52] And it explains why Allen Dulles, as CIA Director in 1957, dealt summarily with Eisenhower's reluctance to authorize more than occasional U-2 overflights of the USSR, by secretly approving a plan with Britain's MI6 whereby U-2 flights could be authorized instead by the U.K. Prime Minister Macmillan.[53]

This mentality exhibited itself in 1952, when Truman's Justice Department sought to break up the cartel agreements whereby Standard Oil of New Jersey (now Exxon) and four other oil majors controlled global oil distribution. (The other four were Standard Oil Company of New York or Socony [later Mobil], Standard Oil of California [now Chevron], Gulf Oil, and Texaco. Together with Royal Dutch Shell and Anglo-Iranian, they comprised the so-called "Seven Sisters" of the cartel.) Faced with a government order to hand over relevant documents, Exxon's lawyer Arthur Dean at Sullivan and Cromwell, where Foster was senior partner, refused: "If it were not for the question of national security, we would be perfectly willing to face either a criminal or a civil suit. But this is the kind of information the Kremlin would love to get its hands on."[54]

At this time the oil cartel was working closely with the British Anglo-Iranian Oil Company (AIOC, later BP) to prevent AIOC's nationalization by Iran's Premier Mossadeq, by instituting, in May 1951, a successful boycott of Iranian oil exports. "In May 1951 the AIOC secured the backing of the other *oil majors*, who had every interest in discouraging nationalisation. . . . None of the large companies would touch Iranian *oil*; despite one or two picturesque episodes, the boycott held."[55]

As a result Iranian oil production fell from 241 million barrels in 1950 to 10.6 million barrels in 1952. "This was accomplished by denying Iran the ability to export its crude oil. At that time, the Seven Sisters controlled almost 99% of the crude oil tankers in the world for such export, and even more importantly, the markets to which it was going."[56] But Truman declined, despite a direct personal appeal from Churchill, to have the CIA participate in efforts to overthrow Mossadeq, and instead dispatched Averell Harriman to Tehran in a failed effort to negotiate a peaceful resolution of Mossadeq's differences with London.[57]

All this changed with the election of Eisenhower in November 1952 (with considerable support from the oil industry), followed by the appointment of the Dulles brothers to be Secretary of State and head of CIA. The Justice Department's criminal complaint against the oil cartel was swiftly replaced by a civil suit, from which the oil cartel eventually emerged unscathed.[58]

> Eisenhower, an open friend of the oil industry . . . changed the charges from criminal to civil and transferred responsibility of the case from the Department of Justice to the Department of State—the first time in history that an antitrust case was handed to State for prosecution. Seeing as how the Secretary of State was John Foster Dulles and the defense counsel for the oil cartel was Dulles' former law firm (Sullivan and Cromwell), the case was soon as good as dead.[59]

Thereafter,

> Cooperative control of the world market by the major oil companies remained in effect, with varying degrees of success, until the oil embargo of 1973–74. That the cooperation was more than tacit can be seen by the fact that antitrust regulations were specifically set aside a number of times during the 1950–1973 period, allowing the major companies to negotiate as a group with various Mideastern countries, and after its inception [in 1960], with the Organization of Petroleum Exporting Countries or OPEC.[60]

Also in November 1952 CIA officials began planning to involve the CIA in the efforts of MI6 and the oil companies in Iran[61]—although its notorious Operation TP/AJAX to overthrow Mossadeq was not finally approved by Eisenhower until July 22, 1953.[62]

The events of 1953 strengthened the role of the oil cartel as a structural component of the American deep state, drawing on its powerful connections to both Wall Street and the CIA.[63] (Another such component was the Arabian-American Oil Company or ARAMCO in Saudi Arabia, which increased oil production in 1951–1953 to offset the loss of oil from Iran. Until it was fully nationalized in 1980, ARAMCO maintained undercover CIA personnel like William Eddy among its top advisors.)[64] The five American oil majors in particular were also strengthened by the success of AJAX, as Anglo-Iranian (renamed BP) was henceforth forced to share 40 percent of the oil from its Iran refinery with them.

Nearly all recent accounts of Mossadeq's overthrow treat it as a covert intelligence operation, with the oil cartel (when mentioned at all) playing a subservient role. However the chronology, and above all the belated approval from Eisenhower, suggest that it was CIA that came belatedly in 1953 to assist an earlier oil cartel operation, rather than vice versa. In terms of the deep state, in 1951 the oil cartel or deep state initiated a process that the American public state only authorized two years later. Yet the inevitable bias in academic or archival historiography, working only with those primary sources that are publicly available, is to think of the Mossadeq tragedy as simply a "CIA coup."

The oil cartel's victories in 1952–1953 left a legacy that was not felt only in Iran. As we shall see, the oil majors now had a license to act in conjunction with the CIA to destabilize or overthrow governments in other countries, such as Indonesia in 1965. Later in this chapter we will see how oil companies, Saudi Arabia, and former CIA personnel all operated together in ways that terminated the presidential career of someone who had earned their disapproval, President Jimmy Carter.

THE CIA, BOOZ ALLEN HAMILTON, AND THE WALL STREET OVERWORLD

In the 1950s Eisenhower further consolidated the role of the private sector in the deep state system by his decision to bring private corporation chiefs into the super-secret COG planning process.[65] (This was the precedent for placing Rumsfeld and Cheney in a position to plan for the suspension of the U.S. Constitution, even in the 1990s under Clinton, when both men, as we shall see in chapter 3, were corporation CEOs and not in the U.S. government.)

But a much larger role for the private sector has come with the increased outsourcing of the government's intelligence budget. Tim Shorrock revealed in 2007 that "about 70 percent of the estimated $60 billion the government spends every year on . . . intelligence" is now outsourced to private intelligence contractors like Booz, Allen & Hamilton (now Booz Allen Hamilton) and SAIC (Science Applications International Corporation).[66]

Indeed the distinction between "public" and "private" fades even more with the "revolving door" mentioned above, which circulates top-level intelligence officials and the chiefs of the contracting firms cleared for intelligence work. For example Mike McConnell "went from being head of the National Security Agency under Bush 41 and Clinton directly to Booz Allen, one of the nation's largest private intelligence contractors, then became Bush's Director of National Intelligence (DNI), then went back to Booz Allen, where he is now Executive Vice President."[67] Intelligence officers in government write the noncompetitive contracts for the private corporations that they may have worked for and may work for again. And over the years the "revolving door" has also exchanged personnel between Booz Allen and the international oil companies served by the firm.

The original firm of Booz, Allen, & Hamilton split in 2008 into Booz Allen Hamilton, focused on USG business, and Booz & Company in New York, assuming the old company's commercial and international portfolio. Booz Allen Hamilton is majority owned by the private equity firm the Carlyle Group, noted for its association with political figures like both Presidents Bush.[68]

Lofgren points to the deep state importance of Booz Allen Hamilton, 99 percent of whose business is dependent on the U.S. government.[69] Booz Allen has been linked in the media to the NSA ever since its employee Edward Snowden decamped with NSA records. Booz Allen is also prominent in the profitable area of "continuity of government" (COG) and "continuity of operations" (COOP) contracts.[70]

But Booz Allen, one of the oldest and largest of the "cleared contractors," has been intertwined with the CIA's covert operations since Allen Dulles became CIA Director in 1953.[71] In the same year, Booz Allen began "to take on several overseas assignments . . . : a land-registration system in the Philippines, a restructuring of Egypt's customs operations and textile industries, and work for Iran's national oil company."[72] All three assignments overlapped with CIA covert operations in 1953, including the Philippine land distribution program that Edward Lansdale promoted in order to fight a Huk insurrection, and the CIA's operation TP/AJAX (with Britain's MI6) to rescue the Anglo-Iranian oil company (later BP).[73]

But the most important CIA-Booz Allen cooperation may have been in Egypt. In March 1953 Miles Copeland, having resigned from the CIA to join Booz Allen, "returned to Cairo under what was, for all practical purposes, a joint CIA-BA&H mission."[74] In addition to offering management advice to the Egyptian government in general, and to a private textile mill, Miles also gave Nasser advice on establishing his intelligence service (the *Mukhabarat*), and "soon became his closest Western advisor" (as well as his top channel to the USG, more important than either the local U.S. ambassador or CIA chief).[75]

Copeland's role with Nasser did not make him a *shaper* of U.S. policy; his pro-Nasser views were largely subordinated to the pro-British anti-Nasserism of the Dulles brothers. But they did establish a bond between Copeland and the Eisenhower White House. By 1967, when Nixon was preparing to run for president, Copeland had taken a leave of absence from Booz Allen to become a prestigious and well-paid consultant for oil companies.

THE CIA, MILES COPELAND, AND ADNAN KHASHOGGI

In 1966 Copeland, while technically on leave from Booz Allen, made close contact with Adnan Khashoggi, a young Arab who was in the course of becoming both a "principal foreign agent" of the United States and also extremely wealthy on the commissions he earned from Lockheed, Northrop, and other military firms on arms sales to Saudi Arabia.[76] ("To give some sense of the size of the business, the company acknowledged in the mid-1970s that it had provided $106 million in commissions to Khashoggi between 1970 and 1975, more than ten times the level of payments made to the next most important connection, Yoshi [sic] Kodama of Japan."[77]

By Copeland's own account in 1989, this encounter with Khashoggi "put the two of us on a 'Miles-and-Adnan' basis that has lasted for more than twenty years of business, parties, and a very special kind of political action."[78] Copeland adds that "Adnan and I, separately had been called on by our respective friends in Langley [i.e., CIA] to . . . have an official [sic], off-the-record exchange of ideas on the emerging crisis in the Middle East, and come up with suggestions that the tame bureaucrats would like to have made but couldn't."[79]

Copeland almost immediately flew to Cairo and immersed himself in a series of high-level but ultimately unsuccessful efforts to forestall what soon became the 1967 Egyptian-Israeli Six-Day War. By his account, his mission, though unsuccessful, gave a "tremendous boost" to his reputation, enabling him "to accelerate the attempt I had already started to establish a 'private CIA' by use of confidential arrangements with politically astute members of the client companies."[80]

Copeland's self-promoting claims are controversial, and a number of establishment writers have described his books as "unreliable."[81] But eyewitness Larry Kolb corroborates that Copeland was close to Khashoggi, and that the two of them "had written a white paper . . . proposing that . . . rich countries, including not only the United States but also the Arab oil states, should establish a 'Marshall Plan' for all the needy countries of the Middle East, including Israel." Rewritten with Kolb's assistance after consultation with the Reagan White House, the plan would be backed by a "Mideast Peace Fund" to which "Adnan was pledging a hundred million dollars of his own money."[82]

The proposal failed, partly because of the Middle East's resistance to negotiated solutions, but also partly because by the 1980s Khashoggi was no longer as rich and influential as he had once been. His function as an agent of influence in the Middle East and elsewhere had been sharply limited after the United States, by the Corrupt Federal Practices Act of 1978, outlawed direct payments by U.S. corporations to foreign individuals. Henceforward the function of bestowing money and sexual favors on client politicians passed primarily from Khashoggi to the bank he used, the recently created Bank of Credit and Commerce International (BCCI, also a CIA connection).[83] A major shareholder in BCCI was Saudi intelligence chief Kamal Adham, Khashoggi's friend and business partner and (according to the Senate BCCI Report) "the CIA's former principal contact in the Arab Middle East."[84]

What the story of the failed "Mideast Peace Fund" reveals is first, that Khashoggi (like BCCI after him) was of interest to Washington because of his financial resources and ability to negotiate with both Israel and Arab countries; and second, that Copeland and what Copeland called his "private CIA,"[85] was in a commanding position as lead adviser to Khashoggi, while still on unpaid leave from Booz Allen Hamilton.

KHASHOGGI, THE CIA'S ASSET EDWARD K. MOSS, AND POLITICAL CORRUPTION

A powerful connection was formed by combining Copeland's political contacts with Khashoggi's millions. And Copeland may have been responsible for Khashoggi's inspired choice of the under-recognized Edward K. Moss, another man with CIA connections, as his public relations agent in Washington.[86]

Back in November 1962, the CIA, as part of its planning to get rid of Castro, decided to use Moss for the Political Action Group of the CIA's Covert Action (CA) staff.[87] This was more than a year after the FBI had advised the CIA that Moss's mistress Julia Cellini and her brother Dino Cellini were alleged to be procurers, while "the Cellini brothers have long been associated with the narcotics and white slavery rackets in Cuba."[88]

This FBI report suggests an important shared interest between Moss and Khashoggi: sexual corruption. Just as his uncle Yussuf Yassin had been a procurer of women for King Abdul-Aziz, so Khashoggi himself was said to have "used sex to win over U.S. executives." The bill for the madam who supplied girls en masse to his yacht in the Mediterranean ran to hundreds of thousands of dollars.[89] Khashoggi made a practice of supplying those he wished to influence with dollars as well as sex.[90]

In the United States, the CIA of course was forbidden to use sex and money in this way or to make the payments to right-wing politicians that characterized its behavior in the rest of the world. But no such prohibition applied to Khashoggi. According to Anthony Summers,

> Khashoggi had courted Nixon in 1967 by putting a plane at his disposal to tour the Middle East after the Six-Day War. Soon afterward, using a proxy, he opened an account at Rebozo's [Bebe Rebozo, Nixon's close confidante] bank in Florida. He did so, he explained to Watergate prosecutors, hoping to "curry favor with Rebozo," to get an entrée to the man who might become president, and to pursue business deals.[91]

Khashoggi in effect served as a "cutout," or representative, in a number of operations forbidden to the CIA and the companies he worked with. Lockheed, for one, was conspicuously absent from the list of military contractors who contributed illicitly to Nixon's 1972 election campaign. But there was no law prohibiting their official representative, Khashoggi, from cycling $200 million through the bank of Nixon's friend Bebe Rebozo.[92] (Pierre Salinger heard from Khashoggi that in 1972 he had donated $1 million to Nixon, corroborating the often-heard claim that Khashoggi had brought it in a briefcase to Nixon's western White House in San Clemente, and then "forgotten" to take it away.)[93]

Khashoggi of course did not introduce such corruption to American politics; he merely joined a milieu where defense companies had used money and girls for years to win defense contracts in Washington and Las Vegas.[94] Prominent in this practice was Howard Hughes, whom Khashoggi soon joined in international investments. (After a Senate investigator on Khashoggi's trail registered at the Hughes-owned Sands Hotel in Las Vegas, a blonde came unexpectedly to his hotel room, and said, "I'm here for your pleasure."[95])

But Khashoggi's corruption channels and targets overlapped with those of others with CIA connections. In 1972 it was alleged that funds from the Paradise Island casino in the Bahamas were being secretly carried to Nixon and his friend Bebe Rebozo, by a casino employee. This was Seymour (Sy) Alter, who was both "a friend of Nixon and Rebozo since 1962" and also an associate of Edward Moss's brother-in-law Eddie Cellini, the casino manager at Paradise Island.[96] The funds came from the Paradise Island Bridge Company, a company partly owned by an officer of Benguet International, a firm represented in America by Paul Helliwell.[97] It is likely that Nixon himself had a hidden interest in the Bridge Company, which might explain the revelation through Operation Tradewinds that a "Richard M. Nixon" (not otherwise identified) had an account at Helliwell's Castle Bank.[98] For decades persons from Booz Allen Hamilton have been among the very small group owning the profitable Paradise Island Bridge Company. (A recent partner in the Paradise Island Bridge Company was Booz Allen Senior Vice-President Robert Riegle.)[99]

Two facts point to a deep state interest in what might otherwise seem a matter of personal corruption. The first is that Paul Helliwell had set up two companies for the CIA—CAT Inc. (later Air America) and Sea Supply Inc. in Bangkok—that became the infrastructure of the CIA's covert operations with drug-trafficking armies in Southeast Asia.[100] The second is that Paul Helliwell's banking partner, E. P. Barry, had been the postwar head of OSS Counterintelligence (X-2) in Vienna, which oversaw the recovery of SS gold in Operation Safehaven.[101] Elsewhere I have reported speculations that in the years between the shutdown of OSS in 1945 and the creation of the CIA in 1947, William Donovan and Allen Dulles, using the resources of a private World Commerce Corporation, were able to use recovered SS gold to initiate the Bangkok drug connection.[102]

MOSS, KHASHOGGI, THE SAFARI CLUB, AND
THE INTERNATIONAL OVERWORLD

The power exerted by Khashoggi and Moss was not limited to Khashoggi's access to funds and women. By the 1970s, Moss was chairman of the elite Safari Club in Kenya, where he invited Khashoggi in as majority owner.[103] The exclusive property was the first venue for an alliance with the same name between national intelligence agencies that wished to compensate for the CIA's retrenchment in the wake of President Carter's election and Senator Church's post-Watergate reforms.[104]

As former Saudi intelligence chief Prince Turki bin Faisal once told Georgetown University alumni,

> In 1976, after the Watergate matters took place here, your intelligence community was literally tied up by Congress. It could not do anything. It could not send spies, it could not write reports, and it could not pay money. In order to compensate for that, a group of countries got together in the hope of fighting Communism and established what was called the Safari Club. The Safari Club included France, Egypt, Saudi Arabia, Morocco, and Iran.[105]

Prince Turki's candid remarks—"your intelligence community was literally tied up by Congress. . . . In order to compensate for that, a group of countries got together . . . and established what was called the Safari Club"—made it clear that the Safari Club, operating at the level of the deep state, was expressly created to overcome restraints established by political decisions of the public state in Washington. Though Turki talked of overriding the intent of Congress, the effect was also to override the explicit intent of President Carter.

Obviously the property owned by Khashoggi and Moss in Kenya should not be confused with the intelligence operation of the same name. But it would be wrong also to make a radical separation between the two: Khashoggi would appear to be part of this supranational intelligence milieu.

Specifically Khashoggi's activities of corruption by sex and money, after they too were somewhat curtailed by Senator Church's post-Watergate reforms, appear to have been taken up by the Bank of Credit and Commerce International (BCCI), a bank where Khashoggi's friend and business partner Kamal Adham, the Saudi intelligence chief and Safari Club financier, was a part-owner.[106]

THE DEEP STATE, THE SAFARI CLUB, AND BCCI

The usual account of the Safari Club's origin is that it was

> the brainchild of Count Alexandre de Marenches, the debonair and mustachioed chief of France's CIA, the SDECE (Service de Documentation Extérieure et de Contre-Espionnage) .... Worried by Soviet and Cuban advances in postcolonial Africa, and by America's post-Watergate paralysis in the field of undercover activity, the swashbuckling de Marenches had come to Turki's father, King Faisal, with a proposition.... [By 1979] Somali president Mohammed Siad Barre had been bribed out of Soviet embrace by $75 million worth of Egyptian arms (paid for ... by Saudi Arabia)....[107]

In this same period de Marenches was also a member of the Pinay Circle, "an international right-wing propaganda group which brings together serving or retired intelligence officers and politicians with links to right-wing intelligence factions from most of the countries in Europe."[108]

However the well-informed Mahmood Mamdani sees it as the product of Washington's search for new proxies after the debacle of the U.S.–South African intervention in Angola in the mid-1970s:

> No matter its military strength and geopolitical importance, apartheid South Africa was confirmed to be a political liability. The recognition only aggravated the search for proxies. Its first success was a regional alliance called the Safari Club, put together with the blessing of Henry Kissinger.[109]

As Kissinger was still Secretary of State when the Safari Club was founded, this would suggest that it was created with U.S. approval. So would the Club's early successes that Mamdani cites, especially when

> it helped bring about the historic rapprochement between two strategic American Allies, Egypt and Israel, laying the ground for Anwar al-Sadat's pathbreaking November 1977 visit to Jerusalem. The suggestion for the meeting was first made in a letter from Israeli Prime Minister Yitzhak Rabin to President Sadat, carried by the Moroccan representative in the club.[110]

But after Carter was elected, according to Joseph Trento, the Safari Club allied itself with Richard Helms and Theodore Shackley against the more restrained intelligence policies of Jimmy Carter. In Trento's account, the dismissal by William Colby in 1974 of CIA counterintelligence chief James Angleton,

> combined with Watergate, is what prompted the Safari Club to start working with [former DCI Richard] Helms [then U.S. Ambassador to Iran] and his most trusted operatives outside of Congressional and even Agency purview. James Angleton said before his death that "Colby destroyed counterintelligence. But because Colby was seen by Shackley and Helms as having betrayed the CIA to Congress, they simply began working with outsiders like Adham and Saudi Arabia. The traditional CIA answering to the president was an empty vessel having little more than technical capability."[111]

Trento adds that "The Safari Club needed a network of banks to finance its intelligence operations. With the official blessing of George Bush as the head of the CIA, Adham transformed . . . the Bank of Credit and Commerce International (BCCI), into a worldwide money-laundering machine."[112] Kevin Phillips agrees that in this period "Bush cemented strong relations with the intelligence services of both Saudi Arabia and the shah of Iran. He worked closely with Kamal Adham, the head of Saudi intelligence, brother-in-law of King Faisal and an early BCCI insider."[113]

Trento claims also that the Safari Club then was able to work with some of the controversial CIA operators who had been forced out of the CIA by Turner, and that this was coordinated by perhaps the most controversial of them all: Theodore Shackley.

> Shackley, who still had ambitions to become DCI, believed that without his many sources and operatives like [Edwin] Wilson, the Safari Club—operating with [former DCI Richard] Helms in charge in Tehran—would be ineffective. . . . Unless Shackley took direct action to complete the privatization of intelligence operations soon, the Safari Club would not have a conduit to [CIA] resources. The solution: create a totally private intelligence network using CIA assets until President Carter could be replaced.[114]

BIG OIL, THE SAUDIS, THE SAFARI CLUB, AND THE DEFEAT OF PRESIDENT CARTER IN 1980

During the 1980 election campaign each party accused the other of plotting an October Surprise to elect their candidate. In the fall of 1980, Jack Anderson charged in the *Washington Post* that the Carter administration, to help get Carter reelected, was preparing a major military operation in Iran to rescue the U.S. hostages held captive in Tehran.[115] Subsequently other journalists, notably Robert Parry, accused CIA veterans on the Reagan campaign, along with Theodore Shackley, of an arguably treasonable but successful plot with

Iranians to delay return of the U.S. hostages until Reagan took office in January 1981.[116]

According to Parry, Alexandre de Marenches of the Safari Club (and Pinay Circle) arranged for William Casey (a fellow Knight of Malta) to meet with Iranian and Israeli representatives in Paris in July and October 1980, where Casey promised delivery to Iran of needed U.S. armaments in exchange for a delay in the return of the U.S. hostages in Iran.[117] This was after a June 1980 meeting of the Pinay Circle, at which "attention was turned towards the American Presidential election that was to bring Reagan to power."[118] Parry also suspects a role of BCCI in both the funding of payoffs for the secret deal and the subsequent flow of Israeli armaments to Iran. We will deal with Parry's charges in chapter 8.

A more usual explanation for Carter's defeat in 1980 was the second oil shock of 1979–1980, in which an acute gas shortage led to both a sudden increase in prices and long gas lines at service stations. It is customary for establishment scholars to blame the shortage on political upheavals in Iran, which led to "a cutoff of Iranian oil."[119]

However Robert Sherrill's close analysis of the American oil industry demonstrates that American oil companies, not Iranian turmoil, were primarily responsible for the gas shortage:

> U.S. companies were up to their own strategy . . . . Although in fact America was importing more oil in January and February [1979], during the Iranian shutdown, than it had imported during the same period in 1978, major oil importers pretended that the Iranian "shortage" . . . was real. It was the excuse they gave for slashing the amount of gasoline they supplied to their retail dealers. . . .
> A CIA study showed that in the first five months of the year, at a time when the Administration was deploring our oil shortage, U.S. companies exported more oil than they had in those glut years 1977 and 1978.[120]

This is only one of the examples Sherrill supplies of the domestic consequences of having liberated the oil majors in 1953 from the disciplinary restraints of antitrust legislation. But in this case their manipulation of domestic oil prices, combined with Carter's failure to bring the hostages home, combined to cause the first defeat for an elected president running for reelection, since that of Herbert Hoover in 1932.

Not mentioned by either mainstream journalists or Sherrill was the role quietly played by Saudi Arabia in augmenting the 1979 gas crisis: "The Saudis had cut production by nearly 1 million barrels a day to 9.5 million at the start of the year [1979], and in April 1979 they made a second cut to 8.5 million. The Saudis had the capacity to produce 12 million barrels a day at that point."[121]

The Saudi manipulation of gas prices reflected their acute displeasure with the Camp David Accords of 1978, which did nothing to change Israeli control of Jerusalem.[122] But what concerns us here is that the concerted policy of big oil in 1979 was closely aligned with their deep state allies in the Saudi government and the Safari Club, to the severe detriment of Americans and their nominal government, the beleaguered Carter administration.

The oil shock and gas shortage contrived by big oil in 1979, together with the October Surprise, were the chief factors in enabling the subsequent Reagan Revolution. This in turn opened the door for a new phase in "continuity of government" or COG plans, that were secretly prepared over two decades by planners like Donald Rumsfeld and Dick Cheney, and then implemented on 9/11.

THE DEEP STATE AND THE BCCI COVER-UP

It is also clear that throughout the 1980s the American deep state in Washington was involved with BCCI and protected it. Acting CIA director Richard Kerr acknowledged to a Senate Committee "that the CIA had also used BCCI for certain intelligence-gathering operations."[123] "Later, a congressional inquiry showed that for more than ten years preceding the BCCI collapse in the summer of 1991, the FBI, the DEA, the CIA, the Customs Service, and the Department of Justice all failed to act on hundreds of tips about the illegalities of BCCI's international activities."[124]

Far less clear is the attitude taken by Wall Street banks toward the miscreant BCCI. The Senate report on BCCI charged however that the Bank of England "had withheld information about BCCI's frauds from public knowledge for 15 months before closing the bank."[125]

Of course the scope and influence of BCCI reflected changes in the global superstructure of finance since the oil price hikes of the 1970s. A recent study of the dangerously unstable concentration of ownership in the world showed only four recognizable Wall Street institutions among the top twenty: JPMorgan Chase & Co., the Goldman Sachs Group, Bank of New York Mellon Corporation, and Merrill Lynch.[126] Of these, Bank of New York, the bank heavily involved in the 1990s looting of Russia, interlocked with BCCI through the Swiss banking activities of the international banker Bruce Rappaport, "thought to have ties to U.S. and Israeli intelligence." (Alfred Hartmann, a board member of BCCI, was both vice-chairman of Rappaport's Swiss bank, Bank of New York-Inter Maritime, and also head of BCCI's Swiss subsidiary, the Banque de Commerce et de Placements.)[127] The mysterious E. P. Barry, the OSS veteran who had overseen the recovery of SS gold in Operation Safehaven before becoming the banking partner of Paul Helliwell, was also a major stockholder in Rappaport's Inter Maritime Bank.[128]

The collapse of BCCI in 1991 did not see an end to systematic Saudi-financed political corruption in the United States and elsewhere. After a proposed major arms sale in the 1980s met enhanced opposition in Congress from the Israeli lobby, Saudi Arabia negotiated a multi-billion pound long-term contract with the United Kingdom—the so-called "al-Yamamah" deal. We shall see in chapter 10 that overpayments for the purchased weapons were siphoned off into a huge slush fund for political payoffs, including "hundreds of millions of pounds to the ex-Saudi ambassador to the United States, Prince Bandar bin Sultan."[129] According to Robert Lacey, the payments to Prince Bandar were said to total one billion pounds over more than a decade and Bandar distributed these funds lavishly: for example: "a suitcase containing more than $10 million" went to a Vatican priest for the CIA's longtime clients, the Christian Democratic Party.[130]

CONCLUSION: A SUPRANATIONAL DEEP STATE

The complex milieu of Khashoggi, the BCCI, and the Safari Club can be characterized as part of a supranational deep state, whose organic links to the CIA may have helped consolidate it. It is clear however that decisions taken at this level by the Safari Club and BCCI were in no way guided by the political determinations of those *elected* to power in Washington. On the contrary, Prince Turki's candid remarks revealed that the Safari Club (with the alleged collaboration of two former CIA Directors, Bush and Helms) was expressly created to overcome restraints established by political decisions in Washington.

A former Turkish president and prime minister once commented that the Turkish deep state was the real state, and the public state was only a "spare state," not the real one.[131] A better understanding of the American deep state is necessary, if we are to prevent it from assuming permanently the same role.

POSTSCRIPT

In accordance with the book's title, this chapter has focused on aspects of the deep state with special relevance to Wall Street and big oil. There are other aspects we could have looked at, such as the roles of the media, of kingmakers like Clark Clifford, William Pawley, and Jackson Stephens, and of opinion managers like Henry Luce, C. D. Jackson, and Joe Alsop. Abroad there are supranational meetings like Bilderberg and Davos, and the Washington and global public relations firm Hill & Knowlton, said to have opened many overseas offices on the advice of friends, including then CIA director Allen W. Dulles.

Yet another aspect, to which we must return, is that of right-wing Texas oilmen and the John Birch Society, opposed to the relative internationalism of Wall Street and big oil.

CHAPTER 3

The Doomsday Project

How COG on 9/11
Subordinated the U.S. Constitution

When the dust finally clears, Americans will see that September
11 was a triumph for the intelligence community, not a failure.[1]

IN JULY 1987, DURING THE IRAN-CONTRA HEARINGS GRILLING OF OLIVER
North, the American public got a glimpse of "highly sensitive" emergency
planning North had been involved in. Ostensibly North had been handling
plans for an emergency response to a nuclear attack (a legitimate concern).
But press accounts alleged that the planning was for a more generalized suspension of the Constitution at the President's determination.

As part of its routine Iran-Contra coverage, the following exchange was
printed in *The New York Times* without journalistic comment or follow-up:

[Congressman Jack] Brooks: Colonel North, in your work at the N.S.C. were you
not assigned, at one time, to work on plans for the continuity of government in
the event of a major disaster?

Both North's attorney and Senator Daniel Inouye, the Democratic Chair of
the Committee, responded in a way that showed they were aware of the issue:

Brendan Sullivan [North's counsel, agitatedly]: Mr. Chairman?
[Senator Daniel] Inouye: I believe that question touches upon a highly sensitive and classified area so may I request that you not touch upon that?
Brooks: I was particularly concerned, Mr. Chairman, because I read in Miami
papers, and several others, that there had been a plan developed, by that same
agency, a contingency plan in the event of emergency, that would suspend the
American Constitution. And I was deeply concerned about it and wondered if
that was an area in which he had worked. I believe that it was and I wanted to
get his confirmation.
Inouye: May I most respectfully request that that matter not be touched upon
at this stage. If we wish to get into this, I'm certain arrangements can be made
for an executive session.[2]

Brooks was responding to a story by Alfonso Chardy in the *Miami Herald* about Oliver North's involvement with the Federal Emergency Management Agency (FEMA) in planning for "Continuity of Government" (COG). According to Chardy, the plans envisaged "suspension of the Constitution, turning control of the government over to the Federal Emergency Management Agency, emergency appointment of military commanders to run state and local governments and declaration of martial law during a national crisis."[3]

Reagan had installed at FEMA a counterinsurgency team that he had already assembled as governor of California. The team was headed by Army Col. Louis Giuffrida, who had attracted Reagan's attention by a paper he had written while at the U.S. Army War College, advocating the forcible warrantless detention of millions of black Americans in concentration camps. Reagan first installed Giuffrida as head of the California National Guard, and called on him "to design Operation Cable Splicer . . . martial law plans to legitimize the arrest and detention of anti-Vietnam war activists and other political dissidents."[4] These plans were refined with the assistance of British counterinsurgency expert Sir Robert Thompson, who had used massive detention and deportations to deal with the 1950s Communist insurgency in what is now Malaysia.

Thompson's plans for concentration camps in Malaysia, adapted first by Giuffrida in California's Operation Cable Splicer, were further refined by Giuffrida and FEMA with the assistance of Oliver North. In 1984 they were the focus of a massive COG exercise, REX-84,

In 1986, the Associated Press reported on a FEMA directive that described a REX-84 exercise across preparing for the detention of more than 400,000 Central American refugees in ten military centers located across the country.[5]

The revelation was a temporary setback for such extreme planning. In the ensuing controversy, Chardy himself suggested that Reagan's Attorney General, William French Smith, had intervened to stop the COG plan from being presented to the President.[6] Earlier, in 1985, Giuffrida was forced out of office for having spent government money to build a private residence. But COG planning not only continued, it expanded.[7]

Seven years later, in 1994, Tim Weiner reported in *The New York Times* that what he called "The Doomsday Project"—the search for "ways to keep the Government running after a sustained nuclear attack on Washington"—had "less than six months to live."[8]

Weiner's language was technically justifiable, but also very misleading. In fact COG planning now simply continued with a new target: terrorism. On the basis of Weiner's article, the first two books to discuss COG planning, by James Bamford and James Mann, both reported that COG planning had been abandoned.[9] Recently Tim Shorrock in 2008 repeated that "the COG program was abandoned during the Clinton administration," and Shirley Anne Warshaw in 2009 wrote that "the Clinton administration . . . shut down the super-secret Project."[10] But on this specific point, all these otherwise excellent and well-informed authors were wrong.

What Weiner and these authors did not report was that in the final months of Reagan's presidency the purpose of COG planning had officially changed: it was no longer for arrangements "after a nuclear war," but for *any* "national security emergency." This was defined in Executive Order 12656 of 1988 as: "any occurrence, including natural disaster, military attack, technological emergency, or other emergency, that seriously degrades or seriously threatens the national security of the United States."[11] In this way a totally legitimate program dating back to Eisenhower, of planning extraordinary emergency measures for an America devastated in a nuclear attack, was now converted to confer equivalent secret powers on the White House for anything it considered an emergency.

In the wake of the Oklahoma City bombing of 1995, Clinton's counterterrorism coordinator Richard Clarke further increased the scope of COG planning.

> On Oct. 21, 1998, President Bill Clinton signed Presidential Decision Directive 67, "Enduring Constitutional Government and Continuity of Government Operations." No longer would only the very few elite leaders responsible for national security be covered. Instead, every single government department and agency was directed to see to it that they could resume critical functions within 12 hours of a warning.[12]

William Arkin later wrote that "after 9/11 . . . these secret [COG] procedures and plans weren't just geared toward the possibility of Doomsday, for some single and distant event, because Doomsday was now every day."[13] But this expanded application of COG was apparently envisaged as early as 1984, when, according to *Boston Globe* reporter Ross Gelbspan,

> Lt. Col. Oliver North was working with officials of the Federal Emergency Management Agency . . . to draw up a secret contingency plan to surveil political dissenters and to arrange for the detention of hundreds of thousands of undocumented aliens in case of an unspecified national emergency. The plan, part of which was codenamed Rex 84, called for the suspension of the Constitution under a number of scenarios, including a U.S. invasion of Nicaragua.[14]

In other words, extreme measures, designed originally to deal with an externally directed and devastating nuclear attack, were being secretly modified to deal whenever desired with domestic dissenters: a situation that still pertains to today.[15]

The revival of Doomsday Project planning under Reagan, which dated back to NSDD 55 of September 14, 1982, was an important but invisible part of the Reagan Revolution. It was explicitly designed to roll back what some of the Doomsday planners, notably Richard Cheney, regarded as the mistakes committed after Watergate, when as William Arkin has written,

> Gerald Ford and Jimmy Carter carried out the largest number of revisions to presidential directives since Eisenhower, carefully rewriting each of the [COG] emergency documents, aware of changes in the Cold War (and the country) since Ike's time, and the recent massive unlawfulness on the part of the secret services.[16]

THE IMPLEMENTATION OF COG ON 9/11

Clearly 9/11 met the conditions for the implementation of COG measures, and we know for certain that COG plans were implemented on that day in 2001, before the last plane had crashed in Pennsylvania. *The 9/11 Report* confirms this twice, on pages 38 and 326.[17] It was under the auspices of COG that Bush stayed out of Washington on that day, and other government leaders like Paul Wolfowitz were swiftly evacuated to Site R, inside a hollowed out mountain near Camp David.[18]

But the implementation of COG went beyond short-term responses, to the installation of what Professor Shirley Anne Warshaw calls a ninety-day alternative "shadow government" outside Washington.

> Cheney jumped into action in his bunker beneath the East Wing to ensure continuity in government. He immediately began to create his shadow government by ordering one hundred mid-level executive officials to move to specially designated underground bunkers and stay there twenty-four hours a day. They would not be rotated out, he informed them, for ninety days, since there was evidence, he hinted, that the terrorist organization al-Qa'ida, which had masterminded the attack, had nuclear weapons. The shadow government, as a result, needed to be ready to take over the government from the bunkers.[19]

In the President's absence, Cheney secured legal authorization for his actions by a path of deputies that would later arouse controversy:

> To accomplish these goals, the vice president and his lawyer [David Addington] had to set the government's legal direction. . . . By the afternoon of September 11, Addington had made contact with Timothy Flanigan, the deputy White House counsel. Flanigan's boss, Alberto Gonzalez, was stranded in Norfolk .
> . . . Flanigan was in the [White House] Situation Room on September 11. When Addington reached him from the [underground] bunker, Flanigan patched in the Justice Department Command Center across town. There he found [sic] a

young attorney named John C. Yoo . . . [who] had taken leave from university life to join the [Justice Department's] Office of Legal Counsel as a deputy.[20]

Apparently by accident, Cheney and his legal counsel had set in motion on 9/11 the ongoing secret back channel of deputies that would later produce the notorious memos justifying torture and warrantless surveillance. (On surveillance, "among those kept out of the circle were Jay Bybee, ostensibly John Yoo's boss . . . and two successive deputy attorneys general".)[21]

The next ninety days after 9/11 saw the swift implementation of the key features attributed to COG planning by Gelbspan and Chardy in the 1980s: *militarization of homeland security, warrantless detentions, warrantless deportations*, and the *warrantless surveillance* that is their logical counterpart. The clearest example was the administration's Project Endgame—a ten-year plan, initiated in September 2001, to expand detention camps, at a cost of $400 million in Fiscal Year 2007 alone.[22] This implemented the central feature of the massive detention exercise, Rex 84, conducted by Louis Giuffrida and Oliver North in 1984.[23]

There was also a flurry of other rapid moves to restructure America's external and domestic structures. Before discussing these, I should acknowledge the obvious: that enhanced measures to deal with terrorism are needed, and for some of them we should be grateful. We should acknowledge also, however, that the most significant achievements against terrorism have been the result of traditional intelligence and police work. As for the war on terror, the most prominent achievement of Cheney's ninety days, many experts have asserted that it has created far more terrorists than it has disposed of.[24]

On September 20, 2001, Bush launched the war on terror in a televised address to a joint session of Congress, when he said, "Our 'war on terror' begins with al Qaeda, but it does not end there. It will not end until every terrorist group of global reach has been found, stopped and defeated."[25] In 2010 the United States had about 100,000 U.S. troops in Afghanistan to deal with an officially estimated sixty members of al-Qaeda. The predictable result has been an expansion of terrorist activities in Somalia, Yemen, and above all Pakistan.

The war on terror was administratively implemented in three National Security Presidential Directives: NSPDs 7, 8, and 9. All three are classified, and the topics of two of them are unknown. The third, NSPD 9 of October 25, 2001, directed the Secretary of Defense to plan military options against both Taliban and al-Qaeda targets in Afghanistan.[26]

The October date is misleading. A version of the directive calling for covert action in Afghanistan had been approved by principals on September 4, 2001, one week *before* 9/11.[27] An enhanced plan for military action in Afghanistan, had been approved by Bush on September 17; and the same document "directed the Pentagon to begin planning military options for an invasion of Iraq."[28]

Perhaps the most significant domestic product from Cheney's *trimester mirabilis* was the Patriot Act of October 25, 2001. Congress was given only one week to pass this 340-page bill, which in the opinion of researchers "was already written and ready to go long before September 11th."[29]

We should not forget that the Patriot Act was only passed after lethal weapons-grade anthrax letters were mailed to two crucial Democratic Senators—Senators Daschle and Leahy—who had initially questioned the bill. After the anthrax letters, however, they withdrew their initial opposition.[30] Someone—we still do not know who—must have planned those anthrax letters well in advance. We should not forget either that some government experts initially blamed the attacks on Iraq. Much later, referring to Fort Detrick, Salon reporter Glenn Greenwald pointed out that the "Government lab where the anthrax attacks themselves came from was the same place where the false reports originated that blamed those attacks on Iraq."[31]

It is generally agreed that, of the three men in National Command Authority on 9/11, Cheney was the ideologue most committed to restoring the power of a presidency that had been weakened by Watergate.[32] Cheney had already declared in his Iran-Contra Minority Report of 1987 his belief that "the Chief Executive will on occasion feel *duty bound* to assert monarchical notions of prerogative that will permit him to exceed the law."[33] And Vice President Cheney, along with Cheney's counsel David Addington and John Yoo, established the legal justifications for declaring that the President had the prerogative power to "deploy military forces preemptively," and that "the Geneva Conventions and other international agreements against torture 'do not protect members of the al Qaeda organization.'"[34]

By Executive Order 13228 of October 8, 2001, the President established an Office of Homeland Security within the presidential Executive Office. This has engendered in turn the Department of Homeland Security (DHS), now the third largest U.S. Cabinet Department, and also a series of Homeland Security Presidential Directives. For example Homeland Security Presidential Directive-6 (HSPD-6) of September 16, 2003, created a Terrorism Screening Center (TSC), to "consolidate the Government's approach to terrorism screening."[35]

Since then we have become inured to repeated stories about nonviolent individuals who are prevented from boarding airplanes, because their names are in TSC computers on the No Fly List and the Terrorist Watch List. Senator Ted Kennedy testified in Congress that he had been repeatedly delayed at airports because a "T Kennedy" was on the No Fly List. Until July 2008, Nelson Mandela was also on the list.

In addition to the No Fly List, with 4,000 names in 2009 and 21,000 in 2012, some people are prevented from flying because they are on the Terrorist Watch List, a much longer list that contained 440,000 names as of December 2010.[36] This is why Walter F. Murphy, a noted professor of constitutional law, was detained in 2007 on his journey to lecture, ironically, about his book *Constitutional Democracy.* According to Professor Murphy, he was asked by an airline employee,

> "Have you been in any peace marches? We ban a lot of people from flying because of that." . . . "I explained," said Murphy, "that I had not so marched but had, in September 2006, given a lecture at Princeton, televised and put on the web, highly critical of George Bush for his many violations of the [C]onstitution." "That'll do it," the man said.[37]

In the end these cases were resolved satisfactorily. But you risk permanent deportation if you have an Arabic-sounding name. The ACLU sued in 2010 on behalf of Ayman Latif, not just a U.S. citizen but a disabled U.S. Marine veteran, who under Obama had been stranded in Egypt for months, because, on orders from the U.S. Embassy, he had not been able to board a plane to come home.

This was a real hardship case: Latif told NPR that "because I missed my appointments in the United States to be evaluated [as a disabled vet], now the VA administration is saying that they're going to cut my benefits from what they are now to zero." On the same program Stewart Baker, a former assistant secretary for policy with the Department of Homeland Security, vigorously defended the No Fly List. But when asked if there is "any *legal* authority by which the United States can say to a citizen who is abroad, you may not return to this country?" Baker replied, "I know of none."[38] This did not seem to concern him.

Ayman Latif's case is far from unique. According to *The New York Times,*

> Advocacy groups say they are trying to help Americans stranded in Yemen, Egypt, Colombia and Croatia, among other countries. At least one American, Raymond Earl Knaeble IV, who studied in Yemen and is now in Colombia, was returned to Colombia by the Mexican authorities after he sought to cross the border into the United States, the groups say.[39]

THE MILITARIZATION OF AMERICAN LAW ENFORCEMENT

Another post-9/11 innovation from the Giuffrida-Oliver North COG plans was the *militarization of domestic United States law enforcement* in 2002, under a new military command, NORTHCOM.[40] Through NORTHCOM the U.S. Army now is engaged with local enforcement in the surveillance and counterterrorism planning of America, in the same way that through CENTCOM it is engaged with local enforcement to police Iraq. Of course army platoons do not patrol roads and break down the doors of Kansas homes, as they routinely do in Iraq or Afghanistan. But behind the scenes, in so-called "fusion centers," the military, the FBI, and state police, along with private intelligence corporations like SAIC, maintain and analyze data to identify potential threats to those in power.[41]

These fusion centers "have been internally promoted by the US Army as means to avoid restrictions preventing the military from spying on the domestic population."[42] In other words, administrative arrangements have been used to fulfill Giuffrida's plans of circumventing the Posse Comitatus Acts on the statute books, without repealing them.

THE PROCLAMATION OF PERMANENT EMERGENCIES

Finally, still in the ninety-day "shadow government" period after 9/11, President Bush proclaimed two important emergencies that are still in force today.

1. On September 14, 2001, Bush issued Proclamation 7463 ("Declaration of National Emergency by Reason of Certain Terrorist Attacks") together with Executive Order 13223 ("Ordering the Ready Reserve of the Armed Forces To Active Duty"). As we shall see, the terms of this proclamation were significantly expanded when it was renewed in 2007.
2. "On September 23, 2001, by Executive Order 13224, the President declared a national emergency with respect to persons who commit, threaten to commit, or support terrorism, pursuant to the International Emergency Economic Powers Act (50 U.S.C. 1701–1706)."[43] This gave the president the power to confiscate without trial or warning the property of individuals providing funds to entities, such as charitable foundations, which were judged to be supporting terrorism. The executive order initially blocked property of twenty-seven designated terrorists. But the list has become enormous. When I looked at it on November 18, 2010, the list included eighty-seven pages just for the letter A. By June 2014 the letter A took 158 pages.

A lawsuit was instituted, asserting that the designation of "alleged terrorists" was arbitrary. A lower court initially agreed that the President's designation authority was unconstitutionally vague; but after the judge reversed herself, the suit lost.[44]

CHENEY AND RUMSFELD ON THE SECRET COMMITTEE TO PLAN COG

From its beginning in 1982, two of the key planners on the secret COG planning committee were Dick Cheney and Donald Rumsfeld, the same two men who implemented COG on 9/11.[45] The committee had been established by Reagan under a secret executive order, NSDD 55 of September 14, 1982. Despite what Weiner implied, the committee continued to meet without interruption until the George W. Bush presidency in 2001.[46]

Thus Cheney and Rumsfeld continued their secret planning during the Clinton presidency; even after both men, both Republicans, were by that time heads of major corporations and not in the government. Andrew Cockburn cites a Pentagon source to support a claim that the Clinton administration had "no idea what was going on."

> Although the exercises continued, still budgeted at over $200 million a year in the Clinton era, the vanished Soviets were now replaced by terrorists. . . . There were other changes, too. In earlier times the specialists selected to run the "shadow government" had been drawn from across the political spectrum, Democrats and Republicans alike. But now, down in the bunkers, Rumsfeld found himself in politically congenial company, the players' roster being filled almost exclusively with Republican hawks. . . . "You could say this was a secret government-in-waiting. The Clinton administration was extraordinarily inattentive, [they had] no idea what was going on."[47]

Cockburn's account requires some qualification. Richard Clarke, a Clinton Democrat, makes it clear that he participated in the COG games in the 1990s and indeed drafted Clinton's Presidential Decision Directive (PDD) 67 on "Enduring Constitutional Government and Continuity of Government."[48] But COG planning involved different teams for different purposes. It is quite possible that the Pentagon official was describing the Department of Defense team dealing with retaliation.

It is important to understand that the COG "Doomsday Project" in the 1980s involved more than planning and exercises. It also oversaw the National Program Office (NPO), also known as "Project 908," the construction of a multibillion-dollar infrastructure for an alternative government. The key element of this was an $8 billion communications and logistics program headquartered at Fort Huachuca, Arizona, the headquarters for Army Intelligence.[49] It also created ground command centers, some of them mobile, to work with the four Boeing E-4 Advanced Airborne Command Posts, or "Doomsday Planes," stationed at Offutt Air Force Base, near Omaha, Nebraska.

Despite initial failures in the communications network, it was ready to be put into operation and utilized on September 11, 2001, by Vice President Cheney.[50] Key commands, including the implementation of COG itself, appear to have been made over this highest-classification security network.[51] This may explain why a Boeing E-4B Advanced Airborne Command Post, the mobile communications center for the National Command Authority (NCA), was seen around 10 a.m. in the prohibited air space above the White House.[52] (The NCA is defined as consisting of the President and the Secretary of Defense or their deputies, though of course none of these men were in an E-4 on that day.)

There is no way to determine how many of the constitutional changes since 9/11 can be traced to COG planning. However we do know that new COG planning measures were still being introduced in 2007, when President Bush issued National Security Presidential Directive 51 (NSPD-51/HSPD-20). This Directive set out what FEMA later called "a new vision to ensure the continuity of our Government," and was followed in August by a new National Continuity Policy Implementation Plan.[53]

Under pressure from his 911truth constituents, Congressman Peter De-Fazio of the Homeland Security Committee twice requested to see these annexes. When his request was denied, DeFazio made a second request, in a letter signed by the chair of his committee. The request was denied again.[54]

COG, THE NATIONAL EMERGENCY, AND THE
NATIONAL EMERGENCIES ACT

I mentioned earlier that the proclamation of a national emergency, issued by Bush on September 14, 2001, and since renewed annually to this day, changed significantly in 2007. All previous annual renewals had enumerated the emergency measures that were being renewed, for example "the measures taken on September 14, 2001, November 16, 2001, and January 16, 2002." After Bush issued NSPD-51 of 2007, with its "new vision" and its new classified COG annexes, the next renewal of the emergency proclamation replaced the previous specific enumerations with a more sweeping general sentence:

> Because the terrorist threat continues, the national emergency declared on September 14, 2001, last extended on September 5, 2006, *and the powers and authorities adopted to deal with that emergency*, must continue in effect beyond September 14, 2007.[55]

"The powers and authorities adopted to deal with that emergency." This language is so vague, it is hard to see how it could not cover the "classified continuity annexes" of NSPD-51 as well. If so, the public proclamation was now proclaiming the continuation of secret powers. (The annual renewals of the emergency by Barack Obama do not repeat this language from 2007, but likewise fail to enumerate just what powers are being extended.)[56]

The National Emergencies Act, one of the post-Watergate reforms that Vice President Cheney so abhorred, specifies that: "Not later than six months after a national emergency is declared, and not later than the end of each six-month period thereafter that such emergency continues, each House of Congress shall meet to consider a vote on a joint resolution to determine whether that emergency shall be terminated."[57] The law does not *permit* Congress to review an emergency; it *requires* Congress to review it.

Yet since 2001 Congress has not once met to discuss the State of Emergency declared by George W. Bush in response to 9/11, a State of Emergency that remains in effect today. Appeals to Congress to meet its responsibilities to review COG have fallen on deaf ears, even during periods when Congress has been dominated by Democrats.[58] Former Congressman Dan Hamburg and I appealed publicly in 2009, both to President Obama to terminate the emergency, and to Congress to hold the hearings required of them by statute.[59] But Obama, without discussion, has extended the 9/11 Emergency again in every year of his presidency.[60] Meanwhile Congress has continued to ignore its statutory obligations.

In 2009 one Congressman explained to a constituent that the provisions of the National Emergencies Act may have now been rendered inoperative by COG. If true, this would indicate that the constitutional system of checks and balances no longer applies, and also that secret decrees now override public legislation as the law of the land.

With a few notable exceptions, there has thus far been scant interest in the media and the public in the extraordinary facts that Cheney and Rumsfeld were able to

1. help plan successfully for constitutional modifications, when they were not in government, and
2. implement these same changes themselves when back in power.

The first of these facts gives us a glimpse of an ongoing power realm, or deep state, independent of the publicly acknowledged state. In the words of James Mann, "Cheney and Rumsfeld were, in a sense, a part of the permanent, though hidden, national security apparatus of the United States, inhabitants of a world in which Presidents come and go, but America always keeps on fighting."[61] A CNN Special Assignment assessment of the COG planners was even more dramatic: "In the United States of America there is a hidden government about which you know nothing."[62]

What is the first step out of this current state of affairs, in which the Constitution appears to have been superseded by a higher, if less legitimate authority? A traditional response would be that people should get Congress to do what the law requires, and determine whether our present proclamation of emergency "shall be terminated."[63] As part of this procedure, Congress should find whether secret COG powers, never submitted to Congress or seen by it, are among "the powers and authorities" that Bush in 2007 included in his prolongation of the 2001 emergency and that are maintained today under Obama.

This would not be a technical or procedural detail. It would be a test of whether the United States is presently governed by its laws and Constitution, or whether, as has been alleged, the laws and Constitution have now in places been superseded by COG. Ideally Congress should go further to look into the activities of Cheney's ninety days of COG shadow government in 2001, and their relationship to the genesis of the Patriot Act, the ten-year program for detention camps, and the permanent militarization of U.S. domestic law enforcement.

But such a traditional recourse to Congress may be impossible, if Congress itself has indeed been subordinated to the higher powers of the deep state.

CHAPTER 4

The Falsified War on Terror

The Deep History of U.S. Protection for al-Qaeda Terrorist Ali Mohamed

BEFORE WORLD WAR II, THE AMERICAN GOVERNMENT, FOR ALL OF ITS glaring faults, also served as a model for the world of limited government, having evolved a system of restraints on executive power through its constitutional arrangement of checks and balances. All that changed with America's emergence as a dominant world power, and changed further after the Vietnam War.

Since 9/11, above all, constitutional American government has been overshadowed by a series of emergency measures to fight terrorism. The latter have mushroomed in size and budget, while traditional government has been shrunk. As a result we have today (as noted in chapter 2) what the journalists Dana Priest and William Arkin have called

> two governments: the one its citizens were familiar with, operated more or less in the open; the other a parallel top secret government whose parts had mushroomed in less than a decade into a gigantic, sprawling universe of its own, visible to only a carefully vetted cadre—and its entirety . . . visible only to God.[1]

More and more, it is becoming common to say that America, like Turkey before it, now has what Marc Ambinder and John Tirman have called a "deep state" behind the public one.[2] And this parallel government is guided in surveillance matters by its own Foreign Intelligence Surveillance Court, known as the "FISA Court," which according to *The New York Times* "has quietly become almost a parallel Supreme Court."[3] Thanks largely to Edward Snowden, it is now clear that the FISA Court has permitted this deep state to expand surveillance beyond the tiny number of known and suspected Islamic terrorists, to any incipient protest movement that might challenge the policies of the American war machine.

Most Americans have by and large not questioned this parallel government, accepting that sacrifices of traditional rights and traditional transparency are necessary to keep us safe from al-Qaeda attacks. However, secret power is unchecked power, and experience of the last century has only reinforced the truth of Lord Acton's famous dictum that unchecked power always corrupts. It is time to consider the extent to which American secret agencies have developed a symbiotic relationship with the forces they are supposed to be fighting—and have even on occasion intervened in a way that let al-Qaeda terrorists proceed with their plots.

For indeed it is certain that on various occasions U.S. agencies have intervened, letting al-Qaeda terrorists proceed with their plots. This alarming statement will be dismissed by some as "conspiracy theory." Yet in this chapter, I will show that this claim does not arise from theory, but from facts that are true, even though they have been systematically suppressed or under-reported in the American mainstream media.

I am describing a phenomenon that occurred not just once, but repeatedly, almost predictably. We shall see that, among the al-Qaeda terrorists who were first protected and then continued their activities were the following:

1. Ali Mohamed, identified in the 9/11 Commission Report as the leader of the 1998 Nairobi Embassy bombing;[4]
2. Mohammed Jamal Khalifa, Osama bin Laden's close friend and, while in the Philippines, financier of both Ramzi Yousef (principal architect of the first World Trade Center [WTC] attack) and his uncle Khalid Sheikh Mohammed;
3. Khalid Sheikh Mohammed, identified in the 9/11 Commission Report as "the principal architect of the 9/11 attacks";[5]
4. Khalid al-Mihdhar and Nawaf al-Hazmi, two of the alleged 9/11 hijackers, whose presence in the United States was concealed from the FBI by CIA officers for months before 9/11.[6]

It might sound from these citations that the 9/11 Commission marked a new stage in the U.S. treatment of these terrorists, and that the report now exposed those terrorists who in the past had been protected. On the contrary, a principal purpose of my chapter is to show that

1. one purpose of protecting these individuals had been to protect a valued intelligence connection (the "al-Qaeda connection," if you will);
2. one major intention of the 9/11 Commission Report was to continue protecting this connection;
3. those on the 9/11 Commission staff who were charged with this protection included at least one commission member (Jamie Gorelick), one staff member (Dietrich Snell), and one important witness (Patrick Fitzgerald) who earlier had figured among the terrorists' protectors.

In the course of writing this chapter, I came to another disturbing conclusion I had not anticipated. This is that a central feature of the protection has been to defend the 9/11 Commission's false picture of al-Qaeda as an example of non-state terrorism, ignoring not just the CIA but also the royal families of Saudi Arabia and Qatar. In reality, as I shall show, royal family protection from Qatar and Saudi Arabia (concealed by the 9/11 Commission) was repeatedly given to key figures like Khalid Sheikh Mohammed, the alleged "principal architect of the 9/11 attacks."

The establishment claims that the wars fought by America in Asia since 9/11 have been part of a global "war on terror." But this "war on terror" has been fought in alliance with Saudi Arabia, Qatar, and Pakistan—precisely the principal political and financial *backers* of the al-Qaedist networks the United States has supposedly been fighting.[7] Meanwhile the most authentic opponents in the region of these Sunni al-Qaedists—the governments of Iraq, Libya, Syria, and Iran—have found themselves overthrown (in the case of Iraq and Libya), subverted with U.S. support (in the case of Syria), or sanctioned and threatened as part of an "axis of evil" (in the case of Iran). We should not forget that, just one day after 9/11, "Rumsfeld was talking about broadening the objectives of our response and 'getting Iraq.'"[8]

To understand U.S. involvement in the area I believe we must look at the complex of networks behind the post-9/11 U.S. campaign against Osama bin Laden and his followers in al-Qaeda. In fact both British and U.S. intelligence have had a deep and complex involvement for decades with the emerging movement of political Islam—a movement exemplified above all by the Muslim Brotherhood (MB) or Ikhwan, and its many spinoffs, of which al-Qaeda is but one.

The MB itself should be regarded more as a movement than as a formal organization. Like the civil rights movement in America, it has been in continuous flux, and comprised of many tendencies, leading to some alliances that are nonviolent, others that are violent. Its complex relationships with the royal families of Saudi Arabia and Qatar have also been in flux.

In the 1950s, when the Soviet Union and Nasserite nationalism were seen as enemies, MI6 and the CIA developed mostly positive links with the MB and its allies. What follows in chapters 4–6 suggests that, even since the fall of the USSR, U.S. officials, particularly in the CIA, have repeatedly chosen on occasion to preserve their long-term relationship with the MB and al-Qaedists.[9]

I conclude that the pseudowar has been fought for other motives than the official one of fighting terrorism—indeed few informed observers would contest the obvious and often-voiced observation, from U.S. intelligence analysts among others, that U.S. wars overseas (as opposed to intelligence and police actions) have radically increased the dangers of terrorism, not reduced them.[10] Among the hidden motives, two stand out. One is the intention to establish a permanent U.S. military presence in the oil- and gas-rich regions of the

Persian Gulf and Central Asia. Another is to justify a permanent domestic apparatus, in part to contain the threat of opposition to militarist policies, opposition either by direct action or by the publication (as in this chapter) of suppressed truths.[11]

The protection to terrorists described in this chapter, in other words, has been sustained partly in order to support the false ideology that has underlain U.S. Asian wars, disguised as a war on terror, for more than a decade. And the blame cannot be assigned all to the Saudis. Two months before 9/11, FBI counterterrorism expert John O'Neill described to the French journalist Jean-Charles Brisard America's "impotence" in getting help from Saudi Arabia concerning terrorist networks. The reason? In Brisard's paraphrase, "Just one: the petroleum interests."[12] Former CIA officer Robert Baer voiced a similar complaint about the lobbying influence of "the Foreign Oil Companies Group, a cover for a cartel of major petroleum companies doing business in the Caspian. . . . The deeper I got, the more Caspian oil money I found sloshing around Washington."[13]

The decade of protection for terrorists demonstrates the power of this extra dimension to the American deep state: the dark forces in our society responsible for protecting terrorists, over and above the parallel government that was strengthened on and after 9/11.[14] Although I cannot securely define these dark forces, I hope to demonstrate that they are related to the black hole at the heart of the complex U.S-Saudi connection, a complex that involves the oil majors like Exxon, the Pentagon's concern with oil and gas movements from the Persian Gulf and Central Asia, offsetting arms sales, Saudi investments in major U.S. corporations like Citibank and the Carlyle Group (the owners of Booz Allen Hamilton), and above all the ultimate United States dependency on Saudi Arabia, Qatar, and OPEC, for the defense of the petrodollar.[15] The apparatus of U.S. security appears to have been hijacked by these deeper forces, in order to protect terrorists who should have been reined in. And the governing media have been complicit in concealing this situation.

In other words, this profound dimension of the deep state, behind its institutional manifestation in our parallel government, could be seen as a greater threat than foreign terrorism to the preservation of U.S. democracy.

THE FBI'S INTERVENTION WITH THE ROYAL CANADIAN MOUNTED POLICE TO RELEASE ALI MOHAMED, 1993

Let me begin my survey of protecting terrorists with the FBI's instruction in 1993 to the Royal Canadian Mounted Police (RCMP) to release the major al-Qaeda organizer Ali Mohamed, who then proceeded to Nairobi in the same year to begin planning the U.S. Embassy bombing of 1998.

In early 1993 a wanted Egyptian terrorist named Essam Hafez Marzouk, a close ally of Osama bin Laden and Ayman al-Zawahiri, arrived at Canada's

Vancouver Airport and was promptly detained by the RCMP. A second terrorist by the name of Ali Mohamed, "the primary U.S. intelligence agent for Ayman al-Zawahiri and Osama bin Laden," came from California to the airport to meet him; and, not finding him, made the mistake of asking about his friend at the Vancouver airport customs office. As a result the RCMP interrogated Ali Mohamed for two days, but finally released him, even though Mohamed had clearly come in order to smuggle a wanted terrorist into the United States.[16]

If the RCMP had detained Ali Mohamed, who was much bigger game than the first terrorist, hundreds of lives might have been saved. After being released, Ali went on to Nairobi, Kenya. There in December 1993 he and his team photographed the U.S. Embassy, and then delivered the photos to Osama bin Laden in Khartoum, leading to the embassy bombing of 1998.[17] Mohamed later told an FBI agent that at some point he also trained al-Qaeda terrorists in using box cutters to hijack airplanes.[18]

The RCMP release of Ali Mohamed was unjustified, clearly had historic consequences, and may have contributed to 9/11. Yet the FBI authorized it: Ali Mohamed gave the RCMP the phone number of an FBI agent, John Zent, in the San Francisco FBI office, and told them, "If they called that number, the agent on the other end of the line would vouch for him." As Ali had predicted, the ensuing phone call led to his release.[19]

Ali Mohamed was an important double agent, of major interest to more important U.S. authorities than Zent. Although Mohamed was at last arrested in September 1998 for his role in the Nairobi Embassy bombing, the U.S. government still had not sentenced him in 2006; and as late as 2011 he may still not have gone to jail.[20]

The story of his Vancouver release and its consequences is another example of the dangers of working with double agents. One can never be sure if the agent is working for his movement, for his agency, or—perhaps most likely— for increasing his own power and influence along with that of both his movement and his agency, by increasing violence in the world.[21]

ALI MOHAMED'S RELEASE AS A DEEP EVENT IGNORED BY THE U.S. MEDIA

Mohamed's release in Vancouver was a deep event, by which I mean an event predictably suppressed in the media and still not fully understandable. A whole chapter in my book *The Road to 9/11* was not enough to describe Mohamed's intricate relationships at various times with the CIA, U.S. Special Forces at Fort Bragg, the murder in New York of Jewish extremist Meir Kahane, and finally, the cover-up of 9/11 perpetrated by the 9/11 Commission and their witness, U.S. Attorney Patrick Fitzgerald (Mohamed's former prosecutor).[22]

The deep event is also an example of deep politics, a mixture of intrigue and suppression involving not just a part of the U.S. government, but also the governing media. According to a 2013 search of LexisNexis, the Vancouver release incident, well covered in Canada's leading newspaper *The Toronto Globe and Mail* (December 22, 2001), has never been mentioned in *any* major American newspaper.

More disturbingly, it is not even hinted at in the otherwise well-informed books and articles about Ali Mohamed by Steven Emerson, Peter Bergen, and Lawrence Wright.[23] Nor is there any mention of it in the best insider's book about the FBI and Ali Mohamed, *The Black Banners*, by former FBI agent Ali Soufan (a book that was itself heavily and inexcusably censored by the CIA, after being cleared for publication by the FBI).[24] Since first publishing this paragraph in 2013, I have noticed that former CIA officer Michael Scheuer also faults both Steve Coll and Lawrence Wright for their "whole-hog acceptance of the Saudi narrative" that minimizes U.S.-Saudi differences.[25]

There is no doubt about the FBI's responsibility for Mohamed's release. It (along with other FBI anomalies in handling Mohamed) is frankly acknowledged in a Pentagon Security bio on Mohamed:

> In early 1993, Mohamed was detained by the Royal Canadian Mounted Police (RCMP) at the Vancouver, Canada, airport. He had come to the airport to meet an Egyptian who had arrived from Damascus but was found to be carrying two forged Saudi passports. When Mohamed was about to be arrested as well, he told the RCMP he was collaborating with the FBI and gave them a name and phone number to call to confirm this. The RCMP made the call and Mohamed was released immediately at the request of the FBI. When the FBI subsequently questioned Mohamed about this incident, he offered information about a ring in California that was selling counterfeit documents to smugglers of illegal aliens. This is the earliest hard evidence that is publicly available of Mohamed being an FBI informant.[26]

Contrast this official candor about the FBI responsibility for Mohamed's release with the suppression of it in the following much longer account of Mohamed (3,200 words) by Benjamin Weiner and James Risen in *The New York Times*:

> [In 1993] he was stopped by the border authorities in Canada, while traveling in the company of a suspected associate of Mr. bin Laden's who was trying to enter the United States using false documents.
>
> Soon after, Mr. Mohamed was questioned by the F.B.I., which had learned of his ties to Mr. bin Laden. Apparently in an attempt to fend off the investigators, Mr. Mohamed offered information about a ring in California that was selling counterfeit documents to smugglers of illegal aliens.[27]

A long *Wall Street Journal* account massages the facts even more evasively:

> At about the same time [1993], the elusive Mr. Mohamed popped up again on the FBI radar screen with information that underscored the emerging bin Laden threat. The Royal Canadian Mounted Police questioned Mr. Mohamed in the spring of 1993 after his identification was discovered on another Arab man trying to enter the U.S. from Vancouver—a man Mr. Mohamed identified as someone who had helped him move Mr. bin Laden to Sudan. The FBI located Mr. Mohamed near San Francisco in 1993, where he volunteered the earliest insider description of al Qaeda that is publicly known.[28]

In 1998, after the Embassy bombings, Mohamed was finally arrested. In the ensuing trial an FBI Agent, Daniel Coleman, entered a court affidavit (approved by prosecutor Patrick Fitzgerald) that summarized the Vancouver incident as follows:

> In 1993, MOHAMED advised the Royal Canadian Mounted Police ("RCMP") that he had provided intelligence and counterintelligence training in Afghanistan to a particular individual. . . . MOHAMED admitted that he had travelled to Vancouver, Canada, in the spring of 1993 to facilitate the entry of that individual into the United States. . . . MOHAMED further admitted that he and the individual had transported Osama bin Laden from Afghanistan to the Sudan in 1991. . . . MOHAMED told the RCMP that he was in the process of applying for a job as an FBI interpreter and did not want this incident to jeopardize the application. (In fact, MOHAMED then had such an application pending though he was never hired as a translator.)[29]

Like the American media, this FBI affidavit suppressed the fact that Mohamed, an admitted ally of Osama bin Laden caught red-handed with another known terrorist, was released at the request of the FBI.

THE TWO LEVELS OF AMERICAN HISTORY: OFFICIAL HISTORY AND DEEP HISTORY

The whole episode illustrates what has become all too common in recent American history, the way in which secret bureaucratic policies can take priority over the public interest, even to the point of leading to mass murder (since it contributed at a minimum to the 1998 Embassy bombings, if not also 9/11). It is also an example of what I mean by the "two levels of history" in America, We can refer to them as those historical facts officially acknowledged, and those facts officially suppressed; or alternatively as those facts fit to be mentioned in the governing media, and those suppressed by the same media. This leads in turn to two levels of historical narrative: official or archival history, which ignores or marginalizes deep events, and a second level—called "deep history" by its practitioners or "conspiracy theory" by its critics—which incorporates them. The task of deep political research is to recover deep events from this second level.

This activity sets deep political research at odds with the governing media, but not, I believe, with the national interest. Quite the contrary. Speaking personally as an ex-diplomat, I should acknowledge clearly that the national interest does occasionally require secrets, at least for a time. Kissinger's trip to China, for example, which led to a normalization of U.S.-Chinese relations, probably required secrecy (at least at the time) in order to succeed.

When insiders and the governing media collaborate in the keeping of a secret, as in the case of the FBI-ordered release of Mohamed, they probably persuade themselves that they are protecting, not just the FBI, but also national security—indeed, the national interest. However national security in this case was conspicuously not served by the subsequent embassy bombings, let alone by 9/11.

In the glaring gap between these two levels of history is a third level—that of the privileged books about Mohamed—"privileged" in the sense that they have access to sources denied to others—that give important but selective parts of the truth. This selectivity is not necessarily culpable; it may for example be due to pressure from lawyers representing Saudi millionaires (a pressure I have yielded to myself).[30] But cumulatively it is misleading.

I owe a considerable debt in particular to Lawrence Wright's book, *The Looming Tower*, which helped expose many problems and limitations in the official account of 9/11. But I see now in retrospect that I, like many others, have been delayed by its selectivity on many matters (including for example Mohamed's RCMP release) from developing a less warped understanding of the truth.

THE LONGER HISTORY OF FBI AND U.S. GOVERNMENT PROTECTION FOR ALI MOHAMED

Why did John Zent vouchsafe for Mohamed in 1993, so that the RCMP released him? The explanation of Peter Lance, the best chronicler of FBI culpability in both the first and second WTC attacks, is that Zent did so because Mohamed was already working as his personal informant, "feeding Zent 'intelligence' on Mexican smugglers who were moving illegal immigrants into the United States from the South."[31] (FBI agent Cloonan confirms that Mohamed had been working as a local FBI informant since 1992.[32]) Elsewhere Lance describes Zent as "trusting and distracted," so that he failed to realize Mohamed's importance.[33]

But the FBI's protection of Ali Mohamed did not begin with Zent, nor was it limited to him. It dated back at least to 1989, according to the following Pentagon Security bio account:

While serving in the Army at Fort Bragg, he traveled on weekends to Jersey City, NJ, and to Connecticut to train other Islamic fundamentalists in surveillance, weapons and explosives. . . . Telephone records show that while at Fort Bragg and later, Mohamed maintained a very close and active relationship with the Office of Services [Maktab Al-Khidamat] of the Mujihadeen, in Brooklyn, which at that time was recruiting volunteers and soliciting funds for the jihad against the Soviets in Afghanistan. This was the main recruitment center for the network that, after the Soviets left Afghanistan, became known as al-Qaida. . . .

The FBI observed and photographed Mohamed giving weapons training to a group of New York area residents during four successive weekends in July 1989. They drove from the Farouq Mosque in Brooklyn to a shooting range in Calverton, Long Island, and they fired AK-47 assault rifles, semiautomatic handguns and revolvers during what appeared to be training sessions. *For reasons that are unknown, the FBI then ceased its surveillance of the group.*[34]

(Similarly in 1993 an FBI supervisor would again abruptly close down surveillance of another group from the al-Kifah Center at a militant training camp in Pennsylvania.)[35]

In the subsequent trial of Mohamed's trainees and others for bombing the World Trade Center, the defense attorney, Roger Stavis, established that Mohamed was giving the al-Kifah trainees "courses on how to make bombs, how to use guns, how to make Molotov cocktails." He showed the court that a training manual seized in Nosair's apartment "showed how to make explosives and some kind of improvised weapons and explosives."[36]

So why would the FBI, after having discovered terrorist training, then *cease* its surveillance? Here the *Wall Street Journal* gives the correct answer: the FBI ceased surveillance because they somehow determined that the men were training "to help the mujahedeen fighting the Soviet puppet government in Afghanistan."[37] (Note however that the mujahedin were no longer fighting the Soviet army itself, which had been withdrawn from Afghanistan as of March 1989.)

AL-KIFAH, ALI MOHAMED, THE FLOW OF ARABS TO AFGHANISTAN

Afghanistan is indeed a plausible explanation for the FBI's terminating its videotaping of al-Qaedists from the Brooklyn Al-Kifah Refugee Center. Incorporated officially in 1987 as "Afghan Refugee Services, Inc.," the Al-Kifah Center "was the recruitment hub for U.S.-based Muslims seeking to fight the Soviets. As many as two hundred fighters were funneled through the center to Afghanistan."[38] More importantly, it was

a branch of the Office of Services [Maktab Al-Khidamat], the Pakistan-based organization that Osama bin Laden helped finance and lead and would later become al Qaeda. In fact, it was Mustafa Shalabi, an Egyptian who founded and ran the center, whom bin Laden called in 1991 when he needed help moving to Sudan.[39]

As we shall see, the Maktab, created in 1984 to organize Saudi financial support to the foreign "Arab Afghans" in the jihad, was part of a project that had the fullest support of the Saudi, Egyptian, and U.S. governments. And Ali Mohamed, who answered bin Laden's call to Shalabi, and who remained in the U.S. Army Reserves until August 1994, was clearly an important trainer in that project—in Egypt, in Afghanistan, and finally in America.

A privileged account of Mohamed's career by Peter Bergen, in *Holy Wars, Inc.*, claims,

> Ali Mohamed . . . was an indispensable player in al-Qaeda. . . . At some point in the early eighties he proffered his services as an informant to the CIA, the first of his several attempts to work for the U.S. government. The Agency was in contact with him for a few weeks but broke off relations after determining he was "unreliable." That would turn out to be a masterful understatement, as Mohamed was already a member of Egypt's terrorist Jihad group.
>
> After being discharged from the Egyptian Army in 1984, Mohamed . . . [took] a job in the counterterrorism department of Egyptair. The following year he moved to the United States.[40]

Bergen's most serious omission here is that Mohamed, though he was on the State Department's visa watch list, had been admitted to the United States in 1984 "on a visa-waiver program that was sponsored by the agency [i.e., CIA] itself, one designed to shield valuable assets or those who have performed valuable services for the country."[41] This should be enough to question the CIA's cover story that it dismissed Mohamed as "unreliable." (Later, one of Mohamed's officers at Fort Bragg was also convinced that Mohamed was "sponsored" by a U.S. intelligence service, "I assumed the CIA.")[42] In addition Bergen omits that, before Mohamed's brief stint as a formal CIA agent, he had been selected out of the Egyptian army in 1981 for leadership training at Fort Bragg—an important point to which we shall return.[43]

THE FBI'S COVER-UP OF ALI MOHAMED'S CONNECTION TO THE KAHANE MURDER

The CIA may have wanted to think that the Al-Kifah training was only for Afghanistan. But the blind Sheikh Omar Abdel Rahman (the mentor of the Center), whom the CIA brought to America in 1990, was preaching for the killing of Jews and also for the destruction of the West.[44] His preachings guided Mohamed's Maktab trainees: as a first step, in November 1990, three of them conspired to kill Meir Kahane, the founder of the Jewish Defense League, in New York City.

Kahane was then shot in Manhattan in November 1990. His actual killer, El Sayyid Nosair, was detained by accident almost immediately, and by luck the police soon found his two coconspirators, Mahmoud Abouhalima and Mohammed Salameh, waiting at Nosair's house. Also at the house, according to John Miller (formerly of the FBI), "were training manuals from the Army Special Warfare School at Fort Bragg [where Ali Mohamed at the time was a training officer]. There were copies of teletypes that had been routed to the Secretary of the Army and the Joint Chiefs of Staff."[45]

And the Pentagon bio, with yet another gentle dig at the FBI, identifies the documents as Mohamed's:

In a search of Nosair's home, the police found U.S. Army training manuals, videotaped talks that Mohamed delivered at the JFK Special Warfare Center at Fort Bragg, operational plans for joint coalition exercises conducted in Egypt, and other materials marked Classified or Top Secret. These documents belonged to Mohamed, who often stayed in New Jersey with Nosair. The documents did not surface during Nosair's 1991 trial for the Kahane murder. It is not known if the FBI investigated Mohamed in connection with these documents.

Yet only hours after the 1990 killing, Joseph Borelli, the chief of the New York Police Department (NYPD) detectives, pronounced Nosair a "lone deranged gunman."[46] A more extended account of his remarks in *The New York Times* actually alluded to Mohamed, though not by name, and minimized the significance of the links to terrorism in a detailed account of the Nosair home cache:

The files contained articles about firearms and explosives apparently culled from magazines, like *Soldier of Fortune*, appealing to would-be mercenaries. But the police said the handwritten papers, translated by an Arabic-speaking officer, appeared to be minor correspondence and did not mention terrorism or outline any plan to kill the militant Jewish leader who had called for the removal of all Arabs from Israel.

"There was nothing [at Nosair's house] that would stir your imagination," Chief Borelli said. . . . A joint anti-terrorist task force of New York City police and the Federal Bureau of Investigation has been set up to look into any possible international links to the slaying, the official said, but so far has not turned up anything.

"Nothing has transpired that changes our opinion that he acted alone," Chief Borrelli [sic] told a news conference yesterday afternoon.[47]

Later an FBI spokesman said the FBI also believed "that Mr. Nosair had acted alone in shooting Rabbi Kahane." "The bottom line is that we can't connect anyone else to the Kahane shooting," an FBI agent said.[48]

Blaming the New York County District Attorney, Robert Morgenthau, the FBI later claimed that the evidence retrieved from Nosair's home was not processed for two or three years.[49] But Robert Friedman suggests that the FBI were not just lying to the public, but also to Morgenthau (who had just helped expose and bring down the CIA-favored Muslim bank BCCI, a Saudi-sponsored ally of the Safari Club).

> According to other sources familiar with the case, the FBI told District Attorney Robert M. Morgenthau that Nosair was a lone gunman, not part of a broader conspiracy; the prosecution took this position at trial and lost, only convicting Nosair of gun charges. Morgenthau speculated the CIA may have encouraged the FBI not to pursue any other leads, these sources say. "The FBI lied to me," Morgenthau has told colleagues. "They're supposed to untangle terrorist connections, but they can't be trusted to do the job."[50]

Using evidence from the Nosair trial transcript, Peter Lance confirms the tension between Morgenthau's office, which wanted to pursue Nosair's international terrorist connections, and the FBI, which insisted on trying Nosair alone.[51]

THE FBI'S PROTECTION OF ALI MOHAMED IN THE 1993 WTC BOMBING

In thus limiting the case, the police and the FBI were in effect protecting, not just Ali Mohamed, but also Nosair's two Arab coconspirators, Mahmoud Abouhalima and Mohammed Salameh, in the murder of a U.S. citizen. The two were thus left free to kill again on February 26, 1993, one month after the FBI secured Mohamed's release in Vancouver. Both Abouhalima and Salameh were ultimately convicted in connection with the 1993 World Trade Center bombing, along with another Mohamed trainee, Nidal Ayyad.

To quote the Pentagon biography yet again,

> In February 1993, the terrorist cell that Mohamed had trained exploded a truck bomb under the World Trade Center that killed six and injured about 1,000 persons. The perpetrators of this bombing included people Mohamed had trained, and Mohamed had been in close contact with the cell during the period leading up to the bombing [i.e., including January 1993, the month of Mohamed's detention and release in Vancouver]. Mohamed's name appeared on a list of 118 potential un-indicted co-conspirators that was prepared by federal prosecutors.[52]

Ali Mohamed was again listed as one of 172 unindicted coconspirators in the follow-up "Landmarks" case, which convicted Sheikh Rahman and others of plotting to blow up the United Nations, the Lincoln and Holland Tunnels, and the George Washington Bridge.[53] The two cases were closely related, as much of the evidence for the Landmarks case came from an informant, Emad Salem, whom the FBI had first planted among the WTC plotters. But the prosecutors' awareness of Ali Mohamed's involvement must be contrasted with the reported intelligence failure at the CIA's Counterterrorism Center (CTC): according to Steve Coll, the CTC "immediately established a seven-day, twenty-four hour task force to collect intelligence about the World Trade Center bombing . . . but nothing of substance came in."[54]

In the WTC bombing case, the FBI moved swiftly to bring the Al-Kifah plotters to trial one month later, in March. Lt. Col. Anthony Shaffer, a Defense Intelligence Agency (DIA) officer, later said,

> we [i.e., DIA] were surprised how quickly they'd [i.e., FBI] made the arrests after the first World Trade Center bombing. Only later did we find out that the FBI had been watching some of these people for months prior to both incidents [i.e., both the 1993 WTC bombing and 9/11].[55]

Shaffer's claim that the FBI had been watching some of the plotters is abundantly corroborated, for example, by Steve Coll in *Ghost Wars*.[56]

THE U.S., EGYPTIAN, AND SAUDI BACKING FOR THE MAKTAB NETWORK

What was being protected here by the FBI? One obvious answer is an extension of Lance's explanation for Zent's behavior: that Mohamed had already been a domestic FBI informant since 1992. However I entirely agree with New York County District Attorney Robert Morgenthau, who suspected that a much larger asset was being protected, the Saudi-sponsored network that we now know was the Maktab Al-Khidamat, by this time already evolving into al-Qaeda.

> On the day the FBI arrested four Arabs for the World Trade Centre bombing, saying it had all of the suspects, Morgenthau's ears pricked up. He didn't believe the four were "self-starters," and speculated that there was probably a larger network as well as a foreign sponsor. He also had a hunch that the suspects would lead back to Sheikh Abdel Rahman. But he worried [correctly] that the dots might not be connected because the U.S. government was protecting the sheikh for his help in Afghanistan.[57]

This "larger network" of the Maktab, although created in 1984, consolidated an assistance program that had been launched by the U.S. government much earlier in Egypt by Zbigniew Brzezinski. At almost the beginning of the Afghan war itself, Brzezinski arranged for a program to train members of the anti-Communist Muslim Brotherhood, a group that the CIA, and the British MI6, had supported in various ways since the 1950s.[58]

In January 1980, Brzezinski visited Egypt to mobilize support for the jihad. Within weeks of his visit, Sadat authorized Egypt's full participation, giving permission for the U.S. Air Force to use Egypt as a base . . . and recruiting, training, and arming Egyptian Muslim Brotherhood activists for battle. . . . Not only were they packaged and shipped to Afghanistan, but [by the end of 1980] they received expert training from U.S. Special Forces.[59]

U.S. military trainers had in fact already been in Egypt since at least 1978 (the year of the Israel-Egypt Camp David peace accords), training Sadat's elite praetorian guard, of which Ali Mohamed was at the time a member. At first the training was handled by a "private" firm, J. J. Cappucci and Associates, owned by former CIA officers Ed Wilson and Theodore Shackley (who is said to have been collaborating at this time with the Safari Club). But after Brzezinski's visit in 1980, the contract was taken over by the CIA.[60]

In 1981 Ali Mohamed was selected out of the U.S.-trained praetorian guard for four months of Special Forces training at Fort Bragg: "Working alongside Green Berets, he learned unconventional warfare, counterinsurgency operations, and how to command elite soldiers on difficult missions."[61] Mohamed was in Fort Bragg as part of the Pentagon's Professional Military Education (PME) program for future leaders; he was being trained to transmit to Egypt the kind of Afghanistan-related skills that he later provided to Al-Kifah on Long Island in 1989.[62]

Mohamed was thus in America when some of his fellow guard members, responding to a *fatwa* or religious order from Muslim Brotherhood member Sheikh Omar Abdel Rahman, assassinated Sadat in October 1981. The assassination only accelerated the export out of Egypt to Afghanistan of Muslim Brotherhood members accused of the murder. These included two of Mohamed's eventual close associates, Sheikh Abdel Rahman and Rahman's then friend Ayman al-Zawahiri, to whom Mohamed swore a *bayat* or oath of allegiance in 1984, after his return to Egypt.[63]

In other words Ali Mohamed was a double agent in a milieu much broader than just the San Francisco FBI office: a milieu involving the United States, Egypt, and al-Qaeda. In the next chapter we shall suggest that in assisting Osama bin Laden, Mohamed was also serving the interests of Saudi Arabia.

CHAPTER 5

The Falsified War on Terror II

How the Deep State Has Protected Gulf Arab States Rather than the American People

THE AL-KIFAH TARGET IN 1993: NOT AFGHANISTAN, BUT BOSNIA

MORGENTHAU'S SUSPICIONS IN 1993 THAT AL-KIFAH WAS RECRUITING AL-Qaedists for Afghanistan were very pertinent. But they were also anachronistic: By 1993, under its new director James Woolsey, both the CIA and al-Kifah had lost interest in Afghanistan. The new interim president of Afghanistan, Mojaddedi, under pressure from Washington, had announced that the Arab Afghans should leave. In January 1993 Pakistan followed suit, closed the offices of all mujahedin in its country, and ordered the deportation of all Arab Afghans.[1]

The al-Kifah support network, in conjunction with wealthy backers in Saudi Arabia, now had new targets in mind elsewhere. After 1991 the Brooklyn Center was focused chiefly on training people for jihad in Bosnia, and at least two sources allege that Ali Mohamed himself visited Bosnia in 1992 (when he also returned to Afghanistan).[2]

> Al-Kifah's English-language newsletter *Al-Hussam* (The Sword) also began publishing regular updates on jihad action in Bosnia. . . . Under the control of the minions of Shaykh Omar Abdel Rahman, the newsletter aggressively incited sympathetic Muslims to join the jihad in Bosnia and Afghanistan themselves. . . . The al-Kifah Bosnian branch office in Zagreb, Croatia, housed in a modern, two-story building, was evidently in close communication with the organizational headquarters in New York. The deputy director of the Zagreb office, Hassan Hakim, admitted to receiving all orders and funding directly from the main United States office of al-Kifah on Atlantic Avenue controlled by Shaykh Omar Abdel Rahman.[3]

One of Ali Mohamed's trainees at al-Kifah, Rodney Hampton-El, assisted in this support program, recruiting warriors from U.S. Army bases like Fort Belvoir, and also training them in New Jersey to be fighters.[4] In 1995 Hampton-El was tried and convicted for his role (along with al-Kifah leader

Sheikh Omar Abdel Rahman) in the plot to blow up New York landmarks. At the trial Hampton-El testified how he was personally given thousands of dollars for this project by Saudi Prince Faisal in the Washington Saudi Embassy.[5] (In addition, "Saudi intelligence has contributed to Sheikh Rahman's legal-defence fund, according to Mohammed al-Khilewi, the former first secretary to the Saudi mission at the U.N.")[6]

Later in this chapter we shall have much more to say about Saudi support for this terrorist network, and in particular about the Saudi embassy in Washington.

AL-KIFAH, AL-QAEDA, TAJIKISTAN, AND DRUGS

Meanwhile the Pakistani Inter-Services Intelligence (ISI) had not lost interest in bin Laden's Arabs, but began to recruit them with bin Laden's support for battle in new areas, notably Central Asia and Kashmir.[7] Bin Laden in the same period began to dispatch his al-Qaedists into areas of the former Soviet Union, notably to the infant Islamic Movement of Uzbekistan (IMU) in Tajikistan.

> The outbreak of Islamist violence in Tajikistan . . . moved bin Laden to send a limited number of al-Qaeda cadre to support Tajik Islamist forces, among them his close associate Wali Khan Amin Shah [an Uzbek later working in the Philippines with Ramzi Yousuf and Khalid Sheikh Mohammed] and the soon-to-be-famous mujahid, Ibn Khattab. In addition, bin Laden, even after his 1991 move to Sudan, continued to run training camps in Afghanistan, where he welcomed the chance to train Tajiks, Uzbeks, Uighurs, and Chechens.[8]

In an al-Qaeda document captured in Iraq, bin Laden wrote:

> With the grace of Allah, we were successful in cooperating with our brothers in Tajikistan in various fields including training. We were able train a good number of them, arm them and deliver them to Tajikistan. Moreover, Allah facilitated to us delivering weapons and ammunition to them; we pray that Allah grants us all victory.[9]

Many other accounts report that the delivery of arms and ammunition was facilitated by the involvement of the IMU and bin Laden in the massive flow of heroin from Afghanistan into the former Soviet Union. According to Ahmed Rashid,

> Much of the I.M.U.'s financing came from the lucrative opium trade through Afghanistan. Ralf Mutschke, the assistant director of Interpol's Criminal Intelligence Directorate, estimated that sixty per cent of Afghan opium exports were moving through Central Asia and that the "I.M.U. may be responsible for

seventy per cent of the total amount of heroin and opium transiting through the area."[10]

Among the experts confirming the IMU–al-Qaeda drug connection is journalist Gretchen Peters:

> The opium trade . . . supported the global ambitions of Osama bin Laden. . . . There was . . . evidence that bin Laden served as middleman between the Taliban and Arab drug smugglers. . . . With Mullah Omar's approval, bin Laden hijacked the state-run Ariana Airlines, turning it into a narco-terror charter service . . . according to former U.S. and Afghan officials. . . . One U.S. intelligence report seen by the author described a smuggling route snaking up through Afghanistan's northwest provinces in Baghdis, Faryab, and Jowzan into Turkmenistan. It was being used as of mid-2004 by "extremists associated with the Taliban, the Islamic Movement of Uzbekistan and al-Qaeda," the report said. Traffickers would move "both heroin and terrorists" along the route and "then onwards into other countries in Central Asia," the CIA document said.[11]

It has been widely reported that in the early 1990s, as U.S. financial support dwindled and bin Laden's finances were being rapidly exhausted in Sudan, his new involvement with the IMU and later the Taliban involved al-Qaeda also in the growing Afghan heroin traffic. Peters saw a CIA document confirming this.[12] Yet *The 9/11 Commission Report*, in contorted language, denied this, as did a Staff Report:

> No persuasive evidence exists that al Qaeda relied on the drug trade as an important source of revenue, had any substantial involvement with conflict diamonds, or was financially sponsored by any foreign government.[13]

This surprising claim was at odds with the views of many U.S. intelligence operatives. It also contradicted the official position of the British government, which told its Parliament in 2001,

> Usama Bin Laden and Al Qaida have been based in Afghanistan since 1996, but have a network of operations throughout the world. The network includes training camps, warehouses, communication facilities and commercial operations able to raise significant sums of money to support its activity. That activity includes substantial exploitation of the illegal drugs trade from Afghanistan.[14]

Meanwhile there were allegations that the Brooklyn al-Kifah Center, as well as bin Laden, was involved in drug trafficking. Back in 1993, *The New York Times* reported that, according to investigators, "Some of the 11 men charged in the [Day of Terror] plot to bomb New York City targets are also suspected of trafficking in drugs."[15] Mujahid Abdulqaadir Menepta, a Muslim suspect in both the 9/11 case and the 1995 Oklahoma City bombing, was linked by telephone numbers on his cell phones to ongoing criminal investigations, involving "organized crime, drugs, and money laundering."[16] And Raed Hijazi, an al-Qaeda terrorist arrested in Jordan in 1999, had previously become an FBI informant in order to avoid drug charges.[17]

The Commission may have covered up and lied about this activity to protect CIA interests in Uzbekistan. It is certain that in the 1980s, the CIA, along with Pakistani and Saudi intelligence, hoped to foment Islamic fundamentalism in Uzbekistan; the CIA even "commissioned an Uzbek exile living in Germany to produce translations of the Koran in the Uzbek language,"[18] for distribution by Islamist factions. Hence it is not surprising that "from the beginning the IMU has received substantial support from Pakistan's Inter-Services Intelligence agency. However . . . . sympathetic foundations and banks in Saudi Arabia and the Arab world, also remain major IMU sponsors."[19]

This would not be the first time that the CIA protected a drug traffic that supported the activities of its assets abroad.[20] If al-Kifah supported its operations through drugs, it would have followed in the tradition of the drug-money–laundering Australian Nugan Hand Bank in the 1970s, founded in part by American veterans of the Vietnam War, with former CIA Director William Colby serving as legal counsel.[21] Nugan Hand had become involved in supplying arms to the UNITA faction of rebels in Angola that was later supported by the Safari Club.[22]

WAS THE U.S. PROTECTION OF THE AL-KIFAH CENTER INTENDED TO HELP EXPORT AND FINANCE AL-QAEDISTS?

There is also no treatment in the 9/11 Report, and almost none elsewhere, of the allegations from Steven Emerson that by 1987, the al-Kifah Center at the Al-Farooq Mosque in Brooklyn "had become a center for counterfeiting tens of thousands of dollars."[23] Similarly there has been no government follow-up of the allegation by Yossef Bodansky, citing FBI informant Emad Salem, that one of the al-Kifah cell leaders (Siddiq Ibrahim Siddig Ali) "had offered to sell a million dollars [of counterfeit currency] for $150,000, well below market value. . . . Quantities of counterfeit $100 bills were later found at the apartment of Sheikh Umar Abdel-Rahman."[24]

J. M. Berger goes further, reporting from court testimony: "In order to support Al Kifah's operations," Mustafa Shalabi, the head of the al-Kifah Center until his murder in 1991, "employed a number of for-profit criminal enterprises, including gunrunning, arson for hire, and a counterfeiting ring set up in the basement of the jihad office."[25] Yet *The 9/11 Commission Report* is silent about these serious charges, which U.S. prosecutors at the time did not pursue.

Why this official reticence? The answer may lie in the fact that by 1996 bin Laden was "supporting Islamists in Lebanon, Bosnia, Kashmir, Tajikistan, and Chechnya."[26] And in step with bin Laden, the al-Kifah Center was also supporting al-Qaedist terrorism after 1992 "in Afghanistan, Bosnia, the Philippines, Egypt, Algeria, Kashmir, Palestine, and elsewhere."[27]

Osama bin Laden and al-Kifah were not acting on their own, they were supporting projects, especially in Bosnia (1992), Tajikistan (1993–1995), and then Chechnya (after 1995), where their principal ally, Ibn al-Khattab (Thamir Saleh Abdullah Al-Suwailem), also enjoyed high-level support in Saudi Arabia.[28]

> Khattab enjoyed a certain amount of logistical and financial support from Saudi Arabia. Saudi sheikhs declared the Chechen resistance a legitimate jihad, and private Saudi donors sent money to Khattab and his Chechen colleagues. As late as 1996, mujahidin wounded in Chechnya were sent to Saudi Arabia for medical treatment, a practice paid for by charities and tolerated by the state.[29]

Ex-FBI agent Ali Soufan adds that America also supported this jihad: by 1996, "the United States had been on the side of Muslims in Afghanistan, Bosnia, and Chechnya."[30]

By protecting the al-Kifah Center and its associates (including Mohamed) and not prosecuting them for their crimes (including murder), the U.S. government was in effect imitating Saudi Arabia and Egypt, by keeping open a channel to export those in America who wished to wage al-Qaedist terrorism—thereby ensuring they would wage it in other countries, not here. (After the arrest of Sheikh Rahman in 1993 al-Kifah closed itself down. But we shall see that an allied institution, Sphinx Trading, continued to be protected after 9/11, even after the FBI knew it had helped one of the alleged 9/11 hijackers.)[31]

Was all this protection *intended* to keep just such a channel open? It was certainly an intentional result of the protection and support for the Maktab al-Khidamat in Saudi Arabia.

SAUDI SUPPORT FOR THE MAKTAB, AND LATER FOR AL-QAEDA

The Saudis, like the Egyptians, had domestic reasons for wishing to export as many Muslim Brotherhood members to possible death in Afghanistan, Bosnia, or anywhere else. Until 1979 Saudi Arabia had provided a home to Brotherhood members fleeing persecution in countries like Syria and Egypt, where some of them had tried to assassinate the Saudis' political enemy Gamel Abdel Nasser. But in 1979 radical Wahhabis, condemning the ruling Saudi family as corrupt infidels, seized the Grand Mosque at Mecca and defended it for weeks.[32] Profoundly shaken, the Saudi family used its foundations, like the World Muslim League (WML), to subsidize the emigration of political Islamists, above all to the new jihad in Afghanistan, which opened one month later against the Soviet Union.[33]

In Afghanistan both Rahman and al-Zawahiri worked with the Maktab al-Khidamat that had been created in 1984 by two other members of the Muslim Brotherhood, the Palestinian Abdullah Azzam, and the Saudi Osama bin Laden.[34] All that *The 9/11 Commission Report* has to say about the Maktab's financing is that "Bin Laden and his comrades had their own sources of support and training, and they received little or no assistance from the United States."[35] But the Pakistani author Ahmed Rashid makes clear the support coming from the Saudi royal family, including Prince Turki (the head of Saudi intelligence), and also royal creations like the World Muslim League:

> Bin Laden, although not a royal, was close enough to the royals and certainly wealthy enough to lead the Saudi contingent. Bin Laden, Prince Turki and General [Hameed] Gul [the head of the Pakistani ISI] were to become firm friends and allies in a common cause. The center for the Arab-Afghans was the offices of the World Muslim League and the Muslim Brotherhood in Peshawar which was run by Abdullah Azam. Saudi funds flowed to Azam and the Makhtab al Khidimat or Services Center which he created in 1984 to service the new recruits and receive donations from Islamic charities. Donations from Saudi Intelligence, the Saudi Red Crescent, the World Muslim League and private donations from Saudi princes and mosques were channeled through the Makhtab. A decade later the Makhtab would emerge at the center of a web of radical organizations that helped carry out the World Trade Center bombing [in 1993] and the bombings of U.S. Embassies in Africa in 1998.[36]

Former Ambassador Peter Tomsen has described how the evolution of the Makhtab into al-Qaeda was accomplished with support from the offices of royally ordained organizations like the World Muslim League (WML) and the World Assembly of Muslim Youth (WAMY):

> Bin Laden's brother-in-law, Mohammad Jamal Khalifa, headed the Muslim World League [MWL] office in Peshawar during the mid-1980s. In 1988, he moved to Manila and opened a branch office of the World Assembly of Muslim Youth. He made the charity a front for bin Laden's terrorist operations in the Philippines and Asia. Al-Qaeda operatives, including Khalid Sheikh Mohammed, mastermind of the 9/11 attacks, and his nephew Ramzi Yusuf [master bomb maker of the 1993 WTC bombing], traveled to Manila in the early 1990s to help Khalifa strengthen al-Qaeda networks in Southeast Asia and plan terrorist attacks in the region.[37]

There are many other examples of WML and WAMY connections to al-Qaeda. For example Maulana Fazlur Rehman Khalil, a signatory of Osama bin Laden's 1998 fatwa to kill Jews and Americans, was invited in 1996 to the 34th WML Congress in Mecca and also spoke there to WAMY.[38] Yet there are only minimal references to Maulana Fazlur Rehman in the western (as opposed to the Asian) media, and none (according to a LexisNexis search in July 2013) linking him to the WML or WAMY.

The FBI's hands-off attitude toward WAMY in America was in keeping with its protection of Ali Mohamed. According to former federal prosecutor John Loftus and others, there was a block in force in the 1980s against antiterrorism enforcement that might embarrass the Saudis.[39] This block explains for example the protection enjoyed by the chair of WAMY in Virginia, Osama bin Laden's nephew Abdullah bin Laden. The FBI opened an investigation of Abdullah bin Laden in February 1996, calling WAMY "a suspected terrorist organization," but the investigation was closed down six months later.[40]

In Pakistan WAMY "shared office space with the Benevolence International Corporation, an al-Qaeda charitable front founded by Osama bin Laden's brother-in-law Mohammed Jamal Khalifa."[41] A decade later,

> In 2002, a raid by Bosnian authorities on the Sarajevo offices of the Benevolence International Foundation, a multimillion-dollar charity, led to the discovery of a document called the "Golden Chain," a list of Al Qaeda sponsors. According to Craig Unger, "The donors of the Golden Chain were not just wealthy Saudis–they were the crème de la crème of the great Saudi industrial and mercantile elite." The list included Osama's brothers who ran the bin Laden Group, and Khalid bin Mahfouz, "the banker of the royal family, and the most powerful banker in Saudi Arabia."[42]

In the 1980s Khalid bin Mahfouz had bought up to 30 percent of the stock of the Bank of Credit and Commerce International (BCCI), the bank cofounded by Kamal Adham, the former Saudi intelligence chief and Safari Club financier.[43]

WHAT SAUDI PRINCE HELPED A PASSPORTLESS OSAMA LEAVE SAUDI ARABIA?

None of the official or privileged sources on Ali Mohamed has linked him to Saudi intelligence activities. But there is at least one such link: his trip, as described in the Coleman FBI affidavit, when in 1991 (still a U.S. Army reservist) he "travelled to Afghanistan to escort Usama bin Laden from Afghanistan to the Sudan."[44] The FBI affidavit presents this, without explanation, as an act in furtherance of an al-Qaeda "murder conspiracy." But Osama's move to Sudan was synchronized with a simultaneous investment in Sudan by his bin Laden brothers, including an airport construction project that was largely subsidized by the Saudi royal family.[45]

A great deal of confusion surrounds the circumstances of bin Laden's displacement in 1991–1992, from Saudi Arabia via Pakistan (and perhaps Afghanistan) to the Sudan. But in these conflicted accounts one important fact is not contested: bin Laden's trip was initially arranged by someone in the royal family.[46] Steven Coll in *Ghost Wars* suggests that the royal family arranged this trip amicably, blaming it on pressure from the United States:

> Peter Tomsen and other emissaries from Washington discussed the rising Islamist threat with [Saudi intelligence chief] Prince Turki in the summer of 1991. . . . At some of the meetings between Turki and the CIA, Osama bin Laden's name came up explicitly. The CIA continued to pick up reporting that he was funding radicals such as Hekmatyar in Afghanistan. . . . "His family has disowned him," Turki assured the Americans about bin Laden. Every effort had been made to persuade bin Laden to stop protesting against the Saudi royal family. These efforts had failed, Turki conceded, and the kingdom was now prepared to take sterner measures. . . . Bin Laden learned of this when Saudi police arrived at his cushion-strewn, modestly furnished compound in Jeddah to announce that he would have to leave the kingdom. According to an account later provided to the CIA by a source in Saudi intelligence, the officer assigned to carry out the expulsion assured bin Laden that this was being done for his own good. The officer blamed the Americans. The U.S. government was planning to kill him, he told bin Laden, by this account, so *the royal family would get him out of the kingdom for his own protection.* The escort put bin Laden on a plane out of Saudi Arabia.[47]

Coll's magisterial but privileged book appeared in February 2004. Six months later the 9/11 Commission Report published a quite different account, implying that by 1991 the Saudi government was estranged from bin Laden:

> The Saudi government . . . undertook to silence Bin Laden by, among other things, taking away his passport. With help from a dissident member of the royal family, he managed to get out of the country under the pretext of attending an Islamic gathering in Pakistan in April 1991.[48]

Lawrence Wright claims, persuasively, that the prince returning Osama's passport was no "dissident," but Interior Minister Prince Naif, after bin Laden persuaded him he was needed in Peshawar "in order to help mediate the civil war among the mujahideen."[49] Prince Naif, the most anti-American of the senior Saudi royals, gave back bin Laden's passport on one condition, that he "sign a pledge that he would not interfere with the politics of South Arabia or any Arab country."[50] This was a common Saudi practice.

The "Islamic gathering" is almost certainly a reference to the ongoing negotiations in Peshawar that eventually produced the Saudi-backed Peshawar Accord (finalized in April 1992) to end the Afghan Civil War. By several well-informed accounts, Bin Laden did play an important part in these negotiations, in furtherance (I would argue) of Prince Turki's own policies.[51] Like Sheikh Rahman before him in 1990, bin Laden tried, vainly, to negotiate a truce between the warring mujahedin leaders, Massoud and Hekmatyar. In these negotiations (according to Peter Tomsen, who was there), Saudi Arabia, Pakistan, the Muslim Brotherhood, and al-Qaeda were all united in seeking the same objective: a united Sunni army (in opposition to American appeals for Shia representation) that could retake Kabul by force.[52]

Thus I believe it is quite clear that bin Laden, in his mediation attempts to bring Hekmatyar into the Peshawar consensus, was acting in line with official Saudi and Pakistani interests. Others disagree. Without documentation, the author of the Frontline biography of bin Laden asserts,

> Contrary to what is always reiterated bin Laden has never had official relations with the Saudi regime or the royal family. All his contacts would happen through his brothers.[53]. . .
>
> Specifically he had no relation with Turki al-Faisal head of Saudi intelligence. He used to be very suspicious of his role in Afghanistan and once had open confrontation with him in 1991 and accused him of being the reason of the fight between Afghan factions.[54]

Michael Scheuer, once head of the CIA's Counterterrorism Center, endorsed this claim, and reinforced it with the testimony of Sa'ad al-Faqih (a critic of the Saudi royal family who has been accused by the U.S. Treasury of being affiliated with al-Qaeda) that, "after the Soviets withdrew 'Saudi intelligence [officers] were actually increasing the gap between Afghani factions to keep them fighting.'"[55]

But this claim if true must have been after Kabul fell to al-Qaedists in 1992, when Massoud, backed by the favored Saudi client Abdul Rasul Sayyaf, began to fight Hekmatyar, the favored client of Pakistan's ISI. Before this time the U.S. State Department's Afghan policy was to promote a broad-based opposition to the rump Communist government in Kabul, while "side-lining the extremists," including both Hekmatyar and Sayyaf.[56]

In the same period, Pakistan's ISI clearly wanted a strong rebel alliance united behind Hekmatyar, and both the CIA and the Saudis continued to support them. As Barnett Rubin reports, "During this period, political 'unity' of some sort among the mujahidin groups was a major goal of U.S.-Pakistani-Saudi policy."[57] And in 1990–1991, as Washington cut its allocation for the CIA's covert Afghan program by 60 percent, Prince Turki more than made up for the shortfall by increased contributions from Saudi Arabia.[58]

I conclude that bin Laden's mediation efforts in Peshawar in 1991 were in accordance with Prince Turki's preferences, just as was Ali Mohamed's effort, in organizing bin Laden's subsequent move from Afghanistan and Pakistan to the Sudan. As Steve Coll reports, the break between bin Laden and the Saudi royal family did not become serious until at least 1993, after the involvement of bin Laden's ally Sheikh Rahman in the first WTC bombing.[59]

CHAPTER 6

Deep State Uses and Protection of al-Qaeda Terrorists

THE STATE DEPARTMENT-CIA SPLIT OVER AFGHANISTAN—AND OIL

IN 1991 THE SOVIET TROOPS HAD BEEN OUT OF KABUL FOR TWO YEARS; AND, as former U.S. Ambassador Tomsen has reported, the CIA's objective of a Pakistan-backed military overthrow in Kabul was at odds with the official U.S. policy of support for "a political settlement restoring Afghanistan's independence."[1] Ambassador Tomsen himself told the CIA Station Chief in Islamabad ("Bill") that, by endorsing Pakistan's military attack on Kabul,

> he was violating fundamental U.S. policy precepts agreed to in Washington by his own agency. American policy was to cut Hekmatyar off, not build him up. Bill looked at me impassively as I spoke. I assumed his superiors in Langley had approved the offensive. The U.S. government was conducting two diametrically opposed Afghan policies.[2]

Steve Coll agrees that "by early 1991, the Afghan policies pursued by the State Department and the CIA were in open competition with each other. ... The CIA ... continued to collaborate with Pakistani military intelligence on a separate military track that mainly promoted Hekmatyar and other Islamist commanders."[3]

This conflict between the State Department and CIA was far from unprecedented. In particular it recalled the CIA-State conflict in Laos in 1959–1960, which led to a tragic war in Laos, and eventually Vietnam.[4] Just as oil companies had a stake in the Indochina conflict, so too was the CIA in 1990–1992 thinking not just of Afghanistan, but also of the oil resources of Central Asia, where some of the al-Kifah-trained "Arab Afghans" were about to focus their attention.

In Afghanistan, the State Department represented the will of the National Security Council and the public state. The CIA, on the other hand, was not "rogue" (as has sometimes been suggested); it was pursuing the goals of oil

companies and their financial backers—or what I have called the deep state—
in preparing for a launch into the former Soviet republics of central Asia.

COVERT OPERATIONS AND OIL IN CENTRAL ASIA

In 1991 the leaders of former Soviet Union states in Central Asia "began to
hold talks with Western oil companies, on the back of ongoing negotiations
between Kazakhstan and the US company Chevron."[5] The first Bush administration actively supported the plans of U.S. oil companies to contract for
exploiting the resources of the Caspian region, and also for building a pipeline
not controlled by Moscow that could bring the oil and gas production out to
the West.

In the same year 1991, Richard Secord, Heinie Aderholt, and Ed Dearborn,
three veterans of CIA Station Chief Theodore Shackley's operations in Laos,
and later of Oliver North's operations with the Contras, turned up in Baku
under the cover of an oil company, MEGA Oil.[6] This was at a time when the
first Bush administration had expressed its support for an oil pipeline stretch-
ing from Azerbaijan across the Caucasus to Turkey.[7] MEGA never did find oil;
but it did contribute materially to the removal of Azerbaijan from the sphere
of post-Soviet Russian influence, and hence to the ultimate construction of the
Baku-Tbilisi-Ceyhan (BTC) pipeline from Baku to Ceyhan in Turkey.

As MEGA operatives in Azerbaijan, Secord, Aderholt, Dearborn, and their
men engaged in military training, passed "brown bags filled with cash" to
members of the government, and above all set up an airline on the model of
Air America that soon was picking up hundreds of mujahedin mercenaries in
Afghanistan.[8] (Secord and Aderholt claim to have left Azerbaijan before the
mujahedin arrived.[9])

Meanwhile, Hekmatyar, who at the time was still allied with bin Laden, was
"observed recruiting Afghan mercenaries [i.e. Arab Afghans] to fight in Azerbaijan against Armenia and its Russian allies."[10] Hekmatyar was a notorious
drug trafficker, and, at this time, heroin flooded from Afghanistan through
Baku into Chechnya, Russia, and even North America.[11]

(In the 1990s, according to Loretta Napoleoni, an al-Qaedist drug route
from Tajikistan transited Azerbaijan to reach Chechnya and Kosovo.[12] And
in 1998, Clinton came to the support of the al-Qaeda–backed Kosovo Liberation Army [KLA]. He did so even though "in 1998, the U.S. State Department
listed the KLA . . . as an international terrorist organization, saying it had
bankrolled its operations with proceeds from the international heroin trade
and from loans from known terrorists like Osama bin Laden."[13] This was
another instance of willingness to make use of al-Qaedist assets in pursuit of
geostrategic goals.)

BIN LADEN, ALI MOHAMED, AND THE SAUDI ROYAL FAMILY

By attempting to negotiate Hekmatyar's reconciliation with the other Peshawar commanders, bin Laden in 1991 was clearly an important part of the CIA's effort to establish a pro-Pakistan regime in Kabul. So, a year earlier, had been the blind Sheikh Omar Abdul Rahman:

> In 1990, after the assassination of Abdullah Azzam, Abd al-Rahman was invited to Peshawar, where his host was Khalid al-Islambouli, brother of one of the assassins of Sadat.... On this trip, reportedly paid for by the CIA, Abd al-Rahman preached to the Afghans about the necessity of unity to overthrow the Kabul regime.[14]

This presumably was shortly before Sheikh Abdul Rahman, even though he was on a State Department terrorist watch list after being imprisoned for the murder of Egyptian president Anwar Sadat, was issued a multiple-entry U.S. visa in 1990 "by a CIA officer working undercover in the consular section of the American embassy in Sudan."[15] This was the same CIA-sponsored program that six years earlier had admitted Ali Mohamed, "a visa-waiver program that was . . . designed to shield valuable assets or those who have performed valuable services for the country."[16]

And Ali Mohamed himself was, according to *The New York Times*, part of the CIA's plan for a military solution: "In the fall of 1992, Mr. Mohamed returned to fight in Afghanistan, training rebel commanders in military tactics, United States officials said."[17] Before this, Mohamed had been charged with the major task of moving bin Laden, his four wives, and his seventeen children from Afghanistan to Sudan. The task was a major one, for Osama moved with his assistants, "a stable of Arabian horses, and bulldozers."[18]

Meanwhile Saudi royal support for this web of radical organizations, in which Ali Mohamed was a central organizer and trainer, continued after the World Trade Center (WTC) bombing of 1993. The Turki-bin Laden connection, which was cemented by Turki's chief of staff and bin Laden's teacher Ahmed Badeeb, may have been renewed as late as 1998:

> In sworn statements after 9/11, former Taliban intelligence chief Mohammed Khaksar said that in 1998 the prince sealed a deal under which bin Laden undertook not to attack Saudi targets. In return, Saudi Arabia would provide funds and material assistance to the Taliban. . . . Saudi businesses, meanwhile, would ensure that money also flowed directly to bin Laden. Turki would deny after 9/11 that any such deal was done with bin Laden. One account has it, however, that he himself met with bin Laden—his old protégé from the days of the anti-Soviet jihad—during the exchanges that led to the deal.[19]

ROYAL SAUDI FINANCING FOR BIN LADEN, INCLUDING
HIS MOVE TO THE SUDAN

Anthony Summers also transmits insider reports

that at least two Saudi princes had been paying, on behalf of the kingdom, what amounted to protection money since 1995. The former official added, "The deal was, they would turn a blind eye to what he was doing elsewhere. 'You don't conduct operations here, and we won't disrupt them elsewhere.'"

American and British official sources, speaking later with Simon Henderson, Baker Fellow at the Washington Institute for Near East Policy, named the two princes in question. They were, Henderson told the authors, Prince Naif, the interior minister, and Prince Sultan. The money involved in the alleged payments, according to Henderson's sources, had amounted to "hundreds of millions of dollars." It had been "Saudi official money—not their own."[20]

It would appear moreover that Saudi royal money may have helped pay for bin Laden's move to the Sudan in 1991–1992: the move organized by Ali Mohamed, possibly in collaboration with bin Laden's family. There is hotly contested evidence that Osama participated with his brothers in the construction of the Port Sudan airport, a project underwritten with funds from the Saudi royal family.[21] According to Lawrence Wright, "the Saudi Binladin Group got the contract to build an airport in Port Sudan, which brought Osama frequently into the country to oversee the construction. He finally moved to Khartoum in 1992."[22]

Not contested, but largely overlooked, is the evidence of how bin Laden financed his move, through investing $50 million in the Sudanese al-Shamal Islamic bank—a bank that also had support from both the bin Laden family and the Saudi royal family. As the *Chicago Tribune* reported in November 2001,

According to a 1996 State Department report on bin Laden's finances, bin Laden co-founded the Al Shamal bank with a group of wealthy Sudanese and capitalized it with $50 million of his inherited fortune. . . .[23]

According to public records, among the investors in the Al Shamal Islamic Bank is a Geneva-based financial services conglomerate headed by Prince Mohamed al-Faisal al-Saud, [brother of Prince Turki], son of the late King [Faisal al-] Saud and a cousin [i.e., nephew] of the current Saudi monarch, King Fahd.

The Al Shamal bank, which opened for business in 1990, admits that Osama bin Laden held three accounts there between 1992 and 1997, when he used Sudan as his base of operations before fleeing to Afghanistan. But the bank insists in a written statement that bin Laden "was never a founder or a shareholder of Al Shamal Islamic Bank."

Told of the bank's statement, the State Department official replied that "we stand by" the assertion that bin Laden put $50 million into the bank.

Al Shamal does acknowledge that among its five "main founders" and principal shareholders is another Khartoum bank, the Faisal Islamic Bank of Sudan.[24] According to public records, 19 percent of the Faisal Islamic Bank is owned by the Dar Al-Maal Al-Islami Trust, headed by Saudi Prince [Mohammed al-Faisal] al-Saud.[25]

The Dar Al-Mal Al-Islami or DMI Trust, "based in the Bahamas and with its operations center in Geneva," was one of a spate of banks, mostly dominated by the Muslim Brotherhood, that were set up with Western guidance and assistance—in DMI's case the assistance came from Price Waterhouse and eventually Harvard University.[26] DMI was one of the two main banks that, according to *Jane's Intelligence Review*, had been funding the Maktab and also the International Islamic Relief Organization (IIRO), about which I say more below.[27]

The $3.5 billion DMI Trust, whose slogan is "Allah is the purveyor of success," was founded 20 years ago to foster the spread of Islamic banking across the Muslim world. Its 12-member board of directors includes Haydar Mohamed Binladen, according to a DMI spokesman, a half-brother of Osama bin Laden. . . .

Though small, the Al Shamal Islamic Bank enabled bin Laden to move money quickly from one country to another through its correspondent relationships with some of the world's major banks, several of which have been suspended since Sept. 11.

The Al Shamal bank was identified as one of bin Laden's principal financial entities during the trial earlier this year [2001] of four Al Qaeda operatives convicted in the 1998 bombings of two U.S. embassies in Africa.[28]

One might have expected this early and revealing insight into bin Laden's finances to have been developed in the spate of privileged bin Laden and al-Qaeda books that appeared in the years after 2001. In fact I have located only one brief inconsequential reference, in Steve Coll's *The Bin Ladens*: "Osama had reorganized his personal banking at the Al-Shamal Bank in Khartoum, but his accounts gradually dried up."[29]

There is of course no mention of the Al-Shamal Bank in *The 9/11 Commission Report*.

U.S. AND SAUDI PROTECTION FOR OSAMA BIN LADEN'S BROTHER-IN-LAW, MOHAMMED JAMAL KHALIFA

It seems clear that the 1980s official U.S. government block against antiterrorism actions that might embarrass the Saudis was still in force in America in 1995. We see this in the extraordinary federal protection extended to Mohammed Jamal Khalifa, Osama bin Laden's best friend and brother-in-law.

On December 16, 1994, the San Francisco FBI arrested Khalifa, in the presence of the Syrian American Mohamed Loay Bayazid, a sometime president of the Benevolence International Foundation.[30] Khalifa's arrest (Bayazid was not detained) took place in Morgan Hills (not far from Ali Mohamed's home). Khalifa's business card had been discovered in a search one year earlier of Sheikh Rahman's residence, after which he had been named as an unindicted coconspirator in the Landmarks case. Soon afterward, a State Department cable described him as "a known financier of terrorist operations and an officer of an Islamic NGO in the Philippines that is a known Hamas front. He is under indictment in Jordan in connection with a series of cinema bombings earlier this year."[31]

Khalifa, in other words, was like Ali Mohamed involved in terrorist operations on an international level. He was an important source of information and talked freely to the FBI agents who arrested him. In his possession they found "documents that connected Islamic terrorist manuals to the International Islamic Relief Organization, the group that he had headed in the Philippines."[32] And in his notebook they found evidence linking him directly to Ramzi Yousef, who at the time was the FBI's *most-wanted terrorist* for his role in the 1993 WTC bombing.

But as Peter Lance narrates, "The Feds never got a chance to question him." Instead, in January 1995, a decision was made by Secretary of State Warren Christopher and supported by Deputy Attorney General Jamie Gorelick to whisk Khalifa from the United States to Jordan for trial, where he was soon "acquitted of terrorism charges and allowed to move to Saudi Arabia."[33] There "Saudi officials greeted him at the airport."[34]

> "I remember people at CIA who were ripshit at the time" over the decision, says Jacob L. Boesen, an Energy Department analyst then working at the CIA's Counterterrorism Center. "Not even speaking in retrospect, but contemporaneous with what the intelligence community knew about bin Laden, Khalifa's deportation was unreal."[35]

Even more unreal was the decision of a court in a civil case to return the contents of his luggage, including his notebook and other computer files, to Khalifa before his deportation.[36]

I believe that Peter Lance, after all his meticulous scholarship, failed to identify who was really being protected by this evasive measure. He writes that Khalifa, from 1983 to 1991, "had been trusted by al Qaeda with running the Philippines branch of the International Islamic Relief Organization (IIRO), one of their key NGOs."[37]

But the IIRO was in the hands of a far greater power than al-Qaeda, which in any case did not exist in 1983. It was a charitable organization that had been authorized in 1979 by Saudi royal decree, as an affiliate of another key institution of the royal family, the Rabita al-Alam al-Islami or World Muslim League (WML).[38] According to former CIA officer Robert Baer, the IIRO was run "with an iron hand" by Prince Salman ibn Abdul-Aziz al Saud (the brother of Saudi King Abdullah), who "personally approved all important appointments and spending."[39]

The creation date of 1979 reflects the important shift in that year of the Saudi royal family's attitude toward the political Islamism of the Muslim Brotherhood or Ikhwan (of which Mohammed Jamal Khalifa was a senior member). As already noted, 1979 was the year radical Wahhabis seized the Grand Mosque at Mecca. In response, the Saudi family foundations like the IIRO began to subsidize the emigration of the Muslim Brotherhood.[40]

Thus Khalifa's status in the IIRO was not anomalous. Besides the bombings in Jordan, the IIRO has also been linked to support of terrorists in the Philippines,[41] India,[42] Indonesia,[43] Canada,[44] Albania, Chechnya, Kenya,[45] and other countries, notably Bosnia.[46] In particular Khalifa personally has been accused of financing the Philippine terrorist group Abu Sayyaf (which in 1993 had kidnapped an American Bible translator).[47] Yet "the U.S. government has not designated Khalifa as a financial supporter of terrorism."[48]

U.S. AND ROYAL PROTECTION FOR AL-QAEDA PLOTTER KHALID SHEIKH MOHAMMED

The Saudi royal protection for Jamal Khalifa was more than matched by the Qatari royal protection of Khalid Sheikh Mohammed (KSM), Ramzi Yousef's uncle and coconspirator in the Philippines. *The 9/11 Commission Report*, which judged KSM to be "the principal architect of the 9/11 attacks," made a muted acknowledgment of this Qatari protection of him:

> Khalid Sheikh Mohammed—Yousef's uncle, then located in Qatar—was a fellow plotter of Yousef's in the Manila air plot and had also wired him some money prior to the Trade Center bombing. The U.S. Attorney obtained an indictment against KSM in January 1996, but an official in the government of Qatar probably warned him about it. Khalid Sheikh Mohammed evaded capture (and stayed at large to play a central part in the 9/11 attacks).[49]

From other sources, notably Robert Baer who was then a CIA officer in Qatar, we learn that the "official" was Sheikh Abdallah bin Khalid bin Hamad al-Thani, the Qatari minister of the Interior and the brother of then Qatari Emir Sheikh Hamad bin Khalid al-Thani.[50] According to ABC News,

> Mohammed is believed to have fled Qatar with a passport provided by that country's government. He is also believed to have been given a home in Qatar

as well as a job at the Department of Public Water Works. Officials also said bin Laden himself visited Abdallah bin Khalid al-Thani in Qatar between the years of 1996 and 2000.[51]

The 9/11 Commission Report itself, in a footnote, notes, "Although KSM claims that Sheikh Abdallah was not a member, financier, or supporter of al Qaeda, he admits that Abdallah underwrote a 1995 trip KSM took to join the Bosnia jihad."[52] This admission is hard to reconcile with the Commission's official finding: "It does not appear that any government other than the Taliban financially supported al Qaeda before 9/11, although some governments may have contained al Qaeda sympathizers who turned a blind eye to al Qaeda's fund-raising activities."[53]

In 2013 the Syrian nightmare finally made U.S. media admit, in the words of *The Atlantic*, that Qatar is "a global financial backer of the Brotherhood."[54] This admission considerably complicates the earlier establishment stereotype of al-Qaedists like KSM as "nonstate actors."[55]

In *Triple Cross*, Peter Lance, who does not mention KSM's escape from Qatar, focuses instead on the way that, later in the same year, U.S. federal prosecutors kept his name out of the trial of Ramzi Yousef in connection with the 1993 World Trade Center bombing:

> Assistant U.S. Attorneys Mike Garcia and Dietrich Snell presented a riveting, evidence-driven case . . . and characterized the material retrieved from Ramzi's Toshiba laptop as "the most devastating evidence of all." . . . While Yousef's Toshiba laptop . . . contained the full details of the plot later executed on 9/11, not a word of that scenario was mentioned during trial. . . . Most surprising, during the entire summer-long trial, the name of the fourth Bojinka conspirator, Khalid Shaikh Mohammed . . . was mentioned by name only *once*, in reference to a letter found in [Yousef's apartment].[56]

Lance repeatedly suggests that U.S. prosecutors in New York, and particularly Dietrich Snell, were responsible for minimizing the role of Khalid Sheikh Mohamed and other shortcomings, because they were seeking "to hide the full truth behind the Justice Department's failures."[57] But the matter of KSM's escape in 1996, like the release of Jamal Khalifa, was sensitive at a much higher level than that of prosecutors. It was a matter that reached back into the black hole that is represented by the ultimate United States dependency on Saudi Arabia, Qatar, and OPEC, for the defense of the petrodollar.

In other words, the suppression of KSM's name was not surprising at all. On the contrary, it was totally consistent with one of the most sensitive and controversial features of the 9/11 story: the much-discussed fact that before 9/11 two counterterrorist officers protected two of the alleged future hijackers from detection and surveillance by the FBI.

FEDERAL PROTECTION FOR ALLEGED 9/11 HIJACKERS

Morgenthau's hypothesis that the CIA was protecting Saudi criminal assets received further corroboration in the wake of 9/11. There is now evidence, much of it systematically suppressed by the 9/11 Commission, that before 9/11, CIA officers Richard Blee and Tom Wilshire inside the CIA's Bin Laden Unit, along with FBI agents such as Dina Corsi, were protecting from investigation and arrest two of the eventual alleged hijackers on 9/11, Khalid al-Mihdhar and Nawaf al-Hazmi—much as the FBI had protected Ali Mohamed from arrest in 1993.

There are also indications that al-Mihdhar and al-Hazmi, like Hampton-El before them, may have been receiving funds indirectly from the Saudi Embassy in Washington:

> Between 1998 and 2002, up to US$73,000 in cashier cheques was funneled by [Saudi Ambassador Prince] Bandar's wife Haifa—who once described the elder Bushes as like "my mother and father"—to two Californian families known to have bankrolled al-Mihdhar and al-Hazmi. . . .
>
> Princess Haifa sent regular monthly payments of between $2,000 and $3,500 to Majeda Dweikat, wife of Osama Basnan, believed by various investigators to be a spy for the Saudi government. Many of the cheques were signed over to Manal Bajadr, wife of [Basnan's close friend] Omar al-Bayoumi, himself suspected of covertly working for the kingdom.
>
> The Basnans, the al-Bayoumis and the two 9/11 hijackers once shared the same apartment block in San Diego. It was al-Bayoumi who greeted the killers when they first arrived in America, and provided them, among other assistance, with an apartment and social security cards. He even helped the men enroll at flight schools in Florida.[58]

The Report of the Joint Congressional Inquiry into 9/11, though very heavily redacted at this point, supplies corroborating information, including a report that Basnan had once hosted a party for the "Blind Sheikh" Omar Abdul Rahman.[59] In other words, the Congressional investigation found indications that those supporting the Islamist conspirators of 1993 were in 2001 supporting those eventually accused of 9/11.[60]

The 9/11 Commission Report, overruling FBI reports, simply denied that Saudi embassy money had supported the two hijackers.[61] It recognized that there had been an intelligence failure with respect to the al-Mihdhar and al-Hazmi, but treated it as an accident that might not have occurred "if more resources had been applied."[62] This explanation, however, has since been rejected by 9/11 Commission Chairman Tom Kean. Asked if the failure to deal appropriately with al-Mihdhar and al-Hazmi could have been a simple mistake, Kean replied, "Oh, it wasn't careless oversight. It was purposeful. No question about that. . . . The conclusion that we came to was that in the DNA of these organizations was secrecy. And secrecy to the point of ya don't share it with anybody."[63]

In 2011 an important book by Kevin Fenton, *Disconnecting the Dots*, demonstrated conclusively that the withholding was purposive, and sustained over a period of eighteen months.[64] This interference and manipulation became particularly blatant and controversial in the days before 9/11.[65]

Before reading Fenton's book, I was satisfied with Lawrence Wright's speculation that the CIA may have wanted to recruit the two Saudis, and that "The CIA may also have been protecting an overseas operation [possibly in conjunction with Saudi Arabia] and was afraid that the F.B.I. would expose it."[66] However, I am now persuaded that Lawrence Wright's explanation, that the CIA was protecting a covert operation, may explain the beginnings of the withholding in January 2000, but cannot explain its renewal, after a quiescent period, in the days just before 9/11.

Fenton analyzes a list of thirty-five different occasions where the two alleged hijackers were protected in this fashion, from January 2000 to about September 5, 2001, less than a week before the hijackings.[67] In his analysis, the incidents fall into two main groups. In the earlier incidents he sees an intention "to cover a CIA operation that was already in progress."[68] However after "the system was blinking red" in the summer of 2001, and the CIA expected an imminent attack, Fenton can see no other explanation than that "the purpose of withholding the information had become to allow the attacks to go forward."[69]

In support of Fenton's conclusion, there is evidence (not mentioned by him) indicating that in mid-2001 the CIA's Counterterrorism Center (CTC), which was the chief supplier of the CIA protection, believed an al-Qaeda attack was imminent, and that al-Mihdhar was important to it. On August 15, CIA Counterterrorism Chief Cofer Black told a secret Pentagon conference, "We're going to be struck soon. . . . Many Americans are going to die, and it could be in the U.S."[70] Three weeks earlier, CTC Deputy Chief Tom Wilshire had written, "When the next big op is carried out . . . Khallad [bin Attash] will be at or near the top . . . Khalid Midhar [sic] should be [of] very high interest."[71] Yet Wilshire (like his superior, Richard Blee), instead of telling the FBI what he knew about al-Mihdhar, did the opposite: he "not only failed to tell anyone else involved in the hunt [for Al-Mihdhar] that Almihdhar would likely soon be a participant in a major al-Qaeda attack inside the US, but also supported a dubious procedure which meant that the FBI was only able to focus a fraction of the resources it had on the hunt."[72]

AN ONGOING COVER-UP THAT DID NOT END WITH 9/11

The homicidal crime suggested by Fenton's meticulous research is one both difficult and painful to contemplate. It has to be considered in the light of the earlier instances of protection we have surveyed:

1. the protection given to Salameh and Abouhalima in the 1990 Kahane murder, leaving them free to participate in the 1993 World Trade Center bombing;
2. the failure for two or three years to process Ali Mohamed's documents seized in 1990, which could have prevented the 1993 World Trade Center bombing;
3. the release of Ali Mohamed from Royal Canadian Mounted Police detention in 1993, leaving him free to participate in the 1998 Nairobi Embassy bombing;
4. the treatment of Ali Mohamed as an "unindicted coconspirator" in the 1993 WTC bombing case and Landmarks case, leaving him free to participate in the 1998 Nairobi Embassy bombing.

There are other indicators that these events were part of a single long-term cover-up, one that is still ongoing. One of the connectors is Sheikh Abdul Rahman's Al-Salaam Mosque in Jersey City, visited by Ali Mohamed and his trainees in 1989, and allegedly frequented by two of the alleged 9/11 hijackers (Mohamed Atta and Marwan al-Shehhi) in 2000–2001.[73]

Next door to the Mosque in Jersey City was the Sphinx Trading Company, whose incorporator and director, Waleed Abouel Nour, was like Ali Mohamed listed as an unindicted coconspirator in the 1995 Landmarks conspiracy case. (*The New York Times* later reported that the FBI had identified Nour as a terrorist.)[74]

> At minimum [sic], two Ali Mohamed-trained members of the New York cell—El Sayyid Nosair and Siddig Ali Siddig—are confirmed to have kept mailboxes at Sphinx Trading during the 1990s, as did the blind Sheikh himself.
>
> A decade later, the mailboxes were still being used by al Qaeda-linked terrorists.
>
> Testifying in a sealed proceeding in 2002, a New Jersey policeman said the FBI told him that "several of the hijackers involved in the September 11th event also had mailboxes at that location."
>
> Police searched the office of a New Jersey businessman [Mohamed el-Atriss] whose name appeared on the Sphinx Trading Co. incorporation papers and found the names and phone numbers of several hijackers among his papers. The businessman eventually admitted having sold fake identification cards to two of the hijackers.[75]

One of the fake IDs was given to Khalid al-Mihdhar.[76]

This important inquiry into the infrastructure of the Ali Mohamed connection was quickly shut down by the FBI:

> The police officer testified in 2002 that the FBI had shut down the New Jersey police investigation of these connections, without explanation but amid unconfirmed rumors (reported by the New York Times) that the businessman was

himself an FBI informant. All terrorism charges against the businessman were eventually dropped.[77]

Just how subordinated official policy could become to deep state needs was demonstrated in November 2001, when Cheney, at the request of Musharraf and the ISI, approved secret airlifts to ferry surrounded Pakistani and high-level al-Qaeda fighters out of Afghanistan, to safety in Pakistan. ("Cheney took charge. . . . The approval was not shared with anyone at State, including Colin Powell, until well after the event. . . . Clearly the ISI was running its own war against the Americans.")[78]

THE SAUDI-AMERICAN PETROLEUM COMPLEX AND THE DEFENSE OF THE PETRODOLLAR

This ongoing cover-up of a terrorist infrastructure spanning a decade is mirrored by the censorship of the Joint Inquiry findings about Osama Basnan, involved in the pass-through of Saudi Embassy funds to al-Mihdhar, and earlier the host of a party for Sheikh Abdul Rahman. One factor enabling the cover-up is the overarching and little understood U.S.-Saudi relationship. To understand it we must also consider the context of petrodollars, OPEC and the major oil companies.

The export of Saudi oil, paid for by all customers in U.S. dollars, and in the U.S. case largely offset by the export of U.S. arms to Saudi Arabia, is a major underpinning of America's petrodollar economy. As I have documented elsewhere, its current strength is supported by OPEC's requirement (secured by a secret agreement in the 1970s between the United States and Saudi Arabia and continuing to this day) that all OPEC oil sales be denominated in dollars.[79] Of the Saudi dollar earnings, $600 billion have been reinvested abroad, most of it in U.S. corporations like Citibank (where the largest shareholder is a member of the Saudi royal family).[80]

This fusion of U.S. and Saudi governing interests is as much political as economic. The first oil price hikes of 1972–1973, arranged by Nixon with the King of Saudi Arabia and the Shah of Iran, helped pay to arm Iran and Saudi Arabia as U.S. proxies in the region, following the withdrawal of British troops from the region in 1971.[81] The oil price hikes of 1979–1980, on the other hand, were assuredly not the intention of President Carter, a political victim of the increases. They have however been credibly attributed to the work of oil majors like BP, possibly acting in collusion with Republicans; and had the result of helping to elect Ronald Reagan (as well as Margaret Thatcher in England).[82]

I am suggesting that there is a high-level fusion of interests between the U.S. and Saudi governments, oil companies and banks (not to mention facilitating alliances like the Carlyle Group) that the CIA tends to represent continuously, and not just ad hoc for the sake of any one particular goal. The ongoing protection given through the years to criminals like Salameh, Ali Mohamed, al-Mihdhar, and al-Hazmi should be seen as consequences of this high-level fusion of interests. Needless to add, the 99 percent of ordinary American people, having as a result now suffered a series of recurring attacks (the first World Trade Center bombing, the 1998 Embassy bombings, possibly even 9/11 itself), have been losers from this arrangement.

I am confident that the mystery of U.S. government protection to terrorists can be traced in part to this "roof" of inscrutable governmental, financial, and corporate relationships between the United States and Saudi Arabia. There is a "black hole" at the center of this roof in which the interests of governments, petrodollar banks, intelligence agencies, and multinational oil companies, are all inscrutably mixed.

This multinational pyramid, with interests at odds with the American people's, is growing stronger. In March 2007 the major U.S. corporation Halliburton, one of the prime forces behind U.S. involvement in the Caspian basin, announced it would "open a corporate headquarters in the United Arab Emirates (U.A.E.) city of Dubai and move its chairman and chief executive, David J. Lesar, there."[83] One can see why. The U.A.E. is a corporate paradise, with low taxes and unions forbidden by law.[84]

Its petrodollars empower it to counter trends toward a more democratic Middle East: for example, the $8 billion aid promised from the U.A.E. and the Saudis to el-Sisi after the 2013 military coup in Egypt now marginalizes the paltry $1.5 billion annual aid package from the United States.[85]

And in the U.A.E. there will be increasingly sophisticated infrastructure for the global reach of the supranational deep state, immune from popular oversight. A secret American-led mercenary army is being put together for the U.A.E. by Erik Prince, the billionaire founder of Blackwater, who is now a U.A.E. resident.[86] In 2013 the U.A.E. also hired Booz Allen, one of the National Security Agency's most important contractors "to replicate the world's largest and most powerful spy agency in the sands of Abu Dhabi."[87]

Still at the apex of this pyramid are probably the banks and the colossi of the military-industrial-petroleum complex. What Franklin Roosevelt wrote to Col. House in 1933 would appear still to be true: "The real truth . . . is, as you and I know, that a financial element in the larger centers has owned the Government ever since the days of Andrew Jackson."[88]

That truth appears to have been reinforced by the introduction of swollen Saudi oil profits into the American financial and political system, so that Citibank's largest shareholder is now a Saudi prince.[89] In 1977 Saudi billionaires Khalid bin Mahfouz and Ghaith Pharaon teamed up with former Texas Governor John Connally to buy the Main Bank in Houston—a bank distinguished by its "highly unusual" practice of obtaining and disbursing "more than ten million dollars a month in hundred dollar bills."[90] Khalid bin

Mahfouz also "helped finance the Houston skyscraper for the Texas Commerce Bank, in which [Reagan's Chief of Staff] James Baker had a significant stake."[91] Repeated investments in the struggling oil company of the young George W. Bush (Arbusto, later part of Harken Energy), led to speculation by "a knowledgeable Saudi source" that they "may have been part of the same strategy the Saudis had of investing in U.S. companies that were connected to powerful politicians."[92]

CONCLUSION: A NEW WORLD DISORDER

All these recent developments are especially disconcerting because of the visible deterioration of governmental relations between Washington and the Gulf states, and the emergence of strong disagreements concerning the Muslim Brotherhood and the future of the region between the Gulf states themselves, particularly Saudi Arabia and Qatar.

Saudi-U.S. relations frayed after the Bush administration's adoption of a neocon agenda of change in the Middle East, particularly by the plans, which King Abdullah publicly opposed, for an Iraqi war in 2003 to topple Saddam Hussein.[93] (The Saudis would have welcomed a Sunni coup to overthrow Saddam, but not a war that, they accurately foresaw, would erode the domination of the country by a Sunni minority.)

This became obvious during the brief regime of Mohamed Morsi, the elected Muslim Brotherhood president of Egypt. Following his overthrow in a military coup, Saudi Arabia, Kuwait, and the United Arab Emirates pledged $8 billion in cash and loans (*The Guardian* said $12 billion) to the successor regime of el-Sisi, countering the strong financial support that Qatar and Turkey had earlier given to Morsi.[94] (Qatar, with a relatively small and easily controlled population, enjoys a secure agreement to support the Muslim Brotherhood abroad in exchange for nondisturbance at home—the kind of agreement that broke down after 1979 in a more vulnerable Saudi Arabia, with ten million migrant workers.)

In March 2014 Saudi Arabia designated the Muslim Brotherhood as terrorist, along with two al-Qaedist groups (the Nusra Front and the Islamic State in Iraq and al-Sham) backed by Qatar in Syria.[95] This was after Prime Minister Erdogan of Turkey, in alliance with Qatar, hailed the Muslim Brotherhood as an ally for creating an emerging new order in the Middle East.[96]

The confusion and bloodletting in the Middle East has increased in the wake of America's Iraq fiasco, and this has seriously weakened the hopes of governmental arrangements and understandings for regional peace and security. But this same decline represents a new frontier of entrepreneurial opportunity for Blackwater, Booz Allen, and other liberated fragments of the American deep state.

Time will tell what this means for a perilous world.

CHAPTER 7

The U.S. Terror War

The CIA, 9/11, Afghanistan, and Central Asia

The engineering of a series of provocations to justify military intervention is feasible and could be accomplished with the resources available.

—Report of May 1963 to U.S. Joint Chiefs of Staff[1]

BUSH'S TERROR WAR AND THE FIXING OF INTELLIGENCE

ON SEPTEMBER 11, 2001, WITHIN HOURS OF THE MURDEROUS 9/11 ATTACKS, Bush, Rumsfeld, and Cheney had committed America to what they later called the "war on terror." It should more properly, I believe, be called the "terror war," one in which terror has been directed repeatedly against civilians by all participants, both states and nonstate actors. A terror war is one in which the major role is played by weapons of indiscriminate destruction, whether they are IEDs planted by the roadside or bombs delivered aerially by a high-tech drone.[2]

Bush's war should also be seen as part of a larger, indeed global, process in which terror has been used against civilians in interrelated campaigns by all major powers, including China in Xinjiang and Russia in Chechnya, as well as the United States.[3] Terror war in its global context should perhaps be seen as the latest stage of the age-long secular spread of transurban civilization into areas of mostly rural resistance—areas where conventional forms of warfare, for either geographic or cultural reasons, prove inconclusive.

Terror war was formally declared by George W. Bush on the evening of September 11, 2001, with his statement to the American nation that "we will make no distinction between the terrorists who committed these acts and those who harbor them."[4] But the notion that Bush was in pursuit of actual terrorists lost credibility in 2003, when it was applied to Saddam Hussein's Iraq, a country known to have been targeted by terrorists but not to have harbored them.[5] It lost still more credibility with the 2005 publication in Britain of the so-called "Downing Street memo," in which the head of the British intelligence service MI6 reported after a visit to Washington in 2002 that "Bush wanted to remove Saddam Hussein, through military action, justified by the conjunction of terrorism and WMD. But the *intelligence and facts were being fixed around the policy.*[6] False stories followed in due course linking Iraq to WMD, anthrax, and Niger yellowcake (uranium).

This chapter will demonstrate that before 9/11 a small element inside the CIA's Bin Laden Unit and related agencies, the so-called "Alec Station group," were also busy, "fixing" intelligence by suppressing it, in a way that, accidentally or deliberately, enabled the terror war. They did so by withholding evidence from the FBI before 9/11 about two of the eventual alleged hijackers on 9/11, Khalid al-Mihdhar and Nawaf al-Hazmi, thus ensuring that the FBI could not surveil the two men or their colleagues.

This failure to share was recognized in *The 9/11 Commission Report*, but treated as an accident that might not have occurred "if more resources had been applied."[7] But as we saw, this explanation has been rejected by 9/11 Commission Chairman Tom Kean, and persuasively demolished in Kevin Fenton's important book, *Disconnecting the Dots.*[8] Fenton described how this interference and manipulation by the "Alec Station group" became particularly blatant and controversial in the days before 9/11; it led one FBI agent, Steve Bongardt, to predict accurately on August 29, less than two weeks before 9/11, that "someday someone will die."[9] I noted in the last chapter Fenton's conclusion that, in the last weeks before 9/11, the Alec Station group's "purpose of withholding the information had become to allow the attacks to go forward."[10]

Fenton's judgment would imply that a homicidal crime was committed by members of the "Alec Station group," even if the crime was one of manslaughter (unintended homicide) rather than deliberate and premeditated murder.[11] One can imagine benign reasons for withholding the information: For example, the CIA may have been tolerating the behavior of the two Saudis in order to track down their associates. In this case, we would be dealing with no more than a miscalculation—albeit a homicidal miscalculation.

THE TERROR WAR AND THE RUMSFELD-CHENEY-WOLFOWITZ PROJECT OF GLOBAL DOMINION

But in the course of this chapter, I shall dwell on the activities of the head of the CIA's Bin Laden Unit, Richard Blee, in Uzbekistan as well as Afghanistan. Uzbekistan was an area of concern not only to Blee and his superior Cofer Black; it was also in an area of major interest to Richard Cheney, whose corporation Halliburton had been active since 1997 or earlier in developing the petroleum reserves of Central Asia. Cheney himself said in a speech to oil industrialists in 1998, "I cannot think of a time when we have had a region emerge as suddenly to become as strategically significant as the Caspian."[12]

I shall suggest that the purpose as well as the result of protecting the two Saudis may have been to fulfill the objectives of Cheney, Rumsfeld, and the Project for the New American Century (PNAC) neocon group for establishing "forward-based forces" in Central Asia.[13] We shall see that a phone call on 9/11 from CIA Director Tenet to Stephen Cambone, a key PNAC figure in the Pentagon, apparently transmitted some of the privileged information that never reached the FBI.

This neocon agenda was partially to maintain American and Israeli domination of the region for security purposes, and (as we shall see) to create the conditions for future unilateral preemptive actions against unfriendly states like Iraq. In particular it was designed to establish new secure bases in the Middle East, anticipating Donald Rumsfeld's predictable announcement in 2003 that the United States would pull "virtually all of its troops, except some training personnel," out of Saudi Arabia.[14] But it was partly also to strengthen American influence in particular over the newly liberated states of Central Asia, with their sizable unproven oil and gas reserves.

Fenton's alarming conclusion about CIA actions leading up to the 9/11 attacks makes more sense in the context of this agenda, and also in the context of three other revealing anomalies about Bush's terror war. The first is the paradox that this supposed pursuit of al-Qaeda was conducted in alliance with the two nations, Saudi Arabia and Pakistan, that were most actively *supporting* al-Qaeda in other parts of the world. In this chapter we shall see U.S. and Saudi intelligence cooperating in such a way as to *protect*, rather than neutralize, Saudi agents in al-Qaeda.

The second anomaly is that although the CIA may have been focused on crushing al-Qaeda, Rumsfeld and Cheney were intent from the outset on a much wider war. In September 2001 there was no intelligence on 9/11 linking the attacks to Iraq, yet Defense Secretary Donald Rumsfeld, supported by his deputy Paul Wolfowitz, was already observing on September 12 "that there were no decent targets for bombing in Afghanistan and that we should consider bombing Iraq, which, he said, had better targets."[15] Rumsfeld's argument was supported by a Defense Department paper prepared for the ensuing Camp David meetings of September 15–16, which "proposed that 'the immediate priority targets for initial action' should be al Qaeda, the Taliban, and Iraq."[16]

Iraq had been a target for Rumsfeld and Wolfowitz since at least 1998, when the two men cosigned a PNAC letter to President Clinton, calling for "the removal of Saddam Hussein's regime from power."[17] But Iraq was not the only target in the Cheney-Rumsfeld-Wolfowitz agenda, which since at least 1992 had been nothing less than global U.S. dominance, or what former U.S. Colonel Andrew Bacevich has called "permanent American global hegemony."[18] It was a high priority for the neocons. Even before Bush had been elected by the Supreme Court in December 2000, Cheney was at work securing key posts for the 1998 letter's cosigners (including Richard Armitage, John Bolton, Richard Perle, along with other PNAC personnel like Stephen Cambone) in the White House, State, and Defense.

The neocon interest in toppling Saddam has been chronicled in a fairly extensive literature. Much less attention has been paid to the fact that the oil majors, and their friends at the Council on Foreign Relations, had also been campaigning, since as early as 1997, for a "policy review toward Iraq including military, energy, economic and political/ diplomatic assessments."[19]

The terror war from its outset was targeted against Iraq. National Security Adviser Condoleezza Rice on September 24 "raised the issue of state sponsorship of terrorism: 'What is our strategy with respect to countries that support terrorism like Iran, Iraq, Libya, Syria, and Sudan?'"[20] In his memoir, General Wesley Clark reports that the question had evolved by November into a Pentagon five-year plan:

> As I went back through the Pentagon in November 2001, one of the senior military staff officers had time for a chat. Yes, we were still on track for going against Iraq, he said. But there was more. This was being discussed as part of a five-year campaign plan, he said, and there were a total of seven countries, beginning with Iraq, then Syria, Lebanon, Libya, Iran, Somalia and Sudan.[21]

Later Clark spoke to the Commonwealth Club in San Francisco about this "policy coup" by a small group. He reported that in the Pentagon back in 1991 Wolfowitz had told him: the United States had "learned that we can use our military . . . in the middle east and the Soviets won't stop us . . . . and we've about five or ten years to clean up those old soviet client regimes—Syria, Iran, Iraq—before the next great superpower comes on to challenge us."[22]

Also in 2001, former CIA officer Reuel Marc Gerecht published an article in *The Weekly Standard* about the need for a change of regime in Iran and Syria.[23] (Gerecht continued for a decade to warn in *The Weekly Standard* about the menace of both nations.)

In the Clinton era Gerecht, like Cheney and Rumsfeld, had been part of the Project for the New American Century, a hawkish group calling both for action against Iraq in particular and also more generally for an expanded defense budget that would "increase defense spending significantly" in "the cause of American leadership." The PNAC report of September 2000, *Rebuilding America's Defenses*, had much to say about Gulf oil and the importance of retaining and strengthening "forward-based forces in the region."[24]

It is relevant that by the end of 2001, in the wake of 9/11 and the terror war, the United States had already established new bases in Uzbekistan,

Tajikistan, and Kyrgyzstan, and was thus better positioned to influence the behavior of the newly liberated governments in the huge oil and gas region east of the Caspian. In the course of this chapter we shall see that the 2001 agreement to use the first and one of the most important of these bases, Karshi-Khanabad or K-2 in Uzbekistan, grew out of an earlier Pentagon arrangement, supplemented by a CIA liaison agreement negotiated in 1999 by Richard Blee of the "Alec Station group," a central figure in this chapter. Most Americans are unaware that on 9/11 United States Special Forces were already at K-2 on an Uzbek training mission, and that by September 22, two weeks before a formal U.S.-Uzbek military agreement, "the CIA was already flying its teams into the massive Karshi-Khanabad, or K2, air base in southern Uzbekistan, where United States army engineers were repairing the runway."[25]

A third anomaly is that the terror war led to a dramatic increase in the resort to terror, and even torture, by America itself, sometimes targeting U.S. citizens. In this context it is relevant that Cheney and Rumsfeld, through their participation in the Defense Department's super-secret Doomsday Project, had also been part of Continuity of Government (COG) planning for undermining the U.S. Bill of Rights by the warrantless surveillance and detention of dissenters.[26] These plans, dating back to the fear of Communists in the McCarthyite 1950s, have been the underpinnings for the elaborate plans in the Pentagon and elsewhere for dealing with antiwar protests against the Pentagon's plans for global domination.

As I have argued elsewhere, the United States is now spending billions every year on Homeland Security, in no small part because of the belief, articulated by Marine Colonel Oliver North, that the Vietnam War was lost in the streets of America, and that this deterrent to U.S. military operations needed to be dealt with.[27] Cheney and Rumsfeld, as part of the so-called "Doomsday Project for Continuity of Government" (COG) planning, had been part of this effort also.[28] In short, 9/11 fulfilled agendas long contemplated by a small group of officials for radical new policies both in Central Asia and also inside America.

The homicidal crime suggested by Fenton's meticulous research is one both difficult and painful to contemplate. America is in a crisis today because of the activities of the Banks Too Big to Fail, which, as has been pointed out, were also Banks Too Big to Jail—for to punish them as criminals would endanger America's already threatened financial structure.[29] This chapter, though detailed, is dealing with something analogous, what may have been a Crime Too Big to Punish.

As will be developed in this chapter, 9/11 has other points in common with the John F. Kennedy assassination.

THE COVER-UP OF 9/11 AND OF THE CIA'S ROLE IN LETTING IT HAPPEN

After ten years it is important to reassess what we know and do not know about the events that culminated in 9/11, particularly the actions of the CIA and the FBI and the denial of critical information to the 9/11 Commission.

Today, we can confidently say,

1. The most important truths still remain unknown, in large part because many of the most important documents are still either unreleased or heavily redacted.
2. The efforts at cover-up continue, if anything more aggressively than before.
3. In addition to the cover-up, there has been what former 9/11 Commission staffer John Farmer has called either "unprecedented administrative incompetence or organized mendacity" on the part of key figures in Washington.[30] These figures include President Bush, Vice President Cheney, Joint Chiefs of Staff Acting Chairman General Richard Myers, and CIA Director George Tenet. They include also President Clinton's National Security Advisor, Samuel Berger, who prior to testifying on these matters, went to the National Archives and removed, and presumably destroyed, key relevant documentation.[31] In his book, Farmer has in effect endorsed both of these alternatives.

Farmer's first alternative, of "unprecedented administrative incompetence," is in effect the explanation offered by *The 9/11 Commission Report*, to deal with a) striking anomalies both on 9/11 itself, and b) the preceding twenty months during which important information was withheld from the FBI by key personnel in the CIA's Bin Laden Unit (the so-called "Alec Station group"). But thanks to the groundbreaking new book by Kevin Fenton, *Disconnecting the Dots*, we can no longer attribute the anomalous CIA behavior to "systemic problems," or what Tony Summers and Robbyn Swan rashly call "bureaucratic confusion."[32]

Building on earlier important books by James Bamford, Lawrence Wright, Peter Lance, and Philip Shenon, Fenton demonstrates beyond a shadow of a doubt that there was a systematic CIA pattern of withholding important information from the FBI, even when the FBI would normally be entitled to it. Even more brilliantly, he shows that the withholding pattern has been systematically sustained through four successive post-9/11 investigations: those of the Congressional Inquiry chaired by Senators Bob Graham and Richard Shelby (still partly withheld), the 9/11 Commission, the Department of Justice inspector general, and the CIA inspector general.

Most importantly of all, he shows that the numerous withholdings, both pre- and post-9/11, were the work of relatively few people. The withholding of information from the FBI was principally the work of the so-called "Alec Station group"—a group within but not identical with the CIA's Bin Laden Unit or "Alec Station," consisting largely of CIA personnel, though including a few FBI as well. Key figures in this group were CIA officer Tom Wilshire (discussed in *The 9/11 Commission Report* as "John"), and his immediate superior at Alec Station, Richard Blee.

The post-9/11 cover-up of Wilshire's behavior was principally the work of one person, Barbara Grewe, who worked first on the Justice Department Inspector General's investigation of Wilshire's behavior, then was transferred to two successive positions with the 9/11 Commission's staff, where, under the leadership of Executive Director Philip Zelikow, she was able to transfer the focus of investigative attention from the performance of the CIA to that of the FBI.[33] Whether or not Grewe conducted the interviews of Wilshire and other relevant personnel, she "certainly drew on them when drafting her sections of the Commission's and Justice Department inspector general's reports."[34]

Grewe's repositioning from post to post is a sign of an intended cover-up at a higher level. So, as we shall see, is Wilshire's transfer in May 2001 from CIA's Alec Station (the Osama Bin Laden Unit) to the FBI, where he began a new phase of interference with the normal flow of intelligence, obstructing the FBI from within it.[35]

The pattern begins with intelligence obtained from surveillance of an important al-Qaeda summit meeting of January 2000 in Malaysia, perhaps the only such summit before 9/11. The meeting drew instant and high-level U.S. attention because of indirect links to a support element (a key telephone in Yemen used by al-Qaeda) suspected of acting as a communications center in the 1998 bombings of U.S. Embassies. As Fenton notes, "The CIA realized that the summit was so important that information about it was briefed to CIA and FBI leaders [Louis Freeh and Dale Watson], National Security Adviser Samuel Berger and other top officials."[36]

Yet inside Alec Station, Tom Wilshire and his CIA subordinate (known only as "Michelle")[37] blocked the effort of an FBI agent detailed there (Doug Miller) to notify the FBI that one of the participants (Khalid al-Mihdhar) had a U.S. visa in his passport.[38] Worse, Michelle then sent a cable to other CIA stations falsely stating that al-Mihdhar's "travel documents, including a multiple entry U.S. visa, had been copied and passed 'to the FBI for further investigation.'"[39] Alec Station also failed to watch-list the participants in the meeting, as was called for by CIA guidelines.[40]

This was just the beginning of a systematic, sometimes lying pattern, where NSA and CIA information about al-Mihdhar and his traveling companion, Nawaf al-Hazmi, was systematically withheld from the FBI, lied about, or manipulated or distorted in such a way as to inhibit an FBI investigation of the two Saudis and their associates. This is a major component of the 9/11 story, because the behavior of these two would-be hijackers was so unprofessional that, without this CIA protection provided by the "Alec Station group," they would almost certainly have been detected and detained or deported, long before they prepared to board Flight 77 in Washington.[41]

Fenton concludes with a list of thirty-five different occasions on which the two alleged hijackers were protected in this fashion, from January 2000 to about September 5, 2001, less than a week before the hijackings.[42] In his analysis, the incidents fall into two main groups. The motive he attributes to the earlier ones, such as the blocking of Doug Miller's cable, was "to cover a CIA operation that was already in progress."[43] However after "the system was blinking red" in the summer of 2001, and the CIA expected an imminent attack, Fenton can see no other plausible explanation than that "the purpose of withholding the information had become to allow the attacks to go forward."[44]

Wilshire's pattern of interference changed markedly after his move to the Bureau. When in the CIA, he had moved to block transmittal of intelligence to the FBI. Now, in contrast, he initiated FBI reviews of the same material, but in such a way that the reviews were conducted in too leisurely a fashion to bear fruit before 9/11. Fenton suspects that Wilshire anticipated a future review of his files; and was laying a false trail of documentation to neutralize his embarrassing earlier performance.[45]

I believe we must now accept Fenton's finding of fact: "It is clear that this information was not withheld through a series of bizarre accidents, but intentionally."[46] However, I suggest a different explanation as to what those intentions originally were, one which is superficially much simpler, more benign, and also more explicative of other parts, apparently unrelated, of the 9/11 mystery.

THE LIAISON AGREEMENTS WITH OTHER INTELLIGENCE AGENCIES

Initially, I believe, al-Mihdhar and al-Hazmi may have been protected because they had been sent to America by the Saudi General Intelligence Directorate (GID) intelligence service, which would explain why after their arrival they were apparently bankrolled indirectly by the Saudi embassy in Washington. (As we saw in the last chapter, up to US$73,000 in cashier cheques was funneled by Saudi Ambassador Prince Bandar's wife to two Californian families known to have bankrolled al-Midhar and al-Hazmi.)[47]

If the two Saudis were in fact sent by the GID, they would almost certainly have been admitted to the United States under the terms of the liaison agreement between the GID and the CIA.[48] Prince Turki bin Faisal, former head of the GID, has said that he shared his al-Qaeda information with the CIA, and that in 1997 the Saudis "established a joint intelligence committee with the United States to share information on terrorism in general and on . . . al Qaeda in particular."[49] The 9/11 Commission Report adds that after a post-millennium review, the Counterterrorism Center (which included Alec Station, the Bin

Laden Unit) intended to proceed with its plan of half a year earlier, "building up the capabilities of foreign security services that provided intelligence via liaison."[50]

This was a Blee specialty. Steve Coll reports that Richard Blee and his superior Cofer Black, excited about the opportunities presented by liaison arrangements for expanding the scope of CIA reach in critical regions, had flown together into Tashkent in 1999, and negotiated a new liaison agreement with Uzbekistan.[51] According to Coll and the *Washington Post*, this arrangement soon led, via Tashkent, to a CIA liaison inside Afghanistan with the Northern Alliance.[52] Thomas Ricks and Susan Glasser reported in the *Washington Post* that, beginning after the embassy bombings in Dar es Salaam and Nairobi in 1998, "The United States and Uzbekistan have quietly conducted joint covert operations aimed at countering Afghanistan's ruling Taliban regime and its terrorist allies . . . , according to officials from both nations."[53]

This involvement in Uzbekistan was part of a wider regional pattern. Beginning in 1997, the United States had begun a series of annual military maneuvers with Kazakh, Kyrgyz, and Uzbek forces, as exercises for possible deployment of combat U.S. forces in the region.

> CENTRAZBAT '97, as it was known, was clearly a test of America's ability to project power into the Caspian basin in the event of a crisis. "There is no nation on the face of the earth that we cannot get to," said General Jack Sheehan . . . the highest-ranking officer to attend the exercise. And, lest anyone doubted the nature of our interests in the region, a deputy assistant secretary of defense accompanying Sheehan, Catherine Kelleher, cited "the presence of enormous energy resources" as a justification for American military involvement. The 1997 operation was the first in an annual series CENTRAZBAT exercises designed to test the speed with which Washington could deploy U.S.-based forces directly to the region and commence combat operations.[54]

In other words, the Pentagon had been active in Uzbekistan for four years before the public Rumsfeld-Karimov agreement of October 2001.

As a former junior Canadian diplomat, let me observe that a liaison arrangement would probably have required special access clearances for those privy to the arrangement and sharing the liaison information.[55] This would explain the exclusion of the FBI agents who were not cleared for this information, as well as the behavior of other noncleared CIA agents who proceeded to collect and disseminate information about the two alleged hijackers. Alec Station needed both to protect the double identity of the two Saudis, and to make sure that they were not embarrassingly detained by the FBI.

Almost certainly the CIA had relevant liaison arrangements, not just with the Saudi GID and Uzbekistan, but also with the Inter-Services Intelligence

(ISI) of Pakistan, as well as the intelligence services of Egypt, and perhaps Yemen and Morocco. As noted earlier, it is possible that Ali Mohamed, a double agent who the FBI protected from being detained in Canada, thus allowing him to help organize the al-Qaeda embassy bombings of 1998, was permitted under such arrangements to enter the United States as an agent of foreign intelligence, presumably Egyptian.[56] Ali Mohamed figures both in the content and as source of the President's Daily Brief (PDB) of August 6, 2001, in which the CIA warned the President, "Bin Ladin Determined to Strike in US."[57] According to Mohamed's FBI handler, Jack Cloonan, "all that information came from Ali," while the PDB itself attributes its key finding to what "an Egyptian Islamic Jihad (EIJ) operative told an [——] service."[58] (Ali Mohamed was definitely EIJ, and this service was probably Egyptian.)

But when Mohamed, like al-Mihdhar and al-Hazmi, was inappropriately admitted to the United States, it was reportedly not by the CIA, but possibly by "some other Federal agency."[59] This was very possibly a Pentagon agency, because from 1987 to 1989, Ali Mohamed "was assigned to the U.S. [Army] Special Operations Command [SOCOM] in Fort Bragg, the home of the Green Berets and the Delta Force, the elite counterterrorism squad."[60] SOCOM, which includes the Joint Special Operations Command (JSOC), has its own intelligence division;[61] and SOCOM is the command that first mounted the Able Danger program in 1999 to track al-Qaeda operatives, and then, inexplicably, both shut it down before 9/11 and destroyed its database.[62] In addition SOCOM was working in Uzbekistan with CIA operatives as a result of the liaison agreement negotiated by Cofer Black and Richard Blee of the Counterterrorist Center (CTC).

For this and other reasons, I suggest reconceptualizing what Fenton calls the anomalous "Alec Station group" as an interagency liaison team (or teams) with special access clearances, including Alec Station personnel, collaborating personnel in the FBI, and possibly SOCOM. (One of these collaborators was FBI agent Dina Corsi, who according to Fenton withheld vital information from fellow agent Steve Bongardt even after the NSA had cleared it for him.)[63]

BACKGROUND: THE SAFARI CLUB AND WILLIAM CASEY

These arrangements can be traced in one form or another, at least back to the 1970s. Then senior CIA officers and ex-officers (notably Richard Helms), who were dissatisfied with the CIA cutbacks instituted under Jimmy Carter's CIA director, Stansfield Turner, organized an alternative network, the so-called "Safari Club." Subordinated to intelligence chiefs from France, Egypt, Saudi Arabia, Morocco and (under the Shah) Iran, the Safari Club is said by Joseph Trento to have been supplemented in Washington by a "private intelligence network" consisting of CIA officers like Theodore Shackley and Thomas

Clines, who had been marginalized or fired by CIA Director Turner.[64] As Prince Turki later explained, the purpose of the Safari Club was not just to exchange information, but to conduct covert operations that the CIA could no longer carry out directly in the wake of the Watergate scandal and subsequent reforms.[65]

In the 1980s, CIA Director William Casey made key decisions in the conduct of the Afghan covert war, not through his own CIA bureaucracy but with the Saudi intelligence chiefs, first Kamal Adham and then Prince Turki. Among these decisions was the creation of a foreign legion to assist the Afghan mujahedin in their war against the Soviets—in other words, the creation of that support network that, since the end of that war, we have known as al-Qaeda.[66] Casey worked out the details with the two Saudi intelligence chiefs, and also with the head of the Bank of Credit and Commerce International (BCCI), the Saudi-Pakistani bank in which Adham and Turki were both shareholders.

In so doing, Casey was in effect running a second or back-channel CIA, building up the future al-Qaeda in Pakistan with the Saudis, even though the official CIA hierarchy underneath him in Langley rightly "thought this unwise."[67] In *American War Machine*, I situated the Safari Club and BCCI in a succession of "second CIA" or "alternative CIA" arrangements dating back to the creation of the Office of Policy Coordination (OPC) in 1948. Thus it is relevant that CIA Director George Tenet, following Casey's precedent, met with Saudi Ambassador Bandar around once a month, and would not tell CIA officers handling Saudi issues what he had discussed.[68]

Fenton himself invokes the example of the Safari Club in proposing the possible explanation that Blee and Wilshire used a "parallel network" to track al-Mihdhar and al-Hazmi inside the United States. In his words, "Withholding the information about Almihdhar and Alhazmi only makes sense if the CIA was monitoring the two men in the United States itself, either officially or off the books."[69] But a third option would be that the GID was monitoring their movements, a situation quite compatible with Saudi Prince Bandar's claim that Saudi security had been "actively following the movements of most of the terrorists with precision."[70]

Joseph and Susan Trento heard from a former CIA officer, once based in Saudi Arabia, that "Both Hazmi and Mihdhar were Saudi agents."[71] If so, they were clearly double agents, acting (or posing) as terrorists at the same time they were acting (or posing) as informants. In espionage, double agents are prized and often valuable; but to rely on them (as the example of Ali Mohamed illustrates) can also be dangerous.

This was particularly the case for the CIA with respect to Saudi Arabia, whose GID supported al-Qaeda energetically in countries like Bosnia, in exchange for a pledge (negotiated by Saudi Interior Minister Naif bin Abdul Aziz with Osama bin Laden) that al-Qaeda "would not interfere with the politics of Saudi Arabia or any Arab country."[72] Pakistan's ISI was even more actively engaged with al-Qaeda, and some elements of ISI were probably closer to the ideological goals of al-Qaeda, than to Pakistan's nominally secular government.

But in all cases the handling of illegal informants is not just dangerous and unpredictable, but corrupting. To act their parts, the informants must break the law; and their handlers, knowing this, must protect them by failing to report them, and then, all too often, intercede to prevent their arrest by others. In this way, handlers, over and over again, become complicit in the crimes of their informants, and later compelled for personal reasons to cover them up.[73]

Even in the best of circumstances, decisions have to be made whether to allow an informant's crime to go forward, or to thwart it and risk terminating the usefulness of the informant. In such moments, agencies are all too likely to make the choice that is not in the public interest.

A very relevant example is the first World Trade Center bombing of 1993—relevant because Khalid Sheikh Mohammed, the alleged mastermind of 9/11, was one of the 1993 plotters as well. As we saw in chapter 4, the FBI had an informant, Emad Salem, among the 1993 plotters; and Salem later claimed, with supporting evidence from tapes of his FBI debriefings, that the FBI deliberately chose not to shut down the plot. Here is Ralph Blumenthal's careful *New York Times* account of this precursor to the mystery of 9/11:

> Law-enforcement officials [i.e., the FBI] were told that terrorists were building a bomb that was eventually used to blow up the World Trade Center, and they planned to thwart the plotters by secretly substituting harmless powder for the explosives, an informer said after the blast.
>
> The informer was to have helped the plotters build the bomb and supply the fake powder, but the plan was called off by an F.B.I. supervisor who had other ideas about how the informer, Emad A. Salem, should be used, the informer said.
>
> The account, which is given in the transcript of hundreds of hours of tape recordings Mr. Salem secretly made of his talks with law-enforcement agents, portrays the authorities as in a far better position than previously known to foil the Feb. 26 bombing of New York City's tallest towers. The explosion left six people dead, more than 1,000 injured and damages in excess of half a billion dollars. Four men are now on trial in Manhattan Federal Court in that attack.[74]

What makes the 1993 plot even more relevant is that Salem, according to many sources, was an agent of the Egyptian intelligence service, sent to America to spy on the actions of the Egyptian "Blind Sheikh" Omar Abdel Rahman.[75] This raises the possibility that the FBI supervisor who had "other ideas" about how to use Emad Salem, was a member of a liaison team, with special knowledge he could not share with other FBI agents. It may have been, for example, that the Egyptian intelligence service declined to let Salem's cover be blown. This suggestion is both speculative and problematic, but it has the advantage of offering a relatively coherent explanation for otherwise baffling behavior.

This explanation does not at all rule out the possibility that some officials had more sinister motives for allowing the bombing to take place and covering it up afterward. Sheikh Omar Abdel Rahman was at this very time a key figure in the sensitive Saudi program, signed on to by U.S. officials as well, to supply mujahedin warriors in Bosnia against Serbia (including some, like Ayman al-Zawahiri, who were later accused of the 9/11 plot).[76] It is clear from both investigative and prosecutorial behavior that a number of different U.S. agencies did not want to disturb Rahman's activities. Even after Rahman himself was finally indicted in the 1995 conspiracy case to blow up New York landmarks, the U.S. government continued to protect Ali Mohamed, a key figure in the conspiracy.

Worse, the performance of the FBI in allowing the bombing to proceed was only one of a series of interrelated bungled performances and missed opportunities, climaxing with 9/11. The first was in connection with the murder in New York of the Jewish extremist Meir Kahane. The FBI and New York police actually detained two of the murderers in that case and then released them, allowing them to take part in the World Trade Center bombing of 1993. A key trainer of the two men was Ali Mohamed while still in U.S. Special Forces, whose name was systematically protected from disclosure by the prosecuting attorney, Patrick Fitzgerald.

Considering all this in the light of the handling of Ali Mohamed, we have to conclude that there is something profoundly dysfunctional going on, and has been going on since before 9/11, indeed under both political parties. The conditions of secrecy created by special clearances have not just masked this dysfunctionality; they have, I would argue, helped create it. The history of espionage demonstrates that secret power, when operating in the sphere of illegal activities, becomes, time after time, antithetical to public democratic power.[77] The more restricted the group of special planners with special clearances, the less likely are their decisions to conform with the dictates of international and domestic law, still less with common morality and common sense.

Add to these conditions of unwholesome secrecy, the fundamentally unhealthy, indeed corrupt, relationship of U.S. intelligence agencies to those of Saudi Arabia and Pakistan. This has been profoundly antidemocratic both at home and in Asia. The U.S. dependency on Saudi oil has in effect subsidized a wealth-generated spread of Islamic fundamentalism throughout the world, while what the 99.9 percent of ordinary Americans pay for oil and gas generates huge sums, which Saudis then recycle into the financial institutions of the one tenth of 1 percent at the pinnacle of Wall Street.

In like manner, America's fraught relationship with the ISI of Pakistan has resulted in a dramatic increase in international heroin trafficking by the two agencies' Afghan clients.[78] In short the bureaucratic dysfunction we are talking about in 9/11 is a symptom of a larger dysfunction in America's relationship with Saudi Arabia, with Pakistan, and through them with the rest of the world.

LIAISON AGREEMENTS AND THE PROTECTION OF AL-MIHDHAR AND AL-HAZMI

Even without the suggestive precedent of the 1993 WTC bombing, it is legitimate to posit that liaison agreements may have inhibited the roundup of Khalid al-Mihdhar and Nawaf al-Hazmi. Let us consider first Fenton's finding of fact: "It is clear that this information [about the two men] was not withheld through a series of bizarre accidents, but intentionally."[79] This finding I consider rock hard. But we cannot be so confident about his explanation: that "the purpose of withholding the information had become to allow the attacks to go forward."[80]

I believe that in fact there are a number of possibilities about the intention, ranging from the relatively innocent (the inhibitions deriving from a liaison agreement) to the nefarious. Before considering these, let us deconstruct the notion of "letting the attacks go forward." Clearly, if the alleged hijackers were not detained at the airport gates, people would probably have been killed—but how many? Recall that in the Operation Northwoods documents, which envisaged planning "false flag" attacks to justify a U.S. military intervention in Cuba, the Joint Chiefs wrote "We could develop a Communist Cuban terror campaign" in which "we could sink a boatload of Cubans."[81] Would the loss of four planeloads of passengers have been a qualitatively different tragedy?

Of course 9/11 became a much greater tragedy when three of the planes hit the two World Trade Center towers and the Pentagon. But it is possible that the liaison minders of the two Saudis did not imagine that their targets were capable of such a feat. Recall that their flying lessons, even in a Cessna, were such a fiasco that the lessons were quickly terminated. Their instructor told them "that flying was simply not for them."[82]

Let me suggest that there are three separable ingredients to the 9/11 attacks: the alleged hijackings, the strikes on the buildings, and the astonishing collapse of the three WTC buildings. It is at least possible that the Alec Station liaison team, as a group, contemplated only the first stage, without ever imagining the two stages that ensued.

A minimal, least malign, initial explanation for the withholding of information about two of the alleged hijackers would be the hypothesis I proposed in the case of Emad Salem—the restricted access created by the special clearance for a liaison agreement. But just as in 1993, the secret power created behind the wall of restrictive clearances may have been exploited for ulterior purposes. The dangerous situation thus created—of potential would-be-hijackers being protected from detention at a time of expected attack—may have inspired some to exploit the resulting conditions of secrecy as an opportunity to plan an incident to justify war. One important analogy with the 1964 false Second Tonkin Gulf Incident that was used to justify attacking North Vietnam is the same presence of a powerful faction—in 2001 the PNAC clique inside government—that was bent on unilateral military action.[83]

One clue to this more sinister intention is that the pattern of withholdings detailed by Fenton is not restricted exclusively to the two Saudis and their CIA station handlers. There are a few concatenating withholdings by other agencies—above all the Able Danger info that was destroyed at SOCOM and the withholding—apparently by the NSA—of an important relevant intercept, apparently about the alleged hijackers and Moussaoui.[84]

If the NSA was withholding information from relevant officials, it would recall the role of the NSA at the time of the second Tonkin Gulf incident in August 1964. Then the NSA, at a crucial moment, forwarded fifteen pieces of signals intelligence (SIGINT) that indicated—falsely—that there had been a North Vietnamese attack on two U.S. destroyers. At the same time NSA withheld 107 pieces of SIGINT that indicated—correctly—that no North Vietnamese attack had occurred.[85] NSA's behavior at that time was mirrored at the CIA: both agencies were aware of a powerful consensus inside the Johnson administration that had already agreed on provoking North Vietnam, in hopes of creating an opportunity for military response.[86]

We know from many accounts of the Bush administration that there was also a powerful pro-war consensus within it, centered on Cheney, Rumsfeld, and the so-called "cabal" of PNAC (the Project for the New American Century) that before Bush's election had been lobbying vigorously for military action against Iraq. We know also that Rumsfeld's immediate response to 9/11 was to propose an attack on Iraq, and that planning for such an attack was indeed instituted on September 17.[87] It is worth considering whether some of those protecting the alleged hijackers from detention did not share these warlike ambitions.[88]

DID RICHARD BLEE HAVE AN ULTERIOR MOTIVE FOR WITHHOLDING INFORMATION?

Fenton speculates that one of those seeking a pretext for an escalated war against al-Qaeda may have been Richard Blee. We saw that Blee, with Cofer Black, negotiated an intelligence-sharing liaison agreement with Uzbekistan.

By 2000 SOCOM had become involved, and "U.S. Special Forces began to work more overtly with the Uzbek military on training missions."[89] In the course of time the Uzbek liaison agreement, as we saw, expanded into a subordinate liaison with the Northern Alliance in Afghanistan. Blee, meeting with Massoud in October 1999, agreed to lobby in Washington for more active support for the Northern Alliance.[90]

After the USS *Cole* bombing in Aden in 2000, Blee was pushing to expand the Uzbek military mission still further into a joint attack force in conjunction with the Northern Alliance forces of Massoud. There was considerable objection to this while Clinton was still president, partly on the grounds that Massoud, with Russian and Iranian support, was fighting Pakistani-backed Taliban forces, and partly because he was known to be supporting his forces by heroin trafficking.[91] But in the spring of 2001 a meeting of department deputies in the new Bush administration revived the plans of Blee and Black (supported by Counterterrorism chief Richard Clarke) for large-scale covert aid to Massoud.[92] On September 4, one week before 9/11, the Bush Cabinet authorized the drafting of a new presidential directive, NSPD-9, authorizing a covert action program along these lines in conjunction with Massoud.[93]

In the new Bush administration Blee was no longer a minority voice, and six weeks after 9/11 he would be named the new CIA station chief in Kabul.[94] Fenton reports that in this capacity Blee became involved in the rendition of al-Qaeda detainees, and suggests that the motive may have been to obtain, by torture, a false confession (by Ibn Shaikh al-Libi) to Iraqi involvement with al-Qaeda. This false confession then became part of the "fixing" of evidence, and "formed a key part of Secretary of State Colin Powell's embarrassing presentation to the UN to support the invasion of Iraq."[95]

DID SOCOM HAVE AN ULTERIOR MOTIVE FOR CLOSING DOWN ABLE DANGER?

What ensued after 9/11 went far beyond Blee's program for paramilitary CIA involvement with the Northern Alliance. The CIA component in Afghanistan was soon dwarfed by the forces of SOCOM: George Tenet reported that by late 2001 the U.S. force in Afghanistan consisted of about 500 fighters, including "110 CIA officers, 316 Special Forces personnel, and scores of Joint Special Operations Command raiders creating havoc behind enemy lines."[96]

In the Bush administration Stephen Cambone, who earlier had collaborated with Rumsfeld and Cheney in signing the PNAC's statement, *Rebuilding America's Defenses,* became one of the active promoters of using SOCOM special forces to operate covertly against al-Qaeda, not just in Afghanistan, but "anywhere in the world."[97]

It is possible that anything Blee may have done in Alec Station to prepare the way for 9/11 was only one part of a larger interagency operation, in which an equivalent role was played by SOCOM's shutting down of the Able Danger project. This might help explain a handwritten notation around 10 p.m. on 9/11 by Stephen Cambone, then one of Cheney's PNAC appointees under Rumsfeld in the Pentagon, after a phone call with George Tenet:

> AA 77—3 indiv[iduals] have been followed since Millennium & Cole
> 1 guy is assoc[iate] of Cole bomber
> 2 entered US in early July
> (2 of 3 pulled aside & interrogated?)[98]

The "guy" here is probably al-Mihdhar, and the "Cole bomber" probably Khallad [or Tawfiq] bin Attash, a major al-Qaeda figure connected not just to the *Cole* bombing but also to the 1998 embassy attacks. One wants to know why Tenet was sharing with a hawk in the Pentagon information that has apparently never been shared by anyone outside the CIA since. And is it a coincidence that Cambone, like Blee, oversaw a program—in this case staffed by SOCOM special operations personnel—using torture to interrogate detainees in Afghanistan?[99]

Just as Blee was reportedly a special protégé of George Tenet at CIA, so Cambone was notorious for his fierce loyalty first to Dick Cheney and later to Donald Rumsfeld in the Pentagon. It is not known whether he was associated with the Continuity of Government (COG) planning project where Rumsfeld and Cheney, among others, prepared for the warrantless surveillance and detention measures that (as I argued in chapter 3) were implemented beginning on the morning of 9/11 and still in force today. Nor is it known if he was associated in any way with Cheney's Counterterrorism Task Force in the Spring of 2001, which has been alleged to have been a source for the war games, including rogue plane attacks, which added to the disarray of the U.S. response, on 9/11.[100]

DEEP EVENTS AS A REPEATED PATTERN OF U.S. ENGAGEMENT IN WAR

I want to conclude with a little historical perspective on the dysfunction we have been looking at. In a sense 9/11 was unprecedented—the greatest mass murder ever committed in one day on U.S. soil. In another sense it represented an example of the kind of signature event with which we have become only too familiar since the Kennedy assassination. I have called these events deep events—events deeply rooted in illegal covert activity in various branches of U.S. intelligence and with a predictable accompanying pattern of official cover-ups backed up by amazing media malfunction and dishonest best-selling books. Some of these deep events, like the Kennedy assassination,

Tonkin Gulf, and 9/11, should be considered structural deep events, because of their permanent impact on history.

It is striking that these structural deep events—the JFK assassination, Tonkin Gulf, and 9/11—should all have been swiftly followed by America's engagement in ill-considered wars. The reverse is also true: all of America's significant wars since Korea—Laos, Vietnam, Afghanistan (twice: once covertly and now overtly), and Iraq—have all been preceded by structural deep events. As I wrote in *American War Machine*, a J-5 Staff Report of 1963 reported to the Joint Chiefs, "The engineering of a series of provocations to justify military intervention is feasible and could be accomplished with the resources available."[101] Tonkin Gulf, 9/11, and even the Kennedy assassination itself can all be seen as events that were indeed "engineered," along the guidelines set out in 1962 in the Joint Chiefs of Staff proposals for Operation Northwoods.[102]

In two recent books I have been slowly persuaded, against my own initial incredulity, to list more than a dozen significant parallels between the Kennedy assassination and 9/11. Thanks to Kevin Fenton's brilliant research, I can list a further analogy. The CIA files on Lee Harvey Oswald, more or less dormant for two years, suddenly became hyperactive in the six weeks before the Kennedy assassination.[103] Fenton has demonstrated a similar burst of activity in FBI files on the two Saudis in the weeks before 9/11—a burst initiated by Tom Wilshire, at a time suspiciously close to when the alleged hijackers settled on a final date for their attack. Then in both cases there were also strange delays, leaving the files open at the time of the deep events.[104]

THE IMPACT OF 9/11 ON U.S. AND INTERNATIONAL LAW

Throughout this chapter we have seen two different and indeed antithetical levels of U.S. foreign policy at work. On the surface level of public diplomacy we see a commitment to international law and the peaceful resolution of differences. On a deeper level, represented by a longtime Saudi connection and covert arrangements to control international oil, we see the toleration and indeed protection of terrorists in fulfillment of both Saudi and American secret goals. We should see the actions in 2000–2001 of the "Alec Station group," with respect to the two alleged hijackers al-Mihdhar and al-Hazmi, in the context of this longtime Saudi connection, as well as of the secret consensus in 2001—just as earlier in 1964—that America's oil and security needs (along with those of Israel) required a new American mobilization for war.

Horrendous as it was, the murder of over 2,000 civilians on 9/11 was not the only major crime of that day. The 9/11 events also initiated a series of ongoing onslaughts on both international and domestic U.S. law. Law and freedom go together, and both had been significantly enhanced by the founding documents of the United States in the eighteenth century. The world benefited; written constitutions soon appeared on every continent; and the Young Europe movements, inspired by America's example, began the long difficult process toward today's European Union.

Starting in 2001, both law and freedom have been progressively eroded. International comity, which depends on each state not doing to others what they would not want done to them, has been supplanted, at least for a while, by U.S. unilateral military engagement without constraint, acting without fear of retribution. Drone killings in far corners of the world have now become routine, causing more than an estimated 2,000 Pakistani deaths (the vast majority of them untargeted civilians) and over 75 percent of them under President Obama.[105] The preemptive war against Iraq, despite being proven both unwarranted and counterproductive, has been followed by the preemptive bombing of Libya, and the prospect of still further campaigns against Syria and Iran.

Writing as a Canadian, let me say that I believe in American exceptionalism, and that at one time America was truly exceptional in its unprecedented replacement of authoritarian with limited constitutional government. Today America is still exceptional, but for its percentage of citizens who are incarcerated, for its disparity in wealth and income between rich and poor (a ratio exceeded among large nations only by China), and for its indiscriminate use of lethal power abroad.

Only the last of these trends began with 9/11. But 9/11 itself should be seen as a dialectical outcome of America's imperial expansion and simultaneous decay—a process inevitably afflicting those superstates that amass and retain more power than is necessary for the orderly management of their own affairs.

POSTSCRIPT (2014)

With the election of Obama in 2008, many hoped that Wolfowitz's PNAC agenda—"we've about five or ten years to clean up those old soviet client regimes—Syria, Iran, Iraq"—would now be history. But Obama has since intervened militarily in Libya, come close to doing so in Syria, and has now recently been using the National Endowment for Democracy to affect the political future of Ukraine, a country that historically is part of Russia itself.

There is great resentment in Moscow, not confined to the Putin government, that when Gorbachev removed Soviet troops from Eastern Europe, NATO troops then moved into the same area. Gorbachev has repeated more than once his charge that "the Americans promised that NATO wouldn't move beyond the boundaries of Germany after the Cold War."[106] Jack Matlock, U.S. ambassador to Moscow at the time, has also said that the West gave a "clear commitment" not to expand.[107] When I visited in Moscow in 2012 I heard from many Russians (even some thought in the West to be relatively "liberal") their sense that NATO was consolidating its encirclement of Russia from Estonia to Iraq to Afghanistan.[108]

In May 2014, as I send this book to its publisher, Putin is endorsing the idea of roundtable discussions to defuse the ominous crisis in Ukraine. Obama meanwhile has reportedly resolved to focus on "isolating . . . Russia by cutting off its economic and political ties to the outside world . . . effectively making it a pariah state."[109] At a recent informed university discussion it was reported that some in Washington still hope to include Ukraine itself in NATO.

One has to be reminded of Tom Hayden's charge, noted in chapter 2, that a "state within the state"—that is, the deep state itself, and not just its neocon friends in PNAC—may be responsible for Obama's failure to follow the guidelines of his friendly speeches.[110]

FURTHER POSTSCRIPT

In the next chapter we will return to the theme of two types of power in U.S. history, in order to see how, in the two decades embracing the Vietnam War, the growing unchecked power of the deep state contested and repeatedly overcame the democratically elected authority of the White House.

Three presidents—Kennedy, Nixon, and Carter—took steps to challenge the growing power of the CIA; and in diverse ways all three saw their political careers terminated in deep events: assassination, Watergate, and the October Surprise. (Less dramatically, the careers of Johnson and Ford were also ended.) The deep state was also affected. The tenures of no less than seven Directors of Central Intelligence (DCIs) were terminated in these two decades, and three of them (Dulles, Helms, and Bush) were reportedly terminated after controversies with their presidents. (A fourth, the relatively liberal Colby, may have been sacked after he incurred the displeasure of some in the deep state.)

This was a new stage in a process of emergent deep state power, climaxing in the Reagan Revolution that ended four decades of power-sharing between American capital and American labor. The two decades opened with presidents seeking détente and coexistence with the Soviet Union. Thanks to deep state manipulations, that trend was reversed. Dulles, Helms, and Bush may have been sacked; but their faction triumphed.

CHAPTER 8

Deep Power Takes Its Toll on U.S. Presidents, 1961–1980

THE DEEP STATE, DEEP EVENTS, AND VIOLENCE

IN FEBRUARY 2011, AT A WASHINGTON PRESS CONFERENCE, SECRETARY OF State Hillary Clinton announced new U.S. government measures to promote freedom of speech throughout the world. At the back of the hall, and wearing a T-shirt with the slogan "Veterans for Peace," Raymond McGovern, a former senior CIA analyst turned nonviolent antiwar activist, conducted a silent, brief protest: he turned his back on Clinton and faced the wall.[1] Two burly men, one of them in plain clothes, pounced on McGovern and wrestled him out of the room. Once out of sight, they beat him so mercilessly that he had wounds over his body and his clothes were bloodied. After being handcuffed and detained at a police station for three hours and then released, he had to be treated for his wounds at a hospital. There he was informed that, as the victim of an assault, it was his responsibility to inform—the Washington police![2]

As I wrote in chapter 1, this episode encapsulates a very old tension in America between two types of power—persuasive and violent. McGovern's example of nonviolent persuasive protest is part of a storied American tradition dating back to Henry Thoreau's arrest in protest of James Polk's Mexican-American War. The violent response is part of an equally American tradition, from the Ku Klux Klan and the Battle of Wounded Knee down to Bull Connor and the Birmingham police in 1963. Both traditions, the persuasive and the violent, are profoundly American.[3]

I wish in this chapter to recapitulate what I said in chapter 1, with a new thesis: that a significant shift in the relationship between public and deep state power occurred in the 1960s and 1970s, culminating in the Reagan Revolution of 1980. In this period five presidents sought to curtail the powers of the deep state. And as we shall see, the political careers of all five were cut off in ways that were unusual. One president, Kennedy, was assassinated. Another, Nixon, was forced to resign.

To some extent the interplay of these two forms of power and political organization is found in all societies. As we saw in chapter 1, the two were defined by Hannah Arendt in the 1960s as "persuasion through arguments" versus "coercion by force." Arendt, following Thucydides, traced these to the common Greek way of handling domestic affairs, which was *persuasion* (πείθειν) as well as the common way of handling foreign affairs, which was force and *violence* (βία)."[4] The two represent not just different techniques of government but different cultures and mindsets, in fundamental tension with each other.[5]

This tension increases, and predictably tips toward violence, if a well-organized open community expands beyond its own borders and is increasingly occupied with the business of supervising an empire. It is repeatedly the case that progressive societies (like America) expand. As their influence expands, their democratic institutions, based at bottom upon persuasive power among equals, are supplemented by new, often secret, institutions of top-down, violent power for the control of alien populations abroad, often speaking different and unfamiliar languages. The more the society expands, the more these institutions of violent power encroach upon and supplant the original democracy.

As a result these nations also experience deeper and deeper politics, much of it a contest between these two types of power. One special feature of American deep politics since World War II is that much of it has been characterized by a series of conspiratorial deep events, emblematic of the ongoing conflict between these two forms of power and their corresponding mindsets. One is the acknowledged public mindset of openness, egalitarianism, and democracy. The other is the global dominance mindset committed to maintaining and expanding American hegemony. In domestic policy we often analyze the two cultures as liberals versus conservatives; in foreign policy, doves versus hawks. (Yet American liberals when they reach power, such as Hillary Clinton and John Kerry, have also been deeply entwined in the militarization of American politics and its global expansion.)

But with the expansion since 9/11 of extra-constitutional agencies like the NSA, it is time to supplement these horizontal distinctions with a vertical one: between those agencies constrained by constitutional checks and balances (the public state) and those not so constrained (the deep state). Although the deep state as we have defined it has always existed, its recent radical expansion has brought it into occasional conspiratorial conflict with the public state—even with the President.

The tension between persuasive and violent power has increased incrementally in recent U.S. history, from the years after World War II through to September 11, 2001. We have seen the emergence to dominance of what used to be called the "military-industrial complex," and what in my 2010 book I called the "American war machine." This is a major change. When Eisenhower warned against the military-industrial complex in 1961, the values, institutions, and resources that comprised it were still subordinate elements in American society. Today it not only dominates both parties, but is also financing threats to both these parties from even further to the right.

That change has been achieved partly by money, but partly also with the assistance of deep events: events, such as the Kennedy assassination, Watergate, the 1980 October Surprise, Iran-Contra, and 9/11, which repeatedly have involved lawbreaking and/or violence, have been mysterious to begin with, and whose mystery has been compounded by systematic falsifications in media and internal government records.[6]

In saying that these deep events have contributed collectively to a major change in American society, I am not attributing them all to a single agent or "secret team." Rather I see them as flowing in part from the sociodynamic processes of violent power itself, power associated with and deployed in the service of the global expansion of American military might, which (as history has shown many times) has the effect to transform both societies with surplus power and the individuals exercising that power.[7] Insofar as these power processes govern America without deriving from its Constitution, we can say that they derive from the milieu of the American deep state.

In discussing the deep events of Dallas, Watergate, Iran-Contra, and 9/11, I will argue that, while the mysteries of these deep events cannot at present be fully dispelled by historical analysis (given the absence of documentation), analysis does point to a pattern linking them. In *American War Machine* I wrote,

> The historical succession of deep events—such as Dallas, Watergate, and 9/11—has impacted more and more profoundly on America's political situation. More specifically, . . . major foreign wars are typically preceded by deep events like the Tonkin Gulf incidents, 9/11, or the 2001 anthrax attacks. This suggests that what I call the war machine in Washington [the forces striving for global U.S. dominance, including elements both inside and outside government, both inside and outside the United States] may have been behind them. . . . Since 1959, virtually all of America's major foreign wars have been wars 1) induced preemptively by the U.S. war machine and/or 2) disguised as responses to unprovoked enemy aggression, with disguises repeatedly engineered by deception deep events, involving in some way elements of the global drug connection.[8]

These deceptions were not designed to deceive America's enemies, but first and foremost to deceive the American people, to accept the unilateral initiation by America of illegal wars.

These successive, deception plots, including the repeated falsified appearances of external attacks or threats (from North Vietnam, Panama, or Iraq) have been part of a larger picture. I will suggest that for at least a half-century the conflict between the two mindsets has given rise to a series of conspiratorial deep events, emanating from the hidden recesses of the American war machine, all designed to deceive and coerce the American people so as to sustain or further military expansion. I will go further, and argue that this continuity underlies yet other significant deep events that led, not to the start of yet another external war, but to the progressive militarization and political repression of domestic American society.

I will document this conflict between the two mindsets, in one way or another, revealing how it underlies all the major deep events in recent American history: Dallas, Tonkin Gulf, Watergate, the 1980 Republican October Surprise, Iran-Contra, and finally 9/11. These events were needed to achieve American acceptance of both militarized domestic security and successive preemptive foreign wars. The neocons of the Project for the New American Century (PNAC) virtually acknowledged this when they wrote that their program for American dominance was unlikely to be adopted soon, "absent some catastrophic and catalyzing event—like a new Pearl Harbor."[9]

MILITARY AND CIA RESENTMENT (1961–1980)

We can trace what has happened over fifty years through the dramatic change in presidential attitudes toward the Soviet Union. Kennedy, Johnson, and above all Nixon believed in détente with the Soviet Union. Starting under Ford and Carter, and climaxing with Reagan, elements in the United States set out to help destroy what Reagan called "the evil empire." Saudi Arabian wealth and influence approved of this change and may have been a factor in achieving it.[10]

The last major achievement of the dove faction was Kennedy's peaceful resolution of the Cuban Missile crisis in 1962. But the Joint Chiefs had been eager to engage with the Soviet Union, and some of them were furious that Kennedy denied them this chance. Air Force Chief General Curtis LeMay "called the settlement 'the greatest defeat in our history,' and urged a prompt invasion."[11] Earlier LeMay had called Kennedy's blockade tactic "almost as bad as the appeasement at Munich," and had threatened to take his dissent public.[12]

There are abundant corroborations for this alarming standoff between the President and his Joint Chiefs. Daniel Ellsberg, who worked in the Pentagon in 1964, told David Talbot that after the Cuban Missile settlement "there was virtually a coup atmosphere in Pentagon circles . . . a mood of hatred and rage. The atmosphere was poisonous, poisonous."[13] Disagreements over how vigorously to pursue the Vietnam War later divided President Johnson from many of his generals, split his party, and finally persuaded LBJ not to run for reelection.

These resentments survived into the Nixon era. Admiral Elmo R. Zumwalt, Jr., came close to accusing Nixon and Kissinger of treason and Kissinger of being a Soviet sympathizer.[14] A book coauthored by retired admiral Chester Ward and published in 1975 charged that Kissinger was not just a Soviet sympathizer but a conscious Soviet agent.[15] (With the rise under George W. Bush and Obama of neocons with aggressive agendas, the Joint Chiefs have tended in contrast to play a restraining role.)[16]

We have to consider that it was no accident that deep events, the Kennedy assassination and Watergate, cut off the presidencies of both Kennedy and Nixon, both bitterly resented by their generals, and also the only presidents not to serve full terms in the postwar era. Less conspicuously, their successors, Ford and Carter, were also afflicted by deep divisions within their respective administrations. Following the wishes of Congress, "Gerald Ford and Jimmy Carter carried out the largest number of revisions to presidential directives since Eisenhower, carefully rewriting each of the [COG] emergency documents."[17] Not coincidentally, each of them faced divisions among their supporters; and they became the first and second incumbent presidents to be defeated for reelection since Herbert Hoover in 1932.[18]

The military figures who protested against presidential restraints on their proposals were not alone in Washington, there was also CIA resistance to presidential efforts to control the agency. The most striking example is perhaps the 1980 election campaign that launched the Reagan Revolution. Robert Parry has demonstrated that this election was preceded by a number of illegal actions—climaxing in the Republican October Surprise—in which both veterans and active employees of the deep state—no longer the obedient servant of the public state—played a significant role. The events of the Republican October Surprise have been characterized—by myself among others—as an escalated reprise of dirty tricks between Republicans and Democrats.[19] It is closer to the truth to see them as Robert Parry has done, as in part a CIA revolt (in alliance with Israel and the Safari Club) against Jimmy Carter and his house-cleaning CIA Director Stansfield Turner. Parry reported that Miles Copeland told him, "'the CIA within the CIA'—the innermost circle of powerful intelligence figures . . . believed Carter and his naïve faith in American democratic ideals represented a grave threat to the nation."[20]

The antagonism between CIA operatives and the White House did not begin with Carter. It was so acute right after the Bay of Pigs and the firing of CIA Director Dulles that Kennedy told one of the highest officials of his administration that he wanted "to splinter the C.I.A. in a thousand pieces and scatter it to the winds."[21] In 1972 Nixon fired Helms after the Watergate break-in because he believed Helms "was out to get him"; and he gave orders to Helms's replacement, James Schlesinger, "to turn the place inside out."[22]

Neither Kennedy nor Nixon finished their terms, let alone their intention to bring the CIA under control. But their successive firings of Dulles and Helms left a toxic resentment inside the CIA, especially after Nixon's CIA Director James Schlesinger then purged more that five hundred analysts and more than one thousand people in all from the clandestine service.[23] CIA veteran Arabist Archibald Roosevelt, who was a significant player along with former CIA Director Bush in the October Surprise, believed that Nixon's appointees as CIA Director—James Schlesinger and William Colby—"had both . . . betrayed their office by pandering to politicians."[24]

CIA resentment and concern was not just directed against presidents. The CIA's Operations Division was also determined to fight a number of limitations imposed on it in the mid-1970s by the responses of a Democratic Congress to the recommendations of the Senate Select Committee chaired by Senator Frank Church. As a result, even before Carter's election, a number of the CIA's allied intelligence services—in France, Egypt, Saudi Arabia, Iran, and Morocco—had allied in the so-called "Safari Club" to serve as an alternative source of funding and financing of covert operations.[25] In this they used the resources and networks of the drug-laundering Bank of Credit and Commerce International (BCCI). CIA assets like Adnan Khashoggi and Bruce Rappaport, assisted by officially retired CIA personnel like Miles Copeland and Jerry Townsend, were part of this global BCCI network. And, as we saw in chapter 2, former Saudi intelligence chief Prince Turki bin Faisal, a key figure in the Safari Club, once admitted candidly that the Safari Club, operating at the level of the deep state, was expressly created to overcome the efforts of Carter and Congress to rein in the CIA.[26]

But as we saw in chapter 2, the efforts of former CIA officers to elect Reagan were only part of a larger effort to ensure the defeat of Carter in 1980. An even more important factor in Carter's defeat was the prior manipulation of oil prices by the U.S. oil majors, to engineer an artificially elevated oil price increase.[27]

The plight of Jimmy Carter in 1979–1980 epitomizes how weak a president can become when he loses the mandate of heaven from the American deep state. First Carter expressed his determination not to admit the deposed Shah of Iran into the United States, knowing very well that this might result in the seizure of the U.S. Embassy in Tehran.[28] But soon thereafter Carter was coerced by the Rockefellers and their man in the White House, Zbigniew Brzezinski, to do just that.[29] (Carter, in caving in to David Rockefeller's demands, asked, "What are you guys going to recommend that we do when they take our embassy and hold our people hostage?")[30] In the remaining months of his presidency, his popularity was battered by his failure to free the Tehran hostages, along with (as previously mentioned) the long waits at gas stations and convenience stores, generated by a largely artificial gas shortage.[31] We can see Carter as a victim of the top-down power of the deep state, which would mean that Carter himself, like Kennedy and Nixon before him, was not on top.

Carter's defeat by Reagan in 1980 ended two tumultuous decades in which one president (along with his candidate brother) was assassinated, the next chose not to run for re-election, the next was forced to resign, and the two last, despite their incumbencies, failed to be re-elected.

Let me state very clearly that I am not blaming all this political confusion on the professional bureaucracies of either the military or the CIA. But as I have been trying to demonstrate, both of these—the military and the CIA—have constituencies among the dark forces of the deep state; and because of their proximity to these other forces, they (and particularly the CIA) have not hesitated on occasion to pursue policies directly at odds with policies that presidents were attempting to impose.

It is not the purpose of this book to try to resolve or even to discuss at length the deep events of the Kennedy assassination, Watergate, and the October Surprise. But in all three cases we have seen for years the withholding of relevant documents, misrepresentation of basic facts by the mainstream media, and systemic resistance to proper investigation of what really happened.

In the next chapter I shall argue that unknown elements in the deep state were responsible for these deep events. And I shall draw particular attention to the presence in all of them of personnel connected to the emergency planning network of the Doomsday Project.

POSTSCRIPT

The door was opened to the Reagan Revolution, and the emergence of two-party agreement on a so-called "Washington consensus" in economics, by which we can mean here the increasing deregulation of the private sector and privatization of the public sector. A crucial step in this was Reagan's decisive end to four decades of power-sharing between labor and capital, by decisively crushing the 1981 strike of the Professional Air Traffic Controllers Organization (PATCO). This completed the transformation of the Republican Party of the 1950s (when the Goldwater conservatives were a fringe right-wing minority) into that of the 1980s (when Goldwater was now to the left of the new conservative majority). The era of the Council on Foreign Relations and the Committee for Economic Development had been replaced by the era of the Heritage foundation and the American Enterprise Institute.

Money, including much new money generated by the Vietnam War, was largely responsible for this change. But as I noted in *American War Machine* (p. 38), the CIA played a hand in promoting Chicago School neoliberalism for application in Chile after the Pinochet takeover in 1973. Since 1981, this program of deregulation has been increasingly applied at home. The result has been a major reversal of the capitalist reforms dating back to FDR in the 1930s and to Theodore Roosevelt before him. Instead we have seen restored the disparities of wealth and income that characterized the "gilded age" of the late nineteenth century. I am not arguing that these unhealthy and dysfunctional disparities were consciously intended. On the contrary I shall argue in the next chapter that it was an overreaction arising from the anxieties of the very wealthy in the 1960s and 1970s, an anxiety urgently shared by other elements in the deep state, that control of the country was slipping away from them.

And as we shall see in chapter 12, the deep state also played an important and perhaps decisive role in ending détente. Seeing its role challenged by a series of post-Watergate reforms, the American and indeed the nascent global deep state (represented by the Safari Club and the Pinay Circle) rallied to revive the covert processes of the Cold War under a new name, the so-called "war on terror." As I have recounted in *The Road to 9/11* (pp. 50–61), the "pivotal shift" of the so-called Halloween Massacre of 1975, overseen by Donald Rumsfeld and Dick Cheney in the Ford White House, resulted in a new defense secretary (Rumsfeld) and a new CIA Director, George H. W. Bush, followed by a somber new reassessment of the "Soviet threat" that helped elect Reagan, and has since been responsible for the massive U.S. defense budget.

Since its success with the Reagan Revolution, the deep state has served chiefly to consolidate a compliant status quo, rather than to change it. But the hegemony of the deep state, emergent in the Vietnam War decades, was not finally established until 9/11 and the implementation of COG.

CHAPTER 9

The Doomsday Project and Deep Events

JFK, Watergate, Iran-Contra, and 9/11

> I know the capacity that is there to make tyranny total in America, and we must see to it that this agency [the National Security Agency] and all agencies that possess this technology operate within the law and under proper supervision, so that we never cross over that abyss. That is the abyss from which there is no return.
>
> —Senator Frank Church (1975)

IN THIS CHAPTER I WILL DISCUSS FOUR MAJOR AND BADLY UNDERSTOOD events—the John F. Kennedy assassination, Watergate, Iran-Contra, and 9/11. I will analyze these deep events as part of a deeper political process linking them, a process that has helped build up repressive power in America at the expense of democracy.

In recent years I have sometimes referred to a "dark force" behind these events, and sometimes to a "deep state," operating both within and outside the public state.[1] In this chapter I want to identify part of that dark force, a part that has operated for five decades or more at the edge of the public state. This part of the dark force has a name not invented by me: the Doomsday Project, the Pentagon's name for the emergency planning "to keep the White House and Pentagon running during and after a nuclear war or some other major crisis."[2]

My point is a simple and important one, to show that the Doomsday Project of the 1980s, and the earlier emergency planning that developed into it, have been an operational factor in the background of all the deep events I shall discuss.

More significantly, they have been a factor behind all four of the disturbing developments that now threaten American democracy. The first of these four is what has been called the conversion of our economy into a plutonomy—with the increasing separation of America into two classes, into the haves and the have-nots, the 1 percent and the 99 percent. The second, already discussed, is the increase in secret top-down power of America's shadow government, the deep state. The third is America's increasing militarization, and above all its inclination, which has become more and more routine and predictable, to wage or provoke wars in remote regions of the globe. It is clear that the operations of this American war machine have served the 1 percent.[3]

The fourth is the important and increasingly deleterious impact on American history of structural deep events (SDEs): mysterious events, like the JFK assassination, the Watergate break-in, or 9/11, which violate the American social structure, have a major impact on American society, repeatedly involve law-breaking or violence, and in many cases proceed from an unknown dark force.

There are any number of analyses of America's current breakdown in terms of income and wealth disparity, also in terms of America's increasing militarization and belligerency. What I shall argue in this chapter is I think new: that both the income disparity—or what has been called our "plutonomy"—and the belligerency have been fostered significantly by deep events.

We must understand that the income disparity of America's current economy was not the result of market forces working independently of political intervention. In large part it was generated by a systematic and deliberate ongoing political process dating from the anxieties of the very wealthy in the 1960s and 1970s that control of the country was slipping away from them.

This was the time when future Supreme Court Justice Lewis Powell, in a 1971 memorandum, warned that survival of the free enterprise system depended on "careful long-range planning and implementation" of a well-financed response to threats from the left.[4] This warning was answered by a sustained right-wing offensive, coordinated by think tanks and funded lavishly by a small group of family foundations.[5] We should recall that all this was in response to serious riots in Newark, Detroit, and elsewhere, and that increasing calls for a revolution were coming from the left (in Europe as well as America). I will focus on the right's response to that challenge, and on the role of deep events in enhancing their response.

What was important about the Powell memorandum was less the document itself than the fact that it was commissioned by the United States Chamber of Commerce, one of the most influential and least discussed lobbying groups in America. And the memorandum was only one of many signs of that developing class war in the 1970s, a larger process working both inside and outside government (including what Irving Kristol called an "intellectual counterrevolution"), which led directly to the so-called "Reagan Revolution."[6]

It is clear that this larger process has been carried on for almost five decades, pumping billions of right-wing dollars into the American political process. What I wish to show is that deep events have also been integral to this right-wing effort, from the John F. Kennedy assassination in 1963 to 9/11. The events of 9/11 resulted in the implementation of "Continuity of Government"

(COG) plans (which in the Oliver North Hearings of 1987 were called plans for "the suspension of the U.S. Constitution").[7] These COG plans, building on earlier COG planning, had been carefully developed since 1982 in the so-called Doomsday Project, by a secret group appointed by Reagan. The group was composed of both public and private figures, including Donald Rumsfeld and Dick Cheney.

I shall try to show that in this respect 9/11 was only the culmination of a sequence of deep events reaching back to the Kennedy assassination if not earlier, and that the germs of the Doomsday Project can be detected behind all of them.

More specifically, I shall try to demonstrate the following about these deep events:

1. Prior bureaucratic misbehavior by the CIA and similar agencies helped to make both the Kennedy assassination and 9/11 happen.
2. The consequences of each deep event included an increase in coercive, repressive power for these same agencies, at the expense of persuasive, democratic power;[8]
3. There are symptomatic overlaps in personnel between the perpetrators of each deep event and the next;
4. One sees in each of these events the involvement of elements of the international drug traffic—suggesting that our current plutonomy is also to some degree a narconomy.
5. In the background of each event (and playing an increasingly important role) one sees the Doomsday Project—the alternative emergency planning structure with its own communications network, operating as a shadow network outside of regular government channels.

BUREAUCRATIC MISBEHAVIOR AS A FACTOR CONTRIBUTING TO BOTH THE JFK ASSASSINATION AND 9/11

Both the JFK assassination and 9/11 were facilitated in part by the way the CIA and FBI manipulated their files about alleged perpetrators of each event (Lee Harvey Oswald in the case of what I shall call "JFK," and the alleged hijackers Khalid al-Mihdhar and Nawaf al-Hazmi in the case of 9/11). Part of this facilitation was the decision on October 9, 1963, of an FBI agent, Marvin Gheesling, to remove Oswald from the FBI watch list for surveillance. This was shortly after Oswald's arrest in New Orleans in August and his reported travel to Mexico in September. Obviously these developments should normally have made Oswald a candidate for *increased* surveillance.[9]

This misbehavior is paradigmatic of the behavior of other agencies, especially the CIA, in both JFK and 9/11. Indeed Gheesling's behavior fits very neatly with the CIA's culpable withholding from the FBI, in the same month of October, information that Oswald had allegedly met in Mexico City with a suspected KGB agent, Valeriy Kostikov.[10] This also helped ensure that Oswald would not be surveilled. Indeed former FBI Director Clarence Kelley in his memoir later complained that the CIA's withholding of information was the major reason why Oswald was not under surveillance on November 22, 1963.[11]

A more ominous provocation in 1963 was that of Army Intelligence, one unit of which in Dallas did not simply withhold information about Lee Harvey Oswald, but manufactured false intelligence in a way that seemed designed to provoke a retaliation against Cuba. I call such provocations "phase-one stories," efforts to portray Oswald as a Communist conspirator (as opposed to the later "phase-two stories," also false, portraying him as a disgruntled loner). A conspicuous example of such phase-one stories was a cable from the Fourth Army Command in Texas, reporting a tip from a Dallas policeman who was also in an Army Intelligence Reserve unit: "Assistant Chief Don Stringfellow, Intelligence Section, Dallas Police Department, notified 112th INTC [Intelligence] Group, this Headquarters, that information obtained from Oswald revealed he had defected to Cuba in 1959 and is a card-carrying member of Communist Party."[12]

This cable was sent late on November 22 directly to the U.S. Strike Command at Fort MacDill in Florida, the base poised for a possible retaliatory attack against Cuba.[13]

The cable was not an isolated aberration. It was supported by other false phase-one stories from Dallas about Oswald's alleged rifle, and specifically by concatenated false translations of Marina Oswald's testimony, to suggest that Oswald's rifle in Dallas was one he owned in Russia.[14]

These last false reports, apparently unrelated, can also be traced to a Dallas Army Intelligence Reserve unit.[15] For the interpreter who first supplied the false translation of Marina's words, Ilya Mamantov, was selected by a Dallas oilman, Jack Crichton, and Deputy Dallas Police Chief George Lumpkin.[16] Crichton and Lumpkin were also the Chief and the Deputy Chief of the 488th Army Intelligence Reserve unit in Dallas.[17] Crichton was an extreme right-winger in the community of Dallas oilmen: He was a trustee of the H. L. Hunt Foundation, and a member of the American Friends of the Katanga Freedom Fighters, a group organized to oppose Kennedy's policies in the Congo.

We have to keep in mind that some of the Joint Chiefs were furious that the 1962 Missile Crisis had not led to an invasion of Cuba, and that in 1963, under new Joint Chiefs of Staff (JCS) Chairman Maxwell Taylor, the Joint Chiefs, in May 1963, still believed "that US military intervention in Cuba is necessary."[18] This was six months after Kennedy, to resolve the Missile Crisis in October 1962, had given explicit assurances to Khrushchev, albeit highly qualified, that the United States would *not* invade Cuba.[19] This did not stop the J-5 of the Joint Chiefs of Staff (the JCS Directorate of Plans and Policy) from producing a menu of "fabricated provocations to justify military intervention."[20] (One proposed example of "fabricated provocations" envisioned violence: "using MIG type aircraft flown by US pilots to . . . attack surface shipping or to attack US military."[21])

The deceptions about Oswald coming from Dallas were immediately post-assassination; thus they do not by themselves establish that the assassination itself was a provocation-deception plot. They do however reveal enough about the anti-Castro mindset of the Army Intelligence Reserve units in Dallas to confirm that it was remarkably similar to that of the J-5 the preceding May— the mindset that produced a menu of "fabricated provocations" to attack Cuba. (According to Crichton there were "about a hundred men in the unit and about forty or fifty of them were from the Dallas Police Department.")[22]

It can hardly be accidental that we see this bureaucratic misbehavior from the FBI, CIA, and military, the three agencies with which Kennedy had had serious disagreements in his truncated presidency.[23] Later in this chapter I shall link Dallas oilman Jack Crichton to the 1963 emergency planning that became the Doomsday Project.

ANALOGOUS BUREAUCRATIC MISBEHAVIOR IN THE CASE OF 9/11

Before 9/11 the CIA, in 2000–2001, again flagrantly withheld crucial evidence from the FBI: evidence that, if shared, would have led the FBI to surveil two of the alleged hijackers, Khalid al-Mihdhar and Nawaz al-Hazmi. This sustained withholding of evidence provoked an FBI agent to predict accurately in August 2001 that "someday someone will die."[24] After 9/11 another FBI agent was even more bitter: "They [CIA] didn't want the bureau meddling in their business—that's why they didn't tell the FBI. . . . And that's why September 11 happened. That is why it happened. . . . They have blood on their hands. They have three thousand deaths on their hands"[25] The CIA's withholding of relevant evidence before 9/11 (which it was required by its own rules to supply) was matched in this case by the NSA.[26]

Without these withholdings, in other words, neither the Kennedy assassination nor 9/11 could have developed in the manner in which they did. As I wrote in *American War Machine*, it would appear that

> Oswald (and later al-Mihdhar) had at some prior point been selected as designated subjects for an operation. This would not initially have been for the commission of a crime against the American polity: on the contrary, steps were probably taken to prepare Oswald in connection with an operation against Cuba and al-Mihdhar [I suspect] for an operation against al-Qaeda. But as [exploitable] legends began to accumulate about both figures, it became possible for some witting people to subvert the sanctioned operation into a plan for murder that would later be covered up. At this point Oswald (and by analogy al-Mihdhar) was no longer just a designated subject but also now a designated culprit.[27]

As we have seen, Kevin Fenton, in his exhaustive book *Disconnecting the Dots*, reached the same conclusion with respect to 9/11: "By the summer of 2001, the purpose of withholding the information had become to allow the attacks to go forward."[28] He also identified the person chiefly responsible for the misbehavior: CIA officer Richard Blee, Chief of the CIA's Bin Laden Unit. While Clinton was still president, Blee had been one of a faction inside CIA pressing for a more belligerent CIA involvement in Afghanistan, in conjunction with the Afghan Northern Alliance.[29] This then happened immediately after 9/11, and Blee himself was promoted to become the new Chief of Station in Kabul.[30]

In like fashion, CIA and NSA withholding of evidence in the Second Tonkin Gulf Incident contributed to war against North Vietnam. The details of this withholding can be found in my *American War Machine*, pages 200–02. But Tonkin Gulf is similar to the Kennedy assassination and 9/11, in that manipulation of evidence helped lead America—in this case very swiftly—into war.

By now, historians such as Fredrik Logevall have agreed with the assessment of former undersecretary of state George Ball that the U.S. destroyer mission in the Tonkin Gulf, which resulted in the Tonkin Gulf incidents, "was primarily for provocation."[31] The planning for this provocative mission came from the J-5 of the Joint Chiefs of Staff, the same unit that in 1963 had reported concerning Cuba that "the engineering of a series of provocations to justify military intervention is feasible."[32]

The NSA and CIA suppression of the truth on August 4, 1964, was in the context of an existing high-level (but controversial) determination to attack North Vietnam. In this respect the Tonkin Gulf incident is remarkably similar to the suppression of the truth by the CIA and NSA leading up to 9/11, when there was again a high-level (but controversial) determination to go to war.

INCREASES IN REPRESSIVE POWER AFTER DEEP EVENTS

All of the deep events discussed here have contributed to the cumulative increase of Washington's repressive powers. It is clear for example that the Warren Commission used the JFK assassination to increase CIA surveillance of Americans. As I wrote in *Deep Politics*, this was the result of

> the Warren Commission's controversial recommendations that the Secret Service's domestic surveillance responsibilities be increased (WR 25–26). Somewhat illogically, the Warren Report concluded both that Oswald acted alone (WR 22), . . . and also that the Secret Service, FBI, CIA, should coordinate more closely the surveillance of organized groups (WR 463). In particular, it recommended that the Secret Service acquire a computerized data bank compatible with that already developed by the CIA.[33]

This pattern would repeat itself four years later with the assassination of Robert Kennedy. In the twenty-four hours between Bobby's shooting and his death, Congress hurriedly passed a statute—drafted well in advance (like the Tonkin Gulf Resolution of 1964 and the Patriot Act of 2001)—that still further augmented the secret powers given to the Secret Service in the name now of protecting presidential candidates.[34] This was not a trivial or benign change: from this swiftly considered act, passed under Johnson, flowed some of the worst excesses of the Nixon presidency.[35]

The change also contributed to the chaos and violence at the Chicago Democratic Convention of 1968. There were army intelligence surveillance agents, seconded to the Secret Service, present both inside and outside the convention hall. Some of them equipped the so-called "Legion of Justice thugs whom the Chicago Red Squad turned loose on local anti-war groups."[36]

In this way the extra secret powers conferred after the Robert F. Kennedy assassination contributed to the disastrous turmoil in Chicago that effectively destroyed the old Democratic Party representing the labor unions: The three Democratic presidents elected since then have all been significantly more conservative.

When we turn to Watergate and Iran-Contra, both of these events were seen in the media as *setbacks* to the repressive powers exercised by Richard Nixon and the Reagan White House, not as expansions of them. On the surface level this is true: both events resulted in a number of legislative reforms that would appear to contradict the thesis of an expanding repressive power.

We need to distinguish here between the two years of the Watergate crisis, and the initial Watergate break-in. The Watergate crisis saw a president forced into resignation by a number of forces, involving both liberals and conservatives. But the key figures in the initial Watergate break-in itself—Hunt, McCord, G. Gordon Liddy, and their Cuban allies—were all far to the right of Nixon and Kissinger. And the end result of their machinations was not finalized until the so-called Halloween Massacre in 1975, when Kissinger was ousted as National Security Adviser and Vice President Nelson Rockefeller was notified he would be dropped from the 1976 Republican ticket. This major shake-up was engineered by two other right-wingers: Donald Rumsfeld and Dick Cheney in the Gerald Ford White House.[37]

That day in 1975 saw the permanent defeat of the so-called Rockefeller or liberal faction within the Republican Party, to be replaced by the conservative Goldwater-Casey faction that would soon capture the nomination and the presidency for Ronald Reagan.[38] This little-noticed palace coup, along with other related intrigues in the mid-1970s, helped achieve the conversion of America from a welfare capitalist economy, with gradual reductions in income and wealth disparity, into a financialized plutonomy where these trends were reversed.[39]

Again in Iran-Contra we see a deeper accumulation of repressive power under the surface of liberal reforms. At the time not only the press but even academics like myself celebrated the termination of aid to the Nicaraguan Contras, and the victory there of the Contadora peace process. Not generally noticed at the time was the fact that, while Oliver North was removed from his role in the Doomsday Project, that project's plans for surveillance, detention, and the militarization of the United States continued to grow after his departure.[40]

Also not noticed was the fact that the U.S. Congress, while curtailing aid to one small drug-financed CIA proxy army, was simultaneously increasing U.S. support to a much larger coalition of drug-financed proxy armies in Afghanistan.[41] While Iran-Contra exposed the $32 million that Saudi Arabia, in collaboration with CIA Director William Casey, had supplied to the Contras, not a word was whispered about the $500 million or more that the Saudis had supplied in the same period to the Afghan mujahedin.[42] In this sense the drama of Iran-Contra in Congress can be thought of as a misdirection play, directing public attention away from America's much more intensive engagement in Afghanistan—a covert policy that has since evolved into America's longest war.

We should expand our consciousness of Iran-Contra to think of it as Iran-Afghan-Contra. And if we do, we must acknowledge that in this complex and misunderstood deep event the CIA in Afghanistan exercised again the paramilitary capacity that Stansfield Turner had tried to terminate when he was CIA Director under Jimmy Carter. This was a victory in short for the faction of men like Richard Blee, the protector of al-Mihdhar as well as the advocate in 2000 for enhanced CIA paramilitary activity in Afghanistan.[43]

PERSONNEL OVERLAPS BETWEEN THE SUCCESSIVE DEEP EVENTS

I will never forget *The New York Times* front page story on June 18, 1972, the day after the Watergate break-in. There on page one were photographs of the Watergate burglars, including one of Frank Sturgis alias Frank Fiorini, whom I had already written about two years earlier in my unpublished book manuscript about the JFK assassination, "The Dallas Conspiracy."[44]

Sturgis was no nonentity; a former contract employee of the CIA, he was also well connected to the mob-linked former casino owners in Havana.[45] My early writings on the Kennedy case focused on the connections between Frank Sturgis and an anti-Castro Cuban training camp near New Orleans in which Oswald had shown an interest. I also noted Sturgis's involvement in false "phase-one" stories portraying Oswald as part of a Communist Cuban conspiracy; these stories were an explicit reason why Johnson wanted a Warren Commission (with its official finding that there was no conspiracy at all).[46]

In spreading these "phase-one" stories in 1963, Sturgis was joined by a number of Cubans who were part of the CIA-supported Central American army of Manuel Artime. Artime's base in Costa Rica was closed down in 1965, allegedly because of its involvement in drug trafficking.[47] In the 1980s some of these Cuban exiles later became involved in drug-financed support activities for the Contras.[48]

The political mentor of Artime's Movimiento de Recuperación Revolucionaria (MRR) movement was future Watergate plotter Howard Hunt; and Artime in 1972 would pay for the bail of the Cuban Watergate burglars. The drug money-launderer Ramón Milián Rodríguez has claimed to have delivered $200,000 in cash from Artime to pay off some of the Cuban Watergate burglars. Later, in support of the Contras, he managed two Costa Rican seafood companies, Frigorificos and Ocean Hunter, that laundered drug money.[49]

It is alleged that Hunt and McCord had both been involved with Artime's invasion plans in 1963.[50] I believe it was no accident that the organization of Hunt's protégé Artime became mired in drug trafficking. I have argued elsewhere that Hunt had been handling a U.S. drug connection since his 1950 post as OPC (Office of Policy Coordination) chief in Mexico City.[51]

But McCord not only had a past in the anti-Castro activities of 1963, he was also part of the nation's emergency planning network that would later figure so prominently in the background of Iran-Contra and 9/11. McCord was a member of a small Air Force Reserve unit in Washington attached to the Office of Emergency Preparedness (OEP), assigned "to draw up lists of radicals and to develop contingency plans for censorship of the news media and U.S. mail in time of war."[52] His unit was part of the Wartime Information Security Program (WISP), which had responsibility for activating "contingency plans for imposing censorship on the press, the mails and all telecommunications (including government communications) [and] preventive detention of civilian 'security risks,' who would be placed in military 'camps.'"[53] In other words, the plans that became known in the 1980s as the Doomsday Project, the Continuity of Government planning on which Dick Cheney and Donald Rumsfeld worked together for twenty years before 9/11.

A COMMON DENOMINATOR FOR STRUCTURAL DEEP EVENTS: PROJECT DOOMSDAY AND COG

McCord's participation in an emergency planning system dealing with telecommunications suggests a common institutional denominator in the backgrounds of almost all the deep events we are considering. Oliver North, the Reagan-Bush point man on Iran-Contra planning, was also the National Security Council action officer for Project 908 planning, and thus he had access to the nation's top-secret Doomsday communications network.[54] North's network, known as Flashboard, "excluded other bureaucrats with opposing viewpoints . . . [and] had its own special worldwide antiterrorist computer network, . . . by which members could communicate exclusively with each other and their collaborators abroad."[55]

Flashboard was used by North and his superiors for extremely sensitive operations that had to be concealed from other hostile parts of the Washington bureaucracy. These operations included the illegal shipments of arms to Iran, but also other activities, some still not known, perhaps even against Olof Palme's Sweden.[56] Flashboard, America's emergency network in the 1980s, was the name in 1984–1986 of the full-fledged Continuity of Government (COG) emergency network that was secretly planned for twenty years, at a cost of billions, by a team including Dick Cheney and Donald Rumsfeld. On 9/11 the same network was activated anew by the two men who had planned it for so many years.[57]

(Since I first advanced the hypothesis that the COG communications network was involved in all our structural deep events, I have found further corroborations for it. For example, John Dean, perhaps the central Watergate figure, had participated in COG activities when serving as the associate deputy attorney general.[58] And an army reserve officer, Norman Katz, revealed in October 2013 that, because of his work in COG communications, he was summoned to Washington in November 1963, in connection with President Kennedy's trip to Dallas.[59])

All this Doomsday planning can be traced back to 1963, when Jack Crichton, head of the 488th Army Intelligence Reserve unit of Dallas, was also part of it. This was in his capacity as chief of intelligence for Dallas Civil Defense, which worked out of an underground Emergency Operating Center. As Russ Baker reports, "Because it was intended for 'continuity of government' operations during an attack, [the Center] was fully equipped with communications equipment."[60] A speech given at the dedication of the Center in 1961 supplies these additional details:

> This Emergency Operating Center [in Dallas] is part of the National Plan to link Federal, State and local government agencies in a communications network from which rescue operations can be directed in time of local or National emergency. It is a vital part of the National, State, and local Operational Survival Plan.[61]

Crichton, in other words, was also part of what became known in the 1980s as the Doomsday Project, like James McCord, Oliver North, Donald Rumsfeld, and Dick Cheney after him. But in 1988 its aim was significantly enlarged—no longer to prepare for an atomic attack, but now to plan for the effective suspension of the American Constitution in the face of *any* emergency.[62] This change in 1988 allowed COG to be implemented in 2001. By this time the Doomsday Project had developed into what the *Washington Post* called "a shadow government that evolved based on long-standing 'continuity of operations plans.'"[63]

It is clear that the Office of Emergency Preparedness (OEP, known from 1961–1968 as the Office of Emergency Planning, and from 1982 to 1994 as the National Program Office or Project 908) supplied a common denominator for key personnel in virtually all of the structural events I have discussed. This is a long way from establishing that the OEP itself (in addition to the individuals I have discussed) was involved in generating any of these events. But I believe that the alternative communications network housed first in the OEP (and later part of Project 908) played a significant role in at least three of them: the JFK assassination, Iran-Contra, and 9/11.

This is easiest to show in the case of 9/11, where it is conceded that the Continuity of Government (COG) plans of the Doomsday Project were implemented by Cheney on 9/11, apparently before the last of the four hijacked planes had crashed.[64] The 9/11 Commission could not locate records of the key decisions taken by Cheney on that day, suggesting that they may have taken place on the "secure phone" in the tunnel leading to the presidential bunker—with such a high classification that the 9/11 Commission was never supplied the phone records.[65] My guess is this was a COG network phone.

It is almost certain that the "secure phone" in the White House tunnel belonged to the Secret Service, and therefore was part of the secure network of the White House Communications Agency (WHCA). If so, it represents a striking link between 9/11 and the JFK assassination. The WHCA boasts on its website that the agency was "a key player in documenting the assassination of President Kennedy."[66] However it is not clear for whom this documentation was conducted, for the WHCA logs and transcripts were in fact withheld, inexcusably, from first the Warren Commission and later the House Select Committee on Assassinations.[67]

The Secret Service had installed a WHCA portable radio in the lead car of the presidential motorcade.[68] This in turn was in contact by police radio with the pilot car ahead of it, carrying Dallas Police Department (DPD) Deputy Chief Lumpkin of the 488th Army Intelligence Reserve unit.[69] Records of the WHCA communications from the motorcade never reached the Warren Commission, the House Select Committee on Assassinations, or the Assassination Records Review Board (ARRB).[70] Thus we cannot tell if they would explain some of the anomalies on the two channels of the Dallas Police Department. They might for example have thrown light upon the unsourced call on the Dallas Police tapes for a suspect who had exactly the false height and weight (5 feet 10 inches, 165 pounds) recorded for Oswald in his FBI and CIA files.[71]

As of June 2014 we were still living under the State of Emergency proclaimed after 9/11 by President Bush. At least some COG provisions are still in effect, and were even augmented by Bush through Presidential Directive 51 of May 2007. Commenting on PD-51, the *Washington Post* reported at that time, "After the 2001 attacks, Bush assigned about 100 senior civilian managers [including Cheney] to rotate secretly to [COG] locations outside of Washington for weeks or months at a time to ensure the nation's survival, a shadow government that evolved based on long-standing 'continuity of operations plans.'"[72]

Presumably this "shadow government" finalized such long-standing COG projects as warrantless surveillance, in part through the Patriot Act, whose controversial provisions were already being refined by Cheney and others well before the bill reached Congress on October 12.[73] Other COG projects implemented included the militarization of domestic surveillance under NORTH-COM, and the Department of Homeland Security's Project Endgame—a ten-year plan to expand detention camps at a cost of $400 million in fiscal year 2007 alone.[74]

For a half century American politics have been constrained and deformed by the unresolved matter of the Kennedy assassination. According to a memo of November 25, 1963, from Assistant Attorney General Nicholas Katzenbach, it was important then to persuade the public that "Oswald was the assassin," and that "he did not have confederates."[75] Obviously this priority became even more important after these questionable propositions were endorsed by the Warren Report, the U.S. establishment, and the mainstream press. It has remained an embarrassing priority ever since for all succeeding administrations, including Obama's. There is or was for example an official in Obama's State Department (Todd Leventhal), whose official job included defense of the lone nut theory against so-called "conspiracy theorists."[76]

If Oswald was not a lone assassin, then it should not surprise us that there is continuity between those who falsified reports about Oswald in 1963, and those who distorted American politics in subsequent deep events beginning with Watergate. Since the deep event of 1963, the legitimacy of America's political system has become vested in a lie—a lie that subsequent deep events have helped to protect.[77]

The usefulness of the Doomsday Project's alternative communications network, the NCS, suggests a commonality among structural deep events on the operational level. In the next chapter I shall suggest that many of them share a commonality on a deeper level, the level of funding from the same off-the-books financial sources.

CHAPTER 10

The American Deep State, Deep Events, and Off-the-Books Financing

THIS CHAPTER WILL DISCUSS HOW RECENT STRUCTURAL DEEP EVENTS (SDEs) have been financed, time after time, from a single deep-state source. But it will help to preface my rather complex argument with a summary of how thinking about deep politics has led me to awareness of the importance of deep events, and these in turn to the mostly undocumented presence of the deep state.

I have been writing about deep politics since 1993, when I gave the example of how the United States after World War II sent American mafia figures to fight communism in Italy, thereby contributing to a corrupted politics that was soon out of control—reminiscent of the influence the mafia once possessed in cities like Marseille, or Chicago.[1]

Since then I have written about deep events, by which I mean mysterious events—like the JFK assassination, the Watergate break-in, or 9/11 that repeatedly involve lawbreaking or violence, and are embedded in fact in deep politics. Some of these may be low-level, as when data is filched from a personal computer, or mid-level, like the murder of Karen Silkwood. But what I have called "structural deep events" are large enough to affect the whole fabric of society, with consequences that enlarge covert government, and are subsequently covered up by systematic falsifications in media and internal government records.

We still live in the official state of emergency imposed after the last great deep event—9/11; and this has left us in a deconstitutionalized era of warrantless surveillance, warrantless detentions, and militarized homeland security. In this chapter, the deep events I refer to will all be structural deep events.

I have come to believe that most structural deep events (or SDEs) are interrelated, and that the study of any one of them helps understand others. Their interrelationship leads to two levels of history in America, and two levels of historical narrative: official or archival history, which ignores or marginalizes deep events, and a second level—called "deep history" by its practitioners or "conspiracy theory" by its critics—which incorporates them.

Others have perceived these interconnections. Back in 1987 Alfonso Chardy wrote, accurately, that the October Surprise Group of 1980—or what Miles Copeland called the "CIA within the CIA" that "concluded that Carter had to be removed from the presidency"—was the "genesis" of the "secret government" that in 1985–1986 used Continuity of Government planning to engineer Iran-Contra.[2] Nixon himself, in the "smoking gun" tape that led to his resignation, said to his chief of staff Bob Haldeman that the Watergate break-in was sensitive because it related to a previous deep event, "the whole Bay of Pigs thing"; Haldeman later speculated with good reason in his memoir that "in all those Nixon references to the Bay of Pigs, he was actually referring to the Kennedy assassination."[3] Without blaming all of these deep events on any single group, such as Copeland's "CIA within the CIA," one can still investigate whether some such group might have contributed to some or all of them.

My study of the interrelationship between deep events has itself deepened over four decades. It began on a superficial level by noticing the overlap of apparently marginal personnel between the deep events of the John F. Kennedy assassination and Watergate; and again between Watergate and Iran-Contra.

In chapter 9 I gave the example of Frank Sturgis (alias Fiorini), the Watergate burglar whom I had already written about two years earlier in my unpublished book manuscript about the JFK assassination, "The Dallas Conspiracy." In 1986 my attention was drawn to the deep events of Iran-Contra when I noticed the involvement in Contra support activities of anti-Castro Cubans in Miami, some of them drug traffickers and some known to Sturgis, who had previously been investigated in connection with deep events ranging from the JFK assassination, to Watergate, to the shooting down in 1976 of a Cuban civilian airliner.[4] Some of these in turn worked in Contra support operations with veterans of Theodore Shackley's drug-financed CIA operations in Laos like Richard Secord.[5] Secord in turn became involved with MEGA Oil's airline for mujahedin in Azerbaijan, along with Gary Best, who was also a veteran of North's Contra support effort, and before that of efforts to support UNITA in Angola.[6]

Since 9/11 my study of structural deep events has progressed from such overlaps of personnel to three deeper levels, which I call the "*operational*," by which I mean a common modus operandi; the "*institutional*," by which I mean a shared agency of implementation; and the "*financial*," by which I mean a common source of funding.

I was myself startled to recognize more than a dozen common operational modalities between two outwardly dissimilar events: the JFK assassination and 9/11. Among the most striking are the following:

1. the almost instant identification of what I call the "designated culprits," Lee Harvey Oswald and the nineteen alleged hijackers;

2. the hidden intelligence backgrounds of the designated culprits; and
3. the protection by the FBI and CIA of the designated culprits in the weeks before the events, to ensure that they would not be placed under surveillance or taken off the streets.[7]

I touched on this in chapter 9, at some length in my 2008 book *The War Conspiracy*, and also elsewhere. But I will repeat a passage here about the last item—protection. In chapter 9, I refer to

the CIA's culpable withholding from the FBI, in . . . October [1963], information that Oswald had allegedly met in Mexico City with a suspected KGB agent, Valeriy Kostikov. This . . . helped ensure that Oswald would not be placed under surveillance. . . . Before 9/11 the CIA, in 2000–2001, again flagrantly withheld crucial evidence from the FBI: evidence that, if shared, would have led the FBI to surveil two of the alleged hijackers, Khalid al-Mihdhar and Nawaz al-Hazmi. This sustained withholding of evidence provoked an FBI agent to predict accurately in August, 2001, [three weeks before 9/11] that "someday someone will die." . . . The CIA's withholding of relevant evidence before 9/11 (which it was required by its own rules to supply) was matched in this case by the NSA.[8]

On the *institutional* level, it is striking that in every structural deep event since the JFK assassination we find some involvement of the National Communications System (NCS), the shadow Doomsday Project network created to ensure continuity of government (COG) in the event of an atomic attack. The NCS was formally established by a JFK Presidential Memorandum on August 21, 1963. By 1969 at least $175 million had been spent "to increase the survivability of national communications resources" in a nuclear attack.[9] In July 1979 the system was tested under Carter, in the first known instance of the exercise GLOBAL SHIELD. By the Reagan era, as we shall see in chapter 11, the NCS had mushroomed into an $8 billion communications and logistics program for an alternative emergency communications network.[10]

As we saw in chapter 9, this alternative network played a central role in Iran-Contra, when Oliver North, arranging for the arms shipments to Iran that eventually cost him his job, used the nation's top secret COG communications network. North's network, known as Flashboard, "excluded other bureaucrats with opposing viewpoints . . . [and] had its own special worldwide antiterrorist computer network, . . . by which members could communicate exclusively with each other and their collaborators abroad."[11] North was also actively developing plans, which originated with Hoover, for emergency detentions on a large scale.[12]

So, before him, was James McCord, famous for having participated in the burglary that precipitated the 1972 Watergate crisis. As we saw in chapter 9, McCord was a member of a small Air Force Reserve unit assigned "to draw up lists of radicals and to develop contingency plans . . . in time of war." His unit was part of the Wartime Information Security Program (WISP), which had responsibility for activating "contingency plans for imposing censorship on the press, the mails and all telecommunications (including government communications) [and] preventive detention of civilian 'security risks,' who would be placed in military 'camps.'"[13]

But 9/11 is the deep event in which the COG network played a most central role. In *The Road to 9/11*, I advance reasons to believe that Cheney and Rumsfeld, during the short period that morning when they were inexplicably not in their command posts, were instead using the COG network to finalize emergency measures, soon to include the first ever implementation that same morning of COG measures.[14]

This is the more remarkable because, for two decades before 9/11, Rumsfeld and Cheney had both been part of a small secret committee planning with the assistance of Oliver North—even in the 1990s when neither man was in the government—for extreme COG measures, including, allegedly, "suspension of the Constitution."[15] In the Iran-Contra Hearings, North was asked about planning to suspend the Constitution, but the Chairman would not allow discussion in an open session.[16]

THE AMERICAN DEEP STATE

In chapter 2, I described an ambiguous symbiosis between two different aspects of the American deep state:

1. the Beltway agencies of the shadow government, like the CIA and NSA, which have been instituted by the public state and now overshadow it, but also including private corporations like Booz Allen Hamilton (Edward Snowden's employers) and SAIC. Seventy percent of intelligence budgets are now outsourced to private companies like Booz Allen Hamilton (owned by the Carlyle Group) and SAIC, the company that, as I wrote in *American War Machine*, helped get the United States to fight in Iraq.
2. the much older power of Wall Street, referring chiefly to the powerful banks and law firms located there, but also to the cartels and other corporate alliances established there, and Wall Street's think tank, the Council on Foreign Relations.

In the 1950s Wall Street, as we saw, was a dominating complex. It included not just banks and other financial institutions but also the oil majors whose cartel arrangements were successfully defended against the U.S. government by the Wall Street law firm Sullivan and Cromwell, home to the Dulles brothers.

Confident that they knew better how to run the world that those whom John Foster Dulles called "highly insular and nationalistic" politicians,[17] the seven major oil companies or Seven Sisters—five American and two British—still operated as a cartel after World War II. Thus when Premier Mossadeq of Iran took steps in 1951–1952 to nationalize the Anglo-Iranian Oil Company (now BP), the oil majors were able to organize a largely successful boycott of Iranian oil exports. They could not however persuade Truman to use the CIA against Mossadeq, and had to wait until Truman was succeeded by Eisenhower in 1953. With the Dulles brothers installed as heads of State and CIA, CIA planning for a coup to restore the shah began immediately, with Eisenhower approving in June.

Mossadeq's removal from power is remembered as a CIA operation, with the oil cartel (when mentioned at all) playing a subservient role. However the chronology suggests that it was CIA that came belatedly in 1953 to assist an earlier oil cartel operation, rather than vice versa. In terms of the deep state, the oil cartel or deep state initiated in 1951 a process that the American public state only authorized two years later.

This shows how the deep state and its overworld are, and to some degree always have been, supranational. In the 1950s, for example, if Allen Dulles as CIA Director wanted to fly a U-2 over Russia on a certain day, and Eisenhower said no, Dulles would simply turn to his British counterparts in MI6 to get permission from Macmillan, and Dulles would get his way.[18]

THE CIA, THE POWER OF THE PURSE, AND OFF-THE-BOOKS FUNDS

Conventional political analysis claims that the CIA is limited by the constitutional system of checks and balances that Congress controls by its power of the purse. Note Lauren Fox's important caveat: "Congress maintains the power of the purse, which gives lawmakers the ability to defund specific programs the federal agency holds dear, but the CIA maintains the documents and information Congress needs to see to effectively conduct oversight in the first place."[19]

Fox, however, ignores the fact that, since its outset, the CIA has always had access to large amounts of off-the-books or offshore funds to support its activities. Indeed, the power of the purse has usually worked in an opposite sense, since those in control of deep-state, offshore funds supporting CIA activities have for decades also funded members of Congress and of the executive—not vice versa. The last six decades provide a coherent and continuous picture of historical direction being provided by this deep-state power of the purse, trumping and sometimes reversing the conventional state.

Let us resume describing some of the CIA's sources of offshore and off-the-books funding for its activities. The CIA's first covert operation was the use of "over $10 million in captured Axis funds to influence the [Italian] election [of

1948]."[20] (The fundraising had begun at the wealthy Brook Club in New York; but Allen Dulles, then still a Wall Street lawyer, persuaded Washington, which at first had preferred a private funding campaign, to authorize the operation through the National Security Council and the CIA.)[21]

Dulles, together with George Kennan and James Forrestal, then found a way to provide a legal source for off-the-books CIA funding, under the cover of the Marshall Plan. The three men "helped devise a secret codicil [to the Marshall Plan] that gave the CIA the capability to conduct political warfare. It let the agency skim millions of dollars from the plan."[22]

At the time of the Marshall Plan slush fund in Europe, the CIA also took steps which resulted in drug money to support anticommunist armies in the Far East. In my book *American War Machine* I tell how the CIA, using former Office of Strategic Services (OSS) operative Paul Helliwell, created two proprietary firms as infrastructure for a Kuomintang (KMT) army in Burma, an army which quickly became involved in managing and developing the opium traffic there. The two firms were Sea Supply Inc. in Bangkok and CAT Inc. (later Air America) in Taiwan. Significantly, the CIA split ownership of CAT Inc.'s plane with KMT bankers in Taiwan. This allowed the CIA to deny responsibility for the flights when CAT planes, having delivered arms from Sea Supply to the opium-growing army, then returned to Taiwan with opium for the KMT. Even after the CIA officially severed its connection to the KMT Army in 1953, its proprietary firm Sea Supply Inc. supplied arms for a CIA-led paramilitary force, PARU, that also was financed, at least in part, by the drug traffic.[23]

Profits from Thailand filtered back, in part through the same Paul Helliwell, as donations to members from both parties in Congress. Thai dictator Phao Sriyanon, a drug trafficker who was then alleged to be the richest man in the world,

hired lawyer Paul Helliwell . . . as a lobbyist in addition to [former OSS chief William] Donovan [who in 1953–1955 was U.S. Ambassador to Thailand]. Donovan and Helliwell divided the Congress between them, with Donovan assuming responsibility for the Republicans and Helliwell taking the Democrats.[24]

The most dramatic use of off-the-books drug profits to finance foreign armies was seen in the 1960s CIA-led campaign in Laos. There the CIA supplied airstrips and planes to support a 30,000-man drug-financed Hmong army. At one point Laotian CIA station chief Theodore Shackley even called in CIA aircraft in support of a ground battle to seize a huge opium caravan on behalf of the larger Royal Laotian Army.[25]

FUNDS FROM ARMS CONTRACTS

In the 1960s and especially the 1970s, America began to import more and more oil from the Middle East. But the negative effect on the U.S. balance of payments was offset by increasing arms and aviation sales to Iran and Saudi Arabia. Contracts with companies like Northrop and especially Lockheed (the builder of the CIA's U-2) included kickbacks to arms brokers, like Kodama Yoshio in Japan and Adnan Khashoggi in Saudi Arabia, who were also important CIA agents. Lockheed alone later admitted to the Church Committee that it had provided $106 million in commissions to Khashoggi between 1970 and 1975, more than ten times what it had paid to the next most important connection, Kodama.[26]

These funds were then used by Khashoggi and Kodama to purchase pro-Western influence. But Khashoggi, advised by a team of ex-CIA Americans like Miles Copeland and Edward Moss, distributed cash, and sometimes provided women, not just in Saudi Arabia, but also around the world—including cash to President Nixon in the United States.[27]

Khashoggi in effect served as a "cutout," or representative, in a number of operations forbidden to the CIA and the companies he worked with. Lockheed, for one, was conspicuously absent from the list of military contractors who contributed illicitly to Nixon's 1972 election campaign. But there was no law prohibiting, and nothing else to prevent their official representative, Khashoggi, from cycling $200 million through the bank of Nixon's friend Bebe Rebozo.[28]

MOSS, KHASHOGGI, THE SAFARI CLUB, AND THE INTERNATIONAL OVERWORLD

As we saw in chapter 2, the power exerted by Khashoggi was not limited to his access to funds and women. By the 1970s, Khashoggi and his aide Edward Moss owned the elite Safari Club in Kenya.[29] The exclusive club became the first venue for another and more important Safari Club: an alliance between Saudi and other intelligence agencies that wished to compensate for the CIA's retrenchment in the wake of President Carter's election and Senator Church's post-Watergate reforms.[30]

Khashoggi's activities involving corruption by sex and money, after they too were somewhat curtailed by Senator Church's post-Watergate reforms, appear to have been taken up quickly by the Bank of Credit and Commerce International (BCCI), a Muslim-owned bank where Khashoggi's friend and business partner Kamal Adham, the Saudi intelligence chief and a principal Safari Club member, was a part-owner.[31] In the 1980s BCCI, and its allied shipping empire owned by the Pakistani Gokal brothers, supplied financing and infrastructure for the CIA's (and Saudi Arabia's) biggest covert operation of the decade, support for the Afghan mujahedin.

To quote from a British book excerpted in the Senate BCCI Report,

BCCI's role in assisting the U.S. to fund the Mujaheddin guerrillas fighting the Soviet occupation is drawing increasing attention. The bank's role began to surface in the mid-1980's when stories appeared in the New York Times show-ing how American security operatives used Oman as a staging post for Arab funds. This was confirmed in the Wall Street Journal of 23 October 1991 which quotes a member of the late General Zia's cabinet as saying "It was Arab money that was pouring through BCCI." The Bank which carried the money on from Oman to Pakistan and into Afghanistan was National Bank of Oman, where BCCI owned 29%.[32]

It is reported in two books that the BCCI money flow through the Bank of Oman was handled in part by the international financier Bruce Rappaport, who for a decade, like Khashoggi, kept a former CIA officer on his staff.[33] Rappaport's partner in his Inter Maritime Bank, which interlocked with BCCI, was E. P. Barry, who earlier had been a partner in the Florida money-laundering banks of Paul Helliwell.[34]

SECRET CLAUSES IN ARMS CONTRACTS

The activities of the Safari Club were exposed after Iranians in 1979 seized the records of the U.S. Embassy in Tehran. But BCCI support for covert CIA operations, including Iran-Contra, continued until BCCI's criminality was exposed at the end of the 1980s.

Meanwhile, with the election of Ronald Reagan in 1980, Washington re-sumed off-budget funding for CIA covert operations under cover of arms contracts to Saudi Arabia. But after Congress in 1977 made it illegal for American corporations to make payments to foreign officials, this was no longer achieved through kickbacks to CIA assets like Khashoggi. Instead ar-rangements were made for payments to be returned, through either informal agreements or secret codicils in the contracts, by the Saudi Arabian govern-ment itself. Two successive arms deals, the airborne warning and control sys-tem (AWACS) deal of 1981 and the al-Yamamah deal of 1985, considerably escalated the amount of available slush funds.

1. The AWACS Deal

In 1981 Vice President Bush and Saudi Prince Bandar, working together, won congressional approval for massive new arms sales of AWACS aircraft to Saudi Arabia. In the $5.5 billion package, only 10 percent covered the cost of the planes. Most of the rest was an initial installment on what was ultimately a $200 billion program for military infrastructure through Saudi Arabia.[35]

It also supplied a slush fund for secret ops, one administered for over a decade in Washington by Prince Bandar, after he became the Saudi Ambas-sador (and a close friend of the Bush family, nicknamed "Bandar Bush"). In the words of researcher Scott Armstrong, the fund was "the ultimate government-off-the-books." . . . Not long after the AWACS sale was approved, Prince Bandar thanked the Reagan administration for the vote by honoring a request by William Casey that he deposit $10 million in a Vatican bank to be used in a campaign against the Italian Communist Party. Implicit in the AWACS deal was a pledge by the Saudis to fund anticommunist guerrilla groups in Afghanistan, Angola, and elsewhere that were supported by the Reagan Administration.[36]

The Vatican contribution, for the CIA's longtime clients, the Christian Democratic Party, of course continued a CIA tradition dating back to 1948.

2. The al-Yamamah Deal

After a second proposed major U.S. arms sale met enhanced opposition in Congress in 1985 from the Israeli lobby, Saudi Arabia negotiated instead a multibillion-pound long-term contract with the United Kingdom—the so-called "al-Yamamah deal." Once again overpayments for the purchased weapons were siphoned off into a huge slush fund for political payoffs, including "hundreds of millions of pounds to the ex-Saudi ambassador to the United States, Prince Bandar bin Sultan."[37] According to Robert Lacey, the payments to Prince Bandar were said to total one billion pounds over more than a decade.[38] The money went through a Saudi Embassy account in the Riggs Bank, Washington. According to Trento, the Embassy's use of the Riggs Bank dated back to the mid-1970s, when, in his words, "the Saudi royal family had taken over intelligence financing for the United States."[39] More accurately, the financing was not "for the United States," but for the supranational deep state, involving both Saudi and American officials.

OFFSHORE FUNDING AND THE CONTINUITY OF DEEP EVENTS

This leads me to the most original and important thing I have to say. I believe that these secret funds from BCCI and Saudi arms deals—first Khashoggi's from Lockheed, and then Prince Bandar's from the AWACS and al-Yamamah deals—are the common denominator in all of the major structural deep events (SDEs) that have afflicted America since the supranational Safari Club was created in 1976.

I am referring specifically to

1. the covert U.S. intervention in Afghanistan (which started about 1978 as a Safari Club intervention, more than a year before the Russian invasion): "Each year the Saudis sent their part of the money to their embassy in Washington. The Saudi ambassador in Washington, Bandar bin Sultan, then transferred the funds to a Swiss bank account controlled by the CIA."[40] The bank in question may have been BCCI, which "handled transfers of funds [for the

mujahedin] through its Pakistani branches and acted as a collection agency
for war matériel and even for the mujahedin's pack animals."[41]

2. the 1980 October Surprise, which together with an increase in Saudi oil prices
and artificially induced shortages helped assure Reagan's election and thus
give us the Reagan Revolution.
3. Iran-Contra in 1984–1986, and
4. last but by no means least—9/11.

That is why I believe it is important to analyze these events at the level of
the supranational deep state.

Let me just cite a few details.

1. The 1980 October Surprise

According to Robert Parry, Alexandre de Marenches (the principal founder
of the Safari Club) arranged for William Casey (a fellow Knight of Malta) to
meet with representatives of the Iranian and Israeli governments in Paris in
July and October 1980, where Casey promised delivery to Iran of needed U.S.
armaments, in exchange for a delay in the return of the U.S. hostages in Iran
until Reagan was in power. Parry suspects a role of BCCI in both the funding of
payoffs for the 1980 secret deal and the subsequent flow of Israeli armaments to
Iran.[42] In addition, John Cooley considers de Marenches to be "the Safari Club
player who probably did most to draw the US into the Afghan adventure."[43]

2. The Iran-Contra Scandal (Including the Funding of the Contras, the Illegal Iran Arms Sales, and Support for the Afghan Mujahedin)

There were two stages to Iran-Contra. For twelve months in 1984–1985, after meeting with Casey, King Fahd of Saudi Arabia, in the spirit of the AWACS
deal, supported the Nicaraguan Contras via Prince Bandar through a BCCI
bank account in Miami.[44] But in April 1985, after the second proposed arms
sale fell through, National Security Advisor Robert McFarlane, fearing AIPAC
opposition, terminated this direct Saudi role. Then Khashoggi, with the help
of Miles Copeland, devised a new scheme in which Iranian arms sales involving Israel would fund the contras. The first stage of Iran-Contra was handled
by Prince Bandar through a BCCI account in Miami; the second channel was
handled by Khashoggi through a different BCCI account in Monte Carlo.

The Kerry-Brown Senate Report on BCCI also transmitted allegations from
a Palestinian-American businessman, Sam Bamieh, that Khashoggi's funds
from BCCI for arms sales to Iran came ultimately from King Fahd of Saudi
Arabia, who "was hoping to gain favor with Ayatollah Ruhollah Khomeini."[45]

The Iran-Contra investigation revealed that BCCI operations, deriving
from Khashoggi's before them, were marked by the ability to deal behind the
scenes with both the Arab countries and also Israel.[46]

Khashoggi and BCCI together, moreover, with the assistance of Khashoggi's case agent Miles Copeland, initiated what we remember as the Iran-Contra arms scandal. According to Theodore Draper, in his exhaustive study of Iran-Contra, "A chance encounter between Adnan Khashoggi and Manucher Ghorbanifar effectively set the Iran affair in motion. As Khashoggi told the story to the French writer Michel Clerc, the meeting took place in Hamburg in April 1985."[47]

Draper notes furthermore that the deal soon involved three Israelis, Yaacov Nimrodi, Adolph (Al) Schwimmer, and David Kimche, for whom "Khashoggi was no newcomer." Together with Israeli Defense Minister Sharon, the three had "met with President Nimeiri of the Sudan [in May 1982] at a safari resort in Kenya owned by Khashoggi"—that is, the Safari Club.[48] But Khashoggi's connection to Schwimmer went even further back: the two men had been introduced in Las Vegas by Schwimmer's partner in gunrunning to the infant state of Israel, Hank Greenspun.[49]

Draper's account of the Hamburg meeting fails however to note that Miles Copeland and his assistant Larry Kolb were (according to their own accounts) also present. Copeland writes that he and Khashoggi met with the Iranian arms dealer Manucher Ghorbanifar, after which Copeland wrote up an Iran arms sales proposal. Copeland claims this had nothing to do with either Contras or hostages, but was intended as a "second paper to McFarlane . . . as an appendix to the 'Marshall Plan' paper. So far as [Khashoggi] was personally concerned, he was attracted to [Ghorbanifar's] proposal only to the extent to which it could be tied into plans for overall Middle Eastern peace."[50]

Copeland's aide Larry Kolb agrees that Copeland, Khashoggi, Schwimmer, and he were all present with Ghorbanifar and others at the 1985 Hamburg meeting. There, according to Kolb, Khashoggi

> said that in recent meetings in Washington, he'd been told that if the American government was going to participate in this venture . . . it would have to be structured in such a way that there would be no trail of arms . . . leading from the United States to Iran. So, Adnan said . . . it had been arranged that the actual goods could come from the Israeli government . . . and be transported directly from Israel to Iran. . . .
>
> But arms trading and spare parts and hostages took up very little of the conversation that day. Most of the time was spent thinking, and talking, . . . about a strategic opening between the United States and Iran—as a means of blunting Soviet attempts to dominate the world's third largest oil producer.[51]

Later he and Copeland wrote up the meeting in a paper "titled 'Adnan Khashoggi's Views on the Possibilities of a Strategic Initiative Between the United States and Iran,'" that "wasn't about an arms deal."[52] They gave it to

Khashoggi to present to McFarlane. "We had no idea then that . . . months later a wild-ass Marine colonel would force the whole thing out into the open by stealing Adnan [Khashoggi]'s fifteen-million-dollar bridge loan which funded the sale and sending the money to the Nicaraguan Contra rebels."[53]

The Congressional investigation of the Iran-Contra Affair agrees with Kolb that "Khashoggi suggested that Ghorbanifar try to develop access to the United States and its arms through Israel."[54] And the Senate investigation of BCCI also reports:

> Both Saudi businessman Adnan Khashoggi and Iranian arms merchant Manucher Ghorbanifar were central agents of the United States in selling arms to Iran in the Iran/Contra affair. According to the official chronologies of the Iran/Contra committees, Khashoggi acted as the middleman for five Iranian arms deals for the United States, financing a number of them through BCCI. . . . According to his own and other published accounts, he provided some $30 million in loans altogether. . . . Both Khashoggi and Ghorbanifar banked at BCCI's offices in Monte Carlo, and for both, BCCI's services were essential.[55]

Both Ghorbanifar and Khashoggi have been presented as mavericks interested in arms sales for their own individual profit. However the participation of Copeland suggests that, once again, what Copeland called "friends in Langley" may have been interested in engaging them in an operation to which both the Secretaries of State and of Defense were resolutely opposed.

3. 9/11

As noted in chapter 6, when the two previously noted alleged hijackers or designated culprits, al-Mihdhar and al-Hazmi, arrived in San Diego, a Saudi named Omar al-Bayoumi both housed them and opened bank accounts for them. Soon afterward Bayoumi's wife began receiving monthly payments from a Riggs bank account held by Prince Bandar's wife, Princess Haifa bint Faisal.[56] In addition, Princess Haifa sent regular monthly payments of between $2,000 and $3,500 to the wife of Bayoumi's close associate Osama Basnan. In all, "between 1998 and 2002, up to US $73,000 in cashier cheques was funneled by Bandar's wife Haifa . . . —to two Californian families known to have bankrolled al-Midhar and al-Hazmi."[57]

Although these sums in themselves are not large, they may have been part of a more general pattern of support for alleged 9/11 hijackers.[58] Author Paul Sperry claims there was possible Saudi government contact with at least four other of the alleged hijackers in Virginia and Florida. For example, "9/11 ringleader Mohamed Atta and other hijackers visited a home owned by Esam Ghazzawi, a Saudi adviser to the nephew of King Fahd."[59]

But it is wrong to think of Bandar's accounts in the Riggs Bank as uniquely Saudi. Recall that Prince Bandar's payments were said to have included "a suitcase containing more than $10 million" that went to a Vatican priest for the CIA's longtime clients, the Christian Democratic Party.[60] And some, as we have just seen, involved former CIA officer Miles Copeland. In 2004, the *Wall Street Journal* reported that the Riggs Bank, which was by then under investigation by the Justice Department for money laundering, "has had a longstanding relationship with the Central Intelligence Agency, according to people familiar with Riggs operations and U.S. government officials."[61]

Meanwhile President Obiang of Equatorial Guinea "siphoned millions from his country's treasury with the help of Riggs Bank in Washington, D.C."[62] For this a Riggs account executive, Simon Kareri, was indicted. But Obiang enjoyed State Department approval for a contract with the private U.S. military firm M.P.R.I., with an eye to defending offshore oil platforms owned by ExxonMobil, Marathon, and Hess.[63]

Behind the CIA relationship with the Riggs Bank was the role played by the bank's overseas clients in protecting U.S. investments, and particularly (in the case of Saudi Arabia and Equatorial Guinea), the nation's biggest oil companies.

CONCLUSION: THE AMERICAN DEEP STATE TODAY

The issue of Saudi Embassy funding of at least two (and possibly more) of the alleged 9/11 hijackers (or designated culprits) is so sensitive that, in the 800-page Joint Congressional Inquiry Report on 9/11, the entire twenty-eight-page section dealing with Saudi financing was very heavily redacted.[64] A similar censorship occurred with the 9/11 Commission Report: According to Philip Shenon, several staff members felt strongly that they had demonstrated a close Saudi government connection to the hijackers, but a senior staff member purged almost all of the most serious allegations against the Saudi government, and moved the explosive supporting evidence to the report's footnotes.[65]

It is probable that this cover-up was not designed for the protection of the Saudi government itself, so much as of the supranational deep state connection described in this chapter, a milieu where American, Saudi, and Israeli elements all interact covertly. One sign of this is that Prince Bandar himself, sensitive to the anti-Saudi sentiment that 9/11 caused, has been among those calling for the U.S. government to make the redacted twenty-eight pages public.[66] (I attach great importance to Bandar's demand: I suspect that the 28 pages may, as he knows, indicate a U.S.-sanctioned Saudi joint operation on 9/11 that is clearly different from the piggy-backed plot to bring down the WTC towers and cause thousands of deaths.)

This limited exposure of the nefarious use of funds generated from Saudi arms contracts has not moved Congress to limit these contracts. On the contrary, in 2010, the second year of the Obama administration,

> The Defense Department . . . notified Congress that it wants to sell $60 billion worth of advanced aircraft and weapons to Saudi Arabia. The proposed sale, which includes helicopters, fighter jets, radar equipment and satellite-guided bombs, would be the largest arms deal to another country in U.S. history if the sale goes through and all purchases are made.[67]

The sale did go through; only a few congressmen objected.[68]

It is clear that for some decades the bottom-upward processes of democracy have been increasingly supplanted by the top-downward processes of the deep state. But the deeper strain in history, I would like to believe, is in the opposite direction: the ultimate diminution of violent top-down forces by the bottom-up forces of an increasingly integrated civil society.[69]

Ultimately, however, whether we see a correction or not will depend, at least in part, on how much people care.

POSTSCRIPT

This chapter attempts to correct a major deficiency of my last book, *American War Machine*, in which I chronicled the rise of the military-industrial complex without reference to Saudi Arabia. In that book I did not, as in earlier books, refer to the underlying triangle of U.S. purchases of Arab oil, U.S. sales of weapons to Arab countries, and Arab investments in the United States, particularly in Texas. (Cf. *The Road to 9/11*, pp. 175–79.)

The growing relevance to the American deep state of Saudi wealth, as just outlined in this chapter, may help explain a little-noticed paradox of American history: how the once marginal anticommunism of Goldwater Republicans, Texas oilmen, the World Anti-Communist League, and the John Birch Society displaced the once dominant coexistence politics of Kennedy, Johnson, and Nixon.

We should not forget that in 1969–70 South Yemen established close relations with the Soviet bloc, turning South Yemen for a while into the major Soviet staging point for infiltration into the region. This was a source of major anxiety for the Saudi monarchy, and, I can only guess, of big oil as well.

In *The Road to 9/11* (pp. 52–61), I analyzed the pivotal deep events of the 1970s that ended détente—the Halloween Massacre and the Team B report—in the context of those pressing for an increase in the U.S. defense budget. The role in these events of oilman George H. W. Bush (who had once, with a CIA veteran, maintained an offshore drilling platform in the Persian Gulf) now makes me suspect that big oil may have been a factor as well.

CHAPTER 11

America's Unchecked Security State

The Continuity of COG Planning, 1936–2001

Dear Bess. . . . Hoover would give his right eye to take over [from the Secret Service] and all Congressmen and Senators are afraid of him. I'm not and he knows it. If I can prevent [it] there'll be no NKVD or Gestapo in this country. Edgar Hoover's organization would make a good start toward a citizen spy system. Not for me.

—President Harry S Truman, 1947[1]

J. EDGAR HOOVER, JOSEPH MCCARTHY, AND OUR DOOMSDAY MANIA

BOTH SCHOLARS AND ORDINARY AMERICANS NOW LOOK BACK WITH RELIEF on McCarthyism and "the anticommunist hysteria of the early 1950s"[2] in the belief that we have outgrown such paranoia and disregard for law and human rights. But the personal excesses of McCarthy were surface manifestations of deeper illegal institutional procedures, mostly initiated by J. Edgar Hoover, which never really ended, and indeed have since proliferated to the point of being omnipresent. Hoover targeted leftists; the NSA targets everybody.

This has been especially true since the implementation of Continuity of Government (COG) measures on 9/11, measures that for two decades had been refined in the Pentagon's "Doomsday Project," by an extragovernmental (and arguably unconstitutional) secret committee including Donald Rumsfeld and Dick Cheney.[3] As Patrick Thronson has observed in a law journal article, "continuity-of-government procedures . . . confer powers on the President—such as the unilateral suspension of habeas corpus—that appear fundamentally opposed to the American constitutional order."[4] Yet some of these measures were then hastily made law in the USA PATRIOT Act of 2001, in support of the so-called "war on terror."[5]

In *The 9/11 Commission Report* we read, "Congress responded, in the immediate aftermath of 9/11, with the Patriot Act."[6] But the Patriot Act, which Congress (nudged by false-flag anthrax attacks) passed without time to read it, did not begin as a *response* to 9/11. Like the infamous Tonkin Gulf Resolution of 1964, with which it deserves to be compared, its contents had been developed well before the event to which it "responded"—in this case slowly and patiently over decades, starting in the 1950s. In other words, it was the product of an almost continuous level of secret emergency planning, going back to J. Edgar Hoover, which I shall show to have underlain both 9/11 and Iran-Contra, and perhaps even Watergate.

As Len Colodny and Tom Schachtman have noted,

> Among the most striking features of the PATRIOT Act was its resurrection of the long-discredited Huston Plan of 1970. The new bill permitted the FBI, CIA, and other agencies to engage in activities that had so horrified Attorney General John Mitchell that he convinced Nixon to rescind the plan four days after it was promulgated. Mitchell considered unconstitutional the Huston Plan's provisions for warrantless wiretapping, opening of mail, "black-bag" burglaries by U.S. agents, surveillance of various sorts, and preventive detention.[7]

And the "threat" which the Huston Plan had addressed (in the same year as the shootings of students at Kent State and Jackson State) was an internal one: the danger that antiwar and other popular movements might force a lasting foreign policy change on Nixon and his successors: a change preventing America from waging future aggressive wars. (At one stage the Huston Plan envisaged the creation of camps in Western states for the detention of antiwar protesters.)

Two of the provisions that Mitchell found unconstitutional—warrantless surveillance and preventive detention—can be found not just in the Patriot Act of 2001, the COG provisions of the 1980s, and the Huston Plan of 1970, but still further back—in the review of emergency detention plans ordered by LBJ after the March 1967 March on the Pentagon,[8] and in the McCarran Internal Security Act of 1950 (eventually overturned).[9] Ultimately the plans derive from secret powers that Hoover illegally arrogated to himself, despite explicit prohibitions from different attorneys general.[10]

At this point one can narrate two different histories of these secret or deep powers. On the public level, the emergency detention provisions of the McCarran Act were never used; and they were repealed in 1971, as Hoover's reputation finally withered and Congress became more responsive to antiwar dissenters.[11] But on a deeper level, Congress had achieved far less than they believed.

"Attorney General John Mitchell approved FBI Director Hoover's recommendation that the FBI continue investigating individuals 'who pose a threat to the internal security of the country' for inclusion in an 'administrative' index for anticipated future detention."[12] In other words, the only practical consequence of the congressional repeal was that Hoover's existing Security Index for the detention of individuals now had a new name.[13]

Also on a deeper level, the planning for detention continued, almost without a break, until it was finally put into effect on 9/11. In like fashion other illicit powers initiated by Hoover were either developed or implemented, first by the Nixon White House and later under Reagan's CIA Director William Casey and Oliver North. On the public level, again, thanks largely to the congressional investigations of Watergate and Iran-Contra, these proliferations were checked. But I hope to show that, while both Nixon and North were ousted, the plans for illegality they encouraged continued, almost continuously, on a deeper level.

This chapter argues that these deep powers are illegal, unchecked, and for the most part unwarranted. Some of them may indeed be needed, because America's dangers both at home and abroad today do in fact call for unusual and perhaps unprecedented responses. The 2013 horror of the Boston Marathon bombings makes this all too clear. But the Boston tragedy was not solved by the grandiose excess of locking down an entire city, but by legal and public methods of police work. The case illustrates one main thesis of this chapter: that the deep powers assembled by the unchecked American security state are vastly in excess of what is needed, to the point of being counterproductive.

Deep powers have not been designed to meet real threats today, but are the result of past unchecked bureaucratic proliferation since the 1950s, mostly after the real Soviet threat to U.S. security had passed.[14] They were refined with sustained energy by COG planners in the 1980s, when the "Soviet threat" had become a phantom resurrected only in the propaganda mills of William Casey's CIA.

The key to the renewed planning was the specter of Soviet-inspired terrorism. The notion that the Soviet Union was behind global terrorism was a successful campaign issue in the 1980 election.[15] It was then forced on CIA professional analysts in 1981 by CIA Director Casey, citing a single book, Claire Sterling's *The Terror Network*, which is now almost universally discredited.[16] Yet the hysterical CIA estimates at that time of the Soviet threat soon became permanently embodied in the hysterical provisions of the Doomsday Project, especially after their implementation in 2001. A thesis of this book is that these unchecked measures, far from being a response to 9/11 and al-Qaeda, actually contributed (perhaps blindly), to the events that now are used to justify them.

And when we compare the 1950s to what is happening in 2014, we must recognize that America in 2014 is caught up in a new hysteria, or collective insanity, which is far more over-reaching and dangerous to personal liberty than the hysteria of either Joe McCarthy or William Casey. Warrantless surveillance and detention, in particular, exist today on a scale that would have been inconceivable then. And, as before, on a scale vastly beyond both the law and what is actually needed for our security.

As in the case of McCarthyism, the people are not the original sources of this hysteria, but receptacles and responders to a hysteria generated by their leaders. There were many reasons for this hysteria in the Cold War, some of them not at all irrational. But central to the origin of Hoover's illegal unchecked powers was his autointoxication with his own power.

Lord Acton wrote: "Power tends to corrupt, and absolute power corrupts absolutely."[17] Even in the absence of absolute power, we can still say, "Power tends to intoxicate, and unchecked power intoxicates irrevocably." Since World War II we have seen the conspicuous examples of Truman's Secretary of Defense James Forrestal and later senior CIA officer Frank Wisner: Both these men went insane, had to be removed from office, and subsequently committed suicide. Less dramatic were the cases of McCarthy and President Nixon: Neither man was ever certified insane, but both lost power rapidly when they succumbed to the follies of their manic or paranoid power overreaches.[18]

I will argue that the same model of manic or paranoid self-destruction applies, less conspicuously, to other figures, less important in public history than in this present narrative of unchecked power—men such as Assistant FBI Director "Crazy" Bill Sullivan, CIA counterintelligence chief James Angleton, Oliver North, and most recently Vice President Cheney and Bush's Defense Secretary Donald Rumsfeld.[19] All these men abused their assigned powers irrationally, to such an extent that their excesses resulted in all of them but Cheney being driven from office.[20] (An important, instructive, but more debatable example is that of Hoover himself. Hoover survived for decades as long as he was restrained in his exercise of power, but both his sanity and his invulnerability were visibly weakening before his death.)

It is a tribute to the long-term sanity and homeostasis of the American political system that all these men—the central figures in this chapter—lost clout to a greater or lesser degree after this inevitable autointoxication from unchecked power. Unfortunately the process I am describing is not a wholly self-correcting one. All of these men (except Cheney and Hoover) were ousted. But the hysteria they had generated not only survived, but in every case became more securely grounded in excessive secret institutional arrangements: the modern unchecked security state.[21]

What shall we call the new hysteria? I was once tempted to call it Cheneyism, after the man who with Donald Rumsfeld planned for almost twenty years for the resurrection of these unconstitutional practices before implementing them on the morning of 9/11. But the new hysteria has outlasted

Cheney, and is by now far more institutionalized than the eccentric vagaries of either McCarthy or even his puppet master, J. Edgar Hoover. But even at this deeper structural level, we see a recurring cycle of manic institutional repressiveness (notably under Richard Nixon) followed by efforts of saner retrenchment (the post-Watergate reforms of the late 1970s instituted chiefly by the Senate Church Committee). Since 9/11 the institutional proliferation of secret, self-defeating repressive powers has become manic again, much as our economy in the same decade has passed through recurring periods of manic exuberant bubbles, followed by recession. [22]

I call our new hysteria the "Doomsday Mania," after the Doomsday Project that (as we saw in chapter 3) was the Pentagon's name for the twenty years of COG planning to suspend parts of the U.S. Constitution. The Doomsday Project was escalated under Reagan in 1982 as emergency planning "to keep the White House and Pentagon running during and after a nuclear war or some other major crisis."[23] Expanded by the end of the Reagan presidency to cover planning for *any* emergency, the planning was entrusted to a secret committee including Donald Rumsfeld and Dick Cheney, even when both men were no longer in the U.S. government.[24] Composed mostly of fellow Republicans, even under Clinton, at least one section of the committee became what a former Pentagon official described as in effect "a secret government-in-waiting."[25]

From its outset in 1982 to its implantation on 9/11, the Doomsday Project was indeed apocalyptic in its baseless determination that America faced a terrorist crisis so dire that the Constitution might need to be partly set aside. A decade before 9/11, its far-reaching arrangements were expanding the groundwork of Oliver North, to create what CNN in 1991 already described as a "shadow government . . . about which you know nothing."[26]

Much less noticed was the revival of warrantless arrest and deportation practices unknown in America since the Palmer Raids of 1919:

> Under Cheney's direction, the United States moved to restore the powers of secret intelligence that had flourished for fifty-five years under J. Edgar Hoover. . . . In top secret orders, they revived the techniques of surveillance that the FBI had used in the war on communism.
>
> The FBI arrested more than 1,200 people within eight weeks of the attacks. Most were foreigners and Muslims. None, so far as could be determined, was a member of al-Qaeda. Some were beaten and abused.[27] . . . Hundreds were imprisoned for months under a "hold until cleared" policy imposed on the FBI by Attorney General Ashcroft. . . . Ashcroft also ordered the indefinite detention of at least seventy people, including at least twenty American citizens. . . . Thirty were never brought before a tribunal. Four were eventually convicted of supporting terrorism.[28]

The post-9/11 Doomsday Mania has also been marked by the widespread use of torture in interrogations, and also by targeted assassinations, even of U.S. citizens. As we shall see, such practices were also used in the Hoover era, but sparingly. President Obama has ordered an end to torture practices, but has radically increased the use of drones for targeted assassinations—a tactic once explicitly forbidden by presidential order.

In a sense drone killings today are not secret, but the Obama administration consistently lies about the program, leading Glenn Greenwald to comment, "People who exercise power inevitably abuse it when they can wield it in secret. They inevitably lie about what they do when they can act in the dark."[29] Even before Edward Snowden, Thomas Drake revealed that the NSA is engaged in a domestic data-mining program that is so extensive, former NSA insiders fear it could help "create an Orwellian state."[30]

Americans are left with a vague sense that their country has changed, but are mostly (as in the era of McCarthyism) either too caught up in the Doomsday Mania to recognize its paranoia, or else frozen in a state of semitraumatized denial (much like the "good Germans" of the 1930s).[31] The minority who oppose the present mania mostly feel either powerless, or uncertain as to what first step must be taken to end it.[32]

Meanwhile we are living under a government that in certain respects is increasingly lawless and out of control. It is true that the government is facing new challenges of a type never experienced before, and that some emergency measures are justifiable in this crisis. But clearly the breakdown of legal restraints is counterproductive in the badly named "war on terror." To give just one example, the number of al-Qaedist warriors in the world has increased, as Tim Weiner notes, after "the images from Abu Ghraib became a recruiting poster across the world."[33] This example of counterproductive, unchecked illegality is not just an anecdote, but only one example of how the so-called "war on terror" has done more to generate and perpetuate terror than to contain it.[34]

Weiner believes that the Doomsday Mania has in some respects abated since the 2001 G. W. Bush administration, because the FBI under Obama has now adopted a 460-page set of guidelines calling for "rigorous obedience to constitutional principles and guarantees."[35] But David Shipler, another *Times* reporter, has dismissed recent headlines about the breaking of "lethal terrorist plots," saying that they were in fact "dramas . . . facilitated by the F.B.I., whose undercover agents and informers posed as terrorists offering a dummy missile, fake C-4 explosives, a disarmed suicide vest and rudimentary training."[36]

Meanwhile there are no comparable moves toward curbing the NSA's controversial data-mining of Americans, or the most illegal and counterproductive programs of all—the Special Forces killer squads and drone attacks, which in August 2012 killed a respected moderate Yemeni cleric, along with the al-Qaeda representatives with whom he was negotiating.[37]

Even within government, there are increasing numbers of people who recognize that the secret powers of other agencies also need to be similarly brought back under legal control. But many congressional attempts to address the problem of state illegality can be considered to have actually aggravated it by regularizing illegal practices in a statute. A prominent example was the National Defense Authorization Act (NDAA) of 2012, which authorized the President, at his urging, to detain U.S. citizens indefinitely.[38]

What is needed instead is a redirection of the U.S. government away from mania and illegality, such as that which ended the McCarthy era. But to so deal with the remaining illegalities of the Doomsday Mania, it will be helpful to understand their illegal origins in steps taken by J. Edgar Hoover, at first against explicit orders from his superiors, the attorneys general. Though there is never any single cure to widespread social problems, it is high time, I believe, for a first step toward normalcy to be taken: to end the source of illegal powers, namely—the state of emergency proclaimed after 9/11. And to take that step I agree with Madison that we must understand how we got here: "A people who mean to be their own governors must arm themselves with the power that knowledge gives."

The purpose of this chapter is to show how we got here: how the emergency surveillance and detention measures contemplated by the Doomsday Project date back to much earlier emergency measures that Hoover had assumed before World War II, some of them illegal, and some of them despite orders from an attorney general to desist.

THE SOURCE OF HOOVER'S ILLICIT POWER: THE FBI'S INTELLIGENCE DIVISION

By the 1960s Hoover had become one of the most powerful political figures in America, thanks chiefly to his ability to use the FBI's notorious Division Five (successively named the National Defense Division, the Security Division, and the Domestic Intelligence Division) to intimidate, blackmail, or destroy the careers of people who were not accused of any crime, but who he deemed to be dangerous.

Hoover had first exercised such powers during the Red Scare of 1919, when, as head of the Justice Department's General Intelligence Division, he had without trial deported hundreds of aliens (along with Emma Goldman, who was arguably an American citizen) in the so-called "Palmer Raids."[39] Hoover had acted at times without consulting or informing President Wilson, in collaboration with a huge army of volunteer spies, the American Protective League, which had been organized by business executives.[40] Hoover did not by any means act alone; to help put down a national steel industry strike at this time, the U.S. Army imposed martial law in certain areas.[41]

One should acknowledge that Hoover himself briefly played a different role, professionalizing the Bureau of Investigation, and accepting for about a decade the directive given him by Attorney General Harlan Stone on May 13, 1924: "The activities of the Bureau are to be limited strictly to investigations of violations of law."[42] Although he had been a major player in the Palmer Raids of 1919–1920, Hoover now (for over a decade) dismantled his General Intelligence Division, concentrated on solving personal crimes already committed, such as bank robberies, and never again involved the Bureau in anything like the Palmer Raids. On the contrary, in 1941 he was a leading opponent within the government of the decision (which originated with a local Army field commander) to round up and intern Japanese Americans.[43] This wholesale internment program overrode Hoover's own proposal for the selective detention of those Japanese already identified on the FBI's Custodial Detention list (described below). It represented, in effect, an unexpected Army rebuff to Hoover.

Instead, the Bureau of Investigation, which in 1935 became the Federal Bureau of Investigation, pursued bootleggers, bank robbers, and other gangsters, from John Dillinger to Al Capone. But noncriminal intelligence files on the general public became the hallmark of the FBI after 1936, when Roosevelt told Hoover he was interested in "'obtaining a broad picture' of the Communist and Fascist movements" in America.[44]

Roosevelt was responding to a troubling message from Hoover about American right-wing activity at the highest level. In 1935 Marine Corps Major General Smedley Butler reported to Hoover that he had been approached by two representatives of Wall Street to lead a right-wing coup d'état against President Roosevelt. Curt Gentry writes that "Hoover informed Butler that since there was no evidence that a federal criminal statute had been violated, he did not have the authority to order an investigation."[45] We see here a key to Hoover's political astuteness: his refusal ever to involve himself in disputes among those whose power was equal to or greater than his own. (We see this again in his refusal, for years, to involve the FBI in the investigation of either organized crime or the international drug traffic.)

However Hoover sought and obtained authority from FDR to reestablish an Intelligence Division, after a second report from General Butler: that the indigenous American Fascist, Father Charles Coughlin, had "approached General Butler and urged him to lead an armed expedition into Mexico, its purpose to oppose the Cárdenas government and restore the church."[46]

This time Hoover reported Butler's information to Roosevelt; and obtained from the President, on August 24, 1936, a verbal go-ahead to conduct investigations on a wide range of domestic political activities, right and left.[47] With this go-ahead, Hoover reestablished an Intelligence Division, which eventually evolved into the source of his power over others, including law-abiding Americans.[48] According to Marc Aronson,

> That secret conversation was the moment when Hoover's life story changed American history. He was given real authority to protect the nation, which he slowly but surely transformed into the right to play by his own rules, even if that totally undermined the laws and principles of the democracy he was protecting.[49]

Because no law or written document had conferred this power on him, Hoover was free to rely increasingly on illegal methods to collect intelligence, ranging from bugs, mail-openings, and wiretaps, to break-ins.[50] He knew very well that information gathered illegally could not be used in prosecutions. But Hoover's aim was to use information, not for prosecution, but to intimidate and control all sectors of society, especially those with other forms of power.

His method of dealing with Father Coughlin is a good example of this. Hoover kept a sharp eye on the outspoken priest, who by 1940 was probably America's most powerful pro-Nazi anti-Semite, with a radio show reaching possibly thirty million listeners. In January 1940 the FBI raided an office of the Christian Front, a group supported by Coughlin, for plotting to overthrow the government. Two years later Coughlin was silenced and his radio show went off the air.

Coughlin's subsequent silence, which lasted for decades, is usually attributed to an order from his bishop, after a deal negotiated with Attorney General Biddle.[51] But after Coughlin's death in 1979, his psychiatrist revealed that what silenced the priest had not been

> sudden obedience to his bishop, whom he had successfully defied for several years. That cover story was circulated in May 1942 by church authorities. . . . Coughlin felt the effects of . . . J. Edgar Hoover [who] had proof of Coughlin's homosexual activity. That proof, communicated in the verbal exchange between Hoover and Coughlin, was sufficient to silence Coughlin's public voice until May 24, 1972. . . . Hoover had died just three weeks earlier, on May 2, 1972.[52]

Hoover's silencing of Coughlin demonstrates that he used his intelligence files, not just against the left, but against any force threatening the somewhat corrupt status quo maintained by his own secret powers.

Armed in 1936 with Roosevelt's verbal authorization, Hoover proceeded to amass a list of files on tens of thousands of Americans. He was not timid in selecting targets. In 1946, bypassing Attorney General Tom Clark whom he knew would be disapproving, Hoover reported in a memo to Truman via George Allen, a wealthy businessman who was a friend, that "There is an enormous Soviet espionage ring in Washington," including "a number of high officials"—specifically including Undersecretary of State Dean Acheson and former Assistant Secretary of War John J. McCloy.[53]

When Truman proved uninterested in Hoover's dire warnings, Hoover turned instead to the House Un-American Activities Committee (HUAC) and the Senate Internal Security Subcommittee (SISS), sharing his files above all with two selected spokesmen, young Congressman Richard Nixon of HUAC in 1947, and later Senator Joseph McCarthy of the SISS in 1950.[54] Armed with information from Hoover to capture headlines, first Nixon and later Ronald Reagan were launched into careers of public prominence that led them to the White House.[55] Both men, in different ways, would then contribute to the further institutionalization of the covert intelligence powers first developed by Hoover.

Hoover eventually collected information on all those with political influence, from members of Congress to the very wealthy; and he retained personal control over this information in his files to protect his position. For example he reportedly had "343 closely held case files on the business activities of Joseph P. Kennedy, starting with the bootlegging years and including coverage of several illegal—treasonous, even—transactions brought off while Kennedy was Ambassador to the Court of Saint James."[56]

By all accounts, Hoover's wealth of such information is what enabled him to retain his office as Director for life, and perhaps influence other major political decisions.[57]

HOOVER'S POWERS AND THE STRENGTHENING OF THE AMERICAN DUAL STATE

The election of Eisenhower in 1952 enhanced Hoover's status in Washington, and also that of his projects.

> Hoover's men . . . oversaw internal security purges throughout the government, destroying lives and careers over suspicions of disloyalty or homosexuality. . . . With the full backing of Secretary of State John Foster Dulles, an FBI agent [personally approved by Hoover] named R. W. "Scott" McLeod took a job as internal security chief at State. His political purges of Washington and embassies and consulates overseas used FBI methods, including wiretaps, to force liberals and suspected leftists out of the foreign service.[58]
>
> Between May 1953 and June 1955 only 8 persons were dismissed as security risks but 273 submitted their resignations. . . . The result was a self-censorship which undoubtedly had an effect on American foreign policy, few daring to express their opinions freely for fear they would be accountable to McLeod and, eventually, McCarthy, with whom he shared the findings of his investigations. Through McLeod and his cadre, Hoover was tapped into every part of the State

Department. Aides say he knew many of [John Foster] Dulles's decisions even before the President did.[59]

The victims particularly affected were old "China hands," like John Paton Davies, who had offended the China lobby by their negative assessments of Chiang Kai-shek and the Kuomintang.

Thus was officially instituted a system whereby one part of government, the FBI, gained the power to install its agents in another, for the purpose of affecting its policies by purging its personnel. The resulting demoralization and re-orientation of State long outlasted the fall of McCarthy. It led to two decades of unreal China policy, accompanied by a long-lasting inability of State to oppose reckless CIA and Pentagon escalations of anticommunist violence in Southeast Asia. State Department veteran James C. Thomson, after resigning in 1966 over the Vietnam War, wrote an important article blaming America's errors and failures in Southeast Asia on the purging of expertise in the McCarthy era, along with Democratic Party remembrance of the "loss of China" charges.[60]

Criticizing this state of affairs from the perspective of someone who had witnessed the SS purges in Nazi Germany, political science professor Hans Morgenthau in 1955 deplored the condition of a similar "dual state" in America, in which the "authorities charged by law" were subordinated to a hostile right-wing clique with "an effective veto over the decisions of the former."[61]

Swedish professor Ola Tunander, expanding on Morgenthau's critique, called the second state a "deep state."[62] Following him in 2007 and 2008, I also defined the deep state somewhat restrictively, as an unrepresentative "restricted locus of top-down power," or as a parallel "hard-edged coalition," consisting primarily of the covert agencies (like the CIA) that are "responsive . . . to the overworld, but with little or no other public constituency."[63]

As noted earlier, I now use the term "deep state" for the larger aggregation of extralegal powers inside and outside government that Hoover helped consolidate, including not just covert agencies like the FBI, but also their media allies and other allied elements both in the wealthy overworld and the criminal underworld. In short my "deep state" is roughly the "deep political system" I defined in 1993 as "one which habitually resorts to decision-making and enforcement procedures outside as well as inside those publicly sanctioned by law and society."[64] Since 1963 this system has included at least some elements responsible for covering up the assassination of a President.

HOOVER AND THE ORIGINS OF COG'S
EMERGENCY DETENTION PLANNING

In November 1939, after the outbreak of war in Europe, Hoover began to compile a list of individuals to be closely monitored and/or detained in the event of a national emergency or war. In June 1940 he sought and gained the approval of Attorney General Robert Jackson for this list, known as the Custodial Detention List. (Late in life, Jackson appears to have regretted the powers that Hoover accumulated.)[65]

The Custodial Detention list played no role in the wholesale displacement in 1942 of Japanese and coastal Italians, which Hoover opposed.[66] In 1943 Attorney General Francis Biddle decided that the Custodial Detention List had outlived its usefulness and that there was no statutory authorization for it. His order to Hoover to close the list was unambiguous: "The [Justice] Department fulfills its proper function by investigating the activities of persons who may have violated the law. It is not aided in this work by classifying persons as to dangerousness."[67] But, as the Church Committee reported, "upon receipt of this order, the FBI Director did not abolish the FBI's list. Instead, he changed its name from Custodial Detention List to Security Index."[68]

Hoover's decision to disregard Biddle's order, leaving his detention program planning without legal authorization, "remained secret until after his death."[69] The plans, along with Hoover's illegal intelligence acquisitions and his use of organized crime as a source for them, were cornerstones in his conversion of the FBI into a powerful bureau that was both publicly funded and in part outside the domain of public law. This in turn became the key element in his aggregation of powers into the "deep state."

In particular the detention list survived a second and third effort to abolish it. When the Security Index was ordered closed in 1971, the names were again transferred, to a new Administrative Index (ADEX). This new ADEX was in turn terminated in 1978 under Jimmy Carter and his Attorney General Griffin Bell.[70] But the list was not destroyed, and remained available for use by the new Reagan administration, when in 1982 a secret committee including Rumsfeld and Cheney began planning for mass detentions under the rubric of Continuity of Government (COG) planning.

HOW HOOVER'S DETENTION PLANS BECAME PART OF NATIONAL EMERGENCY (COG) PLANNING

According to Tim Weiner, it was on July 7, 1950, at the crest of the hysteria fomented by the Korean War and by hearings in HUAC and SISS, that Hoover for the first time formally briefed the White House and the NSC his plans for "the mass detention of political suspects in military stockades, a secret prison system for jailing American citizens, and the suspension of the writ of habeas corpus."[71] He also revealed that he had had since 1939 a list of about twelve thousand individuals, nearly all of them U.S. citizens, who under his plan could be rounded up summarily on the issuance of a single "master warrant."[72] (According to Weiner, Hoover had also approved a plan, never fully implemented, "to put every one of the roughly eighty thousand members of the Communist Party of the United States on the FBI's secret Security [i.e., detention] Index.")[73]

Hoover's plan was soon paralleled in Congress by the passage (over Truman's veto) of the McCarran Internal Security Act in the same year 1950, whose Title II authorized the attorney general in times of emergency to round up and hold individuals in detention centers. Congress, in passing the Emergency Detention Act, was unaware that Hoover had already assumed this power. Moreover the Act established certain protections of individual human rights, which Hoover and some Department of Justice officials considered "unworkable." "Accordingly, Attorney General J. Howard McGrath directed the FBI to ignore the congressionally mandated standards and instead base current and future detention investigation on the administration's secretly authorized program."[74] In this decision we see a sign of America's emerging dual state, in which some U.S. agencies are directed secretly to ignore the law.

The October 1950 entry of China into the Korean War moved Truman, on December 16, 1950, to proclaim "a national emergency, which requires that the military, naval, air, and civilian defenses of this country be strengthened as speedily as possible."[75] Truman's proclamation of a national emergency authorized publicly the military buildup authorized secretly two days earlier in NSC 68/4 of December 14—in the same way that Bush's proclamation of a national emergency on September 14, 2011, became the public authority for the COG measures implemented secretly by Cheney and Rumsfeld (during Bush's absence from Washington) on 9/11.[76]

The Chinese intervention also persuaded Truman to threaten Beijing with possible use of atomic weapons.[77] As the Soviet Union now possessed its own bomb, Truman initiated COG planning to deal with a possible counterattack.[78] Thus in a sense it can be said that today's manic planning for Doomsday is a by-product of the Korean War.

Truman's proclamation of a national emergency lasted until 1977. Under Eisenhower "A series of atomic attack simulations, entitled 'Operation Alert,' were implemented from 1955 to 1960, . . . to test 'the capability of all levels of government to operate following an attack.'"[79] These exercises generated a growing number of Presidential Emergency Action Documents, or PEADs, which have been since defined by FEMA as "final drafts of Presidential messages, proposed legislation proclamations, and other formal documents, including DOJ [Department of Justice]-issued cover sheets addressed to the President, to be issued in event of a Presidentially-declared national emergency."[80]

In 2005 William Arkin wrote tentatively about PEADs:

> Little is known about the highly classified PEADs, which are believed to constitute the highest level contingency planning for the White House and the federal

government, and constitute pre-planned Presidential declarations. PEADs are believed to mostly relate to the Continuity of Government (COG) program and the execution of martial law and other sensitive and secretive operations. They are numbered and approved by the President. PEAD 6 reportedly once provided for the arrest and detention of U.S. citizens as well as aliens considered dangerous to the national defense and public safety, as well as for the seizure of property for which there is a reason to believe may be used to the detriment of national defense and public safety. PEAD 22 was approved in the Reagan Administration.[81]

By 2013 Arkin had established that PEADs and the phrase "continuity of government" were first consolidated under Eisenhower as Annex A to Federal Emergency Plan D, dealing with responses to "a crippling nuclear attack on the United States."[82]

Some PEAD documents have been declassified and posted on the Internet. We learn from an internal FBI memo of June 19, 1958, that one of these PEADs concerned the "apprehension and detention of those dangerous alien enemies presently included in our Security Index."[83] (One wonders what "dangerous alien enemies" were contemplated in the emergency planning of the late 1950s, when the Communist Party was by then clearly moribund, and the U.S. government had not yet begun to stoke xenophobic anxieties about terrorists.)

PEADs contemplated not only detention but also surveillance. According to another FBI document of April 1976,

PEAD #8 authorizes the Secretary of State to initiate measures for the protection, surveillance, and control of certain foreign diplomatic, consular, and other official personnel. PEAD #9 authorizes the Secretary of State to take over property of enemy governments. FBI would assist in the implementation of these PEADs under Procedures for Interning Enemy Diplomatic Consular, United Nations and Official Personnel in the Event of War (PRODIP).[84]

THE EVOLUTION OF MARTIAL LAW PLANNING:
GARDEN PLOT, CABLE SPICER, AND FEMA

Martial law was also envisaged under PEAD #20, "created under Eisenhower and thoroughly revised and signed by President Jimmy Carter on October 13, 1978."[85]

The Army developed a plan for quelling civil disturbance after the difficulties experienced at the Ole Miss riot of 1962, where military commanders "reported back that they were blindsided by a lack of intelligence."[86] As violence increased in the 1960s, first in inner cities but also eventually on campuses, successive plans evolved into Garden Plot. This plan was issued in June 1967, after the riots following the Martin Luther King, Jr. assassination, and one month before being implemented in Detroit. Following these riots, and as part of Garden Plot, two brigades (4,800 troops) were placed on permanent standby to quell unrest. The two brigades were however disbanded in 1971 under Nixon, following the shootings of students at Kent State and Jackson State University, and the embarrassing testimony to Congress by three army undercover agents that Army intelligence had 1,500 plainclothes agents watching every demonstration of twenty people or more throughout the United States.[87]

But Garden Plot plans were resurrected in 1978. This was the year that Harvard Professor Samuel Huntington, who earlier had written of the occasional need to "override the claims of democracy," was named "Coordinator of Security" for the Carter administration.[88] Together with his ally Zbigniew Brzezinski, Huntington redesigned the overall architecture of the COG planning system, notably by creating the Federal Emergency Management Agency (FEMA), to supply infrastructure for an emergency government takeover.[89]

FEMA attracted some notoriety under Reagan, who, as we saw in chapter 3, installed a California counterinsurgency team headed by Army Col. Louis Giuffrida. Earlier Reagan had made Giuffrida the head of the California National Guard, and called on him "to design Operation Cable Splicer. . . . martial law plans to legitimize the arrest and detention of anti-Vietnam war activists and other political dissidents."[90] These plans were refined with the assistance of British counterinsurgency expert Sir Robert Thompson, who had used massive detention and deportations to deal with the 1950s Communist insurgency in what is now Malaysia.

Thompson's plans for massive detention, adapted first by Giuffrida in California's Operation Cable Splicer, were further refined by Giuffrida and FEMA with the assistance of Oliver North. In 1984 they were the focus of a massive COG exercise, REX-84, an exercise preparing for the detention of more than 400,000 Central American refugees in ten military centers located the country.[91] REX-84 was the plan described by *Miami Herald* reporter Alfonso Chardy in 1987 as a "plan to suspend the Constitution in the event of a national crisis, such as nuclear war, violent and widespread internal dissent or national opposition to a U.S. military invasion abroad."[92]

THE NATIONAL COMMUNICATIONS SYSTEM AND THE DOOMSDAY PROJECT

Of primary significance to COG planning in the 1980s and 1990s was the decision by Eisenhower's cabinet to commission new "executive agencies to develop continuity measures—the means by which a fragmented federal government could begin to exercise authority over a devastated nation."[93] One of these, destined to mushroom under Reagan into a billion-dollar boondoggle, was the National Communications Agency (NCA), whose designated task was to "assist in maintaining the flow of essential national telecommunications." Like some of the other such agencies, it was chaired by a corporate executive outside government: in this case by President Frank Stanton of the CBS Television Network.[94] Eisenhower had first brought in Stanton and other prominent private citizens for Doomsday planning, just "a few weeks after the Soviets launched the first manmade satellite in 1957, shattering America's sense of security." The involvement of private leaders from the deep state has been a feature of Doomsday planning ever since.[95]

The NCA was a precursor of the National Communications System (NCS), formally established by a JFK Presidential Memorandum on August 21, 1963. By 1969 at least $175 million had been spent "to increase the survivability of national communications resources" in a nuclear attack.[96] In July 1979 the system was tested under Carter, in the first known instance of the exercise GLOBAL SHIELD. By the Reagan era the NCS had mushroomed into an $8 billion communications and logistics program for an alternative emergency communications network.[97]

Earlier I argued that in the background of 9/11, as well as in all comparable deep events diverting America toward its current dual state, we can see the workings of what in chapter 9 I called the "Doomsday Project—the alternative emergency planning structure with its own communications network, operating as a shadow network outside of regular government channels." The purpose of this chapter has been to note the sporadic but crescive evolution of the COG planning and network, through the presidencies of Roosevelt, Truman, Eisenhower, Kennedy, and Carter. But a barrier was broken when Oliver North, arranging for the arms shipments to Iran that eventually cost him his job, made the first documented use of the Doomsday communications network, Flashboard, to help implement a deep event: Iran-Contra.

From this time forward into the 1990s, COG planning continued to evolve, now under the watchful eyes of neocons like Paul Wolfowitz.[98] The climax of this evolution was 9/11, when COG plans themselves, and not just their network, were implemented for the first time.[99]

CHAPTER 12

America's Unchecked Security State and Lawlessness

This is the way of the post–September 11 world, where whistleblowers and news organizations reveal what would have once been considered illegal and then, years later, find themselves "revealing" it yet again, and then again. So it has been with torture and extrajudicial killing and warrantless wiretapping. We might call these frozen scandals, which begin in revelation and white-hot controversy and end with our learning to live with secret wrongdoing that is in fact no secret at all. This is our new normal—and a vital attribute of the world Dick Cheney bequeathed us.[1]

FROM THE OUTSET OF HIS YEARS AT THE FBI, HOOVER'S POWER WAS REIN-forced by his de facto alliance with the overworld and its own deep state re-sources, combined with his de facto alliance with lawless underworld elements who were also part of the informal power structure in that era.

Back in 1919–1920, Hoover's Bureau, in conducting its nationwide raids and arrests, "coordinated its work closely with a 250,000 member right-wing vigilante group, the American Protective League," supported by business lead-ers.[2] In later years Hoover continued to augment the FBI's spying networks and files with other business-supported organizations, above all the American Legion[3] and its postwar offshoot the American Security Council (ASC).

The second major network supplementing the FBI was the Anti-Defama-tion League (ADL). According to its prominent critic Alfred M. Lilienthal, "the ADL . . . works closely with the Israeli intelligence agency, Mossad, and sometimes with the FBI or CIA."[4]

The author and *Village Voice* journalist Robert Friedman agrees:

At the onset of the Cold War, the ADL was running perhaps the largest private spy agency in America, regularly feeding the FBI information not only on anti-Semitic groups like the KKK and the American Nazi party, but also on Jewish leftists and members of the Communist Party. . . . It supplied not only the FBI, but, according to the Congressional Record, the Commerce Department, which reviewed the files of applicants for government jobs, searching for "subversives." . . . In the '50s and '60s, the ADL continued to penetrate and expose racist and fascist groups. It also championed the civil rights movement, speaking out for fair housing and against job discrimination. Yet as always, there was a darker side. The ADL spied on Martin Luther King and passed its files to J. Edgar Hoover's FBI, according to Henry Schwarz[s]child, who was an ADL officer from 1962 to 1964 and is now an official with the ACLU. "It was common and casually accepted knowledge," Schwarz[s]child told the S.F. Weekly.[5]

Hoover also exploited the close and arguably very improper relationships that he maintained with wealthy, usually independent and self-made, millionaires like Joseph Kennedy, Clint Murchison, Sr., Lewis Rosenstiel, and George Allen (Hoover's backdoor forwarder to Truman of the memo attacking John McCloy).[6]

It is a telling sign of the deep state milieu after Prohibition that every one of these self-made millionaires had intimate connections to organized crime—and there are many reports that through them and their journalistic friends like Walter Winchell, Hoover himself met at New York's Stork Club with organized crime figures like Frank Costello.[7] Burton Hersh asserts that Hoover tactfully maintained this connection to the Stork Club milieu because "Costello was a resource."[8]

For decades Hoover declined to investigate and prosecute organized crime, claiming "that it was a local police problem, outside of the FBI's jurisdiction."[9] As former FBI agent Peter Pitchess (later Sheriff of Los Angeles County) recalled, "Organized crime was just not a concern of the Bureau. We knew it existed, but there were hardly any prosecutions, and we knew this was FBI policy."[10] In this way Hoover tacitly accepted Tammany-style corruption as a reinforcement of the status quo, and also as a resource for dealing with outsiders who threatened it.

Hoover was recognizing and sanctioning, rather than creating, the social status of the mob, which at the time helped elect politicians and perform favors for the wealthy. In particular Hoover was helping to preserve a status quo in which organized crime continued to help wealthy industrialists like Henry Ford (or more precisely his security chief Harry Bennett) fight trade unions like the United Auto Workers, by granting delivery contracts and concessions to prominent mobsters like Joe Adonis, Brooklyn's top man in narcotics.[11]

An important political consequence of this de facto tolerance was to protect and reinforce the enduring influence of organized crime in the local politics of cities like New York, Newark, Boston, Chicago, and San Francisco. This was brought home to me through my research into Jack Ruby, whom I linked in an early manuscript to a nationwide network of mob figures involved in gambling and narcotics. One morning I was surprised to see in our local newspaper that one of Ruby's associates, Benny Barrish, was named for his part in the 1974 lease of a San Francisco City golf course to an East Coast gangster.[12]

Hoover did not just tolerate organized crime; he used it, not just as a source of information, but also as a source of enforcement. A notorious example of the latter was the surrender at the Stork Club of Louis Lepke Buchalter to Hoover personally, negotiated with the approval of Lansky and the aid of newsman Walter Winchell.[13] Enforcement was politically selective. For example when in 1957 a rogue ex-FBI agent, with the assistance of Joe Zicarelli of the Bonanno family, kidnapped the left-wing Dominican journalist Jesús de Galíndez on behalf of Dominican dictator Trujillo (who subsequently had him murdered), Hoover, rather than indict a right-wing dictator, "informed the Justice and State Departments that the case against Trujillo and his henchmen was not 'sufficiently airtight.'"[14]

Hoover used political criteria to recruit and protect individual mafia members as informants, a process that could easily lead to corruption and scandal—some of which still exists. In 1971, as a favor to his political ally, House Speaker John McCormack, Hoover (in a personal memo) directed the Boston FBI office to develop Whitey Bulger, then a minor mob figure, as an informant. (Whitey's brother James was part of the McCormack political machine and a member of the House of Representatives.)[15]

For two decades Bulger fed inside information about the Boston Patriarca crime family to his FBI contact John Connolly (also appointed by Hoover on the recommendation of McCormack). At the same time Whitey Bulger ran a lucrative protection racket targeting drug kingpins and gambling operators. Eventually Bulger was indicted for nineteen murders, including the murder of another FBI informant, a crime for which Connolly also was jailed.[16]

The Connolly-Bulger scandal in Boston was not anomalous. In the 1980s a very similar scandal developed in the FBI's New York office, where agent Lin DeVecchio protected his mafia informant Gregory Scarpa, Sr., from arrest, allowing Scarpa to commit a series of mob murders with impunity.[17] Author Peter Lance has made a persuasive case that the FBI's eagerness to cover up the DeVecchio scandal eventually led it to cover up significant evidence about 9/11.[18]

HOOVER'S USE OF ILLEGAL METHODS TO COMBAT THE KU KLUX KLAN

Those who like myself celebrate the nonviolent desegregation of the South in the 1960s need to recognize that the civil rights movement did not achieve this fundamental change without other efforts to enforce federal laws. The White House deployed federal manpower to enforce rulings of the federal courts—U.S. marshals whenever possible. These were inadequate, however, when Governor Ross Barnett in 1962 sought to block the court-ordered admission of James Meredith to the University of Mississippi, an event that "many historians view as ground zero on the southern counterrevolution against integration and multiculturalism."[19] In this case a well-organized riot forced the Kennedy brothers to send in more than twelve thousand U.S. Army soldiers, climaxing a fixed battle that left two people dead.[20] As we saw in the last chapter, the confusion in the army's response led to a series of plans, resulting in Garden Plot.

The attempt of the Kennedys to use the law against insurrection began to look increasingly counterproductive. Robert Kennedy then moved against General Edwin Walker, who had mobilized the mob at Ole Miss "with his contingent of gunmen from Dallas," by remanding the general for psychiatric examination at the Medical Center for Federal Prisoners in Springfield, Missouri. "The John Birch Society and other far-right groups heralded this as an example of the 'Kennedy police state.'"[21] After five days, the U.S. government backed down and Walker was released, now a "leading light" of the Birch Society in Dallas and elsewhere.[22] And he still had good connections with other right-wing veterans of the U.S. military.

In April 1963 there was a meeting in New Orleans of the Congress of Freedom, Inc., a Miami detective's report of which included the statement that "there was indicated the overthrow of the present government of the United States," including "the setting up of a criminal activity to assassinate particular persons and groups of persons throughout the United States." The report added that "membership within the Congress of Freedom, Inc., contain high ranking members of the armed forces that secretly belong to the organization."[23] Things were beginning to get out of hand.

Characteristically, Hoover took no known steps against this conclave of "high ranking members of the armed forces"; indeed, he took steps to discredit the detective's informant.[24] With respect to the lower middle-class Klan, however, his response was quite different.[25] While the White House used legal means to respond to the phenomenon of Klan violence, Hoover secretly resorted to illegal means to go after the hidden roots of disorder in the Klan and its allies. This may have been more important as well as less disruptive, for as journalist Maryanne Vollers has noted, "the retaliation that followed Meredith's admission to Ole Miss showed a pattern indicating that someone was directing a terror campaign in the state."[26] (It is possible, though not certain, that Hoover had better intelligence than Kennedy on the strength of the deep powers backing Klan resistance to desegregation.)

Admittedly Hoover dealt very belatedly with the problem of racial violence, but in the end he also did so forcefully. He himself was a segregationist by background and inclination. In 1956 he warned Eisenhower's cabinet about the dangers of "mixed education" from desegregation, including the "specter of racial [i.e. interracial] marriage."[27] It has been alleged that, as late as 1961 there were only five African American FBI agents, all of whom "mostly served as drivers."[28]

There were other factors inhibiting his commitment to racial justice. The FBI model for social stability was cooperation with local law enforcement, which in the Deep South was committed to segregation. And much of Hoover's support in Congress came from southern racist committee chairmen like Senator Eastland, the overseer of the Senate Internal Security Subcommittee (SISS).

And yet, as the civil rights movement was answered with more and more bombings and murders from a resurgent Ku Klux Klan, Hoover himself intervened, far more vigorously than is generally recognized. It is widely known that on September 2, 1964, after the murder of three civil rights workers in Mississippi, Hoover matched his COINTELPRO against "Black Nationalist Hate Groups" (including the Southern Christian Leadership Conference [SCLC] and Martin Luther King, Jr.) with a new COINTELPRO—WHITE HATE directed exclusively against the Klan.[29] In the next seven years the FBI conducted 287 separate operations, and by September 1965, the FBI could identify 2,000 Klansmen on its payroll as informants.[30]

It is wrong to dismiss Hoover's anti-Klan campaign as "small" compared to other COINTELPROs.[31] On the contrary, "COINTELPRO activities had a devastating effect on Klan activity. There were so many undercover agents operating in the Klan that Klan leaders became hesitant to make decisions for fear that the FBI would learn of them."[32]

Tim Weiner writes,

> "Mr. Hoover never would have changed by himself" not without LBJ's forceful command [on July 2, 1964], Burke Marshall [RFK's civil rights chief] said. "The FBI was grudging about doing anything" against the Klan. "Mr. Hoover viewed the civil-rights activists as lawbreakers. The FBI was worse than useless, given his mind-set"—until the president ordered him to change his mind.[33]

Marshall's negative judgment of Hoover reflects that voiced at the time by Martin Luther King, Jr. However Athan Theoharis reports that, already in 1963, Hoover had subordinated his distaste for the nonviolent civil rights movement to his concern that certain Klan elements represented an organized violent insurrection against the court-ordered imposition of federal laws. Not only this, Hoover had decided to fight illegal violence with illegal violence— the darker resources of the deep state.

It is alleged that, after the murder of civil rights activist Medgar Evers in June 1963, Hoover may have authorized the use of a mafia killer, "Julio" [possibly Gregory Scarpa], to extract the name of Evers's murderer from a pistol-whipped and terrorized witness.[34] A year later, after the June 1964 murder of three civil rights workers in Mississippi, Scarpa extracted the facts for the FBI from a witness, this time by brandishing a straight-edge razor and unzipping the witness's fly.[35] And in 1966, after the arson-murder of Vernon Dahmer, Scarpa identified the culprit from a witness beaten so violently he was hospitalized and never again the same.[36]

Among those arrested and eventually convicted as a result of Scarpa's interventions was Samuel Holloway Bowers, leader of the White Knights of the Ku Klux Klan, "the most successfully violent KKK subgroup in the nation."[37] Bowers was the power behind murders and bombings across the entire Deep South (including, a recent book has suggested, at least one murder plot against Martin Luther King, Jr.).[38] He had rightly anticipated that he would not be tried in a Mississippi state court; but Scarpa's discoveries helped enable the federal government to establish federal authority and convict him. This ended the impunity of Bowers's Klan, and defused its dangerous "strategy to induce [a] race war."[39]

In 1967, after the conviction of Bowers, remnants of his White Knights began bombing Jewish synagogues and homes.[40] This escalation of violence, to include white as well as black targets, also escalated the FBI's resort to illegalities, far beyond the use of torture to obtain evidence. According to investigative reporter Jack Nelson, who broke the story, the FBI in 1968 helped provoke the attempted bombing of a Jewish businessman's home in Meridian, Mississippi. In Nelson's account, the FBI hired two informants to induce two of Bowers's close associates (Thomas A. Tarrants III and another Klansman) to attempt another bombing, so that police waiting at the scene could execute them during the commission of the crime.[41]

As Nelson pointed out, this represented a new level of FBI illegality:

1. It involved premeditated murder.
2. It involved entrapment—Tarrants (and another victim, not the intended target) "had been lured into a trap by a pair of informants."
3. The informants [one of them out on appeal after being convicted for shooting the three civil rights workers in 1964] were motivated, not just by thousands of dollars in reward money put up by the local Anti-Defamation League, but also by "threats by the local police and the FBI to kill them if they didn't cooperate."[42]

It is difficult to defend such tactics, other than to note (as Nelson does) that 1968 was "a year like no other," with killings and unprecedented rioting around the nation and the world. Nelson himself was so shocked by what he learned that he broke with the local FBI (his source for earlier stories) and alerted the nation to the illegalities.[43]

At the same time Nelson had to concede that, "Since the ambush, there had been no further violence against Jews in Mississippi."[44] His assessment is expanded on by Professor George Michael: "The attack proved effective, as it finally broke the back of the Klan violence in Mississippi."[45]

Let me close this dubious late chapter in Hoover's career with words spoken by Gandhi shortly before his assassination: "No good act can produce an evil result. Evil means, even for a good end, produce evil results."[46] Evil results, in this case, even for the FBI itself.

THE END OF HOOVERISM AND THE DEBATES
OF THE POST-VIETNAM ERA

It can be said that by 1968 Hoover, William Sullivan, the other leaders in Washington, and the country itself were all driven awry from violence, all no longer themselves, all out of control.[47] I wrote earlier that "all power intoxicates; unchecked power intoxicates irrevocably." Like Defense Secretary Forrestal and CIA officer Frank Wisner, both Hoover and Sullivan were by now behaving so oddly that their behavior, especially Sullivan's, was being questioned by their own colleagues.[48] (More recently, both Rumsfeld and Cheney have been analyzed as paranoid.[49])

The point being made here is so important that I should ground it in a larger observation, both very obvious and usually suppressed, that only very abnormal people will seek the U.S. presidency. That abnormality does not of itself derogate from the ability to govern. Indeed a recent book has argued that there is a surprisingly deep correlation between mental illness and successful leadership, pointing to the examples of Abraham Lincoln, Franklin D. Roosevelt, and Martin Luther King, Jr.[50]

But the mania of 1968 was institutional, not just personal, and was inflaming a nation at war with itself. The FBI by then, at Sullivan's urging, had helped instigate a number of other murders, notably that of Black Panther leader Fred Hampton in Chicago, killed with multiple gun wounds while at home sleeping in his bed.[51] Furthermore there were a number of instances where the FBI instigated battles, sometimes lethal, between the Panthers and other groups, making the Bureau, as legal scholar Frank Donner has written, "criminally complicit in the violence" that ensued.[52] Across the country

break-ins and assaults were carried out by right-wing paramilitary groups coordinating their efforts with FBI informants, military intelligence agents, and local police investigative units. . . . The FBI relationship to the far right reached a violent climax in San Diego, where an FBI informant testified the FBI provided him with $10,000 worth of weapons, including explosives used in a bombing by the Secret Army Organization (SAO), a right-wing group which harassed activists protesting the Vietnam war. The FBI even hid a gun used in an SAO assassination attempt against a leftist professor until an ACLU-sponsored lawsuit by a woman wounded in the assault forced the FBI to reveal the weapon's existence.[53]

The FBI's escalation in the use of violence reflected the increasingly independent domination of the its COINTELPROs by Assistant Director William "Crazy Bill" Sullivan.[54] Already in 1967 Sullivan had challenged Hoover's aging leadership, arguing that the Ku Klux Klan was a far greater threat than the Communist Party USA. As Hoover grew increasingly cautious, Sullivan took less and less guidance from his director, and built violence-prone coalitions instead with James Angleton in the CIA, and eventually the Nixon White House.[55]

In a dialectic worthy of a Greek tragedy, the FBI's excesses had seriously undermined Hoover's powers before his death in 1972. Nelson, backed by his newspaper the *L.A. Times*, proceeded, after exposing the Meridian incident, to expose a series of other FBI illegalities, inducing Hoover in turn to put Nelson on his enemies' list and wage a lying war against him as a "jackal" and "a lice-covered ferret."[56] Nelson's sequence of page-one stories had the consequence of eroding Hoover's support in both Congress and the White House: "Suddenly, after years of near idolization, J. Edgar Hoover was no longer untouchable. The FBI director was now fair game."[57]

Before Hoover's death in 1972 Congress had finally begun to expose and condemn Hoover's wiretapping and other illegalities. As Hoover became more and more reluctant to break the law, he became increasingly a curb to the illegalities of others—notably the increasingly obvious efforts of William Sullivan to replace him, with the support of President Nixon. A denouement of sorts was Hoover's blocking of the 1970 "Huston Plan" for a consolidated national police uniting the resources of FBI, CIA, DIA, and NSA. The plan was nominally proposed by Tom Huston in the Nixon White House, but in fact drafted chiefly by Sullivan. The other agencies supported the proposal and Nixon initially signed it; but Hoover, by enlisting Attorney General Mitchell as an ally, succeeded in persuading Nixon to reverse his decision.[58]

This episode was not without consequences. In the short run, the defeat of the Huston Plan drove the White House to engage unilaterally in the series of illegalities we remember as "Watergate."[59] And the coalition of agencies backing the plan was revived during the COG planning (the Doomsday Project) of the 1980s and 1990s. Viewed retrospectively, the Huston Plan looks like an early blueprint for the shadow security state we live under today.

But simultaneously Hoover, increasingly out of touch with reality, began to lose the self-restraint with which he had previously managed his own secret intelligence. In 1971 a congressman who was also a U.S. Navy hero, Commander William Anderson, spoke in the House and "rebuked J. Edgar Hoover . . . for accusing two prominent opponents of the Vietnam War of plotting to kidnap a government official and blow up electrical systems in the Washington area. He termed Hoover's accusations the 'climax' of 'an outrageous pattern of fear and repression.'"[60]

Such a rebuke of Hoover in Congress was unprecedented, and so was Hoover's response. Instead of privately threatening Anderson, he

> had the Congressman investigated. . . . Agents found a madam who "thought" Anderson had visited her place of business several years earlier. Hoover then scribbled "whoremonger" on the memorandum . . . and arranged to have the story leaked to the press in Anderson's home state. . . . In 1972, William Anderson— . . . four-term congressman from Tennessee—was defeated for reelection.[61]

But the spell of the FBI over Congress had been broken; and in a few years Congress, in a turnabout, would begin to investigate the FBI.

THE DEBATE OVER SECRET POWERS IN THE POST-VIETNAM INTERIM BEFORE REAGAN

After the traumas of Watergate and Nixon's resignation, the national mood for more transparency in government increased, at least temporarily. A number of congressional committees, notably the Senate committee chaired by Senator Frank Church, began to examine some of the illegalities of the COINTELPROs, as did an administrative committee of Justice Department officials set up by Attorney General William Saxbe.[62]

It appeared briefly, in short, that the public state might bring this aspect of the deep state under control. And indeed, a number of key FBI programs, such as the Security List for emergency mass detentions, were terminated in 1978—at least on paper. Congress also passed the Foreign Intelligence Surveillance Act (FISA) of 1978, as a compromise effort to regulate wiretapping. In addition two senior FBI officials were convicted in 1980 for having authorized illegal break-ins.[63]

But meanwhile other counterforces were building to reverse what Professor Samuel Huntington, in his 1975 study for the Trilateral Commission, called the "excess of democracy" then current in the American system.[64] In 1974 the new Ford White House, with first Donald Rumsfeld and later Dick Cheney as Chief of Staff, became a focal point for resisting the efforts of Church and others to achieve greater openness in American government.[65]

Rumsfeld and Cheney were not acting alone. Behind them were the neocons of the 1970s Committee on the Present Danger (CPD), who were mobilized to ensure that U.S. defense budget would not shrink (as candidate Jimmy Carter intended) after Vietnam.[66] And behind the CPD were still other, more shadowy international forces, such as the Saudi-backed Safari Club of intelligence chiefs, and the ultra-reactionary political backers of future leaders Reagan and Thatcher (such as Alexandre de Marenches) in the Euro-American Pinay Circle.[67]

Although the predominant issues after the collapse of the Saigon regime in Vietnam were the future of détente and the defense budget, also at stake was the future of the secret powers amassed by Hoover—above all warrantless surveillance. Journalists Lou Dubose and Jake Bernstein write that in this period Cheney, aided by his friend Antonin Scalia (then head of the Justice Department's Office of Legal Counsel) "teamed up to defend executive privilege," including "illegal wiretapping."[68] Rumsfeld, Cheney, and Scalia also united in an unsuccessful campaign to block a major expansion of the Freedom of Information Act (FOIA).[69]

This campaign of Donald Rumsfeld and Cheney in the Ford White House, to protect the FBI and CIA from congressional tampering, was part of a larger campaign, to put an end to Nixon-Kissinger policies of détente and multipolarity, and put America back on the path toward global domination.

In the so-called "Halloween Massacre" of 1975, Rumsfeld and Cheney also arranged to end Kissinger's tenure as national security advisor, and for Nelson Rockefeller to be removed from his expected vice-presidential position on the 1976 Republican ticket. This opened the way to the election of Reagan in 1980 and the subsequent Reagan Revolution, the final victory of the executive forces for secrecy over the congressional efforts at openness.[70] With the appointment of Donald Rumsfeld and Dick Cheney to a secret COG planning committee in 1982 (the so-called Doomsday Project), arrangements resumed for warrantless surveillance, massive emergency detentions, and other suspended features of Hoover's agenda.

In short the post-Vietnam struggle in Washington, between the congressional defenders of a public state, and the administrative defenders of secret powers, was effectively resolved by the launching in 1982 of the so-called "Doomsday Project": plans for an emergency suspension of provisions in the Constitution. Today many of the post-Watergate reforms, such as the FISA Act and the National Emergencies Act, are dead. Programs briefly suspended, such as the maintenance of lists for wide-scale detention, have been restored on a level far, far wider than before.

Of all the post-Watergate reforms, the most visible one to survive was the establishment, by the Intelligence Oversight Act of 1980, of permanent committees in both the Senate and the House for oversight of the CIA and FBI. Those who see this reform as significant point to the Iran-Contra crisis of the 1980s, when a congressional ban on CIA aid to the Nicaraguan Contras (the so-called "Boland Amendments") led to illegal responses by White House officials, and their subsequent exposure. But the intention of the reform can be said to have been effectively reversed, making the committees into constituencies for the intelligence agencies, rather than custodians of them.[71] Thus in the 1980s the Committees not only gave the CIA full leash on their dubious

Afghan operation, but Congressman Charlie Wilson also actually pressed on the CIA a larger budget than many CIA operatives wanted.[72]

To sum up: on the surface, one can date the growth of unchecked secret powers in America to 9/11 and the implementation that morning of Continuity of Government (COG) measures that had been secretly planned for two decades by Cheney and Rumsfeld, even when the two men were not officially part of the U.S. government. But that event had been prepared for, perhaps even made inevitable, by the much earlier Rumsfeld-Cheney victory in the post-Vietnam contest between Congress and the White House—over whether the public state would control the deep state, or vice versa.

HOOVERISM AND THE DOOMSDAY MANIA: THE INSTRUCTIVE DIFFERENCE

The Doomsday Mania, I would once have said, had restored Hooverism. I would now say that COG planning, in restoring specific Hoover techniques, has gone beyond Hooverism to something far more dangerous. In addition, some of the illegalities that Hoover merely *planned for* (like detention), Rumsfeld and Cheney, after also planning for two decades, *implemented* on September 11, 2001.

The COG measures implemented on 9/11 have supplemented Hoover's powers with parallel powers developed by the CIA and NSA (as foreseen in the Huston Plan), plus the worst FBI illegalities from the emergency era of the 1960s. Torture, practiced by the FBI in an extreme situation, became embodied in legal memoranda as a standard way to interrogate suspects. Preemptive murder of opponents, as encouraged by the FBI in Meridian and Chicago, is now the standard practice of the drone program initiated by Bush and Cheney and since expanded by Obama. In brief, as I said earlier, the aims of Hooverism were to maintain the status quo, while the aim of the Doomsday Mania has been explicitly to change it.

Hoover's actions against the Klan were accompanied by similar illegal actions against Martin Luther King, Jr., whom he once characterized, on the record, as "the most notorious liar in the country."[73] The two campaigns, set side by side, reveal Hoover's commitment to the status quo, against any forces, legal or illegal, violent or nonviolent, threatening change.

His tactics to crush the Klan were clearly illegal. But they were in response to murders and a challenge to public order. They were also in their way measured, and in their way less disruptive of the peace than the "legal" tactics of the Kennedy brothers in the 1960s—whose response to the challenge at Ole Miss had resulted not only in lethal violence but the responsive determination of Bowers and others to commit serial murders, in order to induce an apocalyptic race war.[74]

In this respect Hoover's "deep state" illegalities can be distinguished from those we have witnessed since 9/11 against al-Qaeda. Hoover's actions were finite and narrowly targeted, in order to achieve a successful consolidation of federal law. His methods were essentially nonviolent against the nonviolent, violent against the violent.[75] The implementation of COG planning we have seen since 9/11 has been, in contrast, an erosion of law and everyone's liberty, with no end in sight.

In this chapter I have tried to show Hoover's responsibility for developing the traditions of suspending habeas corpus and other constitutional liberties that have been implemented in the last decade. But we should also recognize the huge difference between planning for a suspension of liberty, and the implementation of those plans. There is no evidence that Hoover wanted to see his emergency plans implemented by state institutions including his own FBI. But Donald Rumsfeld and Dick Cheney, after working on COG plans for almost two decades, called publicly in 2000 for "a process of transformation, which even if it brings revolutionary change, is likely to be a long one, absent some catastrophic and catalyzing event—like a new Pearl Harbor."[76]

THE EXPANSION OF SECRET POWERS SINCE 9/11

With the implementation of COG emergency responses to 9/11, we have indeed seen an exponential expansion of America as a dual state, or what Dana Priest and William Arkin called "two governments: the one . . . operated more or less in the open: the other a parallel top secret government . . . visible to only a carefully vetted cadre."[77]

The second government, called by Priest and Arkin "Top Secret America," should not be thought of as identical to the deep state, but rather as the radically expanded institutional base for the deep state, ensuring an ever-greater share of the national budget for top-down programs to constrain dissent both abroad and at home.

The unchecked expansion of this base—much of it now outsourced—has continued under Obama, even as budgetary cutbacks have continued to weaken the public government citizens are familiar with. For example

> CACI . . . recorded $36.4 million in profits in the third quarter of fiscal 2011. It hired four hundred new employees and was looking for another four hundred. Analysts attributed its success to the swelling cybersecurity and intelligence markets and to its lucrative contracts with the army for intelligence and information war services.[78]

A percentage of such profits are inevitably dedicated to supporting those Congressmen who will continue to back swollen budget allocations for security. These flows of funds further trivialize the independence of Congress, to the point where, as *The Nation* editor Katrina vanden Heuvel wrote in 2013, "Bipartisan agreement in Washington usually means citizens should hold on to their wallets or get ready for another threat to peace."[79]

Priest and Arkin note how Obama campaigned in 2008 as a critic of a number of covert programs, including torture, renditions, and secret prisons—yet in the end, torture aside, the new administration, in the words of a CIA observer, "changed virtually nothing."[80] Indeed, after having promised great openness, the Obama administration has proceeded to indict more whistleblowers than all previous administrations combined, with a vindictiveness that has brought a reprimand from a federal judge.[81]

Priest and Arkin's book is of great value for its research into a top secret realm not normally described in the governing media. But it is almost silent about the human agents who have brought us here: in their book Dick Cheney is mentioned only once in passing, and there is nothing at all about the COG planning of the Doomsday Project.

At one point a statement by Janet Napolitano, Obama's cabinet-level Secretary of Homeland Security, reminds Priest and Arkin of J. Edgar Hoover and "the dark days of McCarthyism, when . . . an obsessed and paranoid FBI had drawn up a black list" (the Security Index).[82] There is indeed a sense in which America's Doomsday Mania today is derived from Hoover's obsessive penchant for surveillance and control. But if we were to begin by returning to the dual state as it operated under Hoover, this would represent a return to a far more limited form of secret government than that oppressing us today.

CONCLUSION

Since the 1950s, American history has seen two competing narratives: one relatively stable and benign, and one posing a lawless and dangerous threat to constitutional democracy. On the one hand a succession of power-hungry men have first amassed excessive powers and then in consequence have self-destructed or been ousted: Joe McCarthy in the 1950s, Richard Nixon in 1974, Oliver North in 1986, and Donald Rumsfeld in 2006.[83] Their rise and fall might suggest that American politics essentially comprises a self-correcting, homeostatic system, one in which excessive power generates counterforces to correct it. But this appearance of equilibrium is misleading.

Each of these visible figures exercised power because of their connection to the subterranean accumulation of illegal secret powers assembled originally and principally by J. Edgar Hoover. The departure of individuals did not establish effective legal checks and balances on the deep powers behind them. The one serious congressional effort to do this, after Nixon's resignation in 1974, was successfully stymied, largely by two men (Rumsfeld and Cheney) who went on to plan successfully for the expansion and implementation of these same powers.

The second narrative illustrates the truth of the principle, well understood by America's Founding Fathers, that power, unchecked, will continue to grow like a cancer. This unchecked growth of the security state has been reinforced by a parallel and related development—the unchecked accumulation of gross wealth by the top 1 percent of the 1 percent.[84] (It has been estimated that the top 1 percent now earn 25 percent of the nation's annual income, as opposed to 9 percent in 1976. They now possess 40 percent of the nation's wealth, compared to just 7 percent for the bottom 80 percent of the nation.[85])

The combined growth of great wealth and the security state has radically diminished the powers of the public state (and above all Congress) to restore equilibrium to the American political system. This process, as many have warned, is not at all homeostatic, but threatens disaster if not brought under control.

Corresponding to these two narratives are two opposing prospects for America's future: one optimistic and one gloomy. The development of the Internet has provided new channels of communication for those concerned progressives and dissidents (including "conspiracy theorists") who are unheard in the increasingly corporatized and corrupt governing media. These in turn have supplied a growing constituency in support of those isolated and embattled whistleblowers who have arisen in virtually every agency contributing to the unchecked security state. And we have seen at least two successful bureaucratic revolts in the last decade: first in the FBI and the Justice Department against the Terrorist Surveillance Program memos inspired by Cheney, and then "the revolt of the generals" in 2006 against Donald Rumsfeld.[86]

A pessimist would respond that these developments have somewhat rationalized and heightened the powers of the security state. A rational assessment of the data assembled in this chapter gives no grounds for predicting that the checks needed for democratic checks and balances will soon emerge. If they do not, a veneer of continuity will mask the growing irrelevance of the public state's democratic institutions, leaving them to debate fruitlessly—in the same way that the Roman Senate continued to debate as the Republic slouched into Empire.

In terms of logical analysis, the likely prospect would seem to be the pessimistic one. But neither humans nor their history are wholly logical. The last century has seen a number of nonviolent changes—even revolutions—that few social scientists were able logically to predict. At their head we should list the contribution of Gandhian nonviolence to the liberation of India, one of the world's largest and most exploited nations. Since then we have seen other such contributions: to the largely nonviolent desegregation of the American South, the nonviolent transfer of power in South Africa, and the nonviolent expulsion of Soviet troops from Poland and Eastern Europe.

So it is from faith, rather than from logic, that I am committed to the optimistic prospect. I do so because of the rewards offered by that truth that, as Gandhi wrote, "is like a birth."[87] And I do so from faith, because, to quote Gandhi yet again, "Just as the body cannot exist without blood, so the soul needs matchless and pure strength of faith."[88] Those of us who are old enough have seen such leaders of faith—Gandhi, Martin Luther King, Jr., and Lech Walesa—arise to deal with what is humanly intolerable. As I suggest in the next chapter, I believe that we can see such leaders again.

CHAPTER 13

Why Americans Must End America's Self-Generating Wars

THE MOST URGENT POLITICAL CHALLENGE TO THE WORLD TODAY IS HOW TO prevent the so-called "pax Americana" from progressively degenerating, like the nineteenth-century so-called "pax Britannica" before it, into major global warfare. I say "so-called," because each "pax," in its final stages, became less and less peaceful, less and less orderly, more and more a naked imposition of belligerent, competitive power based on inequality.

To define this prevention of war as an achievable goal may sound pretentious. But the necessary steps to be taken are above all achievable here at home in America. And what is needed is not some radical and untested new policy, but a much-needed realistic reassessment and progressive scaling back of two discredited policies that are themselves new, and demonstrably counterproductive.

I am referring above all to America's so-called "war on terror." American politics, both foreign and domestic, are being increasingly deformed by a war on terrorism that is counter-productive, radically increasing the number of perpetrators and victims of terrorist attacks. It is also profoundly dishonest, in that Washington's policies actually contribute to the funding and arming of the al-Qaedists that it nominally opposes.

Above all the war on terror is a self-generating war, because, as many experts have warned, it produces more terrorists than it eliminates.[1] And it has become inextricably combined with America's earlier self-generating and hopelessly unwinnable war, the so-called War on Drugs.

The two self-generating wars have in effect become one. By launching a War on Drugs in Colombia and Mexico, America has contributed to a para-state of organized terror in Colombia (the so-called AUC) and an even bloodier reign of terror in Mexico (with over 50,000 killed in the last eight years).[2] By launching a war on terror in Afghanistan in 2001, America has contributed to a doubling of opium production there, making Afghanistan now the source of 90 percent of the world's heroin and most of the world's hashish.[3]

Americans should be aware of the overall pattern that drug production repeatedly rises where America intervenes militarily—Southeast Asia in the 1950s and 1960s, Colombia and Afghanistan since then. (Opium cultivation also increased in Iraq after the 2003 U.S. invasion.)[4] And the opposite is also true: where America ceases to intervene militarily, notably in Southeast Asia in the 1970s, drug production declines.[5]

Both of America's self-generating wars are lucrative to the private interests that lobby for their continuance.[6] At the same time, both of America's self-generating wars contribute to an increasing insecurity and destabilization in America and in the world.

Thus, by a paradoxical dialectic, America's New World Order degenerates progressively into a New World Disorder. And at home the seemingly indomitable national security state, beset by the problems of poverty, income disparity, and drugs, becomes, progressively, a national insecurity state.

The purpose of this chapter is to argue, using the analogy of British errors in the late nineteenth century, for a progressive return to a more stable and just international order, by a series of concrete steps, some of them incremental. Using the decline of Britain as an example, I hope to demonstrate that the solution cannot currently be expected from within the current party political system, but must come from people outside that system.

THE FOLLIES OF THE LATE NINETEENTH CENTURY PAX BRITANNICA

The final errors of British imperial leaders are particularly instructive for our predicament today. In both cases power in excess of defense needs led to more and more unjust expansions of influence. My remarks in the following paragraphs about Britain (as later about America) are one-sidedly negative, ignoring positive achievements abroad in the areas of health and education. But the consolidation of British power led to the impoverishment abroad of previously wealthy countries like India, and also of British workers at home.[7]

A main reason for the latter was, as Kevin Phillips has demonstrated, the increasing outward flight of British investment capital and productive capacity:

> Thus did Britain slip into circumstances akin to those of the United States in the 1980s and most of the 1990s—slumping nonsupervisory wage levels and declining basic industries on one hand, and at the other end of the scale a heyday for banks, financial services, and securities, a sharp rise in the portion of income coming from investment, and a stunning percentage of income and assets going to the top 1 percent.[8]

The dangers of increasing income and wealth disparity in Britain were easily recognized at the time, including by the young politician Winston Churchill.[9] But only a few noticed the penetrating analysis by John A. Hobson in his book

Imperialism (1902)—that an untrammeled search for profit-directed capital abroad created a demand for an oversized defense establishment to protect it, leading in turn to wider and wilder use abroad of Britain's armies. Hobson defined the imperialism of his time, which he dated from about 1870, as "a debasement . . . of genuine nationalism, by attempts to overflow its natural banks and absorb the near or distant territory of reluctant and unassimilable peoples."[10]

The earlier British empire could be described by a British historian in 1883 as having been "acquired in a fit of absence of mind," but this could not be said of Cecil Rhodes's advances in Africa. Maldistribution of wealth was an initial cause of British expansion, and also an inevitable consequence of it. Much of Hobson's book attacked Western exploitation of the Third World, especially in Africa and Asia.[11] He thus echoed Thucydides's description of how Athens was undone by the overreaching greed (*pleonexia*) of its unnecessary Sicilian expedition.[12]

Both the apogee of the British empire and the start of its decline can be dated to the 1850s. In that decade London instituted direct control over India, displacing the nakedly exploitative East India Company. But in the same decade Britain sided with France's nakedly expansionist Napoleon III (and the decadent Ottoman empire) in his ambitions against Russia's status in the Holy Land. Although Britain was victorious in that war, historians have since judged that victory to be a chief cause of the breakdown in the balance of power that had prevailed in Europe since the Congress of Vienna in 1815. Thus the legacy of the war for Britain was a more modernized and efficient army, together with a more insecure and unstable world. (Historians may in future come to judge that Obama's ventures in Libya, Syria, and Ukraine played a similar role in ending an era of U.S.-Russian détente.)[13]

The Crimean War also saw the emergence of perhaps the world's first significant antiwar movement in Britain, even though that movement is often remembered chiefly for its role in ending the active political roles of its main leaders, John Cobden and John Bright.[14] In the short run, Britain's governments and leaders moved to the right, leading (for example) to Gladstone's bombardment of Alexandria in 1882 to recover the debts owed by the Egyptians to private British investors.

Reading Hobson's economic analysis in the light of Thucydides, we can focus on the moral factor of emergent hubristic greed (*pleonexia*) fostered by unrestrained British power. In 1886 the discovery of colossal gold deposits in the nominally independent Boer Republic of the Transvaal attracted the attention of Cecil Rhodes, already wealthy from South African diamonds and mining concessions he had acquired by deceit in Matabeleland. Rhodes now saw an opportunity to acquire goldfields in the Transvaal as well, by overthrowing the Boer government with the support of the *uitlanders* or foreigners who had flocked to the Transvaal.

In 1895, after direct plotting with the *uitlanders* failed, Rhodes, in his capacity as Prime Minister of the British Cape Colony, sponsored an invasion of Transvaal with the so-called "Jameson Raid," a mixed band of Mounted Police and mercenary volunteers. The raid was not only a failure, but a scandal: Rhodes was forced to resign as Prime Minister and his brother went to jail. The details of the Jameson raid and resulting Boer War are too complex to be recounted here; but the end result was that after the Boer War the goldfields fell largely into the hands of Rhodes.

The next step in Rhodes's well-funded expansiveness was his vision of a Cape-to-Cairo railway through colonies all controlled by Britain. As we shall see in a moment, this vision provoked a competing French vision of an east-east railway, leading to the first of a series of crises from imperial competition that progressively escalated toward World War I.

According to Carroll Quigley, Rhodes also founded a secret society for the further expansion of the British empire, an offshoot of which was the Round Table that in turn generated the Royal Institute of International Affairs (RIIA). In 1917 some members of a parallel American Round Table also helped found the RIIA's sister organization, the New York–based Council on Foreign Relations (CFR).[15]

Some have found Quigley's argument overstated. But whether one agrees with him or not, one can see a continuity between the expansionist acquisitiveness of Rhodes in Africa in the 1890s and the postwar acquisitiveness of U.K. and U.S. oil corporations in the U.S.-backed coups in Iran (1953), Indonesia (1965), and Cambodia (1970).[16] In all these cases private acquisitive greed (albeit of corporations rather than an individual) led to state violence and/or war as a matter of public policy. And the outcomes enriched and strengthened private corporations in what I have called the American war machine, thus weakening those institutions representing the public interest.

My main point is that the progressive buildup of the British navy and armies provoked, predictably, a responsive buildup from other powers, particularly France and Germany; and this ultimately made World War I (and its sequel, World War II) all but inevitable. In retrospect it is easy to see that the arms buildup contributed, disastrously, not to security but to more and more perilous insecurity, dangerous not just to the imperial powers themselves, but also to the world. Because American global dominance surpasses what Britain's ever was, since the end of the Cold War we have not yet seen a comparable arms race from other states; but increasingly we are beginning to see a backlash buildup (or what the media call "terrorism") from increasingly oppressed peoples.

In retrospect one can see also that the progressive impoverishment of India and other colonies guaranteed that the empire would become progressively more unstable, and doomed in its last days to be shut down. This was not obvious at the time; and comparatively few Britons in the nineteenth century, other than Hobson, challenged the political decisions that led from the Long Depression of the 1870s to the European "Scramble for Africa," and the related arms race.[17] Yet when we look back today on these decisions, and the absurd but ominous crises they led to in distant corners of Africa like Fashoda (1898) and Agadir (1911), we have to marvel at the short-sighted and narrow stupidity of the so-called "statesmen" of that era.[18]

We also note how foolish, international crises could be initially provoked by very small, uncontrolled, bureaucratic cabals. The Fashoda incident in South Sudan involved a small troupe of 132 French officers and soldiers who had trekked for 14 months, in vain hopes of establishing a west-to-east French presence across Africa (thus breaching Rhodes's vision of a north-to-south British presence).[19] The 1911 provocative arrival (in the so-called "*Panzer-sprung*") of the German gunboat Panzer at Agadir in Morocco was the foolish brainchild of a Deputy Secretary of Foreign Affairs; its chief result was the cementing of the Anglo-French Entente Cordiale, thus contributing significantly to Germany's defeat in World War I.[20]

THE PAX AMERICANA IN THE LIGHT OF THE PAX BRITANNICA

The world is not condemned to repeat this tragedy under the Pax Americana. Global interdependence and above all communications have greatly improved. We possess the knowledge, the abilities, and the incentives to understand historical processes more skillfully than before. Above all it is increasingly evident to a global minority that American hypermilitarism, in the name of security, is becoming—much like British hypermilitarism in the nineteenth century—a threat to everyone's security, including America's, by inducing and increasingly seeking wider and wider wars.

There is one consolation for Americans in this increasing global disequilibrium. As the causes for global insecurity become more and more located in our own country, so also do the remedies. More than their British predecessors, Americans have an opportunity that other peoples do not, to diminish global tensions and move toward a more equitable global regimen. Of course one cannot predict that such a restoration can be achieved. But the disastrous end of the Pax Britannica suggests that it is necessary. For American unilateral expansionism, like Britain's before it, is now contributing to a breakdown of the understandings and international legal arrangements (notably those of the U.N. Charter) that for some decades contributed to relative stability.

It needs to be stated clearly that the American arms buildup today is the leading cause in the world of a global arms build-up—one that is ominously reminiscent of the arms race, fuelled by the British armaments industry, which led to the 1911 Agadir incident, and soon after to World War I. But today's arms buildup cannot be called an "arms race": it is so dominated by America (and its NATO allies, required by NATO policy to have compatible armaments) that the responsive arms sales of Russia and China are small by comparison:

> In 2010 . . . the United States maintained its dominating position in the global arms bazaar, signing $21.3 billion in worldwide arms sales, or 52.7 percent of all weapons deals . . . . Russia was second with $7.8 billion in arms sales in 2010, or 19.3 percent of the market, compared with $12.8 billion in 2009. Following the United States and Russia in sales were France, Britain, China, Germany and Italy.[21]

(A year later America's total dominance of overseas arms sales had increased, to represent 79 percent of global arms sales: "Overseas weapons sales by the United States totaled $66.3 billion last year, or more than three-quarters of the global arms market, valued at $85.3 billion in 2011. Russia was a distant second, with $4.8 billion in deals."[22])

And what is NATO's primary activity today requiring arms? Not defense against Russia, but support for America in its self-generating war on terror, in Afghanistan as it had been in Iraq. The war on terror should be seen for what it really is: a pretext for maintaining a dangerously oversized U.S. military, in an increasingly unstable exercise of unjust power.

In other words, America is by far the chief country flooding the world with armaments today. It is imperative that Americans force a reassessment of this incentive to global poverty and insecurity. We need to recall Eisenhower's famous warning in 1953 that "Every gun that is made, every warship launched, every rocket fired signifies, is in the final sense, a theft from those who hunger and are not fed, those who are cold and are not clothed."[23]

It is similarly worth recalling that President Kennedy, in his American University speech of June 10, 1963, called for a vision of peace that would explicitly *not* be "a Pax Americana enforced on the world by American weapons of war."[24] His vision was wise, if short-lived. After sixty years of the American security system—the so-called "pax Americana"—America itself is more and more caught up in an increasingly paranoid condition of psychological insecurity. Traditional features of American culture—such as respect for habeas corpus and international law—are being jettisoned because of a so-called "terrorist threat" that is largely of America's own making. William Arkin has written that Washington's fear has created "the very real predicament—and the danger—of a nation permanently at war."[25]

Small bureaucratic cabals in Washington have also inadvertently contributed to larger disasters. The 1998 destruction of the U.S. embassies in Kenya and Tanzania was two days after a letter from Ayman al-Zawahiri, published in a London Arab newspaper, promised retribution for the CIA's illegal kidnapping and rendition of al-Qaeda militants in Albania, resulting in their torture and killing in Egypt.[26]

The same kidnapping illustrates another risk of small cabals operating within a large bureaucracy: because of the stovepiping of their intelligence, they may end up, as in Bosnia, fighting on opposite sides. The Dutch official observer Cees Wiebes reported a decade ago that, while one CIA cabal was kidnapping al-Qaedists in the Bosnian conflict, another cabal in the Pentagon was supplying al-Qaedists there.

> Arms purchased by Iran and Turkey with the financial backing of Saudi Arabia made their way by night from the Middle East. Initially aircraft from Iran Air were used, but as the volume increased they were joined by a mysterious fleet of black C-130 Hercules aircraft. The report [by Wiebes] stresses that the US was "very closely involved" in the airlift. Mojahedin fighters were also flown in, but they were reserved as shock troops for especially hazardous operations. . . . The CIA's main opponents in Bosnia were now the mojahedin fighters and their Iranian trainers—whom the Pentagon had been helping to supply months earlier.[27]

The result aggravated a chaos profitable only to those private military corporations (PMCs), like MPRI and Blackwater, who were given contracts to deal with it.

THE COVERT U.S.-SAUDI ALLIANCE AND THE WAR ON TERROR

Of the $66.3 billion in U.S. overseas arms sales in 2011, over half, or $33.4 billion, consisted of sales to Saudi Arabia. This included dozens of Apache and Black Hawk helicopters, weapons described by *The New York Times*, as needed for defense against Iran.[28]

These Saudi arms sales are not incidental; they reflect an agreement between the two countries to offset the flow of U.S. dollars to pay for Saudi oil.[29]

The wealth of the two nations, the United States and Saudi Arabia, has become more and more interdependent. This is ironic. In the words of a leaked U.S. cable, "Saudi donors remain the chief financiers of Sunni militant groups like Al Qaeda."[30] As noted in chapter 6, the Rabita al-Alam al-Islami or Muslim World League, launched and largely funded by the Saudi royal family, has provided an international meeting place for international Salafists including some al-Qaeda leaders.[31]

In short, the wealth generated by the Saudi-American relationship is funding both the al-Qaedists of the world today and also America's self-generating war against them. The result is an incremental militarization of the world abroad and America at home, as new warfronts in the so-called "war on terror" spin off, predictably, into previously stable areas like Mali.[32]

The media tend to present the "war on terror" as a conflict between lawful governments and fanatical peace-hating Islamist fundamentalists. In fact in most countries, the United States and Britain not excepted, there is a long history of occasional collaboration with the very forces that at other times they oppose. And it is sometimes American lawlessness that has invited al-Qaeda's terrorist reaction. As previously noted, the destruction of the U.S. embassies in Kenya and Tanzania was two days after a letter from Ayman al-Zawahiri promised retribution for the CIA's illegal kidnapping and rendition of al-Qaeda militants in Albania, resulting in their torture and execution in Egypt.[33]

Today America's foreign policies and above all covert operations are increasingly lawless and chaotic. In some countries, notably Afghanistan, the United States is fighting al-Qaedists that the CIA supported in the 1980s, and that are still supported today by our nominal allies Saudi Arabia and Pakistan. In some countries, notably Libya, the United States has provided protection and indirect support to the same kind of al-Qaedists. In Kosovo, the United States helped bring al-Qaedists to power.[34]

One country where American authorities conceded its clients were supporting al-Qaedists is Yemen. As Christopher Boucek reported some years ago to the Carnegie Endowment of International Peace,

> Islamist extremism in Yemen is the result of a long and complicated set of developments. A large number of Yemeni nationals participated in the anti-Soviet jihad in Afghanistan during the 1980s. After the Soviet occupation ended, the Yemeni government encouraged its citizens to return and also permitted foreign veterans to settle in Yemen. Many of these Arab Afghans were co-opted by the regime and integrated into the state's various security apparatuses. Such co-optation was also used with individuals detained by the Yemeni government after the September 11 terrorist attacks. As early as 1993, the U.S. State Department noted in a now-declassified intelligence report that Yemen was becoming an important stop for many fighters leaving Afghanistan. The report also maintained that the Yemeni government was either unwilling or unable to curb their activities. Islamism and Islamist activists were used by the regime throughout the 1980s and 1990s to suppress domestic opponents, and during the 1994 civil war Islamists fought against southern forces.[35]

In March 2011 the same scholar, Christopher Boucek, observed that America's war on terror had resulted in the propping up of an unpopular government, thus helping it avoid needed reforms:

Our policy on Yemen has been . . . terrorism and security and al-Qaida in the Arabian Peninsula [AQAP], to the exclusion of almost everything else. I think, despite what—what people in the administration say, we have been focused on terrorism. We have not been focused on the systemic challenges that Yemen faces: unemployment, governance abuses, corruption. I think these are the things that will bring down the state. It's not AQAP. . . . everyone in Yemen sees that we're supporting the regimes, at the expense of the Yemeni people.[36]

Stated more bluntly: One major reason why Yemen (like other countries) remains backward and a fertile ground for al-Qaedist terrorism is America's war on terror itself.

America's is not the only foreign security policy contributing to the crisis in Yemen. Saudi Arabia has had a stake in reinforcing the al-Qaedist influence in republican Yemen, ever since the Saudi royal family in the 1960s used conservative hill tribes in northern Yemen to repel an attack on southern Saudi Arabia by the Nasser-backed republican Yemeni government.[37]

These machinations of governments and their intelligence agencies can create conditions of impenetrable obscurity. For example, as Sen. John Kerry has reported, one of the top leaders of al-Qaeda in the Arab Peninsula (AQAP) "is a Saudi citizen who was repatriated to Saudi Arabia from Guantanamo in November 2007 and returned to militancy [in Yemen] after completing a rehabilitation course in Saudi Arabia."[38]

Like other nations, America is no stranger to the habit of making deals with al-Qaedists, to let them fight abroad in areas of mutual interest—such as Bosnia—in exchange for not acting as terrorists at home. This practice clearly contributed to the World Trade Center bombing of 1993, when at least two of the bombers had been protected from arrest because of their participation in a Brooklyn-based program preparing Islamists for Bosnia. As noted earlier, in 1994 the FBI secured the release in Canada of a U.S.-al-Qaeda double agent at the Brooklyn Center, Ali Mohamed, who promptly went on to Kenya where (according to *The 9/11 Commission Report*) he "led" the organizers of the 1998 attack on the U.S. Embassy.[39]

SAUDI ARABIAN SUPPORT FOR TERRORISTS

Perhaps the foremost practitioner of this game is Saudi Arabia, which has not only exported al-Qaedists to all parts of the globe but (as previously noted) also has financed them, sometimes in alliance with the United States. It is estimated that Saudi Arabia has spent at least $87 billion to propagate Wahhabism abroad during two recent decades.[40] And a *New York Times* article in 2010 about leaked diplomatic cables quoted from one of the diplomatic dispatches: "Saudi donors remain the chief financiers of Sunni militant groups like Al Qaeda."[41]

Back in 2007 the London *Sunday Times* also reported that "wealthy Saudis remain the chief financiers of worldwide terror networks. 'If I could somehow snap my fingers and cut off the funding from one country, it would be Saudi Arabia,' said Stuart Levey, the U.S. Treasury official in charge of tracking terror financing."[42]

Similar reports of Saudi funding have come from authorities in Iraq, Pakistan, and Afghanistan, according to Rachel Ehrenfeld:

> Pakistani police reported in 2009 that Saudi Arabia's charities continue to fund al Qaeda, the Taliban and Pakistan's Lashkar-e-Tayyiba. The report said the Saudis gave $15 million to jihadists, including those responsible for suicide attacks in Pakistan and the death of former Pakistani Prime Minister Benazir Bhutto.
>
> In May 2010, *Buratha News Agency*, an independent news source in Iraq, reported on a leaked Saudi intelligence document showing continued Saudi governmental support for al Qaeda in Iraq [now part of the Islamic State of Iraq and al-Sham or ISIS] in the form of cash and weapons. . . . An article in the May 31, 2010, edition of *The Sunday Times* in London revealed that the Afghan financial intelligence unit, FinTRACA, reported that since 2006, at least $1.5 billion from Saudi Arabia was smuggled into Afghanistan, headed most probably to the Taliban.[43]

However the Saudi backing of al-Qaeda was not, according to the London *Sunday Times*, limited to funds:

> In recent months, Saudi religious scholars have caused consternation in Iraq and Iran by issuing *fatwas* calling for the destruction of the great Shi'ite shrines in Najaf and Karbala in Iraq, some of which have already been bombed. And while prominent members of the ruling al-Saud dynasty regularly express their abhorrence of terrorism, leading figures within the kingdom who advocate extremism are tolerated.
>
> Sheikh Saleh al-Luhaidan, the chief justice, who oversees terrorist trials, was recorded on tape in a mosque in 2004, encouraging young men to fight in Iraq. "Entering Iraq has become risky now," he cautioned. "It requires avoiding those evil satellites and those drone aircraft, which own every corner of the skies over Iraq. If someone knows that he is capable of entering Iraq in order to join the fight, and if his intention is to raise up the word of God, then he is free to do so."[44]

THE EXAMPLE OF MALI

Something similar is happening today in Africa, where Saudi Wahhabist fundamentalism "has grown in recent years in Mali with young imams returning from studying on the Arab peninsula."[45] The world press, including Al Jazeera, has reported on the destruction of historic tombs by local al-Qaedists:

> Fighters from the al-Qaeda-linked group Ansar Dine, controlling northern Mali, have destroyed two tombs at the ancient Djingareyber mud mosque in

Timbuktu, an endangered World Heritage site, witnesses say. . . . The new destruction comes after attacks last week on other historic and religious landmarks in Timbuktu that UNESCO called "wanton destruction." Ansar Dine has declared the ancient Muslim shrines "haram," or forbidden in Islam. The Djingareyber mosque is one of the most important in Timbuktu and was one of the fabled city's main attractions before the region became a no-go area for tourists. Ansar Dine has vowed to continue destroying all the shrines "without exception" amid an outpouring of grief and outrage both at home and abroad.[46]

But most of these stories (including al Jazeera's) have failed to point out that the destruction of tombs has long been a Wahhabi practice not only endorsed, but also carried out by the Saudi government:

In 1801 and 1802, the Saudi Wahhabis under Abdul Aziz ibn Muhammad ibn Saud attacked and captured the holy Muslim cities of Karbala and Najaf in Iraq, massacred parts of the Muslim population and destroyed the tombs of Husayn ibn Ali who is the grandson of Muhammad, and son of Ali (Ali bin Abu Talib), the son-in-law of Muhammad. In 1803 and 1804 the Saudis captured Makkah and Medina and destroyed historical monuments and various holy Muslim sites and shrines, such as the shrine built over the tomb of Fatimah, the daughter of Muhammad, and even intended to destroy the grave of Muhammad himself as idolatrous. In 1998 the Saudis bulldozed and poured gasoline over the grave of Aminah bint Wahb, the mother of Muhammad, causing resentment throughout the Muslim World.[47]

THE CHANCE OF PEACE AND INSECURITY, THE CHIEF IMPEDIMENT TO IT

Today one must distinguish between the Saudi Arabian Kingdom and the Wahhabism promoted by senior Saudi clerics and some members of the Saudi royal family. King Abdullah in particular has reached out to other religions, visiting the Vatican in 2007, and encouraged an interfaith conference with Christian and Jewish leaders, which took place in 2008.

In 2002 Abdullah, as Crown Prince, also submitted a proposal for Arab-Israeli peace to a summit of Arab League nations. The plan, which has been endorsed by Arab League governments on many occasions, called for normalizing relations between the entire Arab region and Israel, in exchange for a complete withdrawal from the occupied territories (including East Jerusalem) and a "just settlement" of the Palestinian refugee crisis based on UN Resolution 194. It was spurned in 2002 by Israel's Sharon and also by Bush and Cheney, who at the time were determined to go to war in Iraq. But as David Ottaway of the Woodrow Wilson Center has noted,

Abdullah's 2002 peace plan remains an intriguing possible basis for U.S.-Saudi cooperation on the Israeli-Palestinian issue. Abdullah's proposal was endorsed by the entire Arab League at its 2002 summit; Israeli President Shimon Peres and Olmert both referred to it favorably; and Barack Obama, who chose the Saudi-owned al Arabiya television station for his first interview after taking office, praised Abdullah for his "great courage" in making the peace proposal. However, the presumed new Israeli prime minister, Benjamin Netanyahu, has strongly opposed the Saudi plan, particularly the idea that East Jerusalem should be the capital of a Palestinian state.[48]

Although the plan now has less relevance, in 2009 Israeli President Shimon Peres welcomed the initiative; and George Mitchell, President Obama's special envoy to the Middle East, announced in the same year that President Barack Obama's administration intended to "incorporate" the initiative into its Middle East policy.[49]

These voices of support indicate that a peace agreement in the Middle East is theoretically possible, but by no means do they make it likely. Any peace settlement would require trust, and trust is difficult when all parties are beset by a sense of insecurity about their nations' futures. Pro-Zionist commentators like Charles Krauthammer recall that for thirty years before Camp David, the destruction of Israel was "the unanimous goal of the Arab League."[50] Many Palestinians, and most of Hamas, fear that a peace settlement would leave unsatisfied, and indeed extinguish, their demands for a just settlement of grievances.

Insecurity is particularly widespread in the Middle East because of the widespread resentment there against injustice, which insecurity both grows from and propagates. Most of the global status quo has its origins in injustice; but the injustice in the Middle East, on all sides, is extreme, recent, and ongoing. I say this only to remind Americans that the issues of security and justice cannot be separated.

Above all compassion is needed. We as Americans must understand that both Israelis and Palestinians live in conditions not remote from a state of war; yet both have reason to fear that a peace settlement might leave them even worse off than in their present uncomfortable situation. Too many innocent civilians have been killed in the Middle East. American actions should not increase that number.

This sense of insecurity, the major impediment to peace, is not confined to the Middle East. Since 9/11 Americans have experienced the anguish of insecurity, and this is the major reason why there is so little American resistance to the manifest follies of the Bush-Cheney-Obama Global War on Terror (GWOT).[51]

The war on terror promised to make America more secure, yet as practiced it continues to guarantee the proliferation of America's terrorist enemies. It also continues to disseminate the war into new battlefields, notably Pakistan,

Yemen, Somalia, Mali, and now Kenya. By thus creating its own enemies, the war on terror, now solidly entrenched in bureaucratic inertia, seems likely to continue unabated until it is changed. In this it is much like the equally ill-considered War on Drugs, dedicated to maintaining the high drug costs and drug profits that attract new traffickers.

Above all this contributes to Islamic insecurity as well, causing more and more Muslims to deal with the fear that civilians, not just al-Qaedist terrorists, will be the victims of drone attacks. Insecurity in the Middle East is the major obstacle to peace there. Palestinians live in daily fear of oppression by West Bank settlers and retaliation by the Israeli state. The Israelis live in constant fear of hostile neighbors. So does the Saudi royal family. Insecurity and instability have increased together since 9/11 and the war on terror.

Middle Eastern insecurity replicates itself on a wider and wider scale. Israeli fear of Iran and Hizbollah is matched by Iranian fear of Israeli threats of massive attacks on its nuclear installations. For this reason Zbigniew Brzezinski, a former U.S. hawk, warned in 2012 that an Israeli attack on Iran could lead to a longer war that spread elsewhere.[52]

Above all, in my opinion, Americans should fear the insecurity caused by drone attacks. If not soon stopped, America's drone attacks threaten to do what America's atomic attacks did in 1945: lead to a world in which many powers, not just one, possess this weapon and may possibly use it. In this case the most likely new target by far would be the United States.

How long will it be, I wonder, before a prevailable force of Americans will recognize the predictable course of this self-generating war, and mobilize against it?

WHAT IS TO BE DONE?

As stated above, the purpose of this chapter is to argue, using the analogy of British errors in the late nineteenth century, for a progressive return, on both the official and popular level, to a more stable and just international order, by the following series of concrete steps, some of them incremental:

1. Immediately repeal The Authorization for Use of Military Force (AUMF), Pub. L. 107–40, codified at 115 Stat. 224, passed by the United States Congress on September 14, 2001, and signed into law by President Bush four days later. Because AUMF authorized military force only against targets responsible for 9/11, some have called for a new resolution expanding its scope; but others have pointed to the counterproductivity of expanding the militarization of U.S. foreign policy.[53]
2. Much of the recent intensification of American militarism can be traced to the "state of emergency" proclaimed on September 14, 2001, and renewed annually by American presidents ever since. We need an immediate

termination of this state of emergency, and a reassessment of all the so-called "continuity of government" (COG) measures associated with it—warrant-less surveillance, warrantless detention, and the militarization of domestic American security.[54]

3. Progressively phase-out the violent aspects of the so-called "war on terror," while retaining traditional law enforcement means for dealing with terror-ists.

4. Progressively reduce America's bloated military and intelligence budgets, over and above that already contemplated for financial reasons.

5. Return to strategies for dealing with the problem of terrorists that rely pri-marily on civilian policing and intelligence.

Forty years ago I would have appealed to Congress to take these steps to defuse the state of paranoia we are living under. But I have come to see that today's Congress itself is dominated by the deep state powers that profit from what I have called "America's global war machine." The so-called "statesmen" of America are as dedicated to the preservation of American dominance as were their British predecessors.

But to say this is not to despair of America's ability to change direction. We should keep in mind that four decades ago domestic political protest played a critical role in helping to end an unjustified war in Vietnam. It is true that in 2003 similar protests—involving one million Americans—failed to impede America's entry into an unjustified war in Iraq. Nevertheless, the large num-ber of protesters, assembled under relatively short notice, was impressive. The question is whether protesters can adapt their tactics to new realities.

A healthy nation requires protest. Imagine for a moment that the post-9/11 products of COG, including warrantless surveillance of the entire American people, had operated with equal efficiency in the 1960s and 1970s. America would not have had a powerful antiwar movement; and America might still be fighting in Southeast Asia, much as Russia, since the time of Tolstoy, has been mired in an unwinnable war in the Caucasus. Few today would deny that America was well served to get rid of the Vietnam War; even Mobil, which had lobbied for that war, today has access to Vietnam's offshore oil that it had coveted all along.[55]

But under the guise of Continuity of Government planning, the American war machine has been preparing for forty years to neutralize street antiwar protests.[56] Taking cognizance of this, and using the folly of British hyper-militarism as an example, today's antiwar movement must learn how to apply coordinated pressure within American institutions—not just by "occupying" the streets with the aid of the homeless. It is not enough simply to denounce, as did Churchill in 1908, the increasing disparity of wealth between rich and poor. One must go beyond this to see the origins of this disparity in dysfunctional policies that can be changed. And one of the chief of these is the so-called "war on terror."

The Occupy Movement, which attracted many fine people with energy and enthusiasm, was in my opinion destined never to be a prevailable force in this country. Its amorphousness and lack of leadership guaranteed that it would remain a marginal movement, for it tolerated among its members a few whose violent tactics assured that Occupy would never win the hearts and minds of enough Americans to make a difference.

In my opinion Occupy was a learning experience: one that taught how necessary is disciplined nonviolence to any popular movement that will successfully challenge top-down government. For that discipline there must be leaders; and though leadership at any level of society requires vigilant watching, it is necessary. One has only to look at the rapid erosion of the non-violent civil rights movement after the murder of Martin Luther King, Jr.

No one can predict the success of a new nonviolent movement. But I believe that global developments will persuade more and more Americans that one is necessary. It could and should appeal to a broad spectrum of the American electorate, from the viewers of Democracy Now on the left to the libertarian followers of Murray Rothbard, Ron Paul and Lew Rockwell on the right.

And I believe also that a well-coordinated nonviolent antiwar minority—of from two to five million, acting with the resources of truth and common sense on their side—can win. America's core political institutions are at present both dysfunctional and unpopular: Congress in particular has an approval rating of less than 10 percent. A more serious problem is the determined resistance of corporate and personal wealth to reasonable reforms; but the more nakedly wealth shows its undemocratic influence, the more evident will become the need to organize against it. Currently much wealth has targeted for removal Congress members who have been guilty of compromise to solve government problems. Surely there is an American majority out there to be mobilized for a return to common sense.

Clearly new strategies and techniques of protest will be needed. It is not the purpose here to define them, but I predict that future protests—or cyberprotests—will require more skillful use of the Internet. That is why the revelations of Edward Snowden are so significant: they reveal how the great new hope for a global civil society—the Internet—is being co-opted while few noticed.

I repeat that one cannot be confident of victory in the struggle for sanity against special interests and ignorant ideologues. But with the increasing danger of a calamitous international conflict, the need to mobilize for sanity is increasingly clear. The study of history is one of the most effective ways to avoid repeating it.

Are these hopes for protest mere wishful thinking? Very possibly. But, wishful or not, I consider them to be necessary.

Greek Theater

Mario Savio and the Socratic Quest

> But in changing the city's desires instead of complying with them . . .
> that is the only business of a good citizen.
>
> —Plato, *Gorgias* 517 B-C

It has taken weeks
        of unsettled half-awareness
    for me to recognize

the student wrestled to the ground   *Cohen Freedom's Orator 213*
        by six policemen in uniforms
    a baton menacing his neck and tie

(an arm across his throat
        to keep him from speaking)   *San Francisco Chronicle December 9 1964*
    on the cover of this book   *Rosenfeld Subversives*

about how J. Edgar Hoover
        slipped lies to the *San Francisco Examiner*
    advancing the career of Ronald Reagan   *Rosenfeld Subversives 212, 227*

is Mario Savio   *leader of Berkeley Free Speech Movement*
        on the stage of the Greek Theater   *December 7 1964; Rosenfeld*
    wrecking the well-planned closure   *Subversives 224*

of the assembly called to proclaim
        an end to the protests and sit-ins
    of the Free Speech Movement

and the inauguration
        of a *new era of freedom under law*   *Rosenfeld Subversives 223*
        by an ambitious professor   *Cohen Freedom's Orator 213–14*

hoping thereby to become
        our next Chancellor
        who defended the war on national TV

and is now less googled
        than his daughter a language poet   *Leslie Scalapino*
        The anticlimax when Mario

came back out only to announce
        there would be a Free Speech rally   *Cohen Freedom's Orator 213–14*
        on the Sproul Hall steps   *Rosenfeld Subversives 224*

up-ended my own planned life
        I was just a few yards away
        at the same camera angle

one of those who had urged
        the students to trust
        the decency of those in power

my head then filled with Anglo-Latin
        verse from the ninth century
        why the return of a cuckoo in spring

spoke to the heart
        expressing aspirations of friendship
        more deeply than Virgil could   *Scott Alcuin's Versus de Cuculo*

and did more to invent Europe
        at a higher level—
    Christianus sum   *I am a Christian*

non possum militare—   *I cannot make war*   *Acta Maximiliani 1.3*
        than the battle stopping the Moors
        on the banks of the Loire

two different kinds of power *Douglass Gandhi and the Unspeakable 25*
    βία the *power of dominance* *violence Arendt 93*
    versus πείθειν the power of persuasion *Schell Unconquerable World 218*

the cop who thanked Howard Zinn
    for his talk to the Police Academy
    then pleaded with him desperately

to please leave the antiwar blockade
    before a little later
    battering him with an outsized club *Ellsberg*

versus Mario inspiring the crowd
    to immobilize the campus police car
    till Jack Weinberg inside it was released *Cohen Freedom's Orator 98–12*

the power to transcend enmity
    as I had seen in an iconic moment
    alone reading Plato's *Gorgias*

in the Ambassador's huge bed
    when I was *chargé d'affaires* in Warsaw— *stand-in for absent*
    that the way to change the world *ambassador*

was not through international treaties
    but through *changing the city's desires* *Plato Gorgias 503–21*
    the power of persuasion

versus that of the nightstick
    or even the diplomatic service
    with all its tempting frills—

the cook the chauffeur   that flag up ahead on the limo
    the house party up the Hudson
    where baffled ducks were released

for the half-drunk guests to shoot
    the sit-down banquet at Schönbrunn *Vienna Imperial Palace*
    for six hundred people

served by liveried footmen—
    which I willingly abandoned
    so I could teach in a university

the heritage of the *Patrologia Latina*
      which I had skimmed so greedily
   my first semester back

and then Dante   *la mala condotta*   *misguidance*
      è la cagion che'l mondo ha fatto reo   *is why the world goes wrong*
      e non natura che'n voi sia corrotta   *and not your nature that is corrupt*
                                      Dante Purgatorio 16:103–05

Well—little could I foresee
      how Mario in an instant
   (who himself had been inspired

by *the plays of Sophocles*
      and Aeschylus and Euripides   *Cohen Freedom's Orator 35*
   before being beaten in Mississippi

for walking in public with a black man
      as part of Freedom Summer)   *Cohen Freedom's Orator 59–60*
   had changed me from a Latinist

into an activist
      no longer a mere spectator
   (as I had been five days earlier

when the students filed into Sproul Hall
      singing *We shall overcome*)   *December 2 1964; Rosenfeld 216–22*
   that same evening I spoke   *Scott Charlie Sellers 1*

at the crisis faculty meeting   *Cohen Freedom's Orator 214–15*
      and only one month later
   my first public appeal

to get troops out of Vietnam
      which though I could not know it
   would soon bring a painful end

to my evenings with Milosz
      debating the right English
   for *what is poetry*

that does not save
      nations or peoples?   *Milosz New Collected Poems 78*
     a heartbreaking loss at the time   *Haven An Invisible Rope 69*

but not one that deterred me
      as much as the crazy violence
     that developed after Mario

moved away from leadership   *Cohen Freedom's Orator 253*
      not wanting the Movement
     to become too dependent on him   *Cohen Freedom's Orator 237–38*

in the dramatic struggle between
      two kinds of decency
     one struggling for an end

to racial hiring
      in the local supermarkets   *Rosenfeld Subversives 176–77*
     one that of the U.S. middle class

who did not want their kids dropping acid
      or cursing *Amerikkka*   *Ruether America Amerikkka*
     and so when given a chance

voted for Ronald Reagan
      the great persuader   *Broder Washington Post 6/7/04*
     while Richard Aoki

as a paid FBI informant
      armed the Black Panthers   *Rosenfeld Subversives 418–19, 421*
     But Mario returned in the 1980s

and revived a dormant campus
      changing the city's desires   *Plato Gorgias 517 B-C*
     with his *use of philosophy*

Socrates and Thoreau   *Cohen Freedom's Orator 202*
      when he spoke of shifting *our values*
     for an America *less dominated*

by production for war
  and more *by human needs*   *Cohen Freedom's Orator 280, 348*
  inspiring—yes!—even faculty like myself

to monitor a divestment protest
  in support of the South African resistance *Rosenfeld Subversives 501*
  with white armbands torn from a sheet in our basement

all helping to stoke *a nationwide demonstration* *New York Times 4/17/85*
  till finally the UC Regents
  divested $3 billion in funds   *Skelton Los Angeles Times 12/11/13*

so that—I do believe—
  Mario helped contribute
  to the liberation of South Africa

Mandela himself credited California
  with helping push his country
  toward racial integration   *Skelton Los Angeles Times 12/11/13*

Truth-force as history! Oh John Searle   *Satyagraha*
  you recognized in your student Mario's speeches
  a kind of freshness combined

with *a certain deep intellectual vision* *Cohen Freedom's Orator 189*
  but when you later came to see the movement
  as a bunch of *losers*   *Cohen Freedom's Orator 317*

with *unreasonable expectations*   *Searle Interview 5*
  you were resuming your distinguished career
  as an academic philosopher

while it was Mario
  at what you called a *second-rate* university *Cohen Freedom's Orator*
  who remained on the *straight path*

of the Socratic quest
  to change by persuasion
  our misguided world

curbing the authority of *violence*
>by appealing to those hints of freedom
>encoded in our DNA

that truth-force enabling a movement
>to overcome *the machine*
>*so odious*

you've got to make it stop   Cohen Freedom's Orator 183, 458–59

GREEK THEATER BIBLIOGRAPHY

Acta Maximiliani, ed. H. Musurillo. *The Acts of the Christian Martyrs*. Oxford: Clarendon Press, 1972.

Arendt, Hannah. *Between Past and Future: Eight Exercises in Political Thought*. New York: Penguin Books, 1993.

Broder, David S. "The Great Persuader." *Washington Post*, June 7, 2004. http://www.washingtonpost.com/wp-dyn/articles/A21076-2004Jun6.html.

Cohen, Robert. *Freedom's Orator: Mario Savio and the Radical Legacy of the 1960s*. New York: Oxford University Press, 2009.

Douglass, James W. *Gandhi and the Unspeakable: His Final Experiment with Truth*. Maryknoll, NY: Orbis Books, 2012.

Ellsberg, Daniel. "A Memory of Howard Zinn." AntiWar.com, January 27, 2010. http://antiwar.com/blog/2010/01/27/a-memory-of-howard-zinn/.

Gleason, Ralph J. "The Tragedy at The Greek Theater." *San Francisco Chronicle*, December 9, 1964. http://www.fsm-a.org/stacks/R_Gleason.html.

Haven, Cynthia, ed. *An Invisible Rope: Portraits of Czeslaw Milosz*. Athens: Ohio University Press, 2011. Contains Peter Dale Scott, "A Difficult, Inspirational Giant," 65–73.

New York Times, April 17, 1985. http://www.nytimes.com/1985/04/17/us/15-arrested-on-berkeley-campus-in-protest-on-south-africa-policy.html.

Rosenfeld, Seth. *Subversives: The FBI's War on Student Radicals, and Reagan's Rise to Power*. New York: Farrar, Straus and Giroux, 2012.

Ruether, Rosemary Radford. *America, Amerikkka: Elect Nation and Imperial Violence*. Oakville, CT: Equinox, 2007.

Schell, Jonathan. *The Unconquerable World: Power, Nonviolence, and the Will of the People*. New York: Metropolitan Books, 2003.

Scott, Peter Dale. "Alcuin's *Versus de Cuculo*: The Vision of Pastoral Friendship." *Studies in Philology*, 62 no. 4 (July 1965), 510–30. http://www.enotes.com/alcuin-essays/alcuin/peter-dale-scott-essay-date-july-1965.

Scott, Peter Dale. "Charlie Sellers at Berkeley." A Tribute at the Charles G. Sellers 90th Birthday Symposium, Berkeley, CA, September 7, 2013. http://nature.berkeley.edu/~c-merchant/Sellers/tributes/1.pdf.

John Searle Interview. Conversations with History, Institute of International Studies, University of California, Berkeley. http://globetrotter.berkeley.edu/people/Searle/searle-con5.html.

Skelton, George. "Leading the Way to Justice in South Africa." *Los Angeles Times*, December 11, 2013. http://articles.latimes.com/2013/dec/11/local/la-me-cap-mandela-20131212.

Notes

1. THE DOOMSDAY PROJECT, DEEP EVENTS, AND THE SHRINKING OF AMERICAN DEMOCRACY

1. "'America as the No. 1 Warmonger': President Jimmy Carter Talks to Salon about Race, Cable News, 'Slut-Shaming' and More," Salon, April 10, 2014, http://www.salon.com/2014/04/10/america_as_the_no_1_warmonger_president_jimmy_carter_talks_to_salon_about_race_cable_news_slut_shaming_and_more/.

2. Chalmers Johnson, *Blowback: The Costs and Consequences of American Empire* (New York: Henry Holt, 2000), 217. Cf. Chalmers Johnson, *The Sorrows of Empire: Militarism, Secrecy and the End of the Republic* (New York: Metropolitan Books, 2004).

3. Michael Lind, *Made in Texas: George W. Bush and the Southern Takeover of American Politics* (New York: Basic Books, 2003), 143.

4. Hannah Arendt, *Between Past and Future: Eight Exercises in Political Thought* (New York: Penguin Books, 1993), 93.

5. Hannah Arendt, *Crises of the Republic: Lying in Politics, Civil Disobedience, On Violence, Thoughts on Politics and Revolution* (New York: Harcourt Brace, 1972), 155. Cf. Jonathan Schell, *The Unconquerable World: Power, Nonviolence, and the Will of the People* (New York: Metropolitan Books/Henry Holt, 2003), 218. Arendt also writes of "top down" and "bottom up" power, but this distinction is not quite the same. There can also be top-down, one-sided persuasive power, from Plato's philosopher king to FDR's fireside chats (James MacGregor Burns, *Leadership* [New York: Harper & Row, 1978]). This is on the surface nonviolent. But in recent years we have seen covert CIA and Pentagon intervention in the fields of culture and especially mass culture (Frances Stonor Saunders, *The Cultural Cold War: The CIA and the World of Arts and Letters* [New York: New Press, 1999]; Matthew Alford, *Reel Power: Hollywood Cinema and American Supremacy* [London: Pluto Press, 2010]). One result has been a Hollywood propaganda of violence that has contributed to the propagation of nonstate violence on an unfamiliar scale (Alford, *Reel Power; The Act of Killing*, directed by Joshua Oppenheimer [2012 documentary film, Drafthouse Films]). To discuss the deep state and cultural deep politics would require another book.

6. Samuel P. Huntington, *American Politics: The Promise of Disharmony* (Cambridge, MA: Belknap Press, 1981), 75.

7. Peter Dale Scott, *The Road to 9/11: Wealth, Empire, and the Future of America* (Berkeley: University of California Press, 2007), 267.

8. Grant Barrett, "A Wordnado of Words in 2013," *New York Times*, December 21, 2013, http://www.nytimes.com/2013/12/22/opinion/sunday/a-wordnado-of-words-in-2013.html.

9. Cf. Schell, *The Unconquerable World*, 227–31.

10. Kevin Phillips, *Wealth and Democracy: A Political History of the American Rich* (New York: Broadway Books, 2002), 171–200.

11. Carl A. Huffman, *Archytas of Tarentum: Pythagorean, Philosopher, and Mathematician King* (Cambridge: Cambridge University Press, 2005), 207: "In Diodotus' speech in the Mytilenian debate, wealth is particularly identified as producing arrogant 'overreaching' (*pleonexia*—III.45.4). Thus *pleonexia* seems to be associated with the abuse of power by either a tyrant or a wealthy oligarchy."

12. Paul M. Kennedy, *The Rise and Fall of the Great Powers* (New York: Random House, 1987); Phillips, *Wealth and Democracy*; Johnson, *The Sorrows of Empire*.

13. Scott, *The Road to 9/11*, xiv–xv; Peter Dale Scott, "Atrocity and its Discontents: U.S. Double-Mindedness About Massacre," in Adam Jones, ed., *Genocide, War Crimes and the West: Ending the Culture of Impunity* (London: Zed Press, 2004), 146–63.

14. Johnson, *Blowback*, 221.

15. Peter Dale Scott, *American War Machine: Deep Politics, the CIA Global Drug Connection, and the Road to Afghanistan* (Lanham, MD: Rowman & Littlefield, 2010), 63–142, 239–53. The Karzai regime in Afghanistan is only the latest of CIA client governments to struggle to maintain itself with support from drug traffickers. Cf. Peter Dale Scott, "Can the US Pacify the Drug-Addicted War in Afghanistan? Opium, the CIA and the Karzai Administration," The Asia-Pacific Journal: Japan Focus, April 5, 2010, http://japanfocus.org/-Peter_Dale-Scott/3340; Ryan Grim, "Karzai Releasing Scores of Drug Traffickers in Afghanistan, WikiLeaks Cables Show," *Huffington Post*, December 31, 2010, http://www.huffingtonpost.com/2010/12/27/karzai-releasing-drug-tra_n_801587.html.

16. Tim McGurk, *Time*, August 2, 2004; cf. *USA Today*, October 26, 2004.

17. James Risen, *New York Times*, December 11, 2010. Both traffickers were ultimately arrested by DEA officials: Noorzai in 2005, and Khan in 2008. The United States probably came to prefer Khan over Noorzai, because he was more closely allied to Ahmed Wali Karzai, another drug trafficker and CIA asset, as well as a central figure in the power apparatus of his brother Hamid Karzai, the U.S. client president of Afghanistan.

18. *Time*, November 29, 1993; Scott, *American War Machine*, 14–15.

19. It is too early to report the ultimate fate of Noorzai and Khan after their arrest and indictment by the United States. But it is clear that Guillén Davila's arrest and indictment never led to conviction or imprisonment. On the contrary, he appears to have continued to enjoy CIA favor in Venezuela (Scott, *American War Machine*, 14–15).

20. See chapter 4; also Peter Dale Scott, *The Road to 9/11: Wealth, Empire, and the Future of America* (Berkeley: University of California Press, 2007), 152–58.

21. "D.E.A. Deployed Mumbai Plotter Despite Warning," *New York Times*, November 8, 2009; cf. Scott, *American War Machine*, 246–47. Elsewhere I will develop the thesis that what I call "surplus repressive power"—power developed exclusively by one society for the repressive dominance of others—is doomed, in this and other ways, to encourage the proliferation of its enemies. My point here is a more modest and general one.

22. For details, see Peter Dale Scott, *The War Conspiracy: JFK, 9/11, and the Deep Politics of War* (New York: Skyhorse Publishing, 2013), 368–72.

23. Cf. Peter Dale Scott, "Atrocity and its Discontents: U.S. Double-Mindedness About Massacre," in Adam Jones, ed., *Genocide, War Crimes and the West: Ending the Culture of Impunity* (London: Zed Press, 2004), 146–63.

24. Oliver North Testimony, Iran-Contra Committee, July 7, 1987; quoted in Lou Dubose and Jake Bernstein, *Vice: Dick Cheney and the Hijacking of the American Presidency* (New York: Random House, 2006), 75.

25. Ron Ridenhour with Arthur Lubow, "Bringing the War Home," *New Times*, November 28, 1975; Dave Lindorff, "Planning for Martial Law?" Salon, March 15, 2002, http://dir.salon.com/story/news/feature/2002/03/15/martial_law/index.html.

26. "Brigade homeland tours start Oct. 1," *Army Times*, September 30, 2008, http://www.armytimes.com/article/20080930/NEWS/809300331/Brigade-homeland-tours-start-Oct-1.

27. Scott, *Road to 9/11*, 241–42.

28. Peter Dale Scott, *Deep Politics and the Death of JFK* (Berkeley: University of California Press, 1998), 24–37; *The War Conspiracy*, 285–333; James Galbraith, "Exit Strategy: In 1963, JFK Ordered a Complete Withdrawal from Vietnam," *Boston Review*, October/November 2003, http://new.bostonreview.net/BR28.5/galbraith.html.

2. THE DEEP STATE, THE WALL STREET OVERWORLD, AND BIG OIL

1. "Competition in the Energy Industry": Hearings Before the Subcommittee on Antitrust and Monopoly of the Senate Committee on the Judiciary, Ninety-third Congress, First Session, June 8, 1973 (Washington, DC: U.S. Government Printing Office, 1974).

2. Steve Coll, *Private Empire: ExxonMobil and American Power* (New York: Penguin Press, 2012), 19–20.

3. Dana Priest and William Arkin, *Top Secret America: The Rise of the New American Security State* (New York: Little Brown, 2011), 52.

4. For example, Marc Ambinder and D. G. Grady, *Deep State: Inside the Government Secrecy Industry* (New York: Wiley, 2013); cf. John Tirman, "The Quiet Coup: No, Not Egypt. Here," HuffingtonPost, July 9, 2013, http://www.huffingtonpost.com/john-tirman/nsa-deep-state_b_3569316.html: "Now we know: the United States of America is partially governed by a deep state, undemocratic, secret, aligned with intelligence agencies, spying on friend and foe, lawless in almost every respect."

5. Mike Lofgren, "A Shadow Government Controls America," Reader Supported News, February 22, 2014, http://readersupportednews.org/opinion2/277-75/22216-a-shadow-government-controls.

6. Peter Dale Scott, *Deep Politics and the Death of JFK* (Berkeley: University of California Press, 1998), 7.

7. "Tom Hayden on Venezuela's Current Crisis," *Tikkun*, February 25, 2014, http://www.tikkun.org/tikkundaily/2014/02/28/tom-hayden-on-venezuelas-current-crisis/.

8. Henry Fairlie, "Political Commentary," *The Spectator*, September 23, 1955. Cf. Henry Fairlie, "Evolution of a Term," *New Yorker*, October 19, 1968. The notion of a Wall Street establishment was developed by Carroll Quigley, notably in *Tragedy and Hope: A History of the World in Our Time* (New York: Macmillan, 1966).

9. C. Wright Mills, *The Power Elite* (New York: Oxford University Press, 1956). The deep state, consisting of those whose powers can transcend and override public power, would not include many of Mills's corporate managers, the military, and politicians.

10. C. Wright Mills, *The Causes of World War Three* (London: Secker & Warburg, 1958), 37.

11. David Wise and Thomas B. Ross, *The Invisible Government* (New York: Random House, 1964).

12. To take a single telling example, six of Sam Walton's heirs are now reportedly wealthier than the bottom 30 percent of Americans, or 94.5 million people (Tim Worstall, "Six Waltons Have More Wealth Than the Bottom 30% of Americans," *Forbes*, December 14, 2011, www.forbes.com/sites/timworstall/2011/12/14/six-waltons-have-more-wealth-than-the-bottom-30-of-americans/). Cf. the devastating picture of a disintegrating America in George Packer, *The Unwinding: An Inner History of the New America* (New York: Farrar, Straus and Giroux, 2013).

13. See Kevin Phillips, *The Politics of Rich and Poor: Wealth and the American Electorate in the Reagan Aftermath* (New York: HarperCollins, 1991). Cf. John T. Stinson, *The Reagan Legacy* (Bloomington, IN: iUniverse, 2009), 146; Timothy Noah, *The Great Divergence: America's Growing Inequality Crisis and What We Can Do about It* (New York: Bloomsbury Press, 2012).

14. For the impact of railroads on expanded social awareness, see Benedict Anderson, *Imagined Communities: Reflections on the Origin and Spread of Nationalism* (London: Verso, 1991).

15. "What Is the Deep State?," On Religion, July 4, 2013, http://www.onreligion.co.uk/what-is-the-deep-state/.

16. Gareth Jenkins, "Susurluk and the Legacy of Turkey's Dirty War," *Terrorism Monitor*, May 1, 2008; quoted in Peter Dale Scott, "9/11, Deep State Violence and the Hope of Internet Politics," Global Research, June 11, 2008, http://www.globalresearch.ca/9-11-deep-state-violence-and-the-hope-of-internet-politics.

   For the Susurluk incident, see also Peter Dale Scott, *American War Machine: Deep Politics, the CIA Global Drug Connection, and the Road to Afghanistan* (Lanham, MD: Rowman & Littlefield, 2010), 19–20, etc.

17. Scott, *Deep Politics and the Death of JFK*, xi–xii.

18. Lofgren, "A Shadow Government Controls America."

19. Quoted in Peter Dale Scott, *The Road to 9/11: Wealth, Empire, and the Future of America* (Berkeley: University of California Press, 2007), 1. A year later Senator Gerald Nye, a Republican, presided over a series of influential hearings into munitions companies and banks, after which Senator Nye commented that it was "altogether fair to say that these bankers [referring to the "house of Morgan"] were in the heart and center of a system that made our going to war inevitable" ("Nye Denies Inquiry 'Cleared' Morgan," *New York Times*, February 10, 1936, quoted in Oliver Stone and Peter Kuznick, *The Untold History of the United States* [New York: Gallery Books, 2012], 76).

20. *Forbes* magazine founder Bertie Charles Forbes wrote six years later, "Picture a party of the nation's greatest bankers stealing out of New York on a private railroad car under cover of darkness, stealthily riding hundred[s] of miles South, embarking on a mysterious launch, sneaking onto an island [the appropriately named Jekyll Island] deserted by all but a few servants, living there a full week under such rigid secrecy that the names of not one of them was once mentioned, lest the servants learn the identity and disclose to the world this strangest, most secret expedition in the history of American finance. I am not romancing; I am giving to the world, for the first time, the real story of how the famous Aldrich currency report, the foundation of our new currency system, was written (B. C. Forbes, *Leslie's Weekly*, October 19, 1916, quoted in T. Cushing Daniel, *Real Money Versus False Money—Bank Credits; The Most Important Factor in Civilization and Least Understood by the People* [Washington, DC: The Monetary Educational Bureau, 1924], 169. Cf. B. C. Forbes, *Men Who Are Making America* [New York: Forbes Publishing Co., 1922], 398; cf. G. Edward Griffin, *The Creature from Jekyll Island: A Second Look at the Federal Reserve* [Westlake Village, CA: American Media, 1994]).

    Paul Warburg later wrote that "Though eighteen years have since gone by, I do not feel free to give a description of this most interesting conference, concerning which Senator Aldrich pledged all participants to secrecy" (Paul Warburg, *The Federal Reserve System: Its Origin and Growth* [New York, Macmillan, 1930], 128).

21. Congress was persuaded to provide perfunctory support of the bailout, under an alleged mysterious threat of martial law. See Peter Dale Scott, "Martial Law, the Financial Bailout, and War," Global Research, January 8, 2009, http://www.glob alresearch.ca/index.php?context=va&aid=11681, and reprinted in Michel Chossudovsky and Andrew Gavin Marshall, eds., *The Global Economic Crisis: The Great Depression of the XXI Century* (Montreal: Global Research Publishers, 2010), 219–40; Llewellyn H. Rockwell, Jr., "Sen. Inhofe: [Henry] Paulsen [Secretary of the Treasury and former Chief Executive Officer of Goldman Sachs] Threatened Martial Law To Pass Bailout," LewRockwell.com, November 20, 2008, http://www.lewrockwell.com/lrc-blog/sen-inhofe-paulsen-threatened-martial-law-to-pass-bailout/.

22. Richard Helms, with William Hood, *A Look Over My Shoulder: A Life in the Central Intelligence Agency* (New York: Random House, 2003), 82–83. Cf. Scott, *American War Machine*, 26–28.

23. Laurence H. Shoup and William Minter, *Imperial Brain Trust: The Council on Foreign Relations and United States Foreign Policy* (New York: Monthly Review Press, 1977), 195–99.

24. Gordon Thomas, *Secret Wars: One Hundred Years of British Intelligence Inside MI5 and MI6* (New York: Thomas Dunne Books/ St. Martin's Press, 2009), 98. This may have occurred during Dulles's visit to Europe in the spring of 1947 (James Srodes, *Allen Dulles: Master of Spies* [Washington, DC: Henry Regnery, 1999], 392).

25. Richard Aldrich, *The Hidden Hand: Britain, America, and Cold War Secret Intelligence* (Woodstock, NY: Overlook Press, 2001), 343. Dulles also chaired the executive committee of the companion National Committee for a Free Europe (behind the Iron Curtain), whose legal affairs were handled by Sullivan and Cromwell (Wilson D. Miscamble, *George F. Kennan and the Making of American Foreign Policy, 1947–1950* [Princeton, NJ: Princeton University Press, 1992], 204).

26. Amy B. Zegart, *Flawed by Design: The Evolution of the CIA, JCS, and NSC* (Stanford, CA: Stanford University Press, 1999), 189; citing Christopher Andrew, *For the President's Eyes Only* (New York: HarperCollins, 1995), 172. See also Senate Select Committee to Study Governmental Operations with Respect to Intelligence Activities [Church Committee], *Final Report: Book IV—Supplementary Detailed Staff Reports on Foreign and Military Intelligence* (Washington, DC: U.S. Government Printing Office, 1976), 28–29.

27. David Wise and Thomas B. Ross, *The Espionage Establishment* (New York: Random House, 1967), 166; Scott, *Road to 9/11*, 13.

28. "In January 1946 Dulles outlined in some detail a reconstruction plan that is one of the earliest notions of what would, a year later, be known as the Marshall Plan" (Srodes, *Allen Dulles: Master of Spies*, 374).

29. Tim Weiner, *Legacy of Ashes: The History of the CIA* (New York: Doubleday, 2007), 28. Cf. Daniel J. Leab, *Orwell Subverted: The CIA and the Filming of Animal Farm* (University Park: Pennsylvania State University Press, 2007), 18:

> For each dollar in aid received, as a top ECA administrator later explained, "the recipient had to contribute an equal amount in local currency, 95% would be used for Marshall Plan programs, and 5% (the counterpart of the dollars provided) would be used by the U.S. government." . . . That 5 percent has been estimated to be close to $200 million a year, much of which Wisner appropriated for OPC.

30. Douglas Valentine, "The French Connection Revisited: The CIA, Irving Brown, and Drug Smuggling as Political Warfare," *Covert Action Quarterly*, http://www.covertaction.org/content/view/99/75/.

31. Norbert Schlei, "Japan's 'M-Fund' Memorandum, January 7, 1991," JPRI [Japan Policy Research Institute] Working Paper No. 11: July 1995, http://www.jpri.org/publications/workingpapers/wp11.html: "Incident to the revision of the Security Treaty [in 1960], Vice President Nixon agreed to turn over exclusive control of the M-Fund to Japan. It has been alleged that this action by Nixon was part of a corrupt political bargain, whereby it was agreed that if Japan would assist him to

become President of the United States, Nixon would agree to release control of the Fund to Japan and, if he became President, would return Okinawa to Japan."

32. "C.I.A. Spent Millions to Support Japanese Right in 50's and 60's," *New York Times*, October 9, 1994. Cf. Scott, *American War Machine*, 93–94, 298–99, citing Chalmers Johnson, "The 1955 System and the American Connection: A Bibliographic Introduction," JPRI [Japan Policy Research Institute] Working Paper No. 11: July 1995, http://www.jpri.org/publications/workingpapers/wp11.html.

33. Chalmers Johnson, "The 1955 System and the American Connection: A Bibliographic Introduction," Japan Policy Research Institute, JPRI Working Paper No. 11: July 1995, http://www.jpri.org/publications/workingpapers/wp11.html.

34. Scott, *American War Machine*, 94, etc.

35. Scott, *American War Machine*, 65–67, 87–96.

36. Norman Mailer, "A Harlot High and Low: Reconnoitering Through the Secret Government," *New York*, August 16, 1976 (Hughes); Michael Schaller, *Altered States: The United States and Japan Since the Occupation* (New York: Oxford University Press, 1997), 294 (Lockheed).

37. Johnson, "The 1955 System and the American Connection."

38. David E. Kaplan and Alec Dubro, *Yakuza: Japan's Criminal Underworld* (Berkeley: University of California Press, 2003), 89–90. Cf. Jonathan Marshall, in William O. Walker, III, ed., *Drug Control Policy: Essays in Historical and Comparative Perspective* (University Park: Pennsylvania State University Press, 1992), 108: "Yoshio Kodama's fortune, built of profits from tungsten and opium, established the party that today rules Japan. . . . Kodama contributed to the pervasive corruption of Japanese politics by steering huge corporate contributions into the coffers of favored LDP members. This pattern culminated in the Lockheed scandal, which revealed that multi-million-dollar payoff by American aerospace firms had swayed key procurement decisions by Japan's national airline and defense establishment and raised the possibility that the CIA had used Kodama and corporate funds to influence Japanese politics. The money-laundering channel used for Lockheed's bribes was favored both by the CIA and international drug traffickers."

39. The *San Francisco Chronicle* (October 24, 1983, 22) described a USAF-Lockheed operation in Southeast Asia, "code-named 'Operation Buttercup' that operated out of Norton Air Force Base in California from 1965 to 1972." For the CIA's close involvement in Lockheed payoffs, cf. Anthony Sampson, *The Arms Bazaar* (New York: Viking Press, 1977), 137, 227–28, 238.

40. Sampson, *The Arms Bazaar*, 137, 227–28, 238; cf. Thomas Fensch, ed. *The C.I.A. and the U-2 Program: 1954–1974* (The Woodlands, TX: New Century Books, 2001).

41. William D. Hartung, *Prophets of War: Lockheed Martin and the Making of the Military-Industrial Complex* (New York: Nation Books, 2011), 121; David Boulton, *The Grease Machine* (New York: Harper & Row, 1978), 97 (friends); Kai Bird, *The Chairman: John J. McCloy—The Making of the American Establishment* (New York: Simon & Schuster, 1992), 471–72 (Retinger and Jackson).

42. Andrew Feinstein, *The Shadow World: Inside the Global Arms Trade* (New York: Farrar, Straus and Giroux, 2011), 265; Sampson, *The Arms Bazaar*, 135–36.

43. Committee on Foreign Relations, United States Senate, *Multinational Corporations and United States Foreign Policy, Hearings Before the Subcommittee on Multinational Corporations*, Part 12 (Washington, DC: U.S. Government Printing Office, 1973–1975), 943–51.

44. Bradley R. Simpson, *Economists with Guns: Authoritarian Development and U.S.-Indonesian Relations, 1960–1968* (Stanford, CA: Stanford University Press, 2008), 142, quoting from CIA, "Political Action Project," November 19, 1964; *Foreign Relations of the United States, 1964–1968*, Vol. 26: *Indonesia; Malaysia-Singapore; Philippines* (Washington, DC: U.S. Government Printing Office, 2000), 181–84, https://history.state.gov/historicaldocuments/frus1964-68v26.

45. In addition there was "a U.S. deal to deliver 200 light aircraft to the Indonesian Army in July 1965. . . . [The aircraft went to the army's Diponegoro division, which] as well as supplying the bulk of the [September 30] 'coup' personnel in Java, . . . also provided the bulk of the personnel for its suppression" (Nathaniel Mehr, *"Constructive Bloodbath" in Indonesia: The United States, Britain and the Mass Killings of 1965–66* [Nottingham, UK: Spokesman Books, 2009], 36).

46. Peter Dale Scott, "The United States and the Overthrow of Sukarno, 1965–1967," *Pacific Affairs*, 58, Summer 1985, http://www.namebase.org/scott.html; citing Senate Committee on Foreign Relations, *Multinational Corporations and United States Foreign Policy*, Part 12, 937–65.

47. Scott, "The United States and the Overthrow of Sukarno."

48. Masashi Nishihara, *The Japanese and Sukarno's Indonesia: Tokyo-Jakarta Relations, 1951–1966* (Honolulu: University Press of Hawaii, 1976), 171, 194, 202; Scott, "The United States and the Overthrow of Sukarno."

49. *Fortune*, July 1973, 154, cf. *Wall Street Journal*, April 18, 1967.

50. Ian J. Bickerton, "America's Israel/ Israel's America," in John Dumbrell and Axel R Schäfer, eds., *America's "Special Relationships": Foreign and Domestic Aspects of the Politics of Alliance* (London: Routledge, 2009), 187.

51. John Foster Dulles to Lord McGowan, Chairman of Imperial Chemical Industries, in Nancy Lisagor and Frank Lipsius, *A Law unto Itself: The Untold Story of the Law Firm of Sullivan & Cromwell* (New York: William Morrow, 1988), 127.

52. Charles T. O'Reilly, *Forgotten Battles: Italy's War of Liberation, 1943–1945* (Lanham, MD: Lexington Books, 2001), 288; Peter Dale Scott, "How Allen Dulles and the SS Preserved Each Other," *Covert Action Information Bulletin*, 25 (Winter 1986), 4–14. Dulles's plans to use SS resources in postwar Germany can be seen as part of a successful plan to frustrate the implementation of Roosevelt's so-called "Morgenthau Plan" to deindustrialize Germany.

53. Stephen Dorril, *MI6: Inside the Covert World of Her Majesty's Secret Intelligence Service* (New York: Free Press, 2000), 659–60.

54. Ovid Demaris, *Dirty Business: The Corporate-Political Money-Power Game* (New York: Avon, 1974), 213–14.

55. J. P. D. Dunbabin, *International Relations Since 1945: A History in Two Volumes*, vol. 2, (London: Longman, 1994), 344. The boycott is denied without argumentation in Exxon's corporate history (Bennett H. Wall et al., *Growth in a Changing Environment: A History of Standard Oil Company (New Jersey), Exxon Corpora-*

tion, 1950–1975, vol. 4 (New York: McGraw-Hill, 1988), 476: "Despite oft-printed statements to the contrary, the oil majors did not conspire to boycott NIOC oil."

56. Robert Palmer Smith, *Darkest Truths of Black Gold: An Oil Industry Executive Breaks the Industry's Code of Silence* (New York: iUniverse, 2007), 256. In July 1952 Mossadeq attempted to break the embargo by contracting to sell oil to a small private Italian oil firm. The maneuver was frustrated by the British Royal Navy, which in July 1952 intercepted the Italian tanker Rose Mary and redirected it to Aden. The news dissuaded other tankers from trying to reach Abadan (Mary Ann Heiss, *Empire and Nationhood: The United States, Great Britain, and Iranian Oil, 1950–1954* [New York: Columbia University Press, 1997], 130; Stephen Kinzer, *All the Shah's Men: An American Coup and the Roots of Middle East Terror* [Hoboken, NJ: John Wiley & Sons, 2003], 136).

57. Mostafa Elm, *Oil, Power, and Principle: Iran's Oil Nationalization and Its Aftermath* (Syracuse, NY: Syracuse University Press, 1992), 198–99 (Churchill); Robert Moskin, *American Statecraft: The Story of the U.S. Foreign Service* (New York: Thomas Dunne Books/St. Martin's Press, 2013), 627–28 (Harriman).

58. Demaris, *Dirty Business*, 214–25: "The incoming Eisenhower Administration . . . quickly dropped the criminal case. The civil suit that was instituted alleged that the five American oil companies violated the Sherman Antitrust and the Wilson Tariff Acts by conspiring to divide and control foreign production and distribution . . . . An inadequate staff was assigned to the case and the action finally petered out a decade later with a couple of meaningless consent decrees."

59. Robert Sherrill, *The Oil Follies of 1970–1980: How the Petroleum Industry Stole the Show (and Much More Besides)* (Garden City, NY: Anchor Press/Doubleday, 1983), 221.

60. William R. Freudenburg and Robert Gramling, *Oil in Troubled Waters: Perceptions, Politics, and the Battle over Offshore Drilling* (Albany: State University of New York Press, 1994), 17; citing Shukri Mohammed Ghanem, *OPEC, The Rise and Fall of an Exclusive Club* (London: KPI, 1986); Mira Wilkins, "The Oil Companies in Perspective," in Raymond Vernon, ed., *The Oil Crisis* (New York: W. W. Norton, 1976).

61. William Roger Louis, "Britain and the Overthrow of Mossadeq," in Mark J. Gasiorowski and Malcolm Byrne, eds., *Mohammad Mosaddeq and the 1953 Coup in Iran* (Syracuse, NY: Syracuse University Press, 2004), 168. Cf. William R. Clark, *Petrodollar Warfare: Oil, Iraq and the Future of the Dollar* (Gabriola Island, BC: New Society Publishers, 2005), 125: "The Dulles brothers had already conceived a plot when Eisenhower became president in January 1953."

62. Scot Macdonald, *Rolling the Iron Dice: Historical Analogies and Decisions to Use Military Force in Regional Contingencies* (Westport, CT: Greenwood Press, 2000), 98. Cf. Richard H. Immerman, *John Foster Dulles: Piety, Pragmatism, and Power in U.S. Foreign Policy* (Wilmington, DE: Scholarly Resources, 1999), 67. Allen Dulles played a personal role in TP/AJAX, by flying to Italy and persuading the frightened Shah to return to Tehran.

63. In the past, wishing to dissociate the term "deep state" from organizational connotations, I have written of the American "deep state" as "a milieu both inside

and outside government with the power to steer the history of the public state and sometimes redirect it" (Peter Dale Scott, "William Pawley, the Kennedy Assassination, and Watergate," Global Research, November 29, 2012, http://www .globalresearch.ca/william-pawley-the-kennedy-assassination-and-watergate-tilt -and-the-phase-three-story-of-clare-boothe-luce/5313486. But there are also extragovernmental *structural* components in the deep state system.

64. See Chalmers A Johnson, *The Sorrows of Empire: Militarism, Secrecy, and the End of the Republic* (New York: Metropolitan Books/Henry Holt, 2004), 218–19; Timothy Mitchell, *Carbon Democracy: Political Power in the Age of Oil* (New York: Verso Books, 2011), 212. In 1952 Aramco offered logistical support to a Saudi force in a military dispute with Oman and Abu Dhabi (Mark Curtis, *Secret Affairs: Britain's Collusion with Radical Islam* [London: Profile, 2011], 69).

65. James Bamford, *A Pretext for War: 9/11, Iraq, and the Abuse of America's Intelligence Agencies* (New York: Doubleday, 2004), 71. See discussion in chapter 11.

66. Tim Shorrock, *Spies for Hire: The Secret World of Intelligence Outsourcing* (New York: Simon & Schuster, 2008), 6.

67. Glenn Greenwald, "Mike McConnell, the WashPost & the Dangers of Sleazy Corporatism," Salon, March 29, 2010, http://www.salon.com/2010/03/29/mcconnell_3/.

68. George H. W. Bush was an adviser to Carlyle, which in its early days "backed a management-led buyout of Caterair and appointed George W Bush to the board" (Jamie Doward, "Bush Sr's Carlyle Group Gets Fat On War And Conflict," *The Observer*, March 25, 2003, http://www.rense.com/general36/fat.htm).

69. Lofgren, "A Shadow Government Controls America."

70. A May 2014 Google search for "'Booz Allen' + 'COOP COG'" yielded 478 informative hits.

71. Booz Allen Hamilton's headquarters is now in McLean, Virginia, close to the headquarters of the CIA.

72. Art Kleiner, *Booz Allen Hamilton: Helping Clients Envision the Future* (Old Saybrook, CT: Greenwich Publishing, 2004), 43. http://www.boozallen.com/media/file/90th-History-Book-Complete.pdf

73. John Prados, *Safe for Democracy: The Secret Wars of the CIA* (Chicago: Ivan R. Dee, 2006), 139. Cf. Christine N. Halili, *Philippine History* (Manila: Rex Book Store, 2004), 258 (Philippines land distribution).

74. Miles Copeland, *The Game Player: The Confessions of the CIA's Original Political Operative* (London: Aurum Press, 1989), 158.

75. Ephraim Kahana and Muhammad Suwaed, *Historical Dictionary of Middle Eastern Intelligence* (Lanham, MD: Scarecrow Press, 2009), 65 ("advisor"); Jack O'Connell, *King's Counsel: A Memoir of War, Espionage, and Diplomacy in the Middle East* (New York: W. W. Norton, 2011), 20 (channel).

76. Committee on Foreign Relations, United States Senate, *The BCCI Affair: BCCI, the CIA and Foreign Intelligence, A Report to the Committee on Foreign Relations, United States Senate by Senator John Kerry and Senator Hank Brown, December 1992; 102d Congress, 2d Session, Senate Print 102–140* (Washington, DC: U.S. Government Printing Office), https://www.fas.org/irp/congress/1992_rpt/

bcci/11intel.htm ("agent"). His close friend and fellow architect of the 1953 CIA operation in Iran, Kermit Roosevelt, became a similar agent for first Gulf Oil and then Northrop (Anthony Sampson, *The Arms Bazaar*, 159, 247).

77. William D. Hartung, *Prophets of War*, 126.

78. Copeland, *The Game Player*, 231.

79. Copeland, *The Game Player*, 233.

80. Copeland, *The Game Player*, 239.

81. For example, Evan Thomas, *The Very Best Men: Four Who Dared: The Early Years of the CIA* (New York: Simon & Schuster, 1995), 380.

82. Larry J. Kolb, *Overworld: The Life and Times of a Reluctant Spy* (New York: Riverhead/Penguin, 2004), 237–38. Cf. Copeland, *The Game Player*, 230, 262–63; Ronald Kessler, *The Richest Man in the World: The Story of Adnan Khashoggi* (New York: Warner Books), 300–301: "On May 17, 1983, [Khashoggi] submitted to President Reagan a confidential 'yellow paper' [which] proposed an economic aid program similar to the 1949 Marshall Plan developed by the United States for Europe. Called a Peace Fund, it would provide up to $300 billion in regional economic aid from the United States, Saudi Arabia and Kuwait to Israel and any Arab country that signed a peace treaty with it."

83. Peter Dale Scott, "Deep Events and the CIA's Global Drug Connection," 911Truth .org, October 12, 2008, http://www.911truth.org/deep-events-and-the-cias-global -drug-connection/; Scott, *American War Machine*, 160–65.

84. Committee on Foreign Relations, United States Senate, *The BCCI Affair*. Khashoggi's status had declined, but by no means vanished. As late as 2003, Khashoggi was negotiating with Richard Perle, a member of the Cheney-Rumsfeld clique who at the time was still Chairman of the U.S. Defense Policy Board, to invest considerable Saudi money in Perle's company Trireme (Seymour Hersh, *New Yorker*, March 17, 2003).

85. Copeland, *The Game Player*, 239; cf. 228. For decades Congress has been a field of tensions between Arab and Israeli interests, represented primarily by the oil lobby and by the American Israel Public Affairs Committee (AIPAC). But in a very interesting essay by Robert Dreyfuss for PBS's *Frontline*, former AIPAC official Keith Weissman describes how he

> brought some Conoco guys to AIPAC's policy conference, where half the House and half the Senate usually attend, and they knew that night that they would never win anything against us. So they began to cooperate. A lot of the oil companies realized, "We're not gonna beat these guys in Congress, so we might as well try to tailor their activities, where we at least have some room to work." And I was the go-between. I was the guy. I mean, BP still credits me with being the guy who greased the Baku-Tbilisi-Ceyhan pipeline, because of my work with them. That was originally designed as an anti-Iran project (Robert Dreyfuss, "AIPAC from the Inside," *Frontline*, June 11, 2013, http://www.pbs.org/wgbh/pages/frontline/tehranbureau/2011/06/aipac -from-the-inside-1-isolating-iran.html).

86. Kessler, *The Richest Man in the World*, 84, 188, etc.; Scott, *American War Machine*, 158–62.

87. Scott, *American War Machine*, 158–62; citing "Moss, Edward K. #172 646," CIA Memo of 19 April 1967, NARA #104-10122-10006; CIA Inspector General's Report on CIA-Mafia Plots to Assassinate Fidel Castro, NARA # 104-10213-10101, 38. Cf. memo of 7 November 1962 in CIA's Edward K. Moss folder, 26, NARA #1994.05.03.10:54:53:780005.

88. "Manuel Antonio Varona," FBI Memorandum of January 16, 1961 to A. H. Belmont, 105-76826-20; NARA #124-90055-10139, 2. Cf. "Moss, Edward K. #172 646," CIA Memo of 14 May 1973, in Meyer Lansky Security File, 9, NARA #1993.08.13.17:42:12:560059; CIA letter of 16 December 1960 to FBI, FBI file 105-76826-18; NARA #124-90055-10133. The CIA itself had notified the FBI on December 16, 1960, that Julia "Cellino" had advised that her brothers "have long been associated in the narcotics and white slavery rackets in Cuba" (CIA letter of 16 December 1960 to Director, FBI, FBI File 105-76826-18; NARA #124-90055-10133.

89. Kessler, *The Richest Man in the World*, 29 (Yassin), 275–78 (Khashoggi). A friend of Khashoggi's, Larry Kolb, reports that Khashoggi himself essentially corroborated the story that Khashoggi and John Kennedy had a friendship in the 1950s that "evolved primarily out of whoring together" (Kolb, *Overworld: The Life and Times of a Reluctant Spy*, 236). The woman who destroyed the presidential aspirations of Senator Gary Hart in 1987 was one of Khashoggi's many women.

90. Nor was Khashoggi the first CIA foreign asset to have been accused of using women to acquire political influence in Washington. Similar rumors had circulated about the wealthy Korean Tong Sun Park, owner of the fashionable Georgetown Club, and said to be an associate of the Korean Central Intelligence Agency (KCIA). See Claude A. Buss, *The United States and the Republic of Korea: Background for Policy* (Stanford, CA: Hoover Institution Press, Stanford University, 1982), 127; Jim Hougan, *Secret Agenda: Watergate, Deep Throat, and the CIA* (New York: Random House, 1984), 120–21; Scott, *Deep Politics and the Death of JFK*, 237.

91. Anthony Summers with Robbyn Swan, *The Arrogance of Power: The Secret World of Richard Nixon* (New York: Viking Penguin , 2000), 283. Cf. Kessler, *The Richest Man in the World*, 171: Khashoggi told the prosecutors "that he churned millions through the tiny [Rebozo] bank to win favor with the president."

92. Investigative reporter Jim Hougan reports the incredulity of congressional investigators that Lockheed was the only large corporation not to have made a contribution to Nixon's 1972 election campaign (Jim Hougan, *Spooks: The Haunting of America: The Private Use of Secret Agents* [New York: William Morrow, 1978], 457–58).

93. Scott, *Road to 9/11*, 35; citing Summers, *Arrogance of Power*, 283; Robert Baer, *Sleeping with the Devil* (New York: Crown, 2003), 43. (Baer reports the year of the briefcase as 1968, not 1972.) Kolb ("unequivocally, and from personal experience") denies the briefcase story (Kolb, *Overworld: The Life and Times of a Reluctant Spy*, 299).

94. Scott, *Deep Politics and the Death of JFK*, 234–39.

95. Kessler, *The Richest Man in the World,* 129, 160–61. When Hughes flew from Las Vegas to the Paradise Island casino in the Bahamas (where Edward Moss's brother-in-law Eddie Cellini was casino manager), he did so on a Khashoggi plane. (Kessler, *The Richest Man in the World,* 149–50).

96. Summers, with Swan, *The Arrogance of Power,* 242, 252; Hougan, *Spooks,* 398. Cf. Denny Walsh, *New York Times,* January 21, 1974; Jeff Gerth, in Sidney Blumenthal and Harvey Yazijian, eds., *Government by Gunplay* (New York: New American Library, 1976), 137–39.

97. Alan A. Block, *Masters of Paradise: Organized Crime and the Internal Revenue Service in the Bahamas* (New Brunswick, NJ: Transaction Publishers, 1991), 94–96; Summers with Swan, *The Arrogance of Power,* 244–45. Benguet Mines have also been associated with Yamashita's gold (Seagrave and Seagrave, *Gold Warriors,* 147; Scott, *American War Machine,* 322n15).

98. Summers, with Swan, *The Arrogance of Power,* 244–45, 253–54.

99. Marquis Who's Who, *Who's Who in Finance and Industry,* 1979, 568.

100. Scott, *American War Machine,* 71–72. Cf. *Wall Street Journal,* April 18, 1980: "In 1951, Mr. Helliwell helped set up and run Sea Supply Corp., a concern controlled by the CIA as a front. For almost 10 years, Sea Supply was used to supply huge amounts of weapons and equipment to 10,000 Nationalist Chinese [KMT] troops in Burma as well as to Thailand's police."

101. In the course of Operation Safehaven, the U.S. Third Army took an SS major "on several trips to Italy and Austria, and, as a result of these preliminary trips, over $500,000 in gold, as well as jewels, were recovered" (Anthony Cave Brown, *The Secret War Report of the OSS* [New York: Berkeley, 1976], 565–66).

102. Scott, *American War Machine,* 54–56, 70–72; cf. John Loftus and Mark Aarons, *The Secret War against the Jews* (New York: St. Martin's, 1994), 110–11.

103. Kessler, *Richest Man in the World,* 238–41; Scott, *American War Machine,* 161–62.

104. The operation kept the name "Safari Club" even after moving from Khashoggi's Club to a permanent headquarters in Cairo.

105. Ibrahim Warde, *The Price of Fear: The Truth behind the Financial War on Terror* (Berkeley: University of California Press, 2007), 133. Cf. Robert Lacey, *Inside the Kingdom: Kings, Clerics, Modernists, Terrorists, and the Struggle for Saudi Arabia* (New York: Penguin Books, 2009), 66, 72, 76.

106. Christopher Byron, "The Senate Looks at BCCI," *New York Magazine,* October 28, 1991, 20–21.

107. Lacey, *Inside the Kingdom,* 66. Cf. John Cooley, *Unholy Wars* (London: Pluto Press, 1999), 24–27.

108. David Teacher, "The Pinay Circle and Destabilisation in Europe," *Lobster,* 18, October 1989, http://wikispooks.com/wiki/Document: The_Pinay_Circle.

109. Mahmood Mamdani, *Good Muslim, Bad Muslim: America, the Cold War, and the Roots of Terror* (New York: Pantheon Books 2004), 84.

110. Mamdani, *Good Muslim, Bad Muslim,* 85.

111. Joseph J. Trento, *Prelude to Terror: The Rogue CIA and the Legacy of America's Private Intelligence Network* (New York: Carroll & Graf, 2005), 61.

112. Trento, *Prelude to Terror*, 104–5.

113. Kevin Phillips, "The Barreling Bushes," *Los Angeles Times*, January 11, 2004.

114. Trento, *Prelude to Terror*, 113–14.

115. Rod Lenahan, *Crippled Eagle: A Historical Perspective of U.S. Special Operations 1976–1996* (Charleston, SC: Narwhal Press, 1998), 178.

116. "In 1980, Shackley was set on putting his former boss, George Bush, in the White House and possibly securing the CIA directorship for himself. Shackley volunteered his prodigious skills to Bush in early 1980. Though that fact has come out before, Shackley's involvement in the Iran hostage issue, the so-called 'October Surprise' controversy, has been a closely held secret, until now" (Robert Parry, "Bush & a CIA Power Play—The Consortium," Consortiumnews, http://www.consortiumnews.com/archive/xfile7.html. Cf. "The CIA/Likud Sinking of Jimmy Carter," Consortiumnews, June 24, 2010, http://www.consortiumnews.com/2010/062410.html: "Inside the CIA, Carter and his CIA Director Stansfield Turner were blamed for firing many of the free-wheeling covert operatives from the Vietnam era, for ousting legendary spymaster Ted Shackley, and for failing to protect longtime U.S. allies (and friends of the CIA), such as Iran's Shah and Nicaragua's dictator Anastasio Somoza."

117. Robert Parry, *Trick or Treason: The October Surprise Mystery* (New York: Sheridan Square Press, 1993), 154–55.

118. David Teacher, "The Pinay Circle and Destabilisation in Europe."

119. W. Carl Biven, *Jimmy Carter's Economy: Policy in an Age of Limits* (Chapel Hill: University of North Carolina Press, 2002), 1: "There were more practical consequences of the Iranian crisis that tested the temper of the public; perhaps the most visible were a gasoline shortage and long lines of cars at gas stations caused by the cutoff of Iranian oil." Cf. Daniel Yergin, *The Quest: Energy, Security and the Remaking of the Modern World* (New York: Penguin Press, 2011), 531: "The Iranian Revolution led to chaos in the oil market, rapid increases in prices, new gas lines, and a second oil shock, and the Carter administration started to come unwound."

   In 2007 I myself wrote, "By effectively restricting the access of Iran to the global oil market, the Iranian assets freeze became a factor in the huge oil price increases of 1979 and 1981 (and thus an indirect cause of Carter's electoral defeat in 1980)" (Scott, *The Road to 9/11*, 88). It was indeed a factor. But in the context I was arguing that the Iranian assets freeze attributed to Carter in 1979 was in fact part of a complex strategy arranged by advisers to the Chase Manhattan Bank. Prominent among these was Archibald Roosevelt, a former CIA officer and colleague of Copeland, whom Parry also accuses of involvement in the Republican October Surprise (Scott, *The Road to 9/11*, 91; Parry, *Trick or Treason*, 49, 51, 257).

120. Robert Sherrill, *The Oil Follies of 1970–1980*, 435–37. In like manner, William Engdahl has attributed the European oil crisis in 1979 to the market behavior of BP (F. William Engdahl, *A Century of War: Anglo-American Oil Politics and the New World Order* [London: Pluto Press, 2004], 173).

121. David B. Ottaway, *The King's Messenger: Prince Bandar bin Sultan and America's Tangled Relationship with Saudi Arabia* (New York: Walker, 2008), 41.

122. Robert Lacey, *The Kingdom: Arabia & the House of Sa'ud* (New York: Avon, 1981), 451–55: "Crown Prince Fahad decided he must distance himself from Washington. In February 1979 he cancelled a trip he had scheduled to meet President Carter in the following month" (452). In ensuing months of negotiations, Saudis first increased production in late 1979 and then increased their oil price in 1980. At issue also was the Saudi desire to acquire AWACS (airborne warning and control system) aircraft, which, as we shall see in chapter 10, were not supplied to them until under Reagan (Ottaway, *The King's Messenger*, 42–47).

123. Committee on Foreign Relations, United States Senate, *The BCCI Affair*, Part 11, "BCCI, the CIA and Foreign Intelligence," http://www.fas.org/irp/congress/1992_rpt/bcci/11intel.htm.

124. Dan Bawley, *Corporate Governance and Accountability: What Role for the Regulator, Director, and Auditor?* (Westport, CT: Quorum, 1999), 37.

125. Bawley, *Corporate Governance and Accountability*, 37.

126. "Revealed—the capitalist network that runs the world," *New Scientist*, October 24, 2011, http://www.newscientist.com/article/mg21228354.500-revealed--the-capitalist-network-that-runs-the-world.html#.Uw9X_14ihpi.

127. Scott, *American War Machine*, 163; quoting from Peter Truell and Larry Gurwin, *False Profits: The Inside Story of BCCI, the World's Most Corrupt Financial Empire* (Boston: Houghton Mifflin, 1992), 384 ("ties")

128. Alan A. Block and Constance A. Weaver, *All Is Clouded by Desire: Global Banking, Money Laundering, and International Organized Crime* (Westport, CT: Praeger, 2004), 36–37.

129. "Saudi prince 'received arms cash,'" BBC, June 7, 2007, http://news.bbc.co.uk/2/hi/business/6728773.stm. It is unclear whether payments continued after 2001, when the United Kingdom signed the OECD's Anti-Bribery Convention, making such overpayments illegal.

130. Lacey, *Inside the Kingdom*, 108.

131. Former Turkish President and Prime Minister Suleyman Demirel commented that "In our country . . . there is one deep state and one other state. . . . The state that should be real is the spare one, the one that should be spare is the real one" (Jon Gorvett, "Turkey's 'Deep State' Surfaces in Former President's Words, Deeds in Kurdish Town," *Washington Report on Middle East Affairs*, January/February 2006; quoted in Scott, *American War Machine*, 24.

3. THE DOOMSDAY PROJECT

1. One of the highest-ranking CIA officials, as reported in Robert Baer, *See No Evil: The True Story of a Ground Soldier in the CIA's War on Terrorism* (New York: Crown Publishers, 2002), xix. The comment of Baer, himself an ex-CIA officer: "If that's going to be the official line of thinking at the agency . . . then I am more than angry. I'm scared to death of what lies ahead."

2. *New York Times*, July 14, 1987. We have never heard if there was or was not an executive session, or if the rest of Congress was ever aware of the matter. According to James Bamford, *A Pretext for War: 9/11, Iraq, and the Abuse of America's Intelligence Agencies* (New York: Doubleday, 2004), 74: "The existence of the secret government was so closely held that Congress was completely bypassed. Rather than through legislation, it was created by Top Secret presidential fiat. In fact, Congress would have no role in the new wartime administration. 'One of the awkward questions we faced,' said one of the participants, 'was whether to reconstitute Congress after a nuclear attack. It was decided that no, it would be easier to operate without them.'" Cf. James Mann, *The Rise of the Vulcans: The History of Bush's War Cabinet* (New York: Viking, 2004), 145. But key individuals in Congress, such as Senator Inouye of the Senate Intelligence Committee, were certainly aware of something.

3. *Miami Herald*, July 5, 1987. In September 1984 Jack Anderson reported that FEMA's plans would "suspend the Constitution and the Bill of Rights, effectively eliminate private property, abolish free enterprise, and generally clamp Americans in a totalitarian vise" (*Lawrence* [Kansas] *Journal-World*, September 25, 1984).

4. Diana Reynolds, "The Rise of the National Security State: FEMA and the NSC, Political Research Associates," *Covert Action Information Bulletin*, #33 (Winter 1990), http://www.publiceye.org/liberty/fema/Fema_2.html. Earlier, Governor Reagan in California had authorized the development of a counterinsurgency plan (known as Cable Splicer) and exercises to deal with such crises, in conjunction with the U.S. Sixth Army and the Pentagon (Operation Garden Plot). The cadres developing Cable Splicer (headed by Louis Giuffrida) were with Reagan's elevation to the presidency transferred into FEMA.

5. Glenn Beck, *The Overton Window* (New York: Threshold Editions/Mercury Radio Arts, 2010), 296. Cf. Robert C. Aldridge, *America in Peril* (Pasadena, CA: Hope Publishing House, 2008), 295. It would appear that in REX-84 the Army's Garden Plot plan for martial law became fused with COG's plan for massive detention. But the highly classified details remain obscure.

6. Peter Dale Scott, *The Road to 9/11: Wealth, Empire, and the Future of America* (Berkeley: University of California Press, 2007), 184; citing Ross Gelbspan, *Break-Ins, Death Threats, and the FBI: The Covert War against the Central America Movement* (Boston: South End Press, 1991), 184.

7. Peter Dale Scott, "Northwards without North," *Social Justice* (Summer 1989). Revised as "North, Iran-Contra, and the Doomsday Project: The Original Congressional Cover Up of Continuity-of-Government Planning," Asia-Pacific Journal: Japan Focus, February 21, 2011, http://japanfocus.org/-Peter_Dale-Scott/3491.

8. Tim Weiner, *New York Times*, April 17, 1994. The first public reference to the "Doomsday Project" (the Pentagon in-house term for COG procedures) was apparently Steven Emerson, "America's Doomsday Project," *U.S. News & World Report*, August 7, 1989.

9. Bamford, *A Pretext for War*, 74; cf. Mann, *The Rise of the Vulcans*, 138–45.

10. Tim Shorrock, *Spies for Hire: The Secret World of Intelligence Outsourcing* (New York: Simon & Schuster, 2008), 78; Shirley Anne Warshaw, *The Co-Presidency of Bush and Cheney* (Stanford, CA: Stanford Politics and Policy, 2009), 162.

11. "The provisions of Executive Order 12656 of Nov. 18, 1988, appear at 53 FR 47491, 3 CFR, 1988 Comp., p. 585," http://www.archives.gov/federal-register/codifica tion/executive-order/12656.html. *Washington Post* (March 1, 2002) later claimed, falsely, that Executive Order 12656 dealt only with "a nuclear attack." Earlier there was a similar misrepresentation in *The New York Times* (November 18, 1991).

12. William M. Arkin, "Back to the Bunker," *Washington Post*, June 4, 2006, http://www .washingtonpost.com/wp-dyn/content/article/2006/06/02/AR2006060201410.html. Cf. Peter Dale Scott, "Systemic Destabilization in Recent American History: 9/11, the JFK Assassination, and the Oklahoma City Bombing as a Strategy of Tension," Japan Focus: Asia-Pacific Journal, October 7, 2013, http://japanfocus .org/-Peter_Dale-Scott/3835.

13. William Arkin, *American Coup: How a Terrified Government Is Destroying the Constitution* (New York: Little Brown, 2013), 5.

14. Gelbspan, *Break-Ins, Death Threats, and the FBI*, 184; cf. *New York Times*, November 18, 1991. REX 84 (short for Readiness Exercise 1984) turned out to be part of a series of such exercises (now known as Continuity of Operations Exercises) that have continued under FEMA down into the Obama era. See for example the Department of Homeland Security Press Release, "DHS Conducts Continuity of Operations Exercise," June 17, 2009, http://www.dhs.gov/ynews/releases/ pr_1245258718688.shtm.

15. In stressing the alteration of our present political milieu by an extragovernmental group, I do not intend to exonerate Congress. In 1981 Congress passed the Military Cooperation with Civilian Law Enforcement Agencies Act. According to a brilliant and prescient essay written by an Air Force Colonel at the National War College, the Act "was specifically intended to force reluctant military commanders to actively collaborate in police work" (Air Force Lt. Col. Charles E. Dunlap, "The Origins of the American Military Coup of 2012"; quoted in Harry G. Summers, *The New World Strategy: A Military Policy for America's Future* (New York: Simon & Schuster, 1995), 195.

16. Arkin, *American Coup*, 34–35. The incoming Reagan administration also tried, unsuccessfully until 1985, to persuade Congress to repeal the so-called "Clark Amendment" of 1975 barring aid to private groups engaged in military or paramilitary operations in Angola—a restriction that had led the Safari Club to fill the gap. See Rachel Bronson, *Thicker than Oil: America's Uneasy Partnership with Saudi Arabia* (Oxford: Oxford University Press, 2006), 129, 177–79.

17. National Commission on Terrorist Attacks upon the United States, *The 9/11 Commission Report* (New York: W. W. Norton, 2004), http://www.9-11commission .gov/report/911Report.pdf, 38, 326; Scott, *The Road to 9/11*, 228–29.

18. Alfred Goldberg et al., *Pentagon 9/11* (Washington, DC: Department of Defense, 2007), 132.

19. Warshaw, *The Co-Presidency of Bush and Cheney*, 164–65; cf. *Washington Post*, March 1, 2002; Scott, *Road to 9/11*, 237. Warshaw took the characterization of "shadow government" from earlier reports by *U.S. News and World Report* in 1989, and CNN in 1991 (Warshaw, *The Co-Presidency of Bush and Cheney*, 162).

20. Barton Gellman, *Angler: The Cheney Vice Presidency* (New York: Penguin Press, 2008), 133–35.
21. Gellman, *Angler*, 284. The same channel was used for Yoo's still-withheld fifty-page memo on torture: "In an interview after leaving government, Yoo said Addington and Flanigan assisted in the preparation of that memo" (Gellman, *Angler*, 191).
22. Scott, *Road to 9/11*, 238, 240–41.
23. "The exercise anticipated civil disturbances, major demonstrations and strikes that would affect continuity of government and/or resource mobilization. To fight subversive activities, there was authorization for the military to implement government-ordered movements of civilian populations at state and regional levels, the arrest of certain unidentified segments of the population, and the imposition of martial rule" (Reynolds, "The Rise of the National Security State," http://www.publiceye.org/liberty/fema/Fema_3.html).
24. "The National Consortium for the Study of Terrorism and Responses to Terrorism (START) Global Terrorism Database—part of a joint government-university program on terrorism—is hosted at the University of Maryland.... A quick review of charts from the START database show that terrorism has increased [dramatically] in the last 9 years since the U.S. started its 'war on terror'" ("U.S. 'War On Terror' Has INCREASED Terrorism," Washington's Blog, October 21, 2013, http://www.washingtonsblog.com/2013/10/u-s-war-on-terror-has-increased -terrorism.html).
25. "President Bush Addresses the Nation," *Washington Post*, September 20, 2011.
26. "NSPD-9: Combating Terrorism," Federation of American Scientists, http://fas .org/irp/offdocs/nspd/nspd-9.htm:

   > On April 1, 2004, the White House released the following characterization of this otherwise classified document: "The NSPD called on the Secretary of Defense to plan for military options 'against Taliban targets in Afghanistan, including leadership, command-control, air and air defense, ground forces, and logistics.' The NSPD also called for plans 'against al Qaeda and associated terrorist facilities in Afghanistan, including leadership, command-control-communications, training, and logistics facilities.'"

27. "NSPD-9: Combating Terrorism," Federation of American Scientists, http://fas .org/irp/offdocs/nspd/nspd-9.htm citing testimony of Donald Rumsfeld before 9/11 Commission, March 23, 2304. Cf. Richard Clarke, *Against All Enemies: Inside America's War on Terrorism* (New York: Free Press, 2004), 237–38; Steve Coll, *Ghost Wars: The Secret History of the CIA, Afghanistan, and bin Laden, from the Soviet Invasion to September 10, 2001* (New York: Penguin Press, 2004), 574–76; *Commission Report*, 212–14. A draft of the presidential directive had originally been circulated in June 2001 (*9/11 Commission Report*, 208). But the directive approved on September 4 was for covert action only (*9/11 Commission Report*, 213).
28. Bamford, *A Pretext for War*, 287.

29. Jennifer Van Bergen, "The USA PATRIOT Act Was Planned Before 9/11," Truthout.org, May 20, 2002, http://www.globalissues.org/article/342/the-usa -patriot-act-was-planned-before-911. Van Bergen notes a parallel with the Patriot Act's predecessor, the Antiterrorism Act of 1996: "James X. Dempsey and David Cole state in their book, 'Terrorism & the Constitution: Sacrificing Civil Liberties in the Name of National Security,' that the most troubling provisions of the pre-USAPA antiterrorism laws, enacted in 1996 and expanded now by the USAPA, 'were developed long before the bombings [i.e., the Oklahoma City bombing of 1995] that triggered their final enactment.'"

30. Cf. *Time,* Nov. 26, 2001: "While Daschle, the Senate majority leader, could have been chosen as a representative of all Democrats or of the entire Senate, Leahy is a less obvious choice, most likely targeted for a specific reason. He is head of the Senate Judiciary Committee, which is involved in issues ranging from antitrust action to *antiterror legislation* [emphasis added]." See also Anthony York, "Why Daschle and Leahy?" Salon, November 21, 2001, http://www.salon .com/2001/11/22/anthrax_17/.

31. Glenn Greenwald, "Vital unresolved anthrax questions and ABC News," Salon, August 1, 2008, http://www.salon.com/2008/08/01/anthrax_2/.

32. Lew Dubose and Jake Bernstein, *Vice: Dick Cheney and the Hijacking of the American Presidency* (New York: Random House, 2006), 28: "Dick Cheney . . . would spend the rest of his career working to restore the Nixon vision of an all-powerful executive, by undoing the Watergate reforms that came out of the early seventies."

33. Frederick A. O. Schwarz Jr. and Aziz Z. Huq, *Unchecked and Unbalanced: Presidential Power in a Time of Terror* (New York: The New Press, 2007), 174; emphasis added.

34. Dubose and Bernstein, *Vice: Dick Cheney,* 187–90; citing John Yoo memos of September 25, 2001 ("deploy") and January 2002 ("do not protect").

35. Department of Justice, "Review of the Terrorist Screening Center," www.justice. gov/oig/reports/FBI/a0527/final.pdf.

36. Ellen Nakashima, "Terrorist Watch List: One Tip Now Enough to Put Name in Database, Officials Say," *Washington Post,* December 29, 2010.

37. Naomi Wolf, "Fascist America," *Guardian* (London), April 24, 2007, http://www .guardian.co.uk/world/2007/apr/24/usa.comment.

38. "Former U.S. Marine Placed On 'No Fly' List, Sues FBI," NPR, August 5, 2010, http://www.npr.org/templates/story/story.php?storyId=129002767. On August 28, 2013, a federal court in Portland, Oregon, ruled that constitutional rights are at stake when the government places Americans on the No Fly List, agreeing with the plaintiffs in a lawsuit filed by the American Civil Liberties Union (ACLU of Oregon press release, http://aclu-or.org/nofly).

39. Scott Shane, "American Man in Limbo on No-Fly List," *New York Times,* June 15, 2010, http://www.nytimes.com/2010/06/16/world/middleeast/16yemen.html.

40. U.S. Department of Defense, "U.S. Northern Command," http://www.global security.org/military/agency/dod/northcom.htm. Cf. John R. Brinkerhoff, PBS, Online Newshour, September 28, 2002: "The United States itself is now for the first time since the War of 1812 a theater of war. That means that we should apply, in

my view, the same kind of command structure in the United States that we apply in other theaters of war." Brinkerhoff had earlier developed the martial law provisions of REX 84 in the Reagan era.

41. Shorrock, *Spies for Hire*, 344.

42. Julian Assange, "The spy who billed me twice," Wikileaks, http://wikileaks.org/wiki/The_spy_who_billed_me_twice. The March 2009 Army manual "US Army Concept of Operations for Police Intelligence Operations" contains phrases such as, "It [fusion] does not have constraints that are emplaced on MI [Military Intelligence] activities within the US, because it operates under the auspice and oversight of the police discipline and standards" ("Spying on Anti-War Protesters: US Army Concept of Operations for Police Intelligence Operations, 4 Mar 2009," Wikileaks, May 6, 2009, http://wikileaks.org/wiki/Spying_on_anti-war_protesters:_US_Army_Concept_of_Operations_for_Police_Intelligence_Opera tions,_4_Mar_2009).

43. "Notice—Continuation of the National Emergency With Respect to Persons Who Commit, Threaten To Commit, or Support Terrorism," Daily Compilation Of Presidential Documents" ("Author: Obama, Barack H"), September 16, 2010, http://www.readperiodicals.com//201009/2184118701.html.

44. *Humanitarian Law Project v. United States Department of Treasury.* "In April 2007 Judge Collins lifted her injunction against enforcement of that portion of the EO, satisfied that the new definitions were neither vague nor overbroad. Judge Collins also reversed her decision holding Bush's designations unconstitutional, deciding that she erred in allowing the plaintiffs to use a more relaxed standing analysis for First Amendment claims" (Jason Shepard, "Terrorism Over the Airwaves? Satellite Television and the First Amendment in the War on Terror," http://citation.allacademic.com/meta/p_mla_apa_research_citation/2/0/4/2/5/p204257_index.html).

45. Scott, *The Road to 9/11: Wealth, Empire, and the Future of America* (Berkeley and Los Angeles: University of California Press, 2007), 183–87.

46. Mann, *Rise of the Vulcans*, 142 (order); John Fass Morton, *Next-Generation Homeland Security: Network Federalism and the Course to National Preparedness* (Annapolis, MD: Naval Institute Press, 2012), 57 (NSDD 55); Andrew Cockburn, *Rumsfeld: His Rise, Fall, and Catastrophic Legacy* (New York: Scribner, 2007), 88 (2001).

47. Cockburn, *Rumsfeld*, 88.

48. Clarke, *Against All Enemies*, 8, 165–75.

49. Shorrock, *Spies for Hire*, 72–75, 292–96. Project 908 attracted the attention of Steve Emerson and other journalists in 1989, when it was revealed that there had been huge cost overruns, double billing for the same work, and eventually destruction of many key contract documents in the course of an Army investigation. The son of the Army general overseeing the project, former Congressman Rick Renzi, was eventually indicted in 2008 on related charges of extortion, fraud, money laundering and other crimes (Steven Emerson, "America's Doomsday Project," *U.S. News & World Report*, August 7, 1989, 26–31). After years of delays, he was convicted in 2013 and sentenced to three years in prison (Bob Christie, "Ex-Rep.

Rick Renzi Gets 3 Years in Prison for Corruption Convictions," AP, October 28, 2013). As of June 2014, Renzi was free on appeal.

50. See for example, Clarke, *Against All Enemies*, 91.

51. See discussion in Scott, *Road to 9/11*, 223–36. There were reports that when Bush was airborne in Air Force One on 9/11, there were connectivity problems forcing the President to use an ordinary cell phone (Paul Thompson, *The Terror Timeline: Year by Year, Day by Day, Minute by Minute* [New York: HarperCollins/Regan Books, 2004], 437). This may help explain why Air Force One eventually flew to Offutt Air Force Base near Omaha, where the E4-B "Doomsday Planes" are based.

52. CNN, September 11, 2007, http://www.youtube.com/watch?v=UgF9Fd4UyMY. On the CNN show 9/11 Commission cochair Lee Hamilton said he had a vague memory of the mystery plane story, but that it was never discussed by the 9/11 Commission. CNN promptly withdrew its 9/11 E-4B story from its website ("CNN Pulls 9/11 E4B 'Doomsday' Plane Video over White House," JREF Forum, September 13, 2007, http://forums.randi.org/showthread.php?t=93196.

53. Federal Emergency Management Agency, *Federal Continuity Directive 1*, http://www. fema.gov/media-library/assets/documents/30478. NSPD-51 also nullified PDD 67, Richard Clarke's COG directive of a decade earlier; and it referred to new "classified Continuity Annexes" that shall "be protected from unauthorized disclosure."

54. Dennis Kucinich, David Swanson, and Elizabeth De La Vega, *The 35 Articles of Impeachment and the Case for Prosecuting George W. Bush* (Port Townsend, WA: Feral House, 2008), 81; Peter Dale Scott, "Congress, the Bush Administration and Continuity of Government Planning: The Showdown," CounterPunch, March 31, 2008, http://www.counterpunch.org/2008/03/31/the-showdown/.

55. "Notice: Continuation of the National Emergency with Respect to Certain Terrorist Attacks," Federal Register, September 12, 2007, http://www.gpo.gov/fdsys/pkg/WCPD-2007-09-17/pdf/WCPD-2007-09-17-Pg1204.pdf, emphasis added.

56. E.g. "Notice from the President on the Continuation of the National Emergency with Respect to Certain Terrorist Attacks,": White House, September 10, 2010, (http://www.whitehouse.gov/the-press-office/2010/09/10/notice-president-con tinuation-national-emergency-with-respect-certain-te).

57. Public Law 94-112, Sec. 202, 90 Stat. 1256, http://www.gpo.gov/fdsys/pkg/STAT UTE-90/pdf/STATUTE-90-Pg1255.pdf, 2. This language overruled the specification in President Ford's Executive Order 11921 the same year, that, when a state of emergency was declared by the President, Congress could *not* review the matter for a period of six months.

58. Cf. Peter Dale Scott and Dam Hamburg, "To All Readers: Help Force Congress to Observe the Law on National Emergencies!!!," 911Truth.org, March 24, 2009, http://www.911truth.org/to-all-readers-help-force-congress-to-observe-the-law -on-national-emergencies/.

59. Peter Dale Scott and Dan Hamburg, 911Truth.org, March 24, 2009, http://www.911truth.org/article.php?story=20090324183053848#r7.

60. See for example, White House Press Release, September 10, 2010, http://www. whitehouse.gov/the-press-office/2010/09/10/notice-president-continuation-na tional-emergency-with-respect-certain-te.

61. Mann, *Rise of the Vulcans*, 145.
62. CNN Special Assignment, November 17, 1991.
63. Public Law 94-112, 2.

4. THE FALSIFIED WAR ON TERROR

1. Dana Priest and William Arkin, *Top Secret America: The Rise of the New American Security State* (New York: Little Brown, 2011), 52.
2. For example, Marc Ambinder and D. G. Grady, *Deep State: Inside the Government Secrecy Industry* (New York: John Wiley, 2013); John Tirman, "The Quiet Coup: No, Not Egypt. Here," HuffingtonPost, July 9, 2013, http://www.huffingtonpost .com/john-tirman/nsa-deep-state_b_3569316.html.
3. Erich Lichtblau, "In Secret, Court Vastly Broadens Powers of N.S.A.," *New York Times,* July 6, 2013.
4. National Commission on Terrorist Attacks upon the United States, *The 9/11 Commission Report* (New York: W. W. Norton, 2004), 68, http://www.9-11commission .gov/report/911Report.pdf.
5. *9/11 Commission Report*, 145.
6. In addition there are unproven allegations that the United States granted a green card to Ayman al Zawahiri, identified in the *9/11 Commission Report* as "the most important Egyptian in bin Laden's circle" (*9/11 Commission Report*, 57), and since 2011 the leader of al-Qaeda (Nafeez Mosaddeq Ahmed, *The War On Truth: 9/11, Disinformation and the Anatomy of Terrorism* [Northampton, MA: Olive Branch Press, 2005], 46). It is not contested that "foreign trial transcripts and U.S. court records confirmed that Zawahiri had previously flown to America, once in the early 1990s, and again in 1994. . . . Ali Mohamed, bin-Laden's American-trained military adviser, served as Zawahiri's host during the 1994 American fundraising campaign" (Jayna Davis, *The Third Terrorist: The Middle East Connection to the Oklahoma City Bombing* [Nashville, TN: WND Books, 2004], 318–19).
7. I have chosen to use the term "Al-Qaedist" here in place of what I earlier wrote, "jihadi terrorists." "Jihadist," like "Islamist," can refer in English to someone in a legitimate pursuit of Islam; and it is important to distinguish between jihad and terrorism—not blur the distinction between them. I should make it clear that by the term "al-Qaedist" I refer to any terrorist broadly sharing the terrorist political ideology of al-Qaeda, not just those who have sworn allegiance to Osama bin Laden or his successors. Thus for example it would include "the Islamic State of Iraq and Syria, a jihadist group that is so radical it has broken with al Qaeda, in part because it insisted on being allowed to indiscriminately kill Shiites" (*New York Times*, April 29, 2014, 1).
8. Richard Clarke, *Against All Enemies: Inside America's War on Terror* (New York: Free Press, 2004), 30.
9. It is relevant that in 2011 the United States provided assistance to the armed overthrow of Qaddafi in Libya, by a violent resistance force in which al-Qaedists were prominent.

10. For example, Mark Mazzetti, "Spy Agencies Say Iraq War Worsens Terrorism Threat," *New York Times*, September 23, 2006, http://www.nytimes.com/2006/09/24/world/middleeast/24terror.html?pagewanted=all.

11. A 2013 FBI circular instructs enforcement officials that people should be "considered suspicious" of possible involvement in "terrorist activity" if they hold the "attitude" described as "Conspiracy theories about Westerners" (Ralph Lopez, "FBI calls half of populace with 9/11 doubts potential terrorists," *Crime*, September 19, 2013, http://www.digitaljournal.com/article/358624; citing FBI circular, "Potential Indicators of Terrorist Activities Related to Sleepers").

12. Jean-Charles Brisard and Guillaume Dasquié, *Ben Laden: la vérité interdite* (Paris: Denoël, 2001), 14.

13. Robert Baer, *See No Evil: The True Story of a Ground Soldier in the CIA's War On Terrorism* (New York: Crown Publishers, 2002), 243–44; discussion in Peter Dale Scott, *Drugs, Oil, and War: The United States in Afghanistan, Colombia, and Indochina* (Lanham, MD: Rowman & Littlefield, 2003), 28–31; Peter Dale Scott, *The Road to 9/11: Wealth, Empire, and the Future of America* (Berkeley: University of California Press, 2007), 170–72.

14. Cf. my enlargement of the concept of an American deep state beyond parallel government in Peter Dale Scott, *American War Machine: Deep Politics, the CIA Global Drug Connection, and the Road to Afghanistan* (Lanham, MD: Rowman & Littlefield, 2010), 20–23; Peter Dale Scott, "The 'Deep State' behind U.S. democracy," VoltaireNet, April 6, 2011, http://www.voltairenet.org/article169316.html; etc.

15. All of America's military engagements since 1950 have involved defense of the petrodollar system. See chapter 6.

16. Peter Lance, *Triple Cross: How bin Laden's Master Spy Penetrated the CIA, the Green Berets, and the FBI—and Why Patrick Fitzgerald Failed to Stop Him* (New York: Regan, 2006), 120–25. Cf. *Toronto Globe and Mail*, November 22, 2001; Tim Weiner, *Enemies: A History of the FBI* (New York: Random House, 2012), 397.

17. Ali H. Soufan, *The Black Banners: The Inside Story of 9/11 and the War Against al-Qaeda* (New York: W. W. Norton, 2011), 75–77.

18. Lance, *Triple Cross*, 373. Cf. J. M. Berger, "Paving the Road to 9/11," Intelwire, http://intelwire.egoplex.com/unlocking911-1-ali-mohamed-911.html: "Ali Mohamed was the utility player who created al Qaeda's terrorist infrastructure in the United States—a series of connections, ideas, techniques and specific tools used by the [9/11] plot's hijackers and masterminds. . . . Mohamed described teaching al Qaeda terrorists how to smuggle box cutters onto airplanes."

19. Lance, *Triple Cross*, 123–24.

20. Soufan, *The Black Banners*, 561. The testimony of former FBI agents like Ali Soufan that Mohamed was not incarcerated has been challenged in a curious book by Special Forces veteran Pete Blaber, *The Mission, The Men, and Me: Lessons from a Former Delta Force Commander* (New York: Berkley Trade, 2010). Blaber claims to have interviewed Mohamed in a prison cell, after reading Mohamed's perceptive document on how to track down Osama bin Laden. Blaber argues strenuously

that Mohamed was not a double agent, but fails to deal with any of the countervailing evidence (such as the RCMP release).

21. "D.E.A. Deployed Mumbai Plotter Despite Warning," *New York Times*, November 8, 2009; cf. Scott, *American War Machine*, 246–47. Cf. *The Globe and Mail* (Canada), May 26, 2011: "FBI thought Mumbai massacre plotter worked for them, court told." Another much simpler domestic example of this puzzle is Richard Aoki, the FBI informant who in the 1960s supplied the Black Panthers in Oakland with arms (Seth Rosenfeld, *Subversives: The FBI's War on Student Radicals, and Reagan's Rise to Power* [New York: Macmillan, 2012], 418–24, etc.).

22. Peter Dale Scott, *The Road to 9/11*, 151–60. For a summary, see Peter Dale Scott, "Bosnia, Kosovo, and Now Libya: The Human Costs of Washington's On-Going Collusion with Terrorists," Asian-Pacific Journal: Japan Focus, July 29, 2011, http://japanfocus.org/-Peter_Dale-Scott/3578.

23. Steven Emerson, *American Jihad: The Terrorists Living among Us* (New York: Free Press, 2002), 57–58; Peter L. Bergen, *Holy War, Inc.: Inside the Secret World of Osama bin Laden* (New York: Free Press, 2001), 135; Lawrence Wright, *The Looming Tower: Al-Qaeda and the Road to 9/11* (New York: Alfred A. Knopf, 2006), 181–82. Wright gives a detailed summary of John Zent's ensuing interview with Mohamed in May 1993, but says not a word about Zent's intervention with the RCMP. To my knowledge the only privileged book to do so is Tim Weiner's *Enemies*, 397: "He explained that he was working for the FBI and he offered the telephone number of his Bureau contact in San Francisco. The Canadians released Mohamed after the agent vouched for him." Weiner's relative candor came in 2012, long after this FBI scandal had already been publicized by Lance and other authors, including myself.

24. Cf. *Washington Post*, June 1, 2012: "Soufan's case was unusual because he never worked for the CIA. The PRB's [Publications Review Board's] authority [i.e., legal authority] is grounded in the secrecy agreements signed by agency employees that require them to submit any material prepared for public disclosure 'either during my employment . . . or at anytime thereafter.'" In other words, the CIA's PRB had no legal right to censor Soufan's book, but did so anyway—an example of the blurring of past bureaucratic distinctions in today's shadow state.

25. Michael Scheuer, *Osama bin Laden* (New York: Oxford University Press, 2011), 218n.

26. Lessons from "Ali Mohamed Case," Defense Human Resources Activity (DHRA), Department of Defense, http://www.dhra.mil/perserec/osg/terrorism/mohamedhtm.

27. Benjamin Weiner and James Risen, "The Masking of a Militant: A Special Report; A Soldier's Shadowy Trail In U.S. and in the Mideast," *New York Times*, December 1, 1998. This embarrassing exercise in damage control cannot be found on LexisNexis.

28. Peter Waldman, Gerald F. Seib, Jerry Markon, and Christopher Cooper, "Sergeant Served U.S. Army and bin Laden, Showing Failings in FBI's Terror Policing," *Wall Street Journal*, November 26, 2001.

29. Daniel Coleman, Affidavit, Sealed Complaint, United States of America v. Ali Abdelseoud Mohamed, U.S. District Court, Southern District of New York, Sep-

tember 1998 (obtained by INTELWIRE.com), p.7, http://intelfiles.egoplex.com/ali-mohamed-coleman-affidavit.pdf. In fact Mohamed had been an FBI informant since at least 1992.

30. I had no choice but to remove certain relevant material from *The Road to 9/11*. As British and American lawyers pointed out to me, my sources had already retracted their statements before me.

31. Lance, *Triple Cross*, 125. Cf. Steven Emerson, "Osama bin Laden's Special Operations Man," *Journal of Counterterrorism and Security International*, September 1, 1998, http://www.investigativeproject.org/187/osama-bin-ladens-special-operations-man: "In a seemingly bizarre twist, while in California, Mohammed volunteered to provide information to the FBI on a smuggling operations involving Mexicans and other aliens not connected to terrorist groups. Within time, officials say, the relationship allowed Mohammed to divert the FBI's attention away from looking at his real role in terrorism into examining the information he gave them about other smuggling." But it could not have diverted the FBI's attention for very long. By May 1993, five months later, Mohamed had described to Zent in some detail his activities with Osama and al-Qaeda (Wright, *Looming Tower*, 181–82; J. M. Berger, ed., *Ali Mohamed: An Intelwire Sourcebook* [Intelwire Press, 2006], 31–32).

32. Lance, *Triple Cross*, 95. Cf. Weiner, *Enemies*, 397.

33. Lance, *Triple Cross*, 99. Similarly Tim Weiner writes that the FBI agents handling Mohamed "did not comprehend him" (Weiner, *Enemies*, 397).

34. "Ali Mohamed Case," Defense Human Resources Activity (DHRA), Department of Defense, http://www.dhra.mil/perserec/osg/terrorism/mohamed.htm, emphasis added.

35. John Miller, Michael Stone, and Chris Mitchell, *The Cell: Inside the 9/11 Plot, and Why the FBI and CIA Failed to Stop It* (New York: Hyperion, 2002), 90–91.

36. United States of America v. Omar Abdel Rahman et al., September 11, 1995; quoted in Berger, *Ali Mohamed*, 210; cf. Lance, *Triple Cross*, 48.

37. "Sergeant Served U.S. Army and bin Laden," *Wall Street Journal*, November 26, 2001: "At the time, the FBI wrote them off as harmless zealots, fired up to help the mujahedeen fighting the Soviet puppet government in Afghanistan."

38. Bergen, *Holy War, Inc.*, 134. The al-Kifah Center ("al-Kifah" means "the struggle") was "known informally as 'the jihad office.' . . . There was no problem finding volunteers, who might stay in Afghanistan up to three months at a time. . . . The volunteers joined the forces of the Hezb-I-Islami (Party of Islam), led by Gulbuddin Hekmatyar" (Stephen Franklin, "Slain Muslim Had Link To Radical Cleric," *Chicago Tribune*, July 11, 1993, http://articles.chicagotribune.com/1993-07-11/news/9307110208_1_world-trade-center-bombing-sheik-omar-abdel-rahman-mustafa-shalabi).

39. Mitchell D. Silber, *The Al Qaeda Factor: Plots Against the West* (Philadelphia: University of Pennsylvania Press, 2012), 169–70.

40. Bergen, *Holy War, Inc.*, 130–31.

41. Wright, *Looming Tower*, 180; citing *Boston Globe*, February 3, 1995; cf. Robert Friedman, "The CIA's Jihad," *New Yorker*, March 27, 1995; Paul L. Williams, *Al Qaeda: Brotherhood of Terror* (Parsippany, NJ: Alpha, 2002), 117.

42. Lance Williams and Erik McCormick, "Al Qaeda Terrorist Worked with FBI," *San Francisco Chronicle*, November 4, 2001.

43. "Lessons from Ali Mohamed Case," Pentagon, http://www.dhra.mil/perserec/osg/terrorism/mohamed.htm.

44. Robert Friedman, "The CIA and the Sheik," *Village Voice*, March 30, 1993; Evan Kohlmann, *Al-Qaida's Jihad in Europe* (New York: Berg, 2004), 26.

45. Miller, Stone, and Mitchell, *The Cell*, 44. Cf. J. M. Berger, *Jihad Joe: Americans Who Go to War in the Name of Islam* (Washington, DC: Potomac Books, 2011), 44: "The stash included military training manuals and documents given to Nosair by Sergeant Ali Mohamed, the jihadist mole at Fort Bragg."

46. *Newsday*, November 8, 1990.

47. *New York Times*, November 8, 1990.

48. *New York Times*, December 16, 1990. Compare the Pentagon's terrorist account of the training given by Mohamed ("surveillance, weapons and explosives") with the more benign version in the long article about Mohamed in *The New York Times*: "Mr. Mohamed met the local Muslims at an apartment in Jersey City, and taught them survival techniques, map reading and how to recognize tanks and other Soviet weapons, according to testimony by one of his students at Mr. Nosair's 1995 Federal trial" (Benjamin Weiner and James Risen, "The Masking of a Militant: A Special Report," *New York Times*, December 01, 1998).

49. TV journalist John Miller, a former New York deputy police commissioner who would later become the FBI's Assistant Director for Public Affairs, reported in Miller, Stone, and Mitchell, *The Cell*, 44, that the disputed evidence from Nosair's home was withheld from NYPD officer Edward Norris, who prepared the NYPD case against Nosair:

> On the third day after the shooting, while Norris was out to lunch, the FBI removed Nosair's 16 boxes of files from Norris's squad room. Unfortunately the evidence was about to enter a black hole. The FBI now says it turned the files over to the Manhattan District Attorney's Office, after it was decided, following a series of meetings and phone calls, that the local prosecutor and the NYPD would have exclusive jurisdiction over the murder case. The Manhattan DA's office won't comment on what was done with the files before Nosair's trial, though Norris was never informed they were available. But this much is certain: The bulk of the material remained untranslated and unread for nearly three years.

This last sentence is hard to reconcile with the detailed description given *at the time* by Borelli.

50. Friedman, "The CIA's Jihad."

51. Lance, *Triple Cross*, 58–62.

52. "Lessons from Ali Mohamed Case," DHRA, Department of Defense, http://www.dhra.mil/perserec/osg/terrorism/mohamed.htm.

53. For the list, see Lance, *Triple Cross*, 574–75.

54. Steve Coll, *Ghost Wars: The Secret History of the CIA, Afghanistan, and bin Laden, from the Soviet Invasion to September 10, 2001* (New York: Penguin Press, 2004), 251.

55. Quoted in Lance, *Triple Cross*, 383.
56. Coll, *Ghost Wars*, 255: "Since 1989 the FBI had been running paid informants inside circles of Islamic radicals in New York and New Jersey. In 1990, FBI agents carted away forty-seven boxes of documents and training manuals from the home of El Sayyid Nosair." Cf. Lance, *Triple Cross*, 73–75, etc.
57. Friedman, "The CIA's Jihad."
58. Robert Dreyfuss, *Devil's Game: How the United States Helped Unleash Fundamentalist Islam* (New York: Metropolitan Books, 2003), 73–79, 98–108, 120–25. Cf. Robert Baer [a former CIA officer], *Sleeping with the Devil* (New York: Crown, 2003), 99: "The White House looked on the Brothers as a silent ally, a secret weapon against (what else?) communism. This covert action started in the 1950s with the Dulles brothers . . . when they approved Saudi Arabia's funding of Egypt's Brothers against Nasser"; Scott, *Road to 9/11*, 44.
59. Dreyfuss, *Devil's Game*, 274–75; quoting John Cooley, *Unholy Wars* (London: Pluto Press, 1999), 31–32: "By the end of 1980, U.S. military trainers were sent to Egypt to impart the skills of the U.S. Special Forces to those Egyptians who would, in turn, pass on the training to the Egyptian volunteers flying to the aid of the mujahideen in Afghanistan."
60. Joseph J. Trento, *Prelude to Terror: The Rogue CIA and the Legacy of America's Private Intelligence Network* (New York: Carroll and Graf, 2005), 150, 247.
61. "Lessons from Ali Mohamed Case," http://www.dhra.mil/perserec/osg/terrorism/mohamed.htm.
62. Cf. Emerson, "Osama bin Laden's Special Operations Man": "He had been in the United States earlier that decade, having graduated as a captain from a Special Forces Officers School at Fort Bragg in 1981 in a program for visiting military officials from foreign countries."
63. Lance, *Triple Cross*, 194 (oath).

5. THE FALSIFIED WAR ON TERROR II

1. Peter Dale Scott, *The Road to 9/11: Wealth, Empire, and the Future of America* (Berkeley: University of California Press, 2007), 161–62; citing *Guardian* (London), January 7, 1993; Evan Kohlmann, *Al-Qaida's Jihad in Europe* (New York: Berg, 2004), 16.
2. Ferrukh Mir, *Half Truth* (Bloomington, IN: iUniverse, 2011), 163–64: "In 1992, Ali Mohamed, a double agent and ex-US Special Forces officer with close ties to Al-Kifah, led a group of US militants who were all ex-US soldiers to train and fight in Bosnia. Abu Obadiah Yahiya, an ex-US Marine and security chief at the Brooklyn branch, lead [sic] a second group of US militants to fight in Bosnia." Cf. Mark Huband, *Trading Secrets: Spies and Intelligence in an Age of Terror* (New York: I. B. Tauris, 2013), 112: "Mohamed—using the *nom-de-guerre* Abu 'Abdallah—travelled to Bosnia as part of a team which trained and armed Muslim fighters there until June 1993, when he travelled on to Khartoum and was asked by bin Laden to set up the al-Qaeda cell in Nairobi, Kenya."

3. Kohlmann, *Al-Qaida's Jihad in Europe*, 39–41; citing Steve Coll and Steve LeVine, "Global Network Provides Money, Haven," *Washington Post*, August 3, 1993. Bin Laden also gave money to the Third World Relief Agency to buy weapons for Bosnian fighters (Michael Scheuer, *Through Our Enemies' Eyes: Osama bin Laden, Radical Islam, and the Future of America* [Washington, DC: Potomac Books, Inc., 2006], 151).

4. Scott, *Road to 9/11*, 149–50; Kohlmann, *Al-Qaida's Jihad in Europe*, 45, 73–75.

5. Scott, *Road to 9/11*, 149; Kohlmann, *Al-Qaida's Jihad in Europe*, 73. I have been unable to identify this Prince Faisal securely. He is perhaps Prince Faisal bin Salman bin Abdulaziz al-Saud, who frequently visited the United States in connection with his horse-breeding interests in Kentucky. In 2003 Gerald Posner claimed that Faisal's older brother and business partner Ahmed bin Salman had had ties to al-Qaeda and advance knowledge of 9/11 (Gerald Posner, *Why America Slept: The Failure to Prevent 9/11* [New York: Random House, 2003]), 202. Cf. Anthony Summers and Robbyn Swan, *The Eleventh Day: The Full Story of 9/11 and Osama bin Laden* (New York: Ballantine Books, 2011), 405–7, 419, 563–64.

6. Robert Friedman, "The CIA's Jihad," *New Yorker*, March 27, 1995. About this time, Ayman al-Zawahiri, in 2014 the leader of al-Qaeda, came without difficulty to America to raise funds in Silicon Valley, where he was hosted by Ali Mohamed (Lawrence Wright, "The Man Behind Bin Laden," *New Yorker*, September 16, 2002: "Zawahiri decided to look for money in the world center of venture capitalism—Silicon Valley. He had been to America once before, in 1989, when he paid a recruiting visit to the mujahideen's Services Bureau branch office in Brooklyn. According to the F.B.I., he returned in the spring of 1993, this time to Santa Clara, California, where he was greeted by Ali Mohamed, the double agent.")

7. Bruce O. Riedel, *The Search for Al Qaeda: Its Leadership, Ideology, and Future* (Washington, DC: Brookings Institution Press, 2008), 43: "Osama also worked with ISI in the creation of a key Kashmiri jihadist group in the late 1980s, the Lashkar-e-Tayyiba." Cf. Yossef Bodansky, *Bin Laden: The Man Who Declared War on America* (Rocklin, CA: Forum, 2001), 320.

8. Michael Scheuer, "Central Asia in Al-Qaeda's Vision of the Anti-American Jihad, 1979–2006," *China and Eurasia Forum Quarterly*, 2006, 3.

9. The Black Vault, https://www.ctc.usma.edu/v2/wp-content/uploads/2013/10/Letter-to-Mullah-Mohammed-Omar-from-bin-Laden-Translation.pdf

10. Ahmed Rashid, "They're Only Sleeping: Why Militant Islamicists in Central Asia Aren't Going To Go Away," *New Yorker*, January 14, 2002, http://www.newyorker.com/magazine/2002/01/14/theyre-only-sleeping; cf. Ahmed Rashid, *Jihad* (New Haven: Yale University Press, 2002), 165; Svante Cornell, "Narcotics, Radicalism and Security in Central Asia: The Islamic Movement of Uzbekistan," Uppsala University, December 2004, 19: "Bolot Januzakov, Head of the Kyrgyz Security Council, asserted in 2000 that the IMU controlled the majority, perhaps up to 70%, of the heroin entering Kyrgyzstan."

11. Gretchen Peters, *Seeds of Terror: How Heroin Is Bankrolling the Taliban and Al Qaeda* (New York: Thomas Dunne Books/St. Martin's Press, 2009), 69, 87, 89, 132–33. Cf. Parviz Mullodzhanov, "IMU becomes multinational force," *Central Asia Online*, March 17, 2010, http://centralasiaonline.com/en_GB/articles/caii/

features/main/2010/03/17/feature-03: "IMU leaders are focused on the international black market and drug trafficking."

12. Peters, *Seeds of Terror*, 132–33.

13. 9/11 Commission, "Monograph on Terrorist Financing: Staff Report to the Commission," 7. Cf. National Commission on Terrorist Attacks upon the United States, *The 9/11 Commission Report* (New York: W. W. Norton, 2004), http://counterterrorismblog.org/upload/2008/09/911_TerrFin_Monograph.pdf, 171: "Al Qaeda has been alleged to have used a variety of illegitimate means, particularly drug trafficking and conflict diamonds, to finance itself. . . . While the drug trade was a source of income for the Taliban, it did not serve the same purpose for al Qaeda." The footnote to this sentence adds: "No evidence indicates any such involvement in drug trafficking, and none of the detained al Qaeda operatives has indicated that this was a method of fund-raising" (*9/11 Commission Report*, 499).

14. "Evidence Presented to the British Parliament, 4th October 2001," *Los Angeles Times*, October 4, 2001. Cf. *New York Times*, October 4, 2001. For further documentation, see Peter Dale Scott, *Drugs, Oil, and War: The United States in Afghanistan, Colombia, and Indochina* (Lanham, MD: Rowman & Littlefield, 2003), 32, 36.

15. *New York Times*, July 20, 1993. Cf. J. R. de Szigethy, "Crime Scene—World Trade Center," AmericanMafia.com, September 2004, http://www.americanmafia.com/Feature_Articles_275.html: "The murders [from the 1993 WTC bombing] were the result of a plot by members of an organized crime syndicate involved in drug trafficking."

16. Jayna Davis, *The Third Terrorist: The Middle East Connection to the Oklahoma City Bombing* (Nashville, TN: WND Books, 2004), 303.

17. *Boston Herald*, October 17, 2001; cf. *9/11 Commission Report*, 175.

18. Steve Coll, *Ghost Wars: The Secret History of the CIA, Afghanistan, and bin Laden, from the Soviet Invasion to September 10, 2001* (New York: Penguin Press, 2004), 104.

19. Mullodzhanov, "IMU becomes multinational force."

20. Cf. Peter Dale Scott, *American War Machine: Deep Politics, the CIA Global Drug Connection, and the Road to Afghanistan* (Lanham, MD: Rowman & Littlefield, 2010).

21. Alfred W. McCoy, *The Politics of Heroin: CIA Complicity in the Global Drug Trade* (Brooklyn, NY: Lawrence Hill Books, 1991), 261–78.

22. Jonathan Kwitny, *The Crimes of Patriots* (New York: W. W. Norton, 1987), 115 (Nugan Hand); Rachel Bronson, *Thicker than Oil: America's Uneasy Partnership with Saudi Arabia* (Oxford: Oxford University Press, 2006), 177–80; Elaine Windrich, "The Laboratory of Hate: The Role of Clandestine Radio in the Angolan War," *International Journal of Cultural Studies* 3(2), 2000 (Safari Club).

23. Steven Emerson, *American Jihad: The Terrorists Living among Us* (New York: Free Press, 2002), 28.

24. Yossef Bodansky, *Terror! The Inside Story of the Terrorist Conspiracy in America* (New York: S.P.I. Books, 1994), 166. Similarly Gerald Posner notes "rumors that [Mustafa] Shalabi [the head of the al-Kifah Center until he was murdered in

February 1991] . . . might be involved in counterfeiting" (Posner, *Why America Slept*, 8).

25. Berger, *Jihad Joe*, 37; citing United States of America v. Rahman, S5 93 Cr. 181, court transcript, April 3, 1995.

26. Scheuer, *Through Our Enemies' Eyes*, 151.

27. Emerson, *American Jihad*, 28.

28. Bin Laden's and al-Qaeda's proximity to Khattab is both asserted and disputed at high levels. See Robert W. Schaefer, *The Insurgency in Chechnya and the North Caucasus: From Gazavat To Jihad* (Santa Barbara, CA: Praeger Security International, 2011), 165–66.

29. Thomas Hegghammer, *Jihad in Saudi Arabia: Violence and Pan-Islamism Since 1979* (New York: Cambridge University Press, 2010), 56.

30. Ali H. Soufan, *Black Banners: The Inside Story of 9/11 and the War Against al-Qaeda*, (New York: W. W. Norton, 2011), 62. Jeremy Scahill also writes of Special Operations veterans in Blackwater with previous "experience in Chechnya" (Jeremy Scahill, *Dirty Wars: The World Is a Battlefield* [New York: Nation Books, 2013], 408).

31. Berger, *Ali Mohamed*, 18 (discussed below).

32. Yaroslav Trofimov, *The Siege of Mecca: The 1979 Uprising at Islam's Holiest Shrine* (New York: Anchor, 2008).

33. Peter Tomsen, *The Wars of Afghanistan: Messianic Terrorism, Tribal Conflicts, and the Failures of Great Powers* (New York: PublicAffairs, 2011), 179–82, 195–99.

34. Coll, *Ghost Wars*, 155. For Azzam's and Osama bin Laden's Muslim Brotherhood memberships, see Steve Coll, *The Bin Ladens: An Arabian Family in the American Century* (New York: Penguin Press, 2008), 148, 253.

35. *9/11 Commission Report*, 56.

36. Ahmed Rashid, *Taliban: Militant Islam, Oil and Fundamentalism in Central Asia* (New Haven: Yale University Press, 2001), 131. Cf. Steven A. Yetiv, *The Petroleum Triangle: Oil, Globalization, and Terror* (Ithaca, NY: Cornell University Press, 2011), 65.

37. Tomsen, *The Wars of Afghanistan*, 198.

38. Scott, *Road to 9/11*, 171; citing Rajeev Sharma, *Pak Proxy War* (New Delhi: Kaveri Books, 2002), 145–46.

39. Cf. John J. Loftus, "What Congress Does Not Know about Enron and 9/11," May 2003, http://www.informationclearinghouse.info/article4219.htm:

> The . . . block order, in force since the 1980's, was against any investigation that would embarrass the Saudi Royal family. Originally, it was designed to conceal Saudi support for Muslim extremists fighting against the Soviets in Afghanistan and Chechnya, but it went too far. Oliver North noted in his autobiography, that every time he tried to do something about terrorism links in the Middle East, he was told to stop because it might embarrass the Saudis. This block remains in place.

40. Scott, *Road to 9/11*, 172; citing Greg Palast and David Pallister, "Intelligence: FBI Claims Bin Laden Inquiry Was Frustrated," *Guardian*, November 7, 2001, http://www.theguardian.com/world/2001/nov/07/afghanistan.september11.

41. Andrew C. McCarthy, *The Grand Jihad: How Islam and the Left Sabotage America* (New York: Encounter Books, 2010), 124–25. Andrew C. McCarthy is the former Assistant United States Attorney who led the 1995 terrorism prosecution against Sheikh Omar Abdel Rahman and also contributed to the prosecutions of those (including Ali Mohamed) who bombed U.S. embassies in Kenya and Tanzania. He later became a columnist for *National Review*. His book is biased but contains much useful information.

42. David Livingstone, *Black Terror White Soldiers: Islam, Fascism and the New Age* ([Place of publication not identified]: Sabilillah Publications, 2013), 557, citing Craig Unger, *House of Bush, House of Saud* (New York: Scribner, 2004), 112 (cf. 101). Cf. Coll, *The Bin Ladens*, 342.

43. Nathan Vardi, "Sins of the Father?" *Forbes*, March 18, 2002.

44. Coleman affidavit, 2; in J. M. Berger, ed., *Ali Mohamed: An Intelwire Sourcebook* (Intelwire Press, 2006), 26, 31–32).

45. Coll, *The Bin Ladens*, 399–401.

46. For a summary of some of the conflicting accounts, see Summers and Day, *The Eleventh Day*, 215–16.

47. Coll, *Ghost Wars*, 231, emphasis added. In 2001 Peter Bergen had claimed that bin Laden "used his family connections with King Fahd to convince the [Saudi] government that he needed to leave the country to sort out some business matters in Pakistan. Arriving there in April 1991, he then sent a letter to his family telling them that he would not be able to return home. After some months in Afghanistan he arrived in Sudan" (Peter L. Bergen, *Holy War, Inc.* [New York: Free Press, 2001], 81–82).

48. *9/11 Commission Report*, 57. In the December 2004 paperback edition of *Ghost Wars*, 231–32, Coll adjusted his account to reconcile with *The 9/11 Commission Report*. He replaced his sentence, "The escort put bin Laden on a plane out of Saudi Arabia," with two new ones: "Two associates of bin Laden later offered a different version while under interrogation. They said a dissident member of the royal family helped him leave the country by arranging for bin Laden to attend an Islamic conference in Pakistan during the spring of 1991."

49. Steve Coll also suggests that the "interior ministry" (headed by the Prince) supplied bin Laden with "a one-time exit visa to travel to Pakistan to liquidate investments there" (Coll, *The Bin Ladens*, 381). Both motives may have been present in bin Laden's mind, but his capacity to serve as a mediator may have been more influential in persuading the Saudis to arrange for his departure.

50. Lawrence Wright, *Looming Tower: Al-Qaeda and the Road to 9/11* (New York: Alfred A. Knopf, 2006), 161. For Naif (or Nayef) as anti-American, see Coll, *Ghost Wars*, 399; Coll, *The Bin Ladens*, 437, 626n.

51. Wright, *Looming Tower*, 161; Roy Gutman, *How We Missed the Story: Osama Bin Laden, the Taliban and the Hijacking of Afghanistan* (Washington, DC: Endowment of the United States Institute of Peace, 2008), 34.

52. Tomsen, *The Wars of Afghanistan*, 485: "Al-Qaeda, Muslim Brotherhood extremists, and Prince Turki's General Intelligence Directorate supported the ISI's extremist-centered Afghan strategy."

53. Against this odd claim cf., for example, Coll, *The Bin Ladens*, 251: "Osama developed cordial relations with Prince Turki al-Faisal. . . . He also won audiences with the powerful full brothers of Fahd—Nayef and Ahmed"; Wright, *Looming Tower*, 154: "The minister of the interior, Prince Naif, . . . summoned bin Laden to his office. . . . Bin Laden had reported to Naif . . . many times during the Afghan jihad." As noted above, Ahmed Rashid claims that bin Laden and Prince Turki became "firm friends and allies" in the same cause (Rashid, *Taliban*, 131).

54. "A Biography of Osama bin Laden," Frontline, PBS, http://www.pbs.org/wgbh/pages/frontline/shows/binladen/who/bio2.html.

55. Scheuer, *Through Our Enemies' Eyes*, 131.

56. Coll, *Ghost Wars*, 207.

57. Barnett R. Rubin, *Afghanistan from the Cold War through the War on Terror* (New York: Oxford University Press, 2013), 86.

58. Coll, *Ghost Wars*, 215–16.

59. Coll, *The Bin Ladens*, 403–5: "Osama now became a target; it is not entirely clear why."

6. DEEP STATE USES AND PROTECTION OF AL-QAEDA TERRORISTS

1. Peter Tomsen, *The Wars of Afghanistan: Messianic Terrorism, Tribal Conflicts, and the Failures of Great Powers* (New York: PublicAffairs, 2011), 337.

2. Tomsen, *The Wars of Afghanistan*, 406–7.

3. Steve Coll, *Ghost Wars: The Secret History of the CIA, Afghanistan, and bin Laden, from the Soviet Invasion to September 10, 2001* (New York: Penguin Press, 2004), 225.

4. Peter Dale Scott, *American War Machine* (Lanham, MD: Rowman & Littlefield, 2010), 94–105; Peter Dale Scott, *The War Conspiracy: JFK, 9/11, and the Deep Politics of War* (New York: Skyhorse, 2013), 98–103.

5. Ahmed Rashid, *Taliban: Militant Islam, Oil and Fundamentalism in Central Asia* (New Haven, CT: Yale University Press, 2001), 145.

6. Thomas Goltz, *Azerbaijan Diary: A Rogue Reporter's Adventures in an Oil-Rich, War-Torn, Post-Soviet Republic* (Armonk, NY: M. E. Sharpe, 1999), 272–75. Cf. Mark Irkali, Tengiz Kodrarian, and Cali Ruchala, "God Save the Shah," *Sobaka Magazine*, May 22, 2003, http://16beavergroup.org/articles/2003/07/03/rene-god-save-the-shah-american-guns-oil-and-spies-in-azerbaijan/. A fourth operative in MEGA Oil, Gary Best, was also a veteran of North's Contra support effort, and before that of efforts to support UNITA in Angola. For more on General Secord's and Major Aderholt's roles as part of Ted Shackley's team of off-loaded CIA assets and capabilities, see Jonathan Marshall, Peter Dale Scott, and Jane Hunter, *The Iran-Contra Connection: Secret Teams and Covert Operations in the Reagan Era* (Boston: South End Press, 1987), 26–30, 36–42, 197–98.

7. It was also a time when Congress, under pressure from Armenian voters, had banned all military aid to Azerbaijan (under Section 907 of the Freedom Support Act). This ban, reminiscent of the Congressional ban on aid to the Contras in the 1980s, ended after 9/11. "In the interest of national security, and to help in 'enhancing global energy security' during this War on Terror, Congress granted President

Bush the right to waive Section 907 in the aftermath of September 11th. It was necessary, Secretary of State Colin Powell told Congress, to 'enable Azerbaijan to counter terrorist organizations'" (Irkali, Kodrarian, and Ruchala, "God Save the Shah").

8. Goltz, *Azerbaijan Diary*, 272–75; Peter Dale Scott, *Drugs, Oil, and War* (Lanham, MD: Rowman & Littlefield, 2003), 7. As part of the airline operation, Azeri pilots were trained in Texas. Dearborn had previously helped Secord advise and train the fledgling Contra air force (Marshall, Scott, and Hunter, *The Iran-Contra Connection*, 197). These important developments were barely noticed in the U.S. press, but a *Washington Post* article did belatedly note that a group of American men who wore "big cowboy hats and big cowboy boots" had arrived in Azerbaijan as military trainers for its army, followed in 1993 by "more than 1,000 guerrilla fighters from Afghanistan's radical prime minister, Gulbuddin Hekmatyar" (*Washington Post*, April 21, 1994). Richard Secord was allegedly attempting also to sell Israeli arms, with the assistance of Israeli agent David Kimche, another associate of Oliver North. See Scott, *Drugs, Oil, and War*, 7, 8, 20. Whether the Americans were aware of it or not, the al-Qaeda presence in Baku soon expanded to include assistance for moving al-Qaedists onward into Dagestan and Chechnya.

9. Steve Levine claims that "The Afghans, too, returned home," having achieved little (Steve Levine, *The Oil and the Glory: The Pursuit of Empire and Fortune on the Caspian Sea* [New York: Random House, 2007], 188). But John Cooley reports that "According to the Russian Foreign Intelligence Service . . . they played an important role in the capture from the Armenians of Goradiz"; and that "after suffering high casualties in battles with the Armenians . . . the fighters that remained turned to sabotage and terrorism" (John Cooley, *Unholy Wars* [London: Pluto Press, 1999], 180–81).

10. Cooley, *Unholy Wars*, 180; Scott, *Drugs, Oil, and War*, 7.

11. The bin Laden organization established an NGO in Baku, which became a base for terrorism elsewhere (National Commission on Terrorist Attacks upon the United States, *The 9/11 Commission Report* (New York: W. W. Norton, 2004), http://www.9-11commission.gov/report/911Report.pdf, 58). It also became a transshipment point for Afghan heroin to the Chechen mafia, whose branches "extended not only to the London arms market, but also throughout continental Europe and North America" (Cooley, *Unholy Wars*, 176).

12. Loretta Napoleoni, *Terror Incorporated* (New York: Seven Stories Press, 2005), 90–97.

13. "KLA Funding Tied to Heroin Profits," *Washington Times*, May 3, 1999. Cf. Mark Curtis, *Secret Affairs: Britain's Collusion with Radical Islam* (London: Profile, 2011), 237-47; Marcia Christoff Kurop, *Wall Street Journal Europe*, November 1, 2001:

> Islamist infiltration of the Kosovo Liberation Army advanced, meanwhile. Bin Laden is said to have visited Albania in 1996 and 1997, according to the murder-trial testimony of an Algerian-born French national, Claude Kader, himself an Afghanistan-trained mujahideen fronting at the Albanian-Arab Islamic Bank. He recruited some

Albanians to fight with the KLA in Kosovo, according to the Paris-based Observatoire Geopolitique des Drogues.

14. Barnett R. Rubin, *Afghanistan from the Cold War through the War on Terror* (New York: Oxford University Press, 2013), 86.

15. Peter L. Bergen, *Holy War, Inc.: Inside the Secret World of Osama bin Laden* (New York: Free Press, 2001), 67. Cf. Ali H. Soufan, *The Black Banners: The Inside Story of 9/11 and the War Against al-Qaeda* (New York: W. W. Norton, 2011), 565 (murder of Anwar Sadat, watch list); J. M. Berger, *Jihad Joe: Americans Who Go to War in the Name of Islam* (Washington, DC: Potomac Books, 2011), 24 (watch list).

16. Lawrence Wright, *The Looming Tower: Al-Qaeda and the Road to 9/11* (New York: Alfred A. Knopf, 2006), 180; cf. Paul L. Williams, *Al Qaeda: Brotherhood of Terror* (Parsippany, NJ: Alpha, 2002), 117.

17. "A Soldier's Shadowy Trail in U.S. and in the Mideast," *New York Times*, December 1, 1998, http://www.nytimes.com/1998/12/01/international/120198LADEN_SHADOW.html.

18. Phil Karber, *Fear and Faith in Paradise: Exploring Conflict and Religion in the Middle East* (Lanham, MD: Rowman & Littlefield, 2012), 3; cf. Wright, *Looming Tower*, 164–65.

19. Anthony Summers and Robbyn Swan, *The Eleventh Day: The Full Story of 9/11 and bin Laden* (New York: Ballantine Books, 2011), 393: "Citing a U.S. intelligence source, the author Simon Reeve reported as much in 1999—well before it became an issue after 9/11."

20. Summers and Swan, *The Eleventh Day*, 394.

21. Steve Coll, *The Bin Ladens: An Arabian Family in the American Century* (New York: Penguin Press, 2008), 399–401. Cf. Geoffrey Wawro, *Quicksand: America's Pursuit of Power in the Middle East* (New York: Penguin Press, 2010): "Osama mixed business and religion. He committed to build an airport at Port Sudan"; Karber, *Fear and Faith in Paradise*: "Bin Laden promised the people of Sudan an airport at Port Sudan."

22. Wright, *Looming Tower*, 165.

23. The text of the State Department paper of August 14, 1996, "State Department Issues Factsheet on Bin Laden," is reproduced in Jean-Charles Brisard and Guillaume Dasquié, *Ben Laden: la vérité interdite* (Paris: Denoël, 2001), 257–58.

24. The Faisal Islamic Bank of Sudan and the Faisal Islamic Bank of Egypt were both founded in 1977 with official approval by Prince Mohammed al-Faisal al-Saud, a graduate of Menlo College in California. Cf. "Sudan Islamic Banking," Photius [n.d.], http://www.photius.com/countries/sudan/economy/sudan_economy_islamic_banking.html:

> The Faisal Islamic Bank, whose principal patron was the Saudi prince, Muhammad ibn Faisal Al Saud, was officially established in Sudan in 1977 by the Faisal Islamic Bank Act. The "open door" policy enabled Saudi Arabia, which had a huge surplus after the 1973 Organization of Petroleum Exporting Countries (OPEC) increases in the price of petroleum, to invest in Sudan. Members of the Muslim Brotherhood and

its political arm, the National Islamic Front, played a prominent role on the board of directors of the Faisal Islamic Bank, thus strengthening the bank's position in Sudan.

25. John Crewdson, "Swiss Officials Freeze Bank Accounts Linked to Supporters of Terrorist Groups," *Chicago Tribune*, November 3, 2001, http://articles.chicagotri bune.com/2001-11-03/news/0111030131_1_laden-linked-bin-terror-list.

26. Robert Dreyfuss, *Devil's Game: How the United States Helped Unleash Fundamentalist Islam* (New York: Metropolitan Books, 2005), 180–81.

27. *Jane's Intelligence Review*, August 1, 2001; quoted in Peter Dale Scott, *Road to 9/11: Wealth, Empire, and the Future of America* (Berkeley: University of California Press, 2007), 356.

28. Crewdson, "Swiss Officials Freeze Bank Accounts Linked to Supporters of Terrorist Groups." Cf. Nafeez Mosaddeq Ahmed, *The War on Truth: 9/11, Disinformation, and the Anatomy of Terrorism* (Northampton, MA: Olive Branch Press, 2005), 98; *Financial Times*, November 29, 2001, http://archive.today/PEgwN: "A US State Department report in 1996 and a French investigation into the bank separately concur that bin Laden invested $50m in the bank on his arrival in Sudan in 1991, an allegation Mr. Ismail [of the bank] denies." Cf. also Brisard and Dasquié, *Ben Laden*, 119–21, 308–10, etc.

29. Coll, *The Bin Ladens*, 413. There is a brief reference to the State Department White Paper in Bergen, *Holy Wars, Inc.*, 83: "Bin Laden . . . sank $50 million of his own money into the Al-Shamal Islamic Bank in Khartoum" (cf. 264n). The controversial author Yossef Bodansky links both the Faisal Islamic Bank and the Al-Shamal Bank to significant al-Qaedist activities, as well as possible drug trafficking (Yossef Bodansky, *Bin Laden: The Man Who Declared War on America* [Rocklin, CA: Forum, 2001], 42–43).

30. Tony Rizzo, "KC Man Linked to Early al-Qaida," *Kansas City Star*, September 9, 2006.

31. Peter Lance, *Triple Cross: How Bin Laden's Master Spy Penetrated the CIA, the Green Berets, and the FBI—and Why Patrick Fitzgerald Failed To Stop Him* (New York: Regan, 2006), 157–59, citing State Department Cable 1994STATE335575.

32. Steve A. Yetiv, *The Petroleum Triangle: Oil, Globalization, and Terror* (Ithaca, NY: Cornell University Press, 2011), 114–15.

33. Zachary Abuza, *Militant Islam in Southeast Asia: Crucible of Terror* (Boulder, CO: Lynne Rienner, 2003), 108. At ease in Saudi Arabia, Khalifa became a misleading source, rather than a topic of inquiry, in privileged bin Laden books like Wright's *The Looming Tower*, 112–13, 450.

34. Michael Scheuer, *Through Our Enemies' Eyes: Osama bin Laden, Radical Islam, and the Future of America* (Washington, DC: Potomac Books, 2006), 151.

35. Lance, *Triple Cross*, 161, citing personal interview.

36. Lance, *Triple Cross*, 162.

37. Lance, *Triple Cross*, 157–58.

38. Khalifa also "headed the Muslim World League office in Peshawar in the 1980s. In 1988, he moved to Manila and opened a branch office of the World Assembly of Muslim Youth [an allied royal creation]" (Tomsen, *The Wars of Afghanistan*, 198).

39. Robert Baer, *Sleeping with the Devil* (New York: Crown, 2003), 167, 140.

40. Tomsen, *The Wars of Afghanistan*, 179–82, 195–99.

41. Abuza, *Militant Islam in Southeast Asia*, 93.

42. Baer, *Sleeping with the Devil*, 69; Aaron Mannes, *Profiles in Terror: The Guide to Middle East Terrorist Organizations* (Lanham, MD: Rowman & Littlefield, 2004), 41.

43. Kumar Ramakrishna (ed.), *After Bali: The Threat of Terrorism in Southeast Asia* (Singapore: Institute of Defence and Strategic Studies, 2003), 139.

44. Wesley J. L. Anderson, *Disrupting Threat Finances: Utilization of Financial Information to Disrupt Terrorist Organizations in the Twenty-First Century* (Ft. Belvoir Defense Technical Information Center, 2007), 14.

45. Girma Yohannes Iyassu Menelik, *Europe: The Future Battleground of Islamic Terrorism* (München: GRIN-Verlag, 2010), 95.

46. Evan Kohlmann, *Al-Qaida's Jihad in Europe* (New York: Berg, 2004), 41–42. Before being captured in Pakistan, Ramzi Yousef was being sheltered by his maternal uncle Zahid al-Shaikh, a principal with Mercy International (Peter Lance, *1000 Years for Revenge: International Terrorism and the FBI, the Untold Story* [New York: ReganBooks, 2003], 189). Mercy International was another Islamic NGO involved in recruiting "international volunteers" for the war in Bosnia (Richard Labévière, *Dollars For Terror: The United States and Islam* (New York: Algora, 2000), 151.

47. Larry Niksch, *Abu Sayyaf: Target of Philippine-U. S. Anti-Terrorism Cooperation* (Washington, DC: Congressional Research Service, Library of Congress, 2007), CRS-4.

48. Peter L. Bergen, *The Osama Bin Laden I Know: An Oral History of al Qaeda's Leader* (New York: Free Press, 2006), 408.

49. *9/11 Commission Report*, 73; citing Joint Inquiry Report (classified version), 324–28. Cf. pp. 146, 148: "In 1992, KSM . . . moved his family to Qatar at the suggestion of the former minister of Islamic affairs of Qatar, Sheikh Abdallah . . . , In January 1996, well aware that U.S. authorities were chasing him, he left Qatar for good."

50. Baer, *Sleeping with the Devil*, 18–19, 194–96. Baer heard from another member of the al-Thani family, former police chief Hamad bin Jasim bin Hamad al-Thani, that when KSM came from the Philippines, Abdallah bin Khalid gave him 20 blank Qatari passports. Later, "As soon as the FBI showed up in Doha" in 1996, the emir ordered Abdallah to move KSM out of his apartment to his beach estate, and eventually out of the country (Baer, *Sleeping with the Devil*, 195–96).

51. Brian Ross and David Scott, "Qatari Royal Family Linked to Al Qaeda," ABC-NEWS.com, February 7, 2003, http://abcnews.go.com/WNT/story?id=129838.

52. *9/11 Commission Report*, 488, citing Intelligence report, interrogation of KSM, July 23, 2003.

53. *9/11 Commission Report*, 171. A Sarajevo paper confirmed that KSM worked for a relief group in Bosnia that "was just a cover for the Cairo-based Islamist movement, the Muslim Brotherhood" (*Adnkronos*, January 20, 2009, http://www.adnkronos.com/AKI/English/Security/?id=3.0.2928330465).

54. "How Saudi Arabia and Qatar are the Tortoise and the Hare of the Middle East," *The Atlantic*, August 27, 2013, http://www.theatlantic.com/international/archive/2013/08/how-saudi-arabia-and-qatar-are-the-tortoise-and-the-hare-of-the-middle-east/279090/. Qatar's motives for this support seem to be the same as Saudi support earlier, for protection at home: "By aligning itself with [the Brotherhood] Qatar could extend its influence and protect itself from revolution on its own soil, turning the Muslim Brotherhood into an ally rather than a threat" (Frida Ghitis, "Qatar's Risky Bet on the Muslim Brotherhood," *World Policy Review*, January 31, 2013).

55. For example, Kimberley N. Trapp, *State Responsibility for International Terrorism* (New York: Oxford University Press, 2011), 51.

56. Lance, *Triple Cross*, 253; emphasis in original. Lance does discuss the role of Qatar's Sheikh Abdullah in helping KSM to escape the FBI (Peter Lance, *Cover Up: What the Government is Still Hiding about the War on Terror* [New York: Regan Books, 2004], 168–69).

57. Lance, *Triple Cross*, 342.

58. Paul Church, "Was Saudi Arabia involved?" Asia Times Online, February 11, 2012, http://www.atimes.com/atimes/Middle_East/NB11Ak03.html. Cf. Summers and Swan, *The Eleventh Day*, 410–15, 559–62; Former Senator Bob Graham, *Keys to the Kingdom* (New York : Vanguard Press, 2011), 131–32; David B. Ottaway, *The King's Messenger: Prince Bandar bin Sultan and America's Tangled Relationship with Saudi Arabia* (New York: Walker, 2008), 198–99.

59. *The Report of the Joint Congressional Inquiry into Intelligence Community Activities before and after the Terrorist Attacks of September 11, 2001*, 107th Congress, 2nd Session, S. Rept. 107-351 and H. Rept. 107-792, 173–77, http://www.gpo.gov/fdsys/search/pagedetails.action?browsePath=107/HRPT/[700%3b799]&granuleId=CRPT-107hrpt792&packageId=CRPT-107hrpt792.

60. This is an appropriate point to make clear that, in my mind, referring to deep state supporters for alleged 9/11 hijackers does not imply that those supporters intended the destruction of the WTC towers and the murder of thousands of civilians. I believe that there were at least two and probably three overlapping conspiracies on 9/11: first, a joint operation involving both U.S. government and Saudi officials, along with at least some of the alleged hijackers; second, a plot to steer airplanes, probably by remote control, and regardless of the alleged hijackers' knowledge and intentions, into WTC towers and the Pentagon; third, a plot to bring down the WTC towers in a controlled demolition not caused by the impact of the airplanes. I am not clear whether the first and second plots were the same or different, but I strongly believe the third plot, though cognizant of the second, involved quite different plotters. I can of course prove none of this, but at least I can clarify what I mean by "supporting those eventually accused of 9/11."

61. National Commission on Terrorist Attacks upon the United States, "Monograph on Terrorist Financing," http://counterterrorismblog.org/upload/2008/09/911_Terr Fin_Monograph.pdf, 1:

> Despite persistent public speculation, there is no evidence that the hijackers who initially settled in San Diego, Mihdhar and Hazmi, received funding from Saudi

citizens Omar al Bayoumi and Osama Bassnan, or that Saudi Princess Haifa al Faisal provided any funds to the hijackers either directly or indirectly. A number of internal FBI documents state without reservation that Bayoumi paid rent on behalf of Mihdhar and Hazmi, a claim reflecting the initial view of some FBI agents. More thorough investigation, however, has determined that Bayoumi did not pay rent or provide any funding to the hijackers.

62. *9/11 Commission Report*, 266–72, 272.
63. Rory O'Connor and Ray Nowosielski, "Who Is Rich Blee?" 911Truth.org, September 21, 2111, http://www.911truth.org/article.php?story=20110921153919600; Rory O'Connor and Ray Nowosielski, "Insiders Voice Doubts about CIA's 9/11 Story," Salon, October 14, 2111, http://www.salon.com/2011/10/14/insiders_voice_doubts_cia_911/. O'Connor and Nowosielski add corroboration from former Counterterrorism Chief Richard Clarke:

> Clarke said he assumed that "there was a high-level decision in the CIA ordering people not to share that information." When asked who might have issued such an order, he replied, "I would think it would have been made by the director," referring to Tenet—although he added that Tenet and others would never admit to the truth today "even if you waterboarded them."

64. Kevin Fenton, *Disconnecting the Dots* (Walterville, OR: TrineDay, 2011); cf. Peter Dale Scott, "9/11 as a Deep Event: How CIA Personnel Helped Allow It To Happen," in James R. Gourley, ed., *The 9/11 Toronto Report: International Hearings on the Events of September 11, 2001* (Seattle, WA: CreateSpace Independent Publishing Platform, 2012), 109–27.
65. On August 29, less than two weeks before 9/11, this interference led one FBI agent, Steve Bongardt, to predict accurately that "someday someone will die" (*9/11 Commission Report*, 259, 271; Wright, *Looming Tower*, 352–54; Scott, *American War Machine*, 203).
66. Lawrence Wright, "The Agent," *New Yorker*, July 10 and 17, 2006, 68; cf. Wright, *Looming Tower*, 339–44; discussion in Scott, *The War Conspiracy*, 355, 388–89.
67. Fenton, *Disconnecting the Dots*, 383–86.
68. Fenton, *Disconnecting the Dots*, 48. Cf. Wright, "The Agent," 68; quoted approvingly in Scott, *American War Machine*, 399.
69. Fenton, *Disconnecting the Dots*, 371, cf. 95.
70. Quoted in Jeremy Scahill, *Dirty Wars: The World Is a Battlefield* (New York: Nation Books, 2013), 21.
71. Tom Wilshire, July 23, 2001, in "United States v. Zacarias Moussaoui (No. 01-455), Substitution for the Testimony of 'John.'" U.S. Court for the District of Alexandria, July 31, 2006; quoted in Fenton, *Disconnecting the Dots*, 274, 401.
72. Fenton, *Disconnecting the Dots*, 276.
73. J. M. Berger, ed., *Ali Mohamed: An Intelwire Sourcebook* (Intelwire Press, 2006), 17; citing Wayne Parry, "Mysterious Pair in Custody Perplexes Federal Investigators," Associated Press, November 11, 2001; Falasten M. Abdeljabbar, "Neighborhood Tired of Suspicions and Fear," *The Jersey Journal*, December 18, 2001.

74. Robert Hanley and Jonathan Miller, "4 Transcripts Are Released in Case Tied to 9/11 Hijackers," *New York Times*, June 25, 2003.

75. Berger, *Ali Mohamed*, 18; citing John Kifner, "Kahane Suspect Is a Muslim with a Series of Addresses," *New York Times*, November 7, 1990; Transcript, Sealed Bail Hearing, US v. El-Atriss (no case number, bail hearing [sealed]), November 19, 2002. The transcripts were unsealed after a lawsuit by several organizations including *The New York Times* and the *Washington Post*.

76. Wayne Parry, "September 11 Fake ID Suspect Flees U.S.," Associated Press, July 31, 2003, http://911review.org/Wiki/Mohamed-El-Atriss.html.

77. Berger, *Ali Mohamed*, 18; citing Robert Hanley and Jonathan Miller, "4 Transcripts Are Released in Case Tied to 9/11 Hijackers"; Wayne Parry, "Judge Releases Transcripts in Sept. 11 Fake IDs Case," Associated Press, June 24, 2003. *The New York Times* story is worth quoting further:

    *Mr. Atriss was a co-founder of a Jersey City check-cashing company, Sphinx Trading Company, that had bank accounts with millions of dollars and had as a co-owner Waleed Abouel Nour, whom the F.B.I. had identified as a terrorist.

    *That business was at the same location, on Kennedy Boulevard, used as a mailing address by several of the hijackers and earlier by Sheik Omar Abdel Rahman, whose followers were convicted of the 1993 bombing of the World Trade Center.

78. Ahmed Rashid, *Descent into Chaos: The United States and the Failure of Nation Building in Pakistan, Afghanistan, and Central Asia* (New York: Viking, 2008), 92–93; cf. Seymour M. Hersh, "The Getaway," *New Yorker*, January 28, 2002; Scott, *Road to 9/11*, 134–35, 336.

79. Peter Dale Scott, *Drugs, Oil, and War*, 53. Cf. David E. Spiro, *The Hidden Hand of American Hegemony: Petrodollar Recycling and International Markets* (Ithaca, NY: Cornell University Press, 1999), x:

    In 1974 [Treasury Secretary William] Simon negotiated a secret deal so the Saudi central bank could buy U.S. Treasury securities outside of the normal auction. A few years later, Treasury Secretary Michael Blumenthal cut a secret deal with the Saudis so that OPEC would continue to price oil in dollars. These deals were secret because the United States had promised other industrialized democracies that it would not pursue such unilateral policies.

80. See for example, Michael Quint, "Saudi Prince to Become Citicorp's Top Stockholder," *New York Times*, February 22, 1991.

81. Andrew Scott Cooper, *The Oil Kings: How the U.S., Iran, and Saudi Arabia Changed the Balance of Power in the Middle East* (New York: Simon & Schuster, 2011), 275, etc.; Scott, *Road to 9/11*, 33–34.

82. F. William Engdahl, *A Century of War: Anglo-American Oil Politics and the New World Order* (London: Pluto Press, 2004), 173.

83. "Halliburton to Move Headquarters to Dubai," *New York Times*, March 11, 2007, http://www.nytimes.com/2007/03/11/business/12halliburtoncnd.html?_r=0. Halliburton made this announcement after it was "being investigated

by different government agencies for various allegations of improper business dealings, and it is in the cross hairs of Democrats in Congress for alleged overbilling" (ABC News, March 12, 2007, http://abcnews.go.com/GMA/Politics/story?id=2943017&page=1). In 2013 the hotel conglomerate Starwood, operating Sheraton and Westin hotels, announced a similar move for a month as "a grand experiment" (*Business Insider*, April 11, 2013, http://www.businessinsider.com/starwood-dubai-headquarters-2013-4).

84. Energy analyst Roger Read said that if Halliburton "formally incorporates itself in the U.A.E., the banking mecca of the Middle East, company profits will soar. . . . 'You'd probably be looking at a tax savings of several hundred million [dollars]. . . . It's a win for the shareholders'" (ABC News, March 12, 2007, http://abcnews.go.com/GMA/Politics/story?id=2943017&page=1).

85. "Egypt Is Arena for Influence of Arab Rivals," *New York Times*, July 9, 2015, http://www.nytimes.com/2013/07/10/world/middleeast/aid-to-egypt-from-saudis-and-emiratis-is-part-of-struggle-with-qatar-for-influence.html?pagewanted=all&_r=0.

86. "Secret Desert Force Set Up by Blackwater's Founder," *New York Times*, May 14, 2011, http://www.nytimes.com/2011/05/15/world/middleeast/15prince.html?pagewanted=all&_r=0.

87. David E. Sanger and Nicole Perlroth, "After Profits, Defense Contractor Faces the Pitfalls of Cybersecurity," *New York Times*, June 15, 2013, http://www.nytimes.com/2013/06/16/us/after-profits-defense-contractor-faces-the-pitfalls-of-cyber security.html?pagewanted=all.

88. Kevin Phillips, *Wealth and Democracy: A Political History of the American Rich* (New York: Broadway Books, 2002), 71.

89. Michael Quint, "Saudi Prince to Become Citicorp's Top Stockholder," *New York Times*, February 22, 1991.

90. Russ Baker, *Family of Secrets: The Bush Dynasty, the Powerful Forces that Put It in the White House, and What Their Influence Means for America* (New York: Bloomsbury Press, 2009), 304; citing Craig Unger, *House of Bush, House of Saud: The Secret Relationship between the World's Two Most Powerful Dynasties* (New York: Scribner, 2004), 34.

91. Unger, *House of Bush, House of Saud*, 101.

92. Unger, *House of Bush, House of Saud*, 122; cf. Scott, *Road to 9/11*, 176–78.

93. For a sensitive analysis of the current disarray in U.S.-Saudi relations, see Robert Lacey, *Inside the Kingdom: Kings, Clerics, Modernists, Terrorists, and the Struggle for Saudi Arabia* (New York: Penguin Books, 2009), 284–302. "If 9/11 took the special out of the U.S.-Saudi 'special relationship,' the U.S. invasion of Iraq killed it stone dead—for the time being, at least" (Lacey, *Inside the Kingdom*, 299). Cf. Rachel Bronson, *Thicker than Oil: America's Uneasy Partnership with Saudi Arabia* (Oxford: Oxford University Press, 2006), 248–62.

94. Robert F. Worth, "Egypt Is Arena for Influence of Arab Rivals," *New York Times*, July 9, 2013.

95. "Saudi Arabia Designates Brotherhood, Nusra Front, ISIS Terrorist Groups," *Daily Star* (Lebanon), March 8, 2014, http://www.dailystar.com.lb/News/Mid

dle-East/2014/Mar-08/249645-saudi-arabia-designates-brotherhood-nusra-front-isis-terrorist-groups.ashx#ixzz30aspV3Vj:

> Saudi Arabia has formally designated the Muslim Brotherhood as a terrorist organization, in a move that could increase pressure on Qatar whose backing for the group has sparked a row with fellow Gulf monarchies.
>
> The U.S.-allied kingdom has also designated as terrorists the Nusra Front and the Islamic State in Iraq and Greater Syria, whose fighters are battling Syrian President Bashar Assad, the Interior Ministry said in a statement published by state media.

For nuanced discussions of aid to ISIS from wealthy donors in Kuwait, Qatar, and Saudi Arabia, see Josh Rogin, "America's Allies Are Funding ISIS," TheDailyBeast.com, June 14, 2014; "Qatar's Support of Islamists Alienates Allies Near and Far," New York Times, September 7, 2014.

96. Mohammad Abdel Kader, "Turkey's relationship with the Muslim Brotherhood," *Al-Arabiya*, October 14, 2013, http://english.alarabiya.net/en/perspective/alarabiya-studies/2013/10/14/Turkey-s-relationship-with-the-Muslim-Brotherhood.html:

> Although the Turkish leadership still considers that the alliance with the Brotherhood isn't as harmful, at the national level, as ties with any other sort of Egyptian government, it still sees the rise to power of (Sunni) Islamic movements as an opportunity for the Justice and Development party to rise as a leader of modern Turkey and the post-revolutionary Arab region.

7. THE U.S. TERROR WAR

1. Joint Chiefs of Staff, "Courses of Action Related to Cuba (Case II)," Report of the J-5 to the Joint Chiefs of Staff, May 1, 1963, NARA #202-10002-10018, 21, http://www.maryferrell.org/mffweb/archive/viewer/showDoc.do?docId=167&relPageId=21; discussion in Peter Dale Scott, *American War Machine: Deep Politics, the CIA Global Drug Connection, and the Road to Afghanistan* (Lanham, MD: Rowman & Littlefield, 2010), 193, 196.

2. Terror war evolved out of the aerial attacks on civilians in World War II, beginning with Guernica and ending with the mass bombings of German and Japanese cities. But that aerial war was just one phase of a larger conventional war between armed forces.

3. But perhaps no single act of terror committed in the last decade, whether by Qaddafi in Libya or Bashir Assad in Syria, has surpassed or even come close to the U.S. devastation of the Iraqi city of Fallujah.

4. George W. Bush, "Statement by the President in His Address to the Nation," September 11, 2001, http://georgewbush-whitehouse.archives.gov/news/releases/2001/09/20010911-16.html. On September 20, 2001, Bush said in an address to a joint session of congress, "Our 'war on terror' begins with al-Qaeda, but it does not end there. It will not end until every terrorist group of global reach has been found, stopped and defeated."

5. On this point see the National Commission on Terrorist Attacks upon the United States, *The 9/11 Commission Report* (New York: W. W. Norton, 2004), 66, http://

www.9-11commission.gov/report/911Report.pdf: "To date we have seen no evidence that . . . Iraq cooperated with al Qaeda in developing or carrying out any attacks against the United States."

6. *Sunday Times* (London), May 1, 2005; Mark Danner, *The Secret Way to War: The Downing Street Memo and the Iraq War's Buried History* (New York: New York Review of Books, 2006).

7. *9/11 Commission Report*, 272.

8. Kevin Fenton, *Disconnecting the Dots* (Walterville, OR: TrineDay, 2011).

9. *9/11 Commission Report*, 259, 271; Lawrence Wright, *The Looming Tower: Al-Qaeda and the Road to 9/11* (New York: Alfred A. Knopf, 2006), 352–54; Scott, *American War Machine*, 203.

10. Fenton, *Disconnecting the Dots*, 371, cf. 95.

11. To repeat what I said in a footnote to the last chapter: A belief that there was a joint operation involving both U.S. government and Saudi officials, along with at least some of the alleged hijackers can and perhaps should be distinguished from a plot to bring down the World Trade Center towers.

12. Lutz Kleverman, "The New Great Game," *Guardian* (London), October 19, 2003, http://www.guardian.co.uk/business/2003/oct/20/oil.

13. "Rebuilding America's Defenses: Strategy, Forces and Resources for a New Century: A Report of the Project for the New American Century," September 2000, 17, 27, www.newamericancentury.org/RebuildingAmericasDefenses.pdf (site discontinued). Cf. note 24.

14. "US Pulls out of Saudi Arabia," BBC News, April 29, 2003, http://news.bbc.co.uk/2/hi/middle_east/2984547.stm.

15. Richard A. Clarke, *Against All Enemies: Inside America's War on Terror* (New York: Free Press, 2004), 31.

16. Bradley Graham, *By His Own Rules: The Ambitions, Successes, and Ultimate Failures of Donald Rumsfeld* (New York: PublicAffairs, 2009), 290.

17. PNAC, Letter to President Clinton on Iraq, January 26, 1998, http://www.newamericancentury.org/iraqclintonletter.htm (site discontinued).

18. Gary Dorrien, *Imperial Designs: Neoconservatism and the New Pax Americana* (New York: Routledge, 2004). Bacevich was speaking of a 1992 memo drafted by Wolfowitz for then Defense Secretary Cheney, calling for America to retain the power to act unilaterally. See Lewis D. Solomon, *Paul D. Wolfowitz: Visionary Intellectual, Policymaker, and Strategist* (New York: Praeger, 2007), 52; Andrew Bacevich, *American Empire: The Realities and Consequences of U.S. Diplomacy* (Cambridge MA: Harvard University Press, 2002), 44.

19. Baker Institute, Rice University, and Council on Foreign Relations, "Strategic Energy Policy: Challenges for the 21st Century," Task Force Report, 40, http://www.cfr.org/energy-policy/strategic-energy-policy-challenges-21st-century/p3942, discussion in Scott, *Road to 9/11*, 189. The *Scotland Sunday Herald*, October 6, 2002, claimed that Vice President Cheney himself commissioned this Task Force Report, and that former U.S. Secretary of State James Baker delivered the Report to Cheney. I have been assured that neither claim is true.

20. Bob Woodward, *Bush at War* (New York: Simon & Schuster, 2002), 131. Much earlier, on the afternoon of September 11, Department of Defense official Stephen Cambone recorded notes from his conversation with Rumsfeld : "Near term target needs—Go massive—Sweep it all up, things related and not" (Julian Borger, "Blogger Bares Rumsfeld's Post 9/11 Orders," *Guardian*, February 24, 1006, http://www.theguardian.com/world/2006/feb/24/freedomofinformation.september11).

21. Wesley Clark, *Winning Modern Wars* (New York: PublicAffairs, 2003), 130.

22. Wesley Clark, "Talk to Commonwealth Club," October 3, 2007, http://www.you tube.com/watch?v=Ha1rEhovONU (site terminated).

23. Nicholas Lemann, "The Next World Order," *New Yorker*, April 1, 2002, http://www.newyorker.com/magazine/2002/04/01/the-next-world-order.

24. "Rebuilding America's Defenses—Strategy, Forces and Resources For a New Century: A Report of the Project for the New American Century," September 2000, 17, 27, http://www.informationclearinghouse.info/pdf/RebuildingAmeri casDefenses.pdf.

25. Ahmed Rashid, *Descent into Chaos: The United States and the Failure of Nation Building in Pakistan, Afghanistan, and Central Asia* (New York: Viking, 2008), 70, 69; citing Ahmed Rashid, "US Builds Alliances in Central Asia," *Far Eastern Economic Review*, May 1, 2000: "The CIA and the Pentagon had been closely collaborating with the Uzbek army and secret services since 1997, providing training, equipment, and mentoring in the hope of using Uzbek Special Forces to snatch Osama bin Laden from Afghanistan, a fact I discovered on a trip to Washington in 2000."

26. See chapter 9.

27. Peter Dale Scott, *The Road to 9/11: Wealth, Empire, and the Future of America* (Berkeley: University of California Press, 2007), 9.

28. Estimates of annual spending on Homeland Security range up to a trillion dollars. See Stephan Salisbury, "Weaponizing the Body Politic," TomDispatch .com, March 4, 2012, http://www.tomdispatch.com/post/175511/tomgram%3A _stephan_salisbury%2C_weaponizing_the_body_politic/#more.

29. Cf. Simon Johnson, "Too Big to Jail," Slate, February 24, 2012, http://www.slate .com/articles/business/project_syndicate/2012/02/the_robo_signing_settlement _won_t_help_homeowners_and_it_doesn_t_hurt_the_banks_.html:

> The main motivation behind the administration's indulgence of serious criminality evidently is fear of the consequences of taking tough action on individual bankers. And maybe officials are right to be afraid, given the massive size of the banks in question relative to the economy. In fact, those banks are bigger now than they were before the crisis, and, as James Kwak and I documented at length in our book *13 Bankers*, they are *much* larger than they were 20 years ago.

30. John Farmer, *The Ground Truth: The Untold Story of America under Attack on 9/11* (New York: Riverhead Books, 2009), 288; quoted in Anthony Summers and Robbyn Swan, *The Eleventh Day: The Full Story of 9/11 and Osama bin Laden* (New York: Ballantine Books, 2011), 147.

31. Summers and Swan, *Eleventh Day*, 383–84; cf. Farmer, *Ground Truth*, 41. Although a Democrat, Berger was subsequently protected by the Republican Bush administration from having to testify to Congress about his behavior (a condition of his plea bargain).

32. Summers and Swan, *Eleventh Day*, 334.

33. Fenton, *Disconnecting the Dots*, 72–79. Grewe subsequently left government to work at the Mitre Corp., a private firm doing CIA contract work with the CIA and another private firm, Ptech. Questions about Ptech and Mitre Corp's work on FAA-NORAD interoperability systems were raised in 9/11 testimony presented some years ago by Indira Singh; see Scott, *Road to 9/11*, 175.

34. Fenton, *Disconnecting the Dots*, 78. Kirsten Wilhelm of the National Archives told Fenton (p. 78) that "It appears Barbara Grewe conducted the interviews with 'John' [Wilshire] and Jane [Corsi]," another key figure. Wilhelm could find no "memorandum for the record" (MFR) for the Wilshire interview, which Fenton understandably calls "about the most important interview the Commission conducted" (Fenton, *Disconnecting the Dots*, 79). Summers and Swan, also citing correspondence with Kirsten Wilhelm, disagree, saying that the report of Wilshire's interview exists, but "is redacted in its entirety" (Summers and Swan, *Eleventh Day*, 381, cf. 552). This is an important point to be focused on in future investigations.

35. Fenton, *Disconnecting the Dots*, 225.

36. Fenton, *Disconnecting the Dots*, 38; citing *9/11 Commission Report*, 181–82.

37. Michelle has since been identified on the Internet, but so far basically by only one source.

38. Fenton, *Disconnecting the Dots*, 42–45; summarizing Justice Department Inspector General's [IG] Report, 239–42; cf. Wright, *Looming Tower*, 311–12.

39. Fenton, *Disconnecting the Dots*, 50; summarizing Justice Department IG Report, 242–43; cf. Wright, *Looming Tower*, 311.

40. Fenton, *Disconnecting the Dots*, 45.

41. I do not know whether in fact they boarded the plane. However I am now satisfied that al-Mihdhar and al-Hazmi acted as if they intended to hijack, as evidenced by their al-Qaeda contacts in Malaysia and elsewhere, their attempts to learn to fly, and so forth. For the record, I am not and never have been persuaded that Arabs steered the 9/11 planes into their targets.

42. Fenton, *Disconnecting the Dots*, 383–86.

43. Fenton, *Disconnecting the Dots*, 48. Cf. Lawrence Wright, "The Agent," *New Yorker*, July 10 and 17, 2006, 68; quoted approvingly in Peter Dale Scott, *American War Machine*, 399.

44. Fenton, *Disconnecting the Dots*, 371, cf. 95.

45. Fenton, *Disconnecting the Dots*, 239–42, 310–22. Fenton notes that Corsi worked at FBI headquarters, which coordinated "liaisons with foreign services" (Fenton, *Disconnecting the Dots*, 313).

46. Fenton, *Disconnecting the Dots*, 310.

47. Paul Church, Asia Times Online, February 11, 2012. *The 9/11 Commission Report* discounted the importance of al-Bayoumi (*9/11 Commission Report*, 217–18); but

the Report of the Joint Congressional Inquiry into 9/11 (173–77), even though very heavily redacted at this point, supplied corroborating information, including a report that Basnan had once hosted a party for the "Blind Sheikh" Omar Abdel-Rahman, involved in the first World Trade Center bombing of 1993 (*The Report of the Joint Congressional Inquiry into Intelligence Community Activities before and after the Terrorist Attacks of September 11, 2001*, 107th Congress, 2nd Session, S. Rept. 107-351 and H. Rept. 107-792, 173–77, http://www.gpo.gov/fdsys/search/pagedetails.action?browsePath=107/HRPT/[700%3b799]&granuleId=CRPT -107hrpt792&packageId=CRPT-107hrpt792).

48. At first I suspected, as have others, that the two men were Saudi double agents. Another possibility is that they were sent as designated targets, to be surveilled by the Saudis and the Americans separately or together. One of my few disagreements with Fenton is when he calls al-Mihdhar "one of [the hijackers'] most experienced operatives" (Fenton, *Disconnecting the Dots*, 205). My own impression is that he was either an inexperienced and incompetent young spy, or else a low-level asset deliberately exposing himself to detection, in order to test American responses.

49. Summers and Swan, *Eleventh Day*, 396.

50. *9/11 Commission Report*, 184.

51. Steve Coll, *Ghost Wars: The Secret History of the CIA, Afghanistan, and bin Laden, from the Soviet Invasion to September 10, 2001* (New York: Penguin Press, 2004), 456–57.

52. Thomas E. Ricks and Susan B. Glasser, "U.S. Operated Secret Alliance with Uzbekistan," *Washington Post*, October 14, 2001.

53. Ricks and Glasser, *Washington Post*, October 14, 2001.

54. Michael Klare, *Blood and Oil* (New York: Henry Holt, 2004), 135–36; citing R. Jeffrey Smith, "U.S. Leads Peacekeeping Drill in Kazakhstan," *Washington Post*, September 15, 1997. Cf. Kenley Butler, "U.S. Military Cooperation with the Central Asian States," September 17, 2001, http://cns.miis.edu/archive/wtc01/uscamil.htm.

55. In 1957, I myself, as a junior Canadian diplomat, acquired a special-access, higher-than-top-secret clearance to access intelligence from NATO, a relatively overt and straightforward liaison.

56. For the Ali Mohamed story, see Scott, *Road to 9/11*, especially 151–60.

57. Scott, *Road to 9/11*, 158; citing John Berger, "Unlocking 9/11: Paving the Road to 9/11," Intelwire, [n.d.], http://intelwire.egoplex.com/unlocking911-1-ali-mo hamed-911.html: "Mohamed was one of the primary sources for the infamous Aug. 6, 2001, presidential daily brief (PDB) entitled 'Bin Laden Determined to Strike in U.S.'" The PDB, often cited as an example of the CIA's good performance, is in my opinion more probably another example of the Bin Laden Unit salting the record in preparation for post-9/11 scrutiny. The PDB, without naming Ali Mohamed, refers to him no less than three times as a threat, despite the fact that at the time he was under U.S. government control awaiting sentence for his role in the 1998 embassy plots. The PDB, in other words, appears to have been a performance for the record, analogous to Wilshire's performance in the same month of August at the FBI.

58. Berger, "Unlocking 9/11," 20 (Cloonan); *9/11 Commission Report*, 261 (PDB).

59. James Risen, *New York Times*, October 31, 1998; in Scott, *Road to 9/11*, 346–47.

60. *Raleigh News and Observer*, November 13, 2001; in Scott, *Road to 9/11*, 347. I have added the word "Army." The headquarters for USSOCOM itself is at Fort MacDill Air Force Base in Florida.

61. Dana Priest and William M. Arkin, "'Top Secret America': A Look at the Military's Joint Special Operations Command," *Washington Post*, September 2, 2011, http://www.washingtonpost.com/world/national-security/top-secret-america-a -look-at-the-militarys-joint-special-operations-command/2011/08/30/gIQAvYu AxJ_story.html.

62. Fenton, *Disconnecting the Dots*, 168–69; Summers and Swan, *Eleventh Day*, 371, 550.

63. Fenton, *Disconnecting the Dots*, 372.

64. Joseph J. Trento, *Prelude to Terror: The Rogue CIA and the Legacy of America's Private Intelligence Network* (New York: Carroll and Graf, 2005), 113–14:

> Shackley, who still had ambitions to become DCI, believed that without his many sources and operatives . . . the Safari Club—operating with Helms in charge in Tehran—would be ineffective. Shackley was well aware that Helms was under criminal investigation for lying to Congress about the CIA in Chile. Shackley had testified before the same grand jury. Unless Shackley took direct action to complete the privatization of intelligence operations soon, the Safari Club would not have a conduit to DO resources. The solution: create a totally private intelligence network using CIA assets until President Carter could be replaced.

65. Scott, *American War Machine*, 161; Scott, *Road to 9/11*, 62–63.

66. Ahmed Rashid, *Taliban: Militant Islam, Oil, and Fundamentalism in Central Asia* (New Haven CT: Yale University Press, 2000), 129.

67. John Prados, *Safe for Democracy: The Secret Wars of the CIA* (Chicago: Ivan R. Dee, 2006), 489; discussion in Scott, *American War Machine*, 12–13.

68. James Risen, *State of War: The Secret History of the CIA and the Bush Administration* (New York: Free Press, 2006), 188–89.

69. Fenton, *Disconnecting the Dots*, 104.

70. Summers and Swan, *Eleventh Day*, 397.

71. Joseph J. and Susan B. Trento, in Summers and Swan, *Eleventh Day*, 399. Since I presented a version of this chapter at a conference in Toronto on September 11, 2011, "Bob Kerrey of Nebraska, a Democrat who served on the . . . 9/11 Commission, [has] said in a sworn affidavit . . . that 'significant questions remain unanswered' about the role of Saudi institutions. 'Evidence relating to the plausible involvement of possible Saudi government agents in the September 11th attacks has never been fully pursued.'" ("Saudi Arabia May Be Tied to 9/11, 2 Ex-Senators Say," *New York Times*, February 29, 2012, http://www.nytimes.com/2012/03/01/ us/graham-and-kerrey-see-possible-saudi-9-11-link.html?_r=3.)

72. Wright, *Looming Tower*, 161; in Summers and Swan, *Eleventh Day*, 216.

73. Such corruption is predictable and very widespread. In the notorious cases of Gregory Scarpa and Whitey Bulger, FBI agents in the New York and Boston offices

were accused of giving their mob informants information that led to the murder of witnesses and other opponents. Agents in the New York office of the old Federal Bureau of Narcotics (FBN) became so implicated in the trafficking of their informants that the FBN had to be shut down and reorganized.

74. Ralph Blumenthal, "Tapes Depict Proposal to Thwart Bomb Used in Trade Center Blast," *New York Times*, October 28, 1993, emphasis added. The next day, *The Times* published a modest correction: "Transcripts of tapes made secretly by an informant, Emad A. Salem, quote him as saying he warned the Government that a bomb was being built. But the transcripts do not make clear the extent to which the Federal authorities knew that the target was the World Trade Center (*New York Times*, October 29, 1993).

75. Scott, *Road to 9/11*, 145.

76. Peter Dale Scott, "Bosnia, Kosovo, and Now Libya: The Human Costs of Washington's On-Going Collusion with Terrorists," Asia-Pacific Journal: Japan Focus, July 29, 2011, http://japanfocus.org/-Peter_Dale-Scott/3578. Evan Kohlmann has described how a Zagreb office in support of the Saudi-backed jihad in Bosnia received "all orders and funding directly from the main United States office of Al-Kifah on Atlantic Avenue controlled by Shaykh Omar Abdel Rahman" (Evan Kohlmann, *Al-Qaida's Jihad in Europe* (New York: Berg, 2004), 39–41; citing Steve Coll and Steve LeVine, "Global Network Provides Money, Haven," *Washington Post*, August 3, 1993).

77. The corruption appears to be inevitable in superpowers—states that have accumulated power in access of what is needed for their own defense. The pattern is less discernible in less powerful states like Canada.

78. "America's Afghanistan: The National Security and a Heroin-Ravaged State," Asia-Pacific Journal: Japan Focus, no. 20 (May 18, 2009), http://www.japanfocus .org/-Peter_Dale-Scott/3145. Cf. "U.S. Looks into Afghan Air Force Drug Allegations," CNN, March 8, 2012, http://www.cnn.com/2012/03/08/world/asia/afghanistan-air-drugs-investigation/index.html?eref=mrss_igoogle_cnn:

> The United States is investigating allegations that some members of the Afghan air force have used their planes to transport drugs, a U.S. military spokesman said Thursday. Investigators want to know whether the drug-running allegations, first reported in the *Wall Street Journal*, are linked to the shooting deaths last year of eight U.S. Air Force officers at the airport in the Afghan capital, Kabul. "The allegations of improper use of AAF aircraft is being looked into," said Lt. Col. Tim Stauffer, referring to the allegations that Afghan air force equipment has been used to illegally ferry drugs and arms.

79. Fenton, *Disconnecting the Dots*, 310.

80. Fenton, *Disconnecting the Dots*, 371, cf. 95.

81. Joint Chiefs of Staff, "Courses of Action Related to Cuba (Case II)," in Scott, *American War Machine*, 196.

82. *Washington Post*, September 30, 2001; in Summers and Swan, *Eleventh Day*, 293; cf. *9/11 Commission Report*, 221–22.

83. See Scott, *American War Machine*, 199–203.

84. Fenton, *Disconnecting the Dots*, 360–61, 385. There was also apparent withholding of information at a high level in the U.S. Joint Forces Command (USJFCOM):

> One official who attended the DO5 [a USJFCOM intelligence unit assigned to watch terrorism against the United States] briefing was Vice Adm. Martin J. Meyer, the deputy commander in chief (DCINC), USJFCOM . . . . But despite the red flags raised during the briefing, Meyer reportedly told Maj. Gen. Larry Arnold, the commander of the Continental United States NORAD Region (CONR), and other high-level CONR staffers two weeks before the 9/11 attacks that "their concern about Osama bin Laden as a possible threat to America was unfounded and that, to repeat, 'If everyone would just turn off CNN, there wouldn't be a threat from Osama bin Laden'" (Jason Leopold and Jeffrey Kaye, "EXCLUSIVE: New Documents Claim Intelligence on Bin Laden, al-Qaeda Targets Withheld From Congress' 9/11 Probe," Truthout, June 13, 2011, http://www.truth-out.org/new-documents-claim-intelligence-bin -laden-al-qaeda-targets-withheld-congress-911-probe/1307986777).

85. Scott, *American War Machine*, 201.

86. Scott, *American War Machine*, 200–202.

87. Clarke, *Against All Enemies*, 30–33; Summers and Swan, *Eleventh Day*, 175–76; James Bamford, *A Pretext for War: 9/11, Iraq, and the Abuse of America's Intelligence Agencies* (New York: Doubleday, 2004), 287.

88. Mark Selden has described the pattern of "arousing nationalist passions as a result of attacks out of the blue" as one that has "undergirded the American way of war since 1898" (Mark Selden, "The American Archipelago of Bases, Military Colonization and Pacific Empire: Prelude to the Permanent Warfare State," *International Journal of Okinawan Studies*, 2012).

89. Thomas E. Ricks and Susan B. Glasser, "U.S. Operated Secret Alliance with Uzbekistan," *Washington Post*, October 14, 2001. Significantly, the proposal for a joint attack force with Massoud's Northern Alliance was also resisted by Massoud himself (Peter Tomsen, *The Wars of Afghanistan: Messianic Terrorism, Tribal Conflicts, and the Failures of Great Powers* (New York: PublicAffairs, 2011), 597–98, 796n25). The problem of Massoud's resistance to an American troop presence vanished when he was assassinated on September 9, 2011, two days before 9/11.

90. Coll, *Ghost Wars*, 467–69.

91. Coll, *Ghost Wars*, 513, 534–36, 553.

92. Coll, *Ghost Wars*, 558.

93. Coll, *Ghost Wars*, 573–74.

94. Fenton, *Disconnecting the Dots*, 108.

95. Fenton, *Disconnecting the Dots*, 110–14.

96. George Tenet, *At the Center of the Storm: My Years at the CIA* (New York: HarperCollins, 2007), 255.

97. Jeremy Scahill, "Shhhhhh! JSOC is Hiring Interrogators and Covert Operatives for 'Special Access Programs,'" *Nation*, August 25, 2010, http://www.thenation.com/ blog/154133/shhhhh-jsoc-hiring-interrogators-and-covert-operatives-special -access-programs.

98. Summers and Swan, *Eleventh Day*, 387–88; cf. Fenton, *Disconnecting the Dots*, 127–30.

99. Jason Vest, "Implausible Denial II," *Nation*, May 31, 2004, http://www.the nation.com/article/implausible-denial-ii.

100. Scott, *Road to 9/11*, 216–18.

101. Joint Chiefs of Staff, "Courses of Action Related to Cuba (Case II)," 21, http://www.maryferrell.org/mffweb/archive/viewer/showDoc.do?docId=167 &relPageId=21; Scott, *American War Machine*, 193, 196.

102. Scott, *American War Machine*, 195–205; Northwoods document, Joint Chiefs of Staff, JCS 1969/303 on Northwoods, NARA Record # 202-10002-10104, https://www.maryferrell.org/mffweb/archive/viewer/showDoc.do?docId=1244& relPageId=178, 178ss.

103. Peter Dale Scott, *The War Conspiracy: JFK, 9/11, and the Deep Politics of War* (New York: Skyhorse Publishing, 2013), 387–89.

104. Fenton, *Disconnecting the Dots*, 283–355; Peter Dale Scott, *War Conspiracy: JFK, 9/11, and the Deep Politics of War* (New York: Skyhorse, 2013), 341–96.

105. Jason Ditz, "Report: CIA Drones Killed Over 2,000, Mostly Civilians in Pakistan Since 2006," AntiWar.com, January 2, 2011, http://news.antiwar.com/ 2011/01/02/report-cia-drones-killed-over-2000-mostly-civilians-in-pakistan -since-2006/. Cf. Karen DeYoung, "Secrecy Defines Obama's Drone War," *Washington Post*, December 19, 2011, http://www.washingtonpost.com/world/na tional-security/secrecy-defines-obamas-drone-war/2011/10/28/gIQAPKNR5O _story.html ("hundreds of strikes over three years—resulting in an estimated 1,350 to 2,250 deaths in Pakistan").

106. Adrian Blomfield and Mike Smith, "Gorbachev: US Could Start New Cold War," *Telegraph* (London), May 6, 2008, http://www.telegraph.co.uk/news/worldnews/ europe/russia/1933223/Gorbachev-US-could-start-new-Cold-War.html.

107. Uwe Klussmann, Matthias Schepp, and Klaus Wiegrefe, "NATO's Eastward Expansion: Did the West Break Its Promise to Moscow?" *Spiegel Online International*, November 26, 2009, http://www.spiegel.de/international/world/nato-s -eastward-expansion-did-the-west-break-its-promise-to-moscow-a-663315. html.

108. Peter Dale Scott, "The NATO Afghanistan War and US-Russian Relations: Drugs, Oil, and War," Asia-Pacific Journal: Japan Focus, August 26, 2012, http:// japanfocus.org/-Peter_Dale-Scott/3759.

109. Peter Baker, "In Cold War Echo, Obama Strategy Writes Off Putin," *New York Times*, April 19, 2014, http://www.nytimes.com/2014/04/20/world/europe/in cold-war-echo-obama-strategy-writes-off-putin.html?_r=0.

110. "Tom Hayden on Venezuela's current crisis," *Tikkun*, February 25, 2014, http://www.tikkun.org/tikkundaily/2014/02/28/tom-hayden-on-venezuelas-cur rent-crisis/.

8. DEEP POWER TAKES ITS TOLL ON U.S. PRESIDENTS, 1961–1980

1. A personal disclosure: I am both a friend of Ray McGovern and an admirer of his style of spiritually guided nonviolent resistance.

2. David Swanson, "Police Brutalize Ray McGovern as Hillary Clinton Talks Free Speech," Truthout, February 21, 2011, http://www.truth-out.org/police-brutalize -ray-mcgovern-hillary-clinton-talks-free-speech67888. Clinton remarked in her talk, "The rights of individuals to express their views free . . . are universal." Yet she said and did nothing "while the 71 year old protester was grabbed by campus police, pulled to the ground, and dragged out of the auditorium" (Rory O'Connor, "Hillary Clinton Talks Freedom as Protester Ray McGovern Is Blood-ied," Gather.com, February 17, 2011, http://www.gather.com/viewArticle.action? articleId=281474979063740). Four years earlier, McGovern had attended a Rums-feld press conference and was allowed to challenge Rumsfeld from the public mi-crophone, while an unknown protestor turned his back on Rumsfeld throughout the length of the event and was allowed to leave untouched.

3. Both also are featured in projections of American power abroad. Some of those protesting in the 2011 anti-Mubarak demonstrations in Egypt had been trained in the techniques of nonviolent resistance promulgated by the American Gandhian Gene Sharp (New York Times, February 16, 2011). The police who shot and killed the demonstrators were also U.S.-trained, and were using U.S. weapons and am-munition.

4. Hannah Arendt, Between Past and Future: Eight Exercises in Political Thought (New York: Penguin Books, 1993), 93, emphasis added. Adapting Arendt's dis-tinction, Jonathan Schell made a Gandhian case in support of nonviolent per-suasive or community power as a means of challenging top-down violent power and thus reforming the world. I developed this case myself in The Road to 9/11 (Jonathan Schell, The Unconquerable World: Power, Nonviolence, and the Will of the People [New York: Metropolitan Books, 2003], 227–31; Peter Dale Scott, The Road to 9/11: Wealth, Empire, and the Future of America [Berkeley: University of California Press, 2007], 249–66, 269).

5. It is one of the special features of America's richly diverse history that it has seen extreme examples of both persuasive power (the town meetings of New England's Puritan communities) and violent power (the oppression of slaves and of Native Americans).

6. Peter Dale Scott, American War Machine (Lanham, MD: Rowman & Littlefield, 2010), 3.

7. Scott, American War Machine, 31–34, 175–76, 209–11.

8. Scott, American War Machine, 4, 195. In fact all of the major wars were preceded by deceptions, except for the 1980 proxy war in Afghanistan. There, as Brzezinski boasted later in print, a series of U.S. provocations helped draw the Soviet Union into Afghanistan where it suffered defeat.

9. Project for the New American Century, "Rebuilding Americas Defenses," 2000, www.newamericancentury.org/RebuildingAmericasDefenses.pdf (site discontin-ued); discussion in Scott, Road to 9/11, 23–24, etc.

10. Rachel Bronson, Thicker than Oil: America's Uneasy Partnership with Saudi Ara-bia (Oxford: Oxford University Press, 2006), 168: "After a decade of détente, a policy Saudi Arabia never supported, King Fahd welcomed Reagan's determina-tion to confront Soviet pressure more directly."

11. Robert Dallek, *An Unfinished Life: John F. Kennedy, 1917-1963* (Boston: Little Brown, 2003), 570–71; citing Michael R. Beschloss, *The Crisis Years: Kennedy and Khrushchev, 1960-1963* (New York: Edward Burlingame Books, 1991), 544.

12. Dallek, *An Unfinished Life*, 554–55.

13. David Talbot, *Brothers: The Hidden History of the Kennedy Years* (New York: Free Press, 2007), 172–73; quoted in Andrew Gavin Marshall, "The National Security State and the Assassination of JFK," Global Research, November 23, 2010, http://www.globalresearch.ca/index.php?context=va&aid=22071.

14. Stanley I. Kutler, *The Wars of Watergate: The Last Crisis of Richard Nixon* (New York: Knopf, 1990), 117, cf. 457–58. J. Anthony Lukas called the JCS espionage "a natural response to the increasing concentration of national security-making in Kissinger's NSC" (Anthony Lukas, *Nightmare: The Underside of the Nixon Years* [New York: Viking Press, 1976], 105). But the objection to Kissinger had to do with policy as well as with procedures.

15. See Phyllis Schlafly and Chester Ward, *Kissinger on the Couch* (New Rochelle, NY: Arlington House, 1975). Ward was a retired U.S. admiral.

16. See for example, Seymour Hersh, "The Red Line and the Rat Line," *London Review of Books*, April 17, 2014, http://www.lrb.co.uk/v36/n08/seymour-m-hersh/the-red-line-and-the-rat-line.

17. William Arkin, *American Coup: How a Terrified Government Is Destroying the Constitution* (New York: Little Brown, 2013), 34–35. This may refer in part to Ford's signing into law of the National Emergencies Act (50 U.S.C. 1601–1651) which codified previous emergency grants of power into the U.S. Code.

18. See the discussions of the personnel changes in the so-called "Halloween Massacre" of October 1975 under Ford, and the contest between Brzezinski and Vance under Carter (Scott, *Road to 9/11*, 50–92).

19. In 2007 I wrote that they "had a precedent: Nixon's secret deals with Vietnamese president Nguyen van Thieu in 1968" (Scott, *Road to 9/11*, 100).

20. Robert Parry, "The CIA/Likud Sinking of Jimmy Carter," Consortiumnews, June 24, 2010, http://www.consortiumnews.com/2010/062410.html: "Inside the CIA, Carter and his CIA Director Stansfield Turner were blamed for firing for ousting legendary spymaster Ted Shackley, and for failing to protect longtime U.S. allies (and friends of the CIA), such as Iran's Shah and Nicaragua's dictator Anastasio Somoza."

21. Tom Wicker et al., "C.I.A.: Maker of Policy, or Tool?" *New York Times*, April 25, 1966; quoted in James W. Douglass, *JFK and the Unspeakable: Why He Died and Why It Matters* (Maryknoll, NY: Orbis Books, 2008), 15.

22. Tim Weiner, *Legacy of Ashes: The History of the CIA* (New York: Doubleday, 2007), 374.

23. Weiner, *Legacy of Ashes*, 376.

24. Hugh Wilford, *America's Great Game: The CIA's Secret Arabists and the Shaping of the Modern Middle East* (New York: Basic Books, 2013), 295.

25. Scott, *Road to 9/11*, 62–63.

26. Ibrahim Warde, *The Price of Fear: The Truth behind the Financial War on Terror* (Berkeley: University of California Press, 2007), 133.

27. Robert Sherrill, *The Oil Follies of 1970-1980: How the Petroleum Industry Stole the Show (and Much More Besides)* (Garden City, NY: Anchor Press/Doubleday, 1983).

28. American charge d'affaires Bruce Laingen had warned from Tehran that the Shah should not be admitted until the Embassy had been provided with a protective force, as "the danger of hostages being taken in Iran will persist" (Barry M. Rubin, *Paved with Good Intentions: The American Experience and Iran* [New York: Oxford University Press, 1980], 296-97).

29. Details in Scott, *Road to 9/11*, 80-92.

30. *New York Times*, November 18, 1979; Pierre Salinger, *America Held Hostage: The Secret Negotiations* (New York: Doubleday, 1981), 25. Hamilton Jordan, who was one of those present and advising for the Shah's admission, later gave a more hypothetical version: "What are you guys going to advise me to do if they overrun our embassy and take our people hostages" (Hamilton Jordan, *Crisis: The Last Year of the Carter Presidency* [NewYork: Putnam, 1982], 32). Earlier, on July 27, 1979, Carter had commented that "he did not wish the Shah to be here playing tennis while Americans in Tehran were being kidnapped or even killed" (Zbigniew Brzezinski, *Power and Principle: Memoirs of the National Security Advisor, 1977-1981* [New York: Farrar, Straus, Giroux, 1983], 474).

31. See Sherrill, *The Oil Follies of 1970-1980*, 470-80.

9. THE DOOMSDAY PROJECT AND DEEP EVENTS

1. For "dark force," see for example, Peter Dale Scott, "Norway's Terror as Systemic Destabilization: Breivik, the Arms-for-Drugs Milieu, and Global Shadow Elites," *Asia-Pacific Journal: Japan Focus*, August 22, 2011, http://japanfocus.org/-Peter_Dale-Scott/3590.

2. Tim Weiner, "The Pentagon's Secret Stash," *Mother Jones Magazine*, March-April 1992, 26.

3. J. A. Myerson "War Is a Force That Pays the 1 Percent: Occupying American Foreign Policy," Truth-out, November 14, 2011, http://www.truth-out.org/war-force-pays-1-percent-occupying-american-foreign-policy/1321286925. Cf. Peter Dale Scott, *The Road to 9/11* (Berkeley: University of California Press, 2007), 1-25.

4. Lewis Powell, "Confidential Memorandum: Attack on the Free Enterprise System," August 23, 1971, quoted in Kim Phelps-Fein, *Invisible Hands: The Making of the Conservative Movement from the New Deal to Reagan* (New York: W. W. Norton, 2009), 158, 160.

5. Scott, *Road to 9/11*, 22, 97.

6. Scott, *Road to 9/11*, 21, 51-52; Kristol as quoted in Lewis H. Lapham, "Tentacles of Rage: The Republican Propaganda Mill, a Brief History," *Harper's Magazine*, September 2004, 36.

7. *New York Times*, July 14, 1987. See chapter 3.

8. For example, Peter Dale Scott, *American War Machine: Deep Politics, the CIA Global Drug Connection, and the Road to Afghanistan* (Lanham, MD: Rowman & Littlefield, 2010), 204-5.

9. Peter Dale Scott, *The War Conspiracy: JFK, 9/11, and the Deep Politics of War* (New York: Skyhorse Publishing, 2013), 354.

10. Peter Dale Scott, *Oswald, Mexico, and Deep Politics: Revelations from CIA Records on the Assassination of JFK* (New York: Skyhorse Publishing, 2013), 30–33; Scott, *War Conspiracy*, 387; Scott, *American War Machine*, 152.

11. Clarence M. Kelley, *Kelley: The Story of an FBI Director* (Kansas City, MO: Andrews, McMeel, and Parker, 1987), 268, quoted in Scott, *War Conspiracy*, 389.

12. Cable at http://jfk.hood.edu/Collection/Weisberg%20Subject%20Index%20 Files/D%20Disk/Domestic%20Intelligence/Item%2045.pdf; cf. Peter Dale Scott, *Deep Politics and the Death of JFK* (Berkeley: University of California Press, 1993), 275; Scott, *Oswald, Mexico, and Deep Politics*, 80, 129n. Stringfellow worked under Jack Revill in the Vice Squad of the Dallas Police Department (DPD) Special Services Bureau. As such he reported regularly to the FBI on such close Ruby associates as James Herbert Dolan, a "known hoodlum and strong-arm man" on the FBI's Top Criminal list for Dallas (Robert M. Barrett, FBI Report of February 2, 1963, NARA#124-90038-10026, 12 [Stringfellow]; cf. NARA#124-10212-10012, 4 [hoodlum]; NARA#124-10195-10305, 9 [Top Criminal]). Cf. Warren Commission, *Hearings*, Vol. 14, 601–02 [Ruby and Dolan]). Robert Barrett, who received Stringfellow's reports to the FBI, had Ruby's friend Dolan under close surveillance; he also took part in Oswald's arrest at the Texas Theater, and claimed to have seen DPD Officer Westbrook with Oswald's wallet at the site of the Tippit killing (Dale K. Myers, *With Malice: Lee Harvey Oswald and the Murder of Officer J. D. Tippit* [Milford, MI: Oak Cliff Press, 1998], 287–90).

13. It was sent for information to Washington, which received it three days later (Scott, *Deep Politics*, 275; Scott, *Oswald, Mexico, and Deep Politics*, 80, 129n; Scott, *War Conspiracy*, 382). For another link between this shadow network and the JFK assassination, see Larry Haappanen and Alan Rogers, "A Phone Call from Out of the Blue," *Kennedy Assassination Chronicles*, 8 no. 2 (2002), https://www.mary ferrell.org/mffweb/archive/viewer/showDoc.do?absPageId=223425.

14. Warren Commission Exhibit 1778, FBI report, November 23, 1963, of interview of Marina Oswald, Warren Commission, *Hearings*, Vol. 23, 383. (Marina's actual words, before mistranslation, were quite innocuous: "I cannot describe it [the gun] because a rifle to me like all rifles" [discussion in Scott, *Deep Politics*, 168–72].)

15. Stringfellow himself was the source of one other piece of false intelligence on November 22: that Oswald had confessed to the murders of both the President and Officer Tippit (Dallas FBI File DL 89-43-2381C; Paul L. Hoch, "The Final Investigation? The HSCA and Army Intelligence," *The Third Decade*, 1 no. 5 [July 1985], 3).

16. Warren Commission, *Hearings*, Vol. 9, 106; Scott, *Deep Politics*, 275–76; Russ Baker, *Family of Secrets: The Bush Dynasty, the Powerful Forces that Put It in the White House, and What Their Influence Means for America* (New York: Bloomsbury Press, 2009), 119–22.

17. Rodney P. Carlisle and Dominic J. Monetta, *Brandy: Our Man in Acapulco* (Denton: University of North Texas Press, 1999), 128.

18. Joint Chiefs of Staff, "Courses of Action Related to Cuba (Case II)," Report of the J-5 to the Joint Chiefs of Staff, 1 May 1963, NARA #202-10002-10018, 12, http://www.maryferrell.org/mffweb/archive/viewer/showDoc.do?docId=167&relPageId=12. Cf. pp. 15–16: "The United States should intervene militarily in Cuba and could (a) engineer provocative incidents ostensibly perpetrated by the Castro regime to serve as the cause of invasion."

19. Robert Dallek, *An Unfinished Life: John F. Kennedy, 1917–1963* (Boston: Little Brown, 2003), 568.

20. Joint Chiefs of Staff, "Courses of Action Related to Cuba (Case II)," NARA #202-10002-10018, 12.

21. Joint Chiefs of Staff, "Courses of Action Related to Cuba (Case II)," NARA #202-10002-10018, 20. I see nothing in this document indicating that the President should be notified that these "fabricated provocations" were false. On the contrary, the document called for "compartmentation of participants" to insure that the true facts were not leaked (Joint Chiefs of Staff, "Courses of Action Related to Cuba (Case II)," NARA #202-10002-10018, 19).

22. Quoted in Baker, *Family of Secrets*, 122. One of these, DPD Detective John Adamcik, was a member of the party that retrieved a blanket that was said to have contained Oswald's rifle, and was used by the Warren Commission to link Oswald to the famous Mannlicher Carcano. Adamcik was later present at Mamantov's interview of Marina about the rifle, and corroborated Mamantov's account of it to the Warren Commission. There is now reason to think that Mamantov's translation of Marina's testimony was tendentious (Scott, *Deep Politics*, 268–70, 276).

23. See James Douglass, *JFK and the Unspeakable* (Maryknoll, NY: Orbis Books, 2008).

24. National Commission on Terrorist Attacks upon the United States, *The 9/11 Commission Report* (New York: W. W. Norton, 2004), 259, 271, http://www.9-11commission.gov/report/911Report.pdf; Lawrence Wright, *The Looming Tower: Al-Qaeda and the Road to 9/11* (New York: Alfred A. Knopf, 2006), 352–54 (FBI agent).

25. James Bamford, *A Pretext for War: 9/11, Iraq, and the Abuse of America's Intelligence Agencies* (New York: Doubleday, 2004), 224. For a fuller account of the CIA's withholding before 9/11, see Kevin Fenton, *Disconnecting the Dots*, passim; Rory O'Connor and Ray Nowosielski, "Insiders Voice Doubts about CIA's 9/11 Story," Salon, October 14, 2011, http://www.salon.com/2011/10/14/insiders_voice_doubts_cia_911/.

26. Fenton, *Disconnecting the Dots*, 7–12, 142–47, etc.

27. Scott, *American War Machine*, 203.

28. Fenton, *Disconnecting the Dots*, 371, cf. 95. Quite independently, Richard Clarke, the former White House Counterterrorism Chief on 9/11, has charged, "There was a high-level decision in the CIA ordering people not to share information" (O'Connor and Nowosielski, "Insiders Voice Doubts about CIA's 9/11 Story").

29. Steve Coll, *Ghost Wars: The Secret History of the CIA, Afghanistan, and bin Laden, from the Soviet Invasion to September 10, 2001* (New York: Penguin Press, 2004), 467–69.

30. Fenton, *Disconnecting the Dots*, 107–8.

31. James Bamford, *Body of Secrets: Anatomy of the Ultra-Secret National Security Agency—From the Cold War through the Dawn of a New Century* (New York: Doubleday, 2001), 201. Cf. Fredrik Logevall, *Choosing War: The Lost Chance for Peace and the Escalation of War in Vietnam* (Berkeley: University of California Press, 1999), 200, citing John Prados, *The Hidden History of the Vietnam War* (Chicago: Ivan R. Dee, 1995), 51.

32. Joint Chiefs of Staff, "Courses of Action Related to Cuba (Case II)," NARA #202-10002-10018, http://www.maryferrell.org/mffweb/archive/viewer/showDoc .do?absPageId=48338.

33. Scott, *Deep Politics*, 280.

34. Public Law 90-331 (18 U.S.C. 3056), http://www.gpo.gov/fdsys/pkg/STAT UTE-90/pdf/STATUTE-90-Pg2475.pdf; discussion in Peter Dale Scott, Paul L. Hoch, and Russell Stetler, *The Assassinations: Dallas and Beyond* (New York: Random House, 1976), 443–46.

35. Army intelligence agents were seconded to the Secret Service, and at this time there was a great increase in their number. The *Washington Star* later explained that "the big build-up in [Army] information gathering . . . did not come until after the shooting of the Rev. Martin Luther King" (*Washington Star*, December 6, 1970).

36. George O'Toole, *The Private Sector* (New York: W. W. Norton, 1978), 145, quoted in Scott, *Deep Politics*, 278–79.

37. Scott, *Road to 9/11*, 52–53.

38. Scott, *Road to 9/11*, 53–54.

39. Scott, *Road to 9/11*, 50–64.

40. Peter Dale Scott, "Northwards without North," *Social Justice*, Summer 1989. Revised as "North, Iran-Contra, and the Doomsday Project: The Original Congressional Cover Up of Continuity-of-Government Planning," Asia-Pacific Journal: Japan Focus, February 21, 2011, http://japanfocus.org/-Peter_Dale-Scott/3491.

41. Scott, *Road to 9/11*, 132.

42. Jonathan Marshall, Peter Dale Scott, and Jane Hunter, *The Iran-Contra Connection: Secret Teams and Covert Operations in the Reagan Era* (Boston: South End Press, 1987), 13 (Contras); Richard Coll, *Ghost Wars*, 93–102 (mujahedin).

43. Richard Coll, *Ghost Wars*, 457–59, 534–36.

44. This work circulated as a manuscript, but was never published. However I learn from the Internet that "Southeast Louisiana University has two copies of Peter Dale Scott's THE DALLAS CONSPIRACY listed in their JFK papers archive" (http://educationforum.ipbhost.com/index.php?showtopic=8785; cf. http://www .southeastern.edu/acad_research/programs/csls/historical_collections/archival _collections/h_k/kennedy_john_f_assas.html, Supplemental Material Folders 20 and 21).

45. According to testimony from CIA Deputy Director Vernon Walters, only "Hunt and McCord had ever been CIA full-time employees. The others [including Sturgis] were contract employees for a short duration or a longer duration" (Select Committee on Presidential Campaign Activities, 93rd Congress, First Session, Hearings, 3427, http://archive.org/stream/presidentialcamp09unit/presidential

camp09unit_djvu.txt). Cf. Marshall, Scott, and Hunter, *The Iran-Contra Connection*, 45 (casino owners).

46. Peter Dale Scott, "From Dallas to Watergate," *Ramparts*, December 1973; reprinted in Peter Dale Scott, Paul L. Hoch, and Russell Stetler, *The Assassinations: Dallas and Beyond*, 356, 363. Cf. Scott, *Deep Politics*, 38–39, 120.

47. Peter Dale Scott, *Crime and Cover-Up* (Santa Barbara, CA: Open Archive Press, 1993), 20.

48. Peter Dale Scott and Jonathan Marshall, *Cocaine Politics: Drugs, Armies, and the CIA in Central America* (Berkeley: University of California Press, 1998), 25–32, etc.

49. Alexander Cockburn and Jeffrey St. Clair, *Whiteout: The CIA, Drugs, and the Press* (London: Verso, 1998), 308–9; Martha Honey, *Hostile Acts: U.S. Policy in Costa Rica in the 1980s* (Gainesville: University Press of Florida, 1994), 368 (Frigorificos).

50. Tad Szulc, *Compulsive Spy: The Strange Career of E. Howard Hunt* (New York: Viking, 1974), 96–97.

51. Scott, *American War Machine*, 51–54. Hunt helped put together what became the drug-linked World Anti-Communist League (WACL). Artime's Costa Rica base was on land whose owners were part of the local WACL chapter (Scott and Marshall, *Cocaine Politics*, 87, 220). The Saudi-financed WACL was composed of unofficial right-wing CIA assets and served as a forum for them.

52. Carl Bernstein and Bob Woodward, *All the President's Men* (New York: Simon and Schuster, 1974), 23.

53. Jim Hougan, *Secret Agenda* (New York: Random House, 1984), 16, citing Department of Defense Directive 5230.7, June 25, 1965, amended May 21, 1971.

54. James Bamford, *A Pretext for War* (New York: Anchor Books, 2005), 72.

55. Peter Dale Scott, "North, Iran-Contra, and the Doomsday Project: The Original Congressional Cover Up of Continuity-of-Government Planning," Asia-Pacific Journal: Japan Focus, February 21, 2011, http://japanfocus.org/-Peter_Dale-Scott/3491. Cf. Peter Dale Scott, "Northwards Without North: Bush, Counterterrorism, and the Continuation of Secret Power," *Social Justice* (San Francisco), XVI, no. 2 (Summer 1989), 1–30; Peter Dale Scott, "The Terrorism Task Force," *Covert Action Information Bulletin*, 33 (Winter 1990), 12–15.

56. Scott and Marshall, *Cocaine Politics*, 140–41, 242 (Iran, etc.); Ola Tunander, *The Secret War against Sweden: US and British Submarine Deception in the 1980s* (London: Frank Cass, 2004), 309 (Sweden).

57. Scott, *Road to 9/11*, 183–87.

58. John Dean, *Worse than Watergate: The Secret Presidency of George W. Bush* (New York: Little Brown, 2004), 120.

59. "Former White House Attache to Talk about JFK Assassination," *Cape Cod Times*, October 10, 2013, http://www.capecodonline.com/apps/pbcs.dll/article?AID=/20131010/NEWS/310100345&emailAFriend=1.

60. Russ Baker, *Family of Secrets*, 121.

61. "Statement by Col. John W. Mayo, Chairman of City-County Civil Defense and Disaster Commission at the Dedication of the Emergency Operating Center at Fair Park," May 24, 1961, http://www.civildefensemuseum.com/fallout/dallaseoc

.html (link discontinued). Six linear inches of Civil Defense Administrative Files are preserved in the Dallas Municipal Archives; a Finding Guide is viewable online at http://www.ci.dallas.tx.us/cso/archives/FindingGuides/08001.html. I hope an interested researcher may wish to consult them.

62. Scott, *Road to 9/11*, 183–87.
63. Spencer S. Hsu, "Bush Changes Continuity Plan," *Washington Post*, May 10, 2007.
64. *9/11 Commission Report*, 38, 326, 555n9; Scott, *Road to 9/11*, 224.
65. Scott, *Road to 9/11*, 226–30. A footnote in the 9/11 Commission Report says: "The 9/11 crisis tested the U.S. government's plans and capabilities to ensure the continuity of constitutional government and the continuity of government operations. We did not investigate this topic, except as needed to understand the activities and communications of key officials on 9/11. The Chair, Vice Chair, and senior staff were briefed on the general nature and implementation of these continuity plans" (*9/11 Commission Report*, 555n9).

The other footnotes confirm that no information from COG files was used to document the 9/11 Commission Report. At a minimum these files might resolve the mystery of the missing phone call that simultaneously authorized COG, and (in consequence) determined that Bush should continue to stay out of Washington. I suspect that they might tell us a great deal more.

66. "White House Communications Agency," Signal Corps Regimental History, http://signal.army.mil/OLD/history/white_house_communications_agency.html.
67. The Warren Commission staff knew of the WHCA presence in Dallas from the Secret Service (Warren Commission, *Hearings*, Vol. 17, 598, 619, 630, etc.).
68. Statement of Secret Service Winston Lawson, Warren Commission, *Hearings*, Vol. 17, 630 (WHCA radio).
69. Pamela McElwain-Brown, "The Presidential Lincoln Continental SS-100-X," *Dealey Plaza Echo*, 3, no. 2, 23, http://www.maryferrell.org/mffweb/archive/viewer/showDoc.do?docId=16241&relPageId=27 (police radio); Scott, *Deep Politics and the Death of JFK*, 272–75 (Lumpkin).
70. In the 1990s the WHCA supplied statements to the ARRB concerning communications between Dallas and Washington on November 22 (White House Communications Agency [WHCA] files, NARA #172-10001-10002 to NARA #172-10000-10008). The Assassination Records Review Board also attempted to obtain from the WHCA the unedited original tapes of conversations from Air Force One on the return trip from Dallas, November 22, 1963. (Edited and condensed versions of these tapes had been available since the 1970s from the Lyndon Baines Johnson Library in Austin, Texas.) The attempt was unsuccessful: "The Review Board's repeated written and oral inquiries of the White House Communications Agency did not bear fruit. The WHCA could not produce any records that illuminated the provenance of the edited tapes." See *Assassinations Records Review Board: Final Report*, chapter 6, Part 1, 116, http://www.archives.gov/research/jfk/review-board/report/arrb-final-report.pdf .
71. See Scott, *War Conspiracy*, 347–48, 385–87.
72. *Washington Post*, May 10, 2007.

73. Dick Cheney, *In My Time: A Personal and Political Memoir* (New York: Threshold Editions, 2011), 348: "One of the first efforts we undertook after 9/11 to strengthen the country's defenses was securing passage of the Patriot Act, which the president signed into law on [sic] October 2001." Cf. "The Patriot Act, which the president signed into law on October 2001," emptywheel, October 26, 2011, http://www.emptywheel.net/2011/10/26/the-patriot-act-which-the-president-signed-into-law-on-october-2001/; "Questions and Answers about Beginning of Domestic Spying Program," emptywheel, July 16, 2009, http://www.emptywheel.net/2009/07/16/questions-and-answers-about-beginning-of-domestic-spying-program/.

74. Scott, *Road to 9/11*, 236–45; cf. chapter 3 of this book.

75. "Memorandum for Mr. Moyers" of November 25, 1963, FBI 62-109060, Section 18, p. 29, http://www.maryferrell.org/mffweb/archive/viewer/showDoc.do?absPageId=756877. Cf. Nicholas Katzenbach, *Some of It Was Fun* (New York: W. W. Norton, 2008), 131–36.

76. Leventhal's official title is (or was) "Chief of the Counter-Misinformation Team, U.S. Department of State" (http://2002-2009-fpc.state.gov/44434.htm). In 2010 the U.S. State Department "launched an official bid to shoot down conspiracy theories.... The "Conspiracy Theories and Misinformation" page . . . insists that Lee Harvey Oswald killed John F Kennedy alone, and that the Pentagon was not hit by a cruise missile on 9/11" (*Daily Record* [Scotland], August 2, 2010, http://www.dailyrecord.co.uk/news/science-and-technology/2010/08/02/white-house-launches-new-website-to-debunk-conspiracy-theories-86908-22457938/). The site still existed, in July 2013, but I was unable to find it in June 2014. Cf. Robin Ramsay, "Government vs Conspiracy Theorists: The Official War on 'Sick Think,'" Fortean Times, April 2010, http://www.forteantimes.com/strangedays/conspiracycorner/3211/government_vs_conspiracy_theorists.html; Robin Ramsay, "The State Department vs 'Sick Think': The JFK assassination, 9/11, and the Tory MP spiked with LSD," Fortean Times, July 2010, http://www.forteantimes.com/strangedays/conspiracycorner/3937/the_state_department_vs_sick_think.html; William Kelly, "Todd Leventhal: The Minister of Diz at Dealey Plaza," CTKA, 2010, http://www.ctka.net/2010/Levanthal.html.

77. For Nixon's sensitivity concerning the Kennedy assassination, and the way this induced him into some of the intrigues known collectively as Watergate, see for example, Scott, Hoch, and Stetler, *The Assassinations*, 374–78; Scott, *Crime and Cover-Up*, 33, 64–66.

10. THE AMERICAN DEEP STATE, DEEP EVENTS, AND OFF-THE-BOOKS FINANCING

1. Peter Dale Scott, *Deep Politics and the Death of JFK* (Berkeley: University of California Press, 1993), 6–8.

2. Alfonso Chardy, "Reagan Aides and the Secret Government," *Miami Herald*, July 5, 1987, http://bellaciao.org/en/article.php3?id_article=9877.

3. Anthony Summers with Robbyn Swan, *The Arrogance of Power: The Secret World of Richard Nixon* (New York: Viking, 2000), 198; H. R. Haldeman, with Joseph DiMona, *The Ends of Power* (New York: Times Books, 1978), 68.

4. Jonathan Marshall, Peter Dale Scott, and Jane Hunter, *The Iran-Contra Connection: Secret Teams and Covert Operations in the Reagan Era* (Boston: South End Press, 1987), 42–49.

5. Marshall, Scott, and Hunter, *The Iran-Contra Connection*, 25–30, 36–42, 155–57.

6. Thomas Goltz, *Azerbaijan Diary: A Rogue Reporter's Adventures in an Oil-Rich, War-Torn, Post-Soviet Republic* (Armonk, NY: M. E. Sharpe, 1999), 272–75.

7. Peter Dale Scott, *The War Conspiracy: JFK, 9/11, and the Deep Politics of War* (New York: Skyhorse Publishing, 2013), 341–96. There I list thirteen similarities; I have since thought of another dozen.

8. Chapter 9.

9. Charlie Joyce to Clay Whitehead [director of the White House Office of Telecommunications Policy under Nixon], "Emergency Preparedness for Telecommunications," attachment to memo of November 5, 1969, reproduced at http://claytwhitehead.com/ctwlibrary/Box%20006/002_Domestic%20Satellite%20Policy%20Working%20Group%20%281%20of%202%20folders%29.pdf .

10. Tim Shorrock, *Spies for Hire: The Secret World of Intelligence Outsourcing* (New York: Simon & Schuster, 2008), 72–75.

11. Peter Dale Scott, "North, Iran-Contra, and the Doomsday Project: The Original Congressional Cover Up of Continuity-of-Government Planning," Asia-Pacific Journal: Japan Focus, February 21, 2011, http://japanfocus.org/-Peter_Dale-Scott/3491.

12. Ben Bradlee, Jr., *Guts and Glory: The Rise and Fall of Oliver North* (New York: Donald I. Fine, 1988), 132.

13. Bob Woodward and Carl Bernstein, *All the President's Men* (New York: Simon and Schuster, 1974), 23; Jim Hougan, *Secret Agenda* (New York: Random House, 1984), 16. For more on WISP, see David Wise, *The Politics of Lying: Government Deception, Secrecy, and Power* (New York: Random House, 1973), 134–37.

14. Scott, *Road to 9/11*, 197–235.

15. Alfonso Chardy, "Reagan Aides and the Secret Government," *Miami Herald*, July 5, 1987, http://bellaciao.org/en/article.php3?id_article=9877.

16. Congressional Committees Investigating the Iran-Contra Affair, *Hearings*, July 13, 1987, as reported in *New York Times*, July 14, 1987. Cf. Scott, *Road to 9/11*, 183–90.

17. John Foster Dulles to Lord McGowan, Chairman of Imperial Chemical Industries, in Nancy Lisagor and Frank Lipsius, *A Law unto Itself: The Untold Story of the Law Firm of Sullivan & Cromwell* (New York: William Morrow, 1988), 127.

18. Stephen Dorril, *MI6: Inside the Covert World of Her Majesty's Secret Intelligence Service* (New York: Free Press, 2000), 659–60.

19. Lauren Fox, "Spy Game: Why Congress Is Limited in Its CIA Oversight," *U.S. News & World Report*, March 12, 2014, http://www.usnews.com/news/articles/2014/03/12/spy-game-why-congress-is-limited-in-its-cia-oversight.

20. Amy B. Zegart, *Flawed by Design: The Evolution of the CIA, JCS, and NSC* (Stanford, CA: Stanford UP, 1999), 189; citing Christopher Andrew, *For the President's*

Eyes Only (New York: HarperCollins, 1995), 172. See also Church Committee, Senate Select Committee to Study Governmental Operations with Respect to Intelligence Activities, *Final Report; Book IV—Supplementary Detailed Staff Reports on Foreign and Military Intelligence* (Washington, DC: U.S. Government Printing Office, 1976), 28-29, https://www.maryferrell.org/mffweb/archive/viewer/show Doc.do?docId=1160&relPageId=34.

21. David Wise and Thomas B. Ross, *The Espionage Establishment* (New York: Random House, 1967), 166; Scott, *Road to 9/11*, 13.

22. Tim Weiner, *Legacy of Ashes: The History of the CIA* (New York: Doubleday, 2007), 28. An analogous funding source for the CIA developed in the Far East: the so-called

> "M-Fund," a secret fund of money of enormous size that has existed in Japan [in 1991] for more than forty years. The Fund was established by the United States in the immediate postwar era for essentially the same reasons that later gave rise to the Marshall Plan of assistance by the U.S. to Western Europe, including the Federal Republic of Germany. . . . The M-Fund was used not only for the building of a democratic political system in Japan but, in addition, for all of the purposes for which Marshall Plan funds were used in Europe.

23. Peter Dale Scott, *American War Machine: Deep Politics, the CIA Global Drug Connection, and the Road to Afghanistan* (Berkeley: University of California Press, 2007), 68-96.

24. Fineman, *A Special Relationship*, 214-15; cf. 206.

25. Scott, *American War Machine*, 101-16.

26. William D. Hartung, *Prophets of War: Lockheed Martin and the Making of the Military-Industrial Complex* (New York: Nation Books, 2011), 126.

27. Anthony Summers with Robbyn Swan, *The Arrogance of Power: The Secret World of Richard Nixon* (New York: Viking Penguin, 2000), 283. Cf. Ronald Kessler, *The Richest Man in the World: The Story of Adnan Khashoggi* (New York: Warner Books), 171: Khashoggi told the prosecutors "that he churned millions through the tiny [Rebozo] bank to win favor with the president."

28. Cf. Jim Hougan, *Spooks: The Haunting of America: The Private Use of Secret Agents* (New York: William Morrow, 1978), 457-58.

29. Kessler, *Richest Man in the World*, 238-41; Scott, *American War Machine*, 161-62.

30. The operation kept the name "Safari Club" even after moving from Khashoggi's Club to a permanent headquarters in Cairo.

31. Christopher Byron, "The Senate look at BCCI," *New York Magazine*, October 28, 1991, 20-21.

32. Nick Kochan and Bob Whittington, *Bankrupt: The BCCI Fraud* (London: Gollancz, 1991), 220; quoted in Committee on Foreign Relations, United States Senate, *The BCCI Affair: BCCI, the CIA and Foreign Intelligence, A Report to the Committee on Foreign Relations, United States Senate by Senator John Kerry and Senator Hank Brown, December 1992; 102d Congress, 2d Session, Senate Print 102-140*, Part 11,

"BCCI, the CIA and Foreign Intelligence" (Washington, DC: U.S. Government Printing Office), https://www.fas.org/irp/congress/1992_rpt/bcci/11intel.htm.

33. Jonathan Beaty and S. C. Gwynne, *The Outlaw Bank: A Wild Ride into the Secret Heart of BCCI* (New York: Random House, 1993), 311: "Rappaport and the Bank of Oman's managing director maintained key contacts with the Saudis, who were pumping money through the bank for the Afghan rebels, at Casey's request." Cf. Alan A. Block and Constance A. Weaver, *All Is Clouded by Desire: Global Banking, Money Laundering, and International Organized Crime* (Westport, CT: Praeger Publishers, 2004), 27–28; Scott, *American War Machine*, 163; Scott, *Road to 9/11*, 325n94.

34. Block and Weaver, *All Is Clouded by Desire,* 36–37. Allegedly $10 million obtained from the sultan of Brunei for Oliver North's support of the Contras was deposited by accident for a while into Bruce Rappaport's Swiss bank account (Block and Weaver, *All is Clouded by Desire*, 89–90).

35. Craig Unger, *House of Bush, House of Saud: The Secret Relationship between the World's Two Most Powerful Dynasties* (New York: Scribner, 2004), 59–61. The opposition of Israel and its supporters was mitigated in 1983, when Reagan agreed to preserve Israel's "qualitative edge" by supplying comparable weapons (Bernard Reich, *Securing the Covenant: United States-Israel Relations After the Cold War* [Westport, CT: Greenwood Press, 1995], 53). Cf. Marshall, Scott, and Hunter, *The Iran-Contra Connection*, 93–95.

36. Unger, *House of Bush, House of Saud,* 61; citing Robert Baer, "The Fall of the House of Saud," *Atlantic Monthly*, May 2003, 60.

37. "Saudi Prince 'Received Arms Cash,'" BBC, June 7, 2007, http://news.bbc.co.uk/2/hi/business/6728773.stm. It is unclear whether payments continued after 2001, when the U.K. signed the OECD's Anti-Bribery Convention, making such overpayments illegal.

38. Lacey, *Inside the Kingdom*, 108.

39. Joseph J. Trento, *Prelude to Terror: The Rogue CIA and the Legacy of America's Private Intelligence Network* (New York: Carroll & Graf, 2005), 102.

40. Steve Coll, *Ghost Wars: The Secret History of the CIA, Afghanistan, and bin Laden, from the Soviet Invasion to September 10, 2001* (New York: Penguin Press, 2004), 82.

41. Peter Truell and Larry Gurwin, *False Profits: The Inside Story of BCCI, the World's Most Corrupt Financial Empire* (Boston: Houghton Mifflin, 1992), 133.

42. Robert Parry, *Secrecy and Privilege: Rise of the Bush Dynasty from Watergate to Iraq* (Arlington, VA: Media Consortium, 2004), 112–38; Scott, *Road to 9/11*, 99–107.

43. John K. Cooley, *Unholy Wars: Afghanistan, America, and International Terrorism* (London: Pluto Press, 1999), 26. De Marenches, through a shadowy Pinay Circle, was also accused of interfering in the domestic politics of France, England, and other European countries. See Robin Ramsey, "Brian Crozier, the Pinay Circle and James Goldsmith," *Lobster* 17, November 1988; David Teacher, "The Pinay Circle and Destabilization in Europe," *Lobster* 18, October 1989. A more extreme argu-

ment is that of David G. Guyatt, "The Pinay Circle: An Invisible Power Network," *Nexus Magazine*, August-September 1996.

44. Theodore Draper, *A Very Thin Line* (New York: Hill and Wang, 1991), 80–83.

45. Committee on Foreign Relations, United States Senate, *The BCCI Affair*, Part 19. "Khashoggi, a Saudi Arabian who investigators have found played a significant role in financing the early US arms shipments to Iran, was serving as Fahd's emissary in the deals, Bamieh said. . . . " (*The BCCI Affair*, Part 19, http://fas.org/ irp/congress/1992_rpt/bcci/19rogers.htm). This claim was corroborated by two Khashoggi associates and Farid Ghadry, a Saudi dissident in Washington (*New York Times*, January 17, 1987, 6). Cf. also *Washington Post*, March 7, 1987, A4.

46. There is no published evidence that Copeland was involved in the Safari Club covert operations. But it may be significant that Copeland's activity of advising the Egyptian Army became, after the creation of the Safari Club a franchise, of a "private" U.S. firm, J. J. Cappucci and Associates, owned by Theodore Shackley (Trento, *Prelude to Terror*, 150, 247).

47. Draper, *A Very Thin Line*, 129.

48. Draper, *A Very Thin Line*, 131. Cf. Dan Raviv and Yossi Melman, *Every Spy a Prince: The Complete History of Israel's Intelligence Community* (Boston: Houghton Mifflin, 1990), 261; Mayn Katz, *Song of Spies* (Heliographica Press, 2005), 136–37.

49. Samuel Segev, translated by Haim Watzman, *The Iranian Triangle: The Untold Story of Israel's Role in the Iran-Contra* (New York: The Free Press, 1988), 10. For the collaboration of Greenspun, Schwimmer, and Meyer Lansky in gunrunning, see Leonard Slater, *The Pledge* (New York: Simon and Schuster, 1970). Paul Helliwell may have been part of this operation; see Scott, *American War Machine*, 71, 164.

50. Miles Copeland, *The Game Player: The Confessions of the CIA's Original Political Operative* (London: Aurum Press, 1989), 263.

51. Larry J. Kolb, *Overworld: The Life and Times of a Reluctant Spy* (New York: Riverhead/Penguin, 2004), 246.

52. Kolb, *Overworld*, 247.

53. Kolb, *Overworld*, 247.

54. *Iran-Contra Affair*, Report of the congressional committees investigating the Iran-Contra Affair (U.S. Congress, H. Rept. No. 100–433, S. Rept. No. 100–216), 164.

55. Committee on Foreign Relations, United States Senate, *The BCCI Affair*, Part 11, "BCCI, the CIA and Foreign Intelligence."

56. In his 2009 book, Phillip Shenon, *The Commission: The Uncensored History of the 9/11 Investigation* (New York: Twelve, 2009), 52–55, 184, 309–11, 398–99, *New York Times* reporter Shenon discusses Bayoumi and his ties to the Saudi government. Cf. David Ray Griffin, *The New Pearl Harbor Revisited: 9/11, the Cover-Up, and the Exposé* (Northampton, MA: Olive Branch Press, 2008), 224–27.

57. Paul Church, "Was Saudi Arabia involved?," Asia Times Online, February 11, 2012, http://www.atimes.com/atimes/Middle_East/NB11Ak03.html. Cf. Anthony Summers and Robbyn Swan, *The Eleventh Day: The Full Story of 9/11 and Osama bin Laden* (New York: Ballantine Books, 2011), 410–15, 559–62; cf. David B. Ot-

taway, *The King's Messenger: Prince Bandar bin Sultan and America's Tangled Relationship with Saudi Arabia* (New York: Walker, 2008), 198–99.

58. Let me clarify yet again that what I mean by "support for alleged 9/11 hijackers" means support for a joint operation on 9/11 involving both U.S. government and Saudi officials, along with at least some of the alleged hijackers, and not, in my mind at least, of a plot to bring down the World Trade Center towers in a controlled demolition, which I believe may have involved quite different plotters.

59. Paul Sperry, "Inside the Saudi 9/11 Coverup," *New York Post*, December 15, 2013, http://nypost.com/2013/12/15/inside-the-saudi-911-coverup/: "FBI agents investigating the connection in 2002 found that visitor logs for the gated community and photos of license tags matched vehicles driven by the hijackers. Just two weeks before the 9/11 attacks, the Saudi luxury home was abandoned. Three cars, including a new Chrysler PT Cruiser, were left in the driveway. Inside, opulent furniture was untouched."

60. Lacey, *Inside the Kingdom*, 108.

61. Glenn R. Simpson, "Riggs Bank Had Longstanding Link To the CIA," *Wall Street Journal*, December 31, 2004. The *Journal* added that the former Chilean chief of secret police under Pinochet, Manuel Contreras, also banked at Riggs.

62. Peter Maass, "A Touch of Crude," *Mother Jones*, January/February 2005, http://www.motherjones.com/politics/2005/01/obiang-equatorial-guinea-oil-riggs.

63. Steve Coll, *Private Empire: ExxonMobil and American Power* (New York: Penguin Press, 2012), 283, 290.

64. *The Report of the Joint Congressional Inquiry into Intelligence Community Activities before and after the Terrorist Attacks of September 11, 2001*, 107th Congress, 2nd Session, S. Rept. 107-351 and H. Rept. 107-792, http://www.gpo.gov/fdsys/search/page-details.action?browsePath=107/HRPT/[700%3b799]&granuleId=CRPT-107hrpt792&packageId=CRPT-107hrpt792, 173ss. Discussion in Ottaway, *The King's Messenger*, 198–99.

65. Shenon, *The Commission*, 398–99.

66. Ottaway, *The King's Messenger*, 198–99. Cf. *Arab News*, July 26, 2003, http://www.arabnews.com/node/234848:

> What has been produced is nothing less than a charter for Saudi-bashing, all the more so because of the 28 pages supposedly dealing with Saudi links to the hijackers, blocked on White House orders. Anyone who thinks that President Bush is doing us a favor can forget it. Whatever the intention, this is an invitation to the US and other media to speculate. It would be far better if the section were published.

This financial involvement from the supranational deep state is a dimension overlooked by those who describe 9/11 as a conspiracy, or "State Crime Against Democracy" (SCAD), to be blamed on the U.S. Government. See Lance deHaven-Smith, "Beyond Conspiracy Theory: Patterns of High Crime in American Government," *American Behavioral Scientist*, 53 (February 1, 2010), 796; and my discussion in *The Asia-Pacific Journal: Japan Focus*, September 23, 2012, http://japanfocus.org/-Peter_Dale-Scott/3835.

67. Dana Hedgpeth, "Pentagon Plans $60 Billion Weapons Sale to Saudi Arabia," *Washington Post*, October 21, 2010.
68. The leader of the congressional opposition was Rep. Anthony Weiner of New York. Less than a year later, in 2011, he was forced to resign, after exposure of sexually provocative pictures that he had sent to female admirers on the Internet.
69. Cf. Jonathan Schell, *The Unconquerable World: Power, Nonviolence, and the Will of the People* (New York: Metropolitan Books, 2003), 227–31.

11. AMERICA'S UNCHECKED SECURITY STATE

1. Robert H. Ferrell (ed.), *Dear Bess: The Letters from Harry to Bess Truman, 1910–1959* (New York: W. W. Norton, 1983), 550.
2. Brian Fitzgerald, *McCarthyism: The Red Scare* (Minneapolis, MN: Compass Point Books, 2007), 16.
3. See chapter 3.
4. Patrick A. Thronson, "Toward Comprehensive Reform of America's Emergency Law Regime," *University of Michigan Journal of Law Reform*, 46, No. 2 (Winter 2013), 737.
5. See "How the Anti-Terrorism Bill Allows for Detention of People Engaging in Innocent Associational Activity," ACLU, October 23, 2001, http://www.aclu .org/national-security/how-anti-terrorism-bill-allows-detention-people-engaging -innocent-associational-ac.
6. National Commission on Terrorist Attacks upon the United States, *The 9/11 Commission Report* (New York: W. W. Norton, 2004), 394, http://www.9-11commis sion.gov/report/911Report.pdf.
7. Len Colodny and Tom Schachtman, *The Forty Years War: The Rise and Fall of the Neocons, from Nixon to Obama* (New York: HarperCollins, 2009), 390. As we shall see below, Mitchell blocked implementation of the Huston Plan at the urging of Hoover, who was opposed to such cooperation between the FBI and CIA.
8. Church Committee, Senate Select Committee to Study Governmental Operations with Respect to Intelligence Activities, *Final Report; Book II—Intelligence Activities and the Rights of Americans* (henceforth Church Committee, *Book II*) (Washington, DC: U.S. Government Printing Office, 1976), 91, https://www.maryferrell. org/mffweb/archive/viewer/showDoc.do?docId=1158&relPageId=107. For whatever reason, the Church Committee *Final Report* is silent about the detention provisions of the Huston Plan (Church Committee, *Book II*, 112–15).
9. Benjamin O. Fordham, *Building the Cold War Consensus: The Political Economy of U.S. National Security Policy, 1949–51* (Ann Arbor: University of Michigan Press, 1998), 153: "Title II of the act authorized the arrest and detention of suspected subversives in the event of an 'internal security emergency.'"
10. See for example Athan Theoharis, *Spying on Americans: Political Surveillance from Hoover to the Huston Plan* (Philadelphia: Temple University Press, 1978), 99–100; Paul D. Borman, "The Selling of Preventive Detention 1970," *Northwest Law Review*, 65 (January-February 1971), 879–931.

11. A major factor in the rapid decline of Hoover's reputation was the revelation of COINTELPRO programs, discovered in the burglary by activists of a suburban FBI office in Media, PA, on March 8, 1971. See Mark Mazzetti, "Burglars Who Took On F.B.I. Abandon Shadows," *New York Times*, January 7, 2014, http://www.nytimes.com/2014/01/07/us/burglars-who-took-on-fbi-abandon-shadows.html; Betty Medsger, *The Burglary: The Discovery of J. Edgar Hoover's Secret FBI* (New York: Alfred A. Knopf, 2014).

12. Athan Theoharis, ed., *The FBI: A Comprehensive Reference Guide* (Phoenix, AZ: Oryx Press, 1999), 158. We shall see below (in the text at n. 74) that Hoover had never been constrained by the procedures of the Internal Security Act when it was passed.

13. As we shall see below (in the text at n. 70) the new Administrative Index (ADEX) was in turn discontinued in 1978. But the list was again not destroyed, and remained available for use by a committee of Continuity of Government (COG) planners (including Rumsfeld and Cheney) in the new Reagan administration. It has been in active use since 9/11.

14. In three magisterial books (*Blowback, Nemesis*, and *Dismantling the Empire*) Chalmers Johnson documented how America's imperial overstretch abroad has become a threat to the republic itself. This chapter looks at a parallel threat to the republic that has arisen from within.

15. The concept of a "war on terror" had earlier been promoted in 1979 at the Jerusalem Conference on International Terrorism organized by future Israeli Prime minister Benjamin Netanyahu. George H. W. Bush spoke there in support of a "war on terror." In April 1980 a follow-up conference in Washington was addressed by Henry Kissinger, future National Security Adviser Richard Allen, and Richard Pipes. See Raymond L. Garthoff, ed., *The Great Transition: American-Soviet Relations and the End of the Cold War* (Washington, DC: Brookings Institution, 1994), 23n14.

16. See Mark Perry, *Eclipse: The Last Days of the CIA* (New York: William Morrow, 1992), 47–49, 319–20; Gregory F. Treverton, *Covert Action: The Limits of Intervention in the Postwar World* (New York: Basic Books, 1987); David Aaron, *Los Angeles Times*, October 18, 1987, http://articles.latimes.com/1987-10-18/books/bk-15321_1_covert-action: "CIA Director William Casey, angry at his experts on terrorism for coming up with little evidence linking the Soviet Union to terror groups, ordered them to read Claire Sterling's famous book 'The Terror Network.' They did and found that virtually all of the examples she cited turned out to be CIA disinformation—false stories planted in the foreign press that she unwittingly used in good faith."

17. Lord Acton to the Anglican Bishop of London, Mandell Creighton, letter, April 1887, in John Emerich Edward Dalberg-Acton, *Essays on Freedom and Power* (Boston: Beacon Press, 1949), 364.

18. McCarthy's "certain manic brilliance" was noted at the time by commentator Eric Sevareid (Conrad Black, *Richard Milhous Nixon: The Invincible Quest* [London: Quercus, 2007], 310). Cf. Eli Sagan, *Citizens and Cannibals, the French Revolution, the Struggle for Modernity, and the Origins of Ideological Terror* (Lanham, MD: Rowman & Littlefield), 328:

Richard Nixon . . . manifested many attributes that can accurately be called "para-noid." But when the Watergate crisis came to its frightful climax, many sensitive, thoughtful people in Washington were fearful that the president would go over the line and move on from paranoid behavior to paranoia itself. In the last days before Nixon resigned, Secretary of Defense James Schlesinger apparently informed all U.S. commanders that any orders from the White House concerning troops or weapons had to be approved by him, before being executed.

In his important book, *A First-Rate Madness*, Nassir Ghaemi makes an interest-ing case that "the best crisis leaders are either mentally ill or mentally abnormal"; however I am completely unpersuaded by his attempt to prove that "Nixon was *not* mentally ill or abnormal" (Nassir Ghaemi, *A First-Rate Madness: Uncovering the Links between Leadership and Mental Illness* [New York: Penguin Press, 2011], 17, 223; emphasis in original).

19. For Angleton as "the CIA's manic molehunter," see Lori Lyn Bogle, ed. *The Cold War* (New York: Routledge, 2001), 64. For North's "nearly manic devotion to duty," see Donald Worster, *Rivers of Empire: Water, Aridity, and the Growth of the American West* (New York: Oxford University, 1992), 153. Cf. Paul Berman, *Power and the Idealists* (Brooklyn, NY: Soft Skull Press), 135: "Rumsfeld . . . in the judgment of his non-admirers . . . gave off a manic and scary vibe."

20. Likewise Rumsfeld's and Cheney's fellow Vulcan, Paul Wolfowitz, after leav-ing the Pentagon, was forced out of his position as president of the World Bank because of similar hubristic excesses, such as granting his mistress salary raises far in excess of those allowable under Bank rules. Both Rumsfeld and Wolfowitz were ousted after successful revolts by their own subordinates. For Rumsfeld's downfall after "the revolt of the generals" against his "reign of terror," see Andrew Cockburn, *Rumsfeld: His Rise, Fall, and Catastrophic Legacy* (New York: Scribner, 2007), especially 210–23.

21. Peter Dale Scott, "Northwards without North: Bush, Counterterrorism, and the Continuation of Secret Power," *Social Justice*, Summer 1989; revised as "North, Iran-Contra, and the Doomsday Project: The Original Congressional Cover Up of Continuity-of-Government Planning," Asia-Pacific Journal: Japan Focus, Febru-ary 21, 2011, http://japanfocus.org/-Peter_Dale-Scott/3491. I offer the notion of personal power autointoxication as a more personalized and more sympathetic interpretation of the phenomenon increasingly described by some criminologists as "state criminality." See for example, G. Barak, "Crime, Criminology and Hu-man Rights: Towards an Understanding of State Criminality," *Journal of Human Justice*, 1990; Lance deHaven-Smith, "Beyond Conspiracy Theory: Patterns of High Crime in American Government," *American Behavioral Scientist*, February 2010, 795–825. Some of my critique of "state crimes" analysis can be found in Peter Dale Scott, "Systemic Destabilization in Recent American History: 9/11, the JFK Assassination, and the Oklahoma City Bombing as a Strategy of Tension," The Asia-Pacific Journal: Japan Focus, September 23, 2012, http://japanfocus .org/-Peter_Dale-Scott/3835.

22. Our economy's recent recurrent flux between exaggerated bubble (moving in Alan Greenspan's terms from "irrational exuberance" to "infectious greed") and then recession, has been compared by a psychologist to "the cycle of manic depression" (Peter C. Whybrow, *American Mania: When More is Not Enough* [New York: W. W. Norton, 2005], 127).

23. Tim Weiner, "The Pentagon's Secret Stash," *Mother Jones Magazine*, March-April 1992, 26.

24. Peter Dale Scott, *The Road to 9/11: Wealth, Empire, and the Future of America* (Berkeley: University of California Press, 2007), 185–87; citing Executive Order 12656 of 18 November 1988.

25. Cockburn, *Rumsfeld*, 88; quoted in Scott, *Road to 9/11,* 187.

26. CNN, November 17, 1991, quoted in Shirley Anne Warshaw, *The Co-Presidency of Bush and Cheney* (Stanford, CA: Stanford Politics and Policy, 2009), 162.

27. In 2014, at a memorial service for a member of the University of California, Berkeley, one of the speakers was a colleague who was also an Iranian Muslim, not an Arab. He told me personally after his talk that he had been detained without a warrant right after 9/11, held for eighty days, and beaten so severely that there was blood in his urine.

28. Tim Weiner, *Enemies: A History of the FBI* (New York: Random House, 2012), 419–20.

29. Glenn Greenwald, "Three Key Lessons from the Obama Administration's Drone Lies," *Guardian* (London), April 11, 2013, http://www.guardian.co.uk/comment isfree/2013/apr/11/three-lessons-obama-drone-lies. Cf. Micah Zenko, "An Inconvenient Truth: Finally, Proof that the United States Has Lied in the Drone Wars," *Foreign Policy*, April 11, 2013, http://www.foreignpolicy.com/articles/2013/04/10/an_inconvenient_truth_drones#.UWXow7ir6Xk.twitter.

30. William Binney, quoted in Jane Mayer, "The Secret Sharer: Is Thomas Drake an Enemy of the State?" *New Yorker*, May 23, 2011, http://www.newyorker.com/magazine/2011/05/23/the-secret-sharer.

31. "Even as some senior former American security officials question whether the strikes are beginning to do more harm than good, 65 percent of Americans questioned in a Gallup poll last month approved of strikes to kill suspected foreign terrorists; only 28 percent were opposed" (Scott Shane, "Targeted Killing Comes to Define War on Terror," *New York Times*, April 8, 2013, 3). As in the McCarthy era, public xenophobia is trumping common sense. See Martha Stout, *The Paranoia Switch: How Terror Rewires Our Brains and Reshapes Our Behavior—and How We Can Reclaim Our Courage* (New York: Farrar, Straus and Giroux, 2007), which the publisher describes as "a groundbreaking clinical, neuropsychological, and practical examination of what terror and fear politics have done to our minds, and to the very biology of our brains."

32. See for example, Tom Engelhardt, "The Enemy-Industrial Complex," TomDispatch, April 15, 2013, http://www.tomdispatch.com/post/175687/tomgram%3A_engelhardt%2C_the_cathedral_of_the_enemy/:

All these years, we've been launching wars and pursuing a "global war on terror." We've poured money into national security as if there were no tomorrow. From our police to our borders, we've up-armored everywhere. We constantly hear about "threats" to us and to the "homeland." And yet, when you knock on the door marked "Enemy," there's seldom anyone home.

Few in this country have found this striking. Few seem to notice any disjuncture between the enemy-ridden, threatening, and deeply dangerous world we have been preparing ourselves for (and fighting in) this last decade-plus and the world as it actually is, even those who lived through significant parts of the last anxiety-producing, bloody century.

Engelhardt accurately blames this psychotic condition on neocons, who "needed an American public anxious, frightened, and ready to pay." But his trenchant essay ends of a note of gloom, even despair:

They may indeed be a crew of Machiavellis, but they are also acolytes in the cult of terror and global war. . . . It's their religion. They are, after all, the enemy-industrial complex and if we are in their grip, so are they.

33. Weiner, *Enemies*, 443. A classified U.S. intelligence report of around 2006 concluded that Iraq had become a "cause célèbre for jihadists, breeding a deep resentment of U.S. involvement in the Muslim world and cultivating supporters for the global jihadist movement" (Mark Mazzetti, *The Way of the Knife: The CIA, a Secret Army, and a War at the Ends of the Earth* [New York: Penguin Press, 2013], 138).
34. The counter-productivity is of course welcome to those who profit from the American war machine, as well as to those multinational corporations who welcome an American military presence around the globe. See chapter 12.
35. FBI manual quoted in Weiner, *Enemies,* 447–48.
36. David K. Shipler, "Terrorist Plots, Hatched by the F.B.I.," *New York Times*, April 28, 2012, http://www.nytimes.com/2012/04/29/opinion/sunday/terrorist-plots -helped-along-by-the-fbi.html?pagewanted=all&_r=0. Cf. Trevor Aaronson, *The Terror Factory: Inside the FBI's Manufactured War on Terrorism* (Brooklyn, NY: Ig Publishing, 2013); Rick Perlstein, "How FBI Entrapment Is Inventing 'Terrorists'—and Letting Bad Guys Off the Hook," *Rolling Stone*, May 15, 2012, http:// www.rollingstone.com/politics/blogs/national-affairs/how-fbi-entrapment-is -inventing-terrorists-and-letting-bad-guys-off-the-hook-20120515; Spencer Ackerman, "Government agents 'directly involved' in most high-profile US terror plots," *Guardian*, July 21, 2014, http://www.theguardian.com/world/2014/jul/21/ government-agents-directly-involved-us-terror-plots-report.
37. Robert W. Worth, Mark Mazzetti, and Scott Shane, "Drone Strikes' Risks to Get Rare Moment in the Public Eye," *New York Times*, February 5, 2013, http:// www.nytimes.com/2013/02/06/world/middleeast/with-brennan-pick-a-light-on -drone-strikes-hazards.html?pagewanted=all&_r=0. On CIA and Joint Special Operations Command (JSOC) killer squads in general, see Mazzetti, *The Way of the Knife*.
38. Jonathan Turley, "The NDAA's historic assault on American liberty," *Guardian* (London), January 2, 2012:

The almost complete failure of the mainstream media to cover this issue is shocking. . . . On the NDAA, reporters continue to mouth the claim that this law only codifies what is already the law. That is not true. The administration has fought any challenges to indefinite detention to prevent a true court review. Moreover, most experts agree that such indefinite detention of citizens violates the constitution.

39. Weiner, *Enemies*, 24–25, 29, 31.

40. Weiner, *Enemies*, 15–16.

41. Weiner, *Enemies*, 28.

42. Curt Gentry, *J. Edgar Hoover: The Man and the Secrets* (New York: W. W. Norton, 1991), 127.

43. Gentry, *J. Edgar Hoover*, 244–45.

44. Gentry, *J. Edgar Hoover*, 207. However Hoover had already begun to violate Stone's edict by 1933, when he began to collect "derogatory information" on Alfred Einstein (Fred Jerome, *The Einstein File: J. Edgar Hoover's Secret War against the World's Most Famous Scientist* [New York: St. Martin's Press, 2002], jacket, http://www.theeinsteinfile.com/) and 1934, when on FDR's urging he ordered what he termed a "so-called intelligence investigation" of pro-Nazi elements, primarily the German-American Bund (Gentry, *J. Edgar Hoover*, 205).

45. Gentry, *J. Edgar Hoover*, 204. Cf. Jules Archer, *The Plot to Seize the White House: The Shocking True Story of the Conspiracy to Overthrow FDR* (New York: Skyhorse Publishing, 2007); Sally Denton, *The Plots Against the President: FDR, a Nation in Crisis, and the Rise of the American Right* (New York: Bloomsbury Press, 2012), 200–201.

46. Gentry, *J. Edgar Hoover*, 205.

47. Hersh, *Bobby and J. Edgar*, 51; Gentry, *J. Edgar Hoover*, 206–8; Church Committee, *Book II*, 30.

48. Hoover first named the revived Division Five of the FBI as the National Defense Division, then the Security Division, then the Domestic Intelligence Division, and then the Intelligence Division.

49. Marc Aronson, *Master of Deceit: J. Edgar Hoover and America in the Age of Lies* (Somerville, MA: Candlewick, 2012), 85. Aronson erroneously attributes FDR's authorization to the first Butler contact with Hoover, instead of the second.

50. "Intelligence Division operations were cloaked in secrecy; were less accountable to public scrutiny . . . and spilled over into unethical or illegal conduct. Coexisting with the professional culture of the criminal division was a 'counterculture' that developed in the hidden side of the Bureau's intelligence operations" (Theoharis, *The FBI: A Comprehensive Reference Guide*, 183).

51. Sheldon Marcus, *Father Coughlin: The Tumultuous Life of the Priest of the Little Flower* (Boston: Little, Brown, 1972), 214–17.

52. A. S. Richard Sipe, *The Serpent and the Dove: Celibacy in Literature and Life* (Westport, CT: Praeger, 2007), 44–45.

53. Weiner, *Enemies*, 144; Gentry, *J. Edgar Hoover*, 350n. Cf. Kai Bird, *The Chairman: John J. McCloy, the Making of the American Establishment* (New York: Simon & Schuster, 1992), 281.

54. Anthony Summers with Robbyn Swan, *The Arrogance of Power: The Secret World of Richard Nixon* (New York: Viking, 2000), 64–65; Gentry, *J. Edgar Hoover*, 378–80.

55. For Hoover's role in shaping Reagan's political career, see Seth Rosenfeld, *Subversives: The FBI's War on Student Radicals, and Reagan's Rise to Power* (New York: Macmillan, 2012).

56. Burton Hersh, *Bobby and J. Edgar: The Historic Face-Off between the Kennedys and J. Edgar Hoover that Transformed America* (New York: Carroll & Graf, 2007), 15.

57. Robert A. Caro, *The Years of Lyndon Johnson: The Passage of Power* (New York: Alfred A. Knopf, 2012), 291. Burton Hersh believes the allegation that LBJ used information from Hoover to secure his position on the 1960 Democratic ticket (Hersh, *Bobby and J. Edgar,* 15–16).

58. Weiner, *Enemies,* 179–80. McLeod's staff also consisted mostly of former FBI agents, using extralegal techniques such as "surveillances, mail openings, wiretaps, and break-ins" (Gentry, *J. Edgar Hoover,* 408–9). McLeod's office was established during the Eisenhower administration by Presidential Executive Order 10450 of April 27, 1953 (http://www.archives.gov/federal-register/codification/executive-order/10450.html).

59. Gentry, *J. Edgar Hoover,* 409.

60. James C. Thomson, "How Could Vietnam Happen? An Autopsy," *Atlantic Monthly,* April, 1968, http://www.theatlantic.com/magazine/archive/1968/04/how-could-vietnam-happen-an-autopsy/306462/. Cf. Christopher Gerard, "On the Road to Vietnam: 'The Loss of China Syndrome,' Pat McCarran, and J. Edgar Hoover," *Nevada Historical Society Quarterly* 37 (1994).

61. Hans Morgenthau, "The Corruption of Patriotism," *New Republic,* 1955; reprinted in Hans Morgenthau, ed. *Politics in the Twentieth Century,* vol. I (Chicago: University of Chicago Press, 1962), 407. Cf. Eric Wilson, ed. *The Dual State: Parapolitics, Carl Schmitt and the National Security Complex* (Farnham, UK: Ashgate, 2012), 1–3, 21–27, etc.

62. Ola Tunander, "Democratic State versus Deep State: Approaching the Dual State of the West," in *Government of the Shadows: Parapolitics and Criminal Sovereignty,* ed. Eric Wilson and Tim Lindsey (London: Pluto Press, 2008), 56–72.

63. Scott, *Road to 9/11,* 252, 258; cf. Peter Dale Scott, *The War Conspiracy: JFK, 9/11, and the Deep Politics of War* (New York: Skyhorse Publishing, 2013), 15–16; Peter Dale Scott, *American War Machine: Deep Politics, the CIA Global Drug Connection, and the Road to Afghanistan* (Lanham, MD: Rowman & Littlefield, 2010), 21.

64. Scott, *Deep Politics and the Death of JFK* (Berkeley: University of California Press, 1993), xi–xii; discussion in Eric Wilson, "The Concept of the Parapolitical," in Wilson, *The Dual State,* 1–27.

65. Athan G. Theoharis, *The FBI & American Democracy: A Brief Critical History* (Lawrence: University Press of Kansas, 2004), 20–21; Church Committee, Senate Select Committee to Study Governmental Operations with Respect to Intelligence Activities, *Final Report, Book III—Supplementary Detailed Staff Reports on Intelligence Activities and the Rights of Americans* (henceforth Church Committee, *Book III*) (Washington, DC: U.S. Government Printing Office, 1976) 411–17, https://www.maryferrell.org/mffweb/archive/viewer/showDoc.do?docId=1159&relPageId=417.

66. Church Committee, *Book III,* 417.

67. Attorney-General Biddle directive to the FBI, 1943; quoted in Church Committee, *Book III*, 420–21.

68. Church Committee, *Book III*, 420–21.

69. Weiner, *Enemies*, 122: "[The Security Index] included—in addition to 'both aliens and citizens of the United States [of] German, Italian, and Communist sympathies'—radical labor leaders, journalists critical of the administration, writers critical of the FBI, and certain members of Congress." In 1955 about half the names on the Security Index were transferred to a less punitive Communist Index (later renamed the Reserve Index), including "professors, teachers, and educators: labor union organizers and leaders; writers, lecturers newsmen and others in the mass media field; lawyers, doctors, and scientists; other potentially influential persons on a local or national level; individuals who could potentially furnish financial or material aid" (Church Committee, *Book II*, 55). Among those included were Norman Mailer and Martin Luther King, Jr. (Theoharis, *The FBI: A Comprehensive Reference Guide*, 123).

70. FBI, *FBI Privacy Act Systems* (63 FR 8659, 8671 / 02-20-98), http://www.fbi.gov/foia/privacy-act/63-fr-8659:

     The following indices are no longer being used by the FBI and are being maintained at FBIHQ pending receipt of authority to destroy: Black Panther Party Photo Index; Black United Front Index; Security Index; and Wounded Knee Album.

     Administrative Index (ADEX). Consists of cards with descriptive data on individuals who were subject to investigation in a national emergency because they were believed to constitute a potential or active threat to the internal security of the United States. When ADEX was started in 1971, it was made up of people who were formerly on the Security Index, Reserve Index, and Agitator Index. This index is maintained in two separate locations in FBI Headquarters. ADEX was discontinued in January 1978. This list is inactive at FBI Headquarters and 29 Field Offices.

71. Weiner, *Enemies*, 161. Theoharis asserts however that Truman had already secretly approved the detention plan in 1948 (Theoharis, *The FBI: A Comprehensive Reference Guide*, 151).

72. Weiner, *Enemies*, 160–61. The primary targets for detention were Communist Party members and their supporters. Each detained person would eventually get a hearing, which under Hoover's plan would "not be bound by the rules of evidence." The plan was declassified in 2007; see "Hoover plan for mass arrests," Public record media, February 2011, http://publicrecordmedia.com/2011/02/hoover-plan-for-mass-arrests/. The FBI at this time became what Victor Navasky called "the vanguard of an extraordinary internal-security bureaucracy"—including the Subversive Activities Control Board, established, over Truman's veto, by the McCarran Act of 1950 (Victor Navasky, *Naming Names* [New York: Penguin, 1981], 22). That security bureaucracy has morphed today into a second, shadow government.

73. Weiner, *Enemies*, 144–45.

74. Theoharis, *The FBI: A Comprehensive Reference Guide*, 151, 158; cf. Church Committee, *Book II*.

75. Presidential Proclamation 2914 of December 16, 1950; reproduced in Brian Tuohy, *Disaster Government: National Emergencies, Continuity of Government, & You* (San Bernardino, CA: Mofo Press, 2013), 44–45.

76. For NSA 68/4 of December 14, 1950, see *Foreign Relations of the United States, 1950*, vol. 1, 1950, 467–74, https://history.state.gov/historicaldocuments/frus1950v01; cf. Michael J. Hogan, *A Cross of Iron: Harry S. Truman and the Origins of the National Security State, 1945–1954* (Cambridge: Cambridge University Press, 1998), 322, etc.

77. Dennis Wainstock, *Truman, MacArthur, and the Korean War* (Westport, CT: Greenwood Press, 1999), 99.

78. William Arkin cites as the first Presidential Emergency Action Document (PEAD) Executive Order 10346: Preparation by Federal Agencies of Civil Defense Emergency Plans (William Arkin, *American Coup: How a Terrified Government Is Destroying the Constitution* [New York: Little Brown, 2013], 238n4).

79. Matthew L. Conaty, "The Atomic Midwife: The Eisenhower Administration's Continuity-of-Government Plans and the Legacy of 'Constitutional Dictatorship,'" *Rutgers Law Review*, 62, no. 3 (Spring 2010), 7.

80. Federal Emergency Management Agency [FEMA], FEMA MANUAL 5400.2 (effective Feb. 29, 2000), http://www.fema. gov/pdf/library/5400_2.pdf, 111; quoted in Thronson, "Toward Comprehensive Reform of America's Emergency Law Regime," 762.

81. William Arkin, "National Security Contingency Plans of the U.S. Government (Supplement to Code Names: Deciphering U.S. Military Plans, Programs, and Operations in the 9/11 World)," ca. 2005, arkins-contingency-plans-of-the-us -government.pdf.

82. Arkin, *American Coup*, 39.

83. A. H. Belmont to L. F. Boardman, FBI memo of June 19, 1958 (FBI HQ file 66-19016-6), reproduced in Federal Bureau of Investigation (FBI), Defense Plans—Presidential Emergency Action Documents, 1958—1979, http://www .governmentattic.org/4docs/FBI-Presid-Emerg-Action-Docs_1958-1979.pdf .

84. J. Edgar Hoover to Assistant Attorney General for Administration, FBI letter of April 22, 1976, reproduced in Federal Bureau of Investigation (FBI), Defense Plans—Presidential Emergency Action Documents, 1958—1979, www.government attic.org.

85. Arkin, *American Coup*, 43.

86. Arkin, *American Coup*, 97.

87. "Ex-agents Describe Spying on Civilians," UPI, February 25, 1971, http://phil ochs.blogspot.com/2011/02/ex-agents-describe-spying-on-civilians.html.

88. Michel Crozier, Samuel P. Huntington, and Joji Watanuki, *The Crisis of Democracy: Report on the Governability of Democracies to the Trilateral Commission* (New York: New York University Press, 1975), 113.

89. Two dates are given for the creation of FEMA: June 1978, and March 1979, the date of its formal authorization in Presidential Review Memorandum 32.

90. Diana Reynolds, "The Rise of the National Security State: FEMA and the NSC, Political Research Associates," *Covert Action Information Bulletin*, no. 33 (Winter 1990), http://www.publiceye.org/liberty/fema/Fema_2.html. Earlier, Governor Reagan in California had authorized the development of a counterinsurgency plan (known as Cable Splicer) and exercises to deal with such crises, in conjunction with the U.S. Sixth Army and the Pentagon (Operation Garden Plot). The cadres developing Cable Splicer (headed by Louis Giuffrida), were with Reagan's elevation to the presidency transferred into FEMA.

91. Glenn Beck, *The Overton Window* (New York: Threshold Editions/Mercury Radio Arts, 2010), 296. Cf. Robert C. Aldridge, *America in Peril* (Pasadena, CA: Hope Publishing House, 2008), 295.

92. Alfonso Chardy, "Reagan Aides and the Secret Government," *Miami Herald*, July 5, 1987, http://bellaciao.org/en/article.php3?id_article=9877: "Some of President Reagan's top advisers have operated a virtual parallel government outside the traditional Cabinet departments."

93. Conaty, "The Atomic Midwife," 7–8.

94. Conaty, "The Atomic Midwife," 14.

95. Hope Yen, "Eisenhower Letters Reveal Doomsday Plan: Citizens Tapped to Take Over in Case of Attack," AP, *Deseret News*, March 21, 2004, http://www.deseretnews.com/article/595050502/Eisenhower-letters-reveal-doomsday-plan.html?pg=all. Other emergency responses to the launching of the Soviet sputnik included acceleration of the military programs to launch an American satellite, and the creation of the Defense Department's Advanced Research Projects Agency (ARPA, now DARPA), which developed the Internet.

96. Charlie Joyce to Clay Whitehead [director of the White House Office of Telecommunications Policy under Nixon], "Emergency Preparedness for Telecommunications," attachment to memo of November 5, 1969, reproduced at http://www.docstoc.com/docs/128597200/NSA-USCSB_1940-1980.

97. Tim Shorrock, *Spies for Hire: The Secret World of Intelligence Outsourcing* (New York: Simon & Schuster, 2008), 72–75. Cf. Arkin, *American Coup*, 68.

98. Cf. for example, Office of Secretary of Defense (OSD), "Promulgation and Administration of OSD Crisis Action Packages (CAPs)," December 13, 1990, www.dtic.mil/dtic/tr/fulltext/u2/a270081.pdf: "The Director. Crisis Coordination Center shall: . . . d. Develop and maintain an automated data base interfacing CAPs [Crisis Action Packages] with related presidential emergency action documents (PEADs), Federal Emergency Management Agency (FEMA) major emergency actions (MEAs), and Joint Staff fact sheets."

    These programs were under the purview of the Undersecretary of Defense for Policy, who in 1990 was the neocon Paul Wolfowitz. Crisis Action Planning is today intensively developed inside and outside government: for example, James L. Jacobs, Michael C. Dorneich, and Patricia M. Jones, "'Activity Representation and Management for Crisis Action Planning,' *1998 IEEE International Conference on Systems, Man, and Cybernetics,* San Diego, CA, October 11–14, 1998. (Invited)."

99. National Commission on Terrorist Attacks upon the United States, *The 9/11 Commission* Report, 38, 326; Scott, *Road to 9/11*, 228–29.

12. AMERICA'S UNCHECKED SECURITY STATE AND LAWLESSNESS

1. Mark Danner, "Cheney: 'The More Ruthless the Better,'" *New York Review of Books*, May 8, 2014, http://www.nybooks.com/articles/archives/2014/may/08/ruthless-dick-cheney/?insrc=toc.
2. Brian Glick, *War at Home: Covert Action against U.S. Activists and What We Can Do about It* (Boston: South End Press, 1999), 34; cf. Curt Gentry, *J. Edgar Hoover: The Man and the Secrets* (New York: W. W. Norton, 1991), 71 (business); Tim Weiner, *Enemies: A History of the FBI* (New York: Random House, 2012), 15–16.
3. Athan G. Theoharis and John Stuart Cox, *The Boss: J. Edgar Hoover and the Great American Inquisition* (New York: Bantam, 1990), 224–29; Gentry, *J. Edgar Hoover*, 413; Mike Forrest Keen, *Stalking Sociologists: J. Edgar Hoover's FBI Surveillance of American Sociology* (New Brunswick, NJ: Transaction Publishers, 2004), 51 (Legion); Charles R. Geisst, *Undue Influence: How the Wall Street Elite Puts the Financial System at Risk* (Hoboken, NJ: John Wiley & Sons, 2005), 139 (business).
4. Alfred M. Lilienthal, "The Changing Role of B'nai B'rith's Anti-Defamation League," Washington Report on Middle East Affairs, June 1993, http://www.wrmea.org/wrmea-archives/148-washington-report-archives-1988-1993/june-1993/7212-the-changing-role-of-bnai-briths-anti-defamation-league.html.
5. Robert Friedman, "The ADL: The Jewish Thought Police," *Village Voice*, May 11, 1993; citing Henry Schwarzschild, *SF Weekly*, April 28, 1993.
6. Gentry, *J. Edgar Hoover*, 329 (Allen), 432 (Murchison, Kennedy, Rosenstiel), 470n (Kennedy).
7. Gentry, *J. Edgar Hoover*, 329. Burton Hersh claims that Hoover dined at Clint Murchison's club in La Jolla, the del Charro, with John Roselli (Burton Hersh, *Bobby and J. Edgar: The Historic Face-Off between the Kennedys and J. Edgar Hoover that Transformed America* [New York: Carroll & Graf, 2007], 107. Cf. Sanford J. Ungar, *FBI* (Boston: Little Brown, 1976), 393: "Some of the director's own wealthy friends were involved in dealings with the underworld."
8. Hersh, *Bobby and J. Edgar*, 49; cf. 198.
9. Athan Theoharis, ed., *The FBI: A Comprehensive Reference Guide* (Phoenix, AZ: Oryx Press, 1999), 189. Hoover's refusal to investigate American organized crime was ended by the embarrassing news stories about the 1957 Apalachin, New York, crime summit. After Robert Kennedy, then working for a Senate Subcommittee, approached the FBI for information, it developed that the FBI had no information at all on about forty of them. The Federal Bureau of Narcotics (FBN), in contrast, "had something on every one of them" (Gentry, *J. Edgar Hoover*, 454n). In all, fifty-eight mobsters were apprehended at Apalachin, while about fifty more escaped through the woods and fields. Cf. Gil Reavill, *Mafia Summit: J. Edgar Hoover, the Kennedy Brothers, and the Meeting That Unmasked the Mob* (New York: Thomas Dunne Books, 2012).
10. Anthony Summers, *Official and Confidential: The Secret Life of J. Edgar Hoover* (New York: G. P. Putnam's Sons, 1993), 228.

11. Stephen H. Norwood, *Strikebreaking and Intimidation: Mercenaries and Masculinity in Twentieth-Century America* (Durham: University of North Carolina Press, 2001), 178.

12. Peter Dale Scott, *Crime and Cover-Up: The CIA, the Mafia, and the Dallas-Watergate Connection* (Berkeley, CA: Westworks, 1977), 40; citing *San Francisco Chronicle*, September 26, 1974; *San Francisco Chronicle*, January 11, 1975.

13. Gentry, *J. Edgar Hoover*, 218–21; Albert Fried, *The Rise and Fall of the Jewish Gangster in America* (New York: Columbia University Press, 1994), 213.

14. Weiner, *Enemies*, 487. In like manner, when Carmine Galante of the Bonanno family avoided conviction for the murder of the left-wing journalist Carlo Tresca in 1943, a sycophantic admirer of Hoover and Winchell, Guenther Reinhardt, blamed the murder on the Communists (Nunzio Pernicone, *Carlo Tresca: Portrait of a Rebel* [Edinburgh: AK Press, 2010], 296; cf. Thomas A. Reppetto, *Battleground New York City: Countering Spies, Saboteurs, and Terrorists since 1861* [Washington, DC: Potomac Books, 2012], 190–94).

15. Howie Carr, *Hitman: The Untold Story of Johnny Martorano: Whitey Bulger's Enforcer and the Most Feared Gangster in the Underworld* (New York: Forge Books, 2011), 170ss.

16. *Boston Globe*, September 6, 2006, http://www.boston.com/news/local/articles/2006/09/06/fbi_found_liable_for_bulger_flemmi/.

17. John Kroger, *Convictions: A Prosecutor's Battles against Mafia Killers, Drug Kingpins, and Enron Thieves* (New York: Farrar, Straus and Giroux, 2009), 146–52, etc.

18. Peter Lance, *Triple Cross: How bin Laden's Master Spy Penetrated the CIA, the Green Berets, and the FBI—and Why Patrick Fitzgerald Failed to Stop Him* (New York: Regan, 2006), 221–38, etc.

19. Stuart Wexler and Larry Hancock, *The Awful Grace of God* (Berkeley, CA: Counterpoint, 2012), 34.

20. Arthur M. Schlesinger, Jr., *Robert Kennedy and His Times* (New York: Ballantine Books, 1979), 341–50; cf. Taylor Branch, *At Canaan's Edge: America in the King Years, 1965–68* (New York: Simon & Schuster, 2006); Henry T. Gallagher, *James Meredith and the Ole Miss Riot: A Soldier's Story* (Jackson: University Press of Mississippi, 2012).

21. Richard D. Mahoney, *Sons & Brothers: The Days of Jack and Bobby Kennedy* (New York: Arcade, 1999), 186, 188.

22. Anthony Summers, *Not in Your Lifetime* (New York: Marlowe & Co., 1998), 162.

23. Statement of Miami Detective Lochart F. Gracey to Detective Sergeant C. H. Sapp, April 10, 1963, http://jfk.hood.edu/Collection/Weisberg%20Subject%20Index%20Files/M%20Disk/Milteer%20J%20A/Item%2009.pdf. Cf. http://jfk.hood.edu/Collection/Weisberg%20Subject%20Index%20Files/M%20Disk/Milteer%20J%20A/Item%2012.pdf. Peter Dale Scott, *Deep Politics and the Death of JFK* (Berkeley: University of California Press, 1993), 49–50.

24. A few days before the JFK assassination, the source, Joseph Milteer, also told Miami police informant Willie Somersett that the President would be shot "from an office building with a high-powered rifle" ("Conversation between William Somersett [Informant] and Joseph Milteer [Subject]," in Peter Dale Scott, Paul

L. Hoch, and Russell Stetler, eds., *The Assassinations: Dallas and Beyond—A Guide to Cover-Ups and Investigations* [New York: Random House, 1976], 124). FBI headquarters received this information on November 10, 1963; but did not transmit it to the Warren Commission (in a rewritten form making it less credible) until August 7, 1964, when the Commission had already written its report and was winding up its work. Meanwhile FBI headquarters had ordered its Miami office to "amend the reliability statement to show that some of the information . . . could not be verified or corroborated." See Scott, *Deep Politics*, 49–51. Later, in August 1968, the FBI ignored a credible report from Somersett connecting a Klan murderer, Tommy Tarrants, to the murder of Martin Luther King, Jr., in Memphis four months before (Wexler and Hancock, *The Awful Grace of God*, 95–97).

25. Although the Klan were generally people with little status in society, Tommy Tarrants told Patsy Sims that one of the people responsible for planning the White Klan violence in which he participated was "a high-ranking military officer" (Patsy Sims, *The Klan* [Lexington: University Press of Kentucky, 1996], 240).

26. Maryanne Vollers, *Ghosts of Mississippi: The Murder of Medgar Evers, the Trials of Byron de la Beckwith, and the Haunting of the New South* (Boston: Little, Brown, 1995), 229–30; quoted in Michael Newton, *The Ku Klux Klan in Mississippi: A History* (Jefferson, NC: McFarland & Co., 2010), 125.

27. Theoharis, *The FBI: A Comprehensive Reference Guide*, 33; Arthur M. Schlesinger, Jr., *Robert Kennedy and His Times* (New York: Ballantine Books, 1979), 313.

28. Schlesinger, *Robert Kennedy and His Times*, 314; citing Church Committee, Senate Select Committee to Study Governmental Operations with Respect to Intelligence Activities, *Final Report; Volume 6—Hearings on the Federal Bureau of Investigations* (Washington, DC: U.S. Government Printing Office, 1976), 33, https://www.maryferrell.org/mffweb/archive/viewer/showDoc.do?docId=1168&relPageId=43. "Mr. Sullivan who was the Assistant Director of the FBI . . . claims . . . 'It so happened that during the war [Hoover] had five Negro chauffeurs, so he automatically made them special agents. . . . none of them conducted investigations: they were just drivers.'" This claim, by William Sullivan, has been disputed.

29. Weiner, *Enemies*, 247.

30. Glenn Peter Hastedt, ed., *Spies, Wiretaps, and Secret Operations: An Encyclopedia of American Espionage* (Santa Barbara, CA: ABC-CLIO, 2011), 180. One of the agents later commented, "There would be a Klan meeting with ten people there, and six of them would be reporting back the next day" (Weiner, *Enemies*, 247).

31. Hastedt, *Spies, Wiretaps, and Secret Operations*, 180. By way of comparison, the FBI COINTELPRO against the Socialist Workers' Party, over a much longer period, involved only 208 operations.

32. Steven E Atkins, *Encyclopedia of Right-Wing Extremism in Modern American History* (Santa Barbara, CA: ABC-CLIO, 2011), 24.

33. Weiner, *Enemies*, 244.

34. Theoharis, ed., *The FBI: A Comprehensive Reference Guide*, 70; Anthony Villano, *Brick Agent: Inside the Mafia for the FBI* (New York: Quadrangle/New York Times Books, 1977); M. Susan Orr Klopfer, Fred Klopfer, Barry Klopfer, *Where Rebels*

Roost: Mississippi Civil Rights Revisited ([Fort Madison, Iowa?]: M. S. Orr Klopfer, 2006), 399.

35. Sandra Harmon, *Mafia Son: The Scarpa Mob Family, the FBI, and a Story of Betrayal* (New York: St. Martin's Griffin, 2010), 57–64; Richard H. Stratton, *Altered States of America: Icons and Outlaws, Hitmakers and Hitmen* (New York: Nation Books, 2005), 226–27.

36. Fredric L. Dannen "The G-Man and the Hit Man," *New Yorker*, December 16, 1996, http://www.newyorker.com/magazine/1996/12/16/the-g-man-and-the-hit-man. The involvement of Scarpa in the two earlier investigations has been challenged (Jerry Mitchell, "A mobster takes on the KKK," *Jackson Clarion-Ledger*, February 17, 2010), but on the basis of evidence introduced into the trial of Scarpa's FBI handler Lindley DeVecchio, the interpretation of which has itself been challenged (Brad Hamilton, *New York Post*, May 27, 2012, http://nypost.com/2012/05/27/mafia-daughter-says-dad-was-grim-reaper/; Lance, *Triple Cross*, 421–25; Jack Cashill, "The Trials of Angela Clemente: Why the Department of Justice is Destroying America's Best PI," WorldNetDaily.com, May 31, 2007, http://www.cashill.com/twa800/trials_angela_clemente.htm). The year 1966 was also when Hoover authorized the FBI's "Operation Hoodwink," a program described in its leadoff memo as "designed to provoke a dispute between the Communist Party, USA, and La Cosa Nostra" (Michael Newton, *Encyclopedia of American Law Enforcement* [New York: Facts On File, 2007], 71).

37. Wexler and Hancock, *The Awful Grace of God*, 25: "The FBI would connect the White Knights with more than three hundred acts of racial violence."

38. Wexler and Hancock, *The Awful Grace of God*, 20: "Sam Bowers had himself targeted King for murder and . . . was part of a network that had incited and planned attacks on King over a period of years."

39. Wexler and Hancock, *The Awful Grace of God*, 275. In contrast Hoover should be severely faulted for his obstruction of the investigation of the Martin Luther King, Jr., assassination. FBI files contained evidence that, if "collated and cross-referenced . . . could have developed a powerful circumstantial case for a conspiracy to murder King [against Bowers and followers of an allied racist, Wesley Swift]." But after the FBI had developed evidence pointing to James Earl Ray as the assassin, "Hoover issued a directive to several field offices . . . to 'hold all leads in abeyance concerning whereabouts and activities of various individuals, including Dr. Wesley Swift, in view of the present information regarding Galt [i.e., Ray]'" (Wexler and Hancock, *The Awful Grace of God*, 253, 256).

40. Jack Nelson, *Scoop: The Evolution of a Southern Reporter* (Jackson: University Press of Mississippi, 2013), 147–48.

41. Nelson, *Scoop*, 146–52. Cf. David Mark Chalmers, *Backfire: How the Ku Klux Klan Helped the Civil Rights Movement* (Lanham, MD: Rowman & Littlefield, 2003), 83–86.

42. Nelson, *Scoop*, 150, 152. Cf. Wyn Craig Wade, *The Fiery Cross: The Ku Klux Klan in America* (New York: Simon and Schuster, 1986), 362–63. Tarrants, who became a repentant born-again Christian while in prison, later discounted the entrapment

issue: "My feelings are . . . that I was a willing participant" (Sims, *The Klan,* 243; cf. Wade, *The Fiery Cross,* 363).

43. Nelson, *Scoop,* 152.

44. Nelson, *Scoop,* 150.

45. George Michael, *Confronting Right-Wing Extremism and Terrorism in the USA* (London: Routledge, 2003), 128. Cf. Wexler and Hancock, *The Awful Grace of God,* 91–95.

46. Jim Douglass, *Gandhi and the Unspeakable* (Maryknoll, NY: Orbis Books, 2012), 83.

47. Hoover gave increasing signs of being out of touch, even senile (Ronald Kessler, *The Bureau: The Secret History of the FBI* [New York: St. Martin's Press, 2002], 172). Meanwhile leadership in the once nonviolent Students for a Democratic Society (SDS) passed to people like Bernardine Dohrn, who said in a 1970 address to an SDS convention, "Offing those rich pigs with their own forks and knives, far out! The Weathermen dig Charles Manson" (Vincent Bugliosi, with Curt Gentry, *Helter Skelter: The True Story of the Manson Murders* [New York: W. W. Norton, 1994], 297).

48. Cf. Ray Wannall's not wholly unfriendly assessment of his former colleague Sullivan: "With respect to some of Sullivan's FBI associates referring to him as 'Crazy Bill,' there surely were signs of certain irrationalities on his part beginning about a year before he retired from the FBI [in 1971]. . . . Those of us who came to know him well felt that he may have suffered a mental collapse the last year or so he was in the Bureau, perhaps brought on by his obsession to become FBI Director" (Ray Wannall, *The Real J. Edgar Hoover: For the Record* [Paducah, KY: Turner, 2000], 146).

49. For example, Anne McClintock, "Paranoid Empire," in Russ Castronovo and Susan Gillman, eds., *States of Emergency: The Object of American Studies* (Chapel Hill: University of North Carolina Press, 2009), 107. Cf. Jane Mayer, *The Dark Side: The Inside Story of How the War on Terror Turned into a War on American Ideals* (New York: Doubleday, 2008), 6: "In the view of some detractors, such as Lawrence Wilkerson, the chief of staff to former Secretary of State Colin Powell, 'Cheney was traumatized by 9/11. The poor guy became paranoid.'"

50. Nassir Ghaemi, *A First-Rate Madness: Uncovering the Links between Leadership and Mental Illness* (New York: Penguin Press, 2013).

51. Gentry, *J. Edgar Hoover,* 621; Scott, *Deep Politics,* 308–9.

52. Frank J. Donner, *The Age of Surveillance: The Aims and Methods of America's Political Intelligence System* (New York: Vintage Books, 1981), 223; quoted in Gentry, *J. Edgar Hoover,* 621–22n: "more specifically it [the FBI] engaged in a conspiracy to deprive individuals of their constitutionally protected rights."

53. "The Hunt for Red Menace:—4, Information Collection & Sharing," Political Research Associates, http://www.publiceye.org/huntred/Hunt_For_Red_Menace-03.html.

54. "By 1970 Sullivan was, largely unbeknownst to Hoover, almost obsessively pursuing factions of the New Left, pushing field offices to open files on every known individual affiliated with SDS or living on a commune. Such excesses were halted

only when they were discovered by another assistant director, Inspection Division head W. Mark Felt" (David Cunningham, *There's Something Happening Here: The New Left, the Klan, and FBI* [Berkeley: University of California Press, 2004], 253).

55. Gentry, *J. Edgar Hoover*, 687–88. Cf. Wannall, *The Real J. Edgar Hoover*, 145–46. The Angleton-Sullivan alliance may have developed after their collaboration in 1964 to establish a common FBI-CIA version of how John F. Kennedy was killed. Cf. Gentry, *J. Edgar Hoover*, 646; Peter Dale Scott, *Oswald, Mexico, and Deep Politics: Revelations from CIA Records on the Assassination of JFK* (Skyhorse Publishing, 2013), 20. However Mark Riebling writes that the Angleton-Sullivan mostly developed (unknown to Hoover) after Hoover terminated its formal liaison with the CIA in 1970 (Mark Riebling, *Wedge: The Secret War between the FBI and CIA* [New York: Alfred A. Knopf, 1994], 276).

56. Gentry, *J. Edgar Hoover*, 670; Nelson, *Scoop*, 157 ("ferret").

57. Gentry, *J. Edgar Hoover*, 670–72. Cf. B. Hersh, *Bobby and J. Edgar*, 500.

58. Loch K. Johnson, *America's Secret Power: The CIA in a Democratic Society* (New York: Oxford University Press, 1989), 145; Joan Hoff, *Nixon Reconsidered* (New York: Basic Books, 1994), 243.

59. "Huston's legacy lived on in a way he could not have anticipated. . . . Nixon had *formally approved* this extension of buggings and break-ins. . . . The president wanted this development; some of the official organs of the state were frustrating his wishes. . . . When in the following year the next peril presented itself, the urge for the White House to take over and run some police functions itself was irresistible" (Fred Emery, *Watergate: The Corruption of American Politics and the Fall of Richard Nixon* [New York: Random House/Times Books, 1994], 28; emphasis in original). Cf. Hoff, *Nixon Reconsidered*, 243–44.

60. Dennis Hevesi, "William Anderson, Navy Hero, Dies at 85," *New York Times*, March 6, 2007.

61. Gentry, *J. Edgar Hoover*, 666.

62. Church Committee, Senate Select Committee to Study Governmental Operations with Respect to Intelligence Activities, *Final Report; Book III—Supplementary Detailed Staff Reports on Intelligence Activities and the Rights of Americans*, (Washington, DC: U.S. Government Printing Office, 1976), especially 10–11, 33–61, https://www.maryferrell.org/mffweb/archive/viewer/showDoc.do?absPageId=149292.

63. The two men (Edward Miller and Mark Felt) were pardoned by Reagan in 1981, while their cases were still on appeal.

64. Michael Crozier, Samuel P. Huntington, and Joji Watanuki, *The Crisis of Democracy: A Report on the Governability of Democracies to the Trilateral Commission* (New York: New York University Press, 1976).

65. John Prados, *Safe for Democracy: The Secret Wars of the CIA* (Chicago: Ivan R. Dee, 2006), 435: "The [Ford] White House saw the [congressional] inquiries as a major threat."

66. Scott, *Road to 9/11*, 57–64; citing Jerry Sanders, *Peddlers of Crisis: The Committee on the Present Danger and the Politics of Containment* (Boston: South End Press, 1983), 61–65, 197–202, etc.; James Carroll, *House of War: The Pentagon and the Disastrous Rise of American Power* (Boston: Houghton Mifflin, 2006), 321–27, etc.

67. David Teacher reports that at a June 1980 Pinay Circle meeting in Zurich, a German member present (Graf Huyn) reported on propaganda arrangements he had made with "with the head of the Saudi security service" (David Teacher, "The Pinay Circle and Destabilisation in Europe," *Lobster* 18, October 1989, http://wikispooks.com/wiki/Document:The_Pinay_Circle); cf. Scott, *Road to 9/11*, 98; Edward S. Herman, *The Terrorism Industry: The Experts and Institutions that Shape Our View of Terror* (New York: Pantheon Books, 1990), 109, 111.

68. Lou Dubose and Jake Bernstein, *Vice: Dick Cheney and the Hijacking of the American Presidency* (New York: Random House, 2006), 36. For an extended analysis of the Ford-Rumsfeld-Cheney-inspired "counterattack" on the various congressional investigations of the FBI and CIA, and its overall success, see Kathryn Olmstead, *Challenging the Secret Government: The Post-Watergate Investigations of the CIA and FBI* (Chapel Hill: University of North Carolina Press, 1996), 147–89.

69. "Veto Battle 30 Years Ago Set Freedom of Information Norms: Scalia, Rumsfeld, Cheney Opposed Open Government Bill," National Security Archive, November 23, 2004, http://www.gwu.edu/~nsarchiv/NSAEBB/NSAEBB142/index.htm.

70. Scott, *Road to 9/11*, especially 50–113; Olmstead, *Challenging the Secret Government*, 177–78.

71. Cf. Olmstead, *Challenging the Secret Government*, 180–81.

72. Scott, *Road to 9/11*, 132: "Wilson even put an extra $200 million into the CIA's Afghan pipeline in 1991, after the Russians had withdrawn from Afghanistan."

73. *Newsweek*, November 30, 1964. Hoover added, off the record, "He is one of the lowest characters in the country" (Church Committee, *Book III*, 157). For the illegalities in Hoover's obsessive campaign to destroy King, see Gentry, *J. Edgar Hoover*, 571–75; Church Committee, *Book III*, 158–61.

74. Wexler and Hancock, *The Awful Grace of God*, 275, etc.

75. This assumes, as I do, that Hoover was not personally involved in the murder of Martin Luther King, Jr. Having surprised myself by coming to this relatively benign assessment of Hoover, I was pleased and again surprised to find it corroborated by Burton Hersh, *Bobby and J. Edgar*, 514–15.

76. Project for the New American Century [PNAC], *Rebuilding America's Defenses: Strategy, Forces and Resources for a New Century* (Washington, DC: Project for the New American Century, [2000]), 51. Contrary to what some have suggested, the focus of this transformation was clearly on forcing the Department of Defense, for the sake of "military preeminence," "to exploit the emerging revolution in military affairs." But to fulfill the Rumsfeld-Cheney-Wolfowitz PNAC agenda of future preemptive wars, it was also vital to shift America to the more robust techniques we have since seen for silencing antiwar opposition.

77. Dana Priest and William Arkin, *Top Secret America: The Rise of the New American Security State* (New York: Little Brown, 2011), 52.

78. Priest and Arkin, *Top Secret America*, 277. No fiscal cliff threatens CACI's growth. In April 2013 its website advertised 1,014 job openings for people with security clearances, along with another 46 job openings with no clearance required.

79. Katrina vanden Heuvel, "The Corporate 'Predator State.'" *Washington Post*, March 26, 2013.

80. Priest and Arkin, *Top Secret America*, 275; quoting CIA general counsel John Rizzo.

81. Judge Richard D. Bennett of the Federal District Court, commenting on the case of NSA whistleblower Thomas Drake, whose felony charges were dropped in exchange for a guilty plea to a misdemeanor. Judge Bennett said that it was "unconscionable" to charge a defendant with a list of serious crimes that could have resulted in thirty-five years in prison, only to drop all of the major charges on the eve of trial. For more on the Drake case, see Jane Mayer, "The Secret Sharer: Is Thomas Drake an Enemy of the State?" *New Yorker*, May 23, 2011, http://www.newyorker.com/magazine/2011/05/23/the-secret-sharer?currentPage=all. Obama's behavior is reminiscent of Jimmy Carter's, who was elected after promising to reduce the defense budget, but presided instead over a huge increase. I suspect that neither president was duplicitous; rather, they are just less powerful than the covert processes over which they preside.

82. Priest and Arkin, *Top Secret America*, 132.

83. Some might wish to add to this list: General MacArthur in 1952 and General Westmoreland in 1968.

84. "In America in particular the share of national income going to the top one percent has followed a great U-shaped arc. Before World War I the one percent received around a fifth of total income in both Britain and the United States. By 1950 that share had been cut by more than half. But since 1980 the one percent has seen its income share surge again—and in the United States it's back to what it was a century ago" (Paul Krugman, "Why We're in a New Gilded Age" [a review of *Capital in the Twenty-First Century* by Thomas Piketty], *New York Review of Books*, May 8, 2014, http://www.nybooks.com/articles/archives/2014/may/08/thomas-piketty-new-gilded-age/). Cf. Bill Moyers and Michael Winship, "Dr. King's 'Two Americas' Truer Now than Ever," Moyers @ Company, April 10, 2013, http://billmoyers.com/2013/04/10/dr-king%E2%80%99s-%E2%80%9Ctwo-americas%E2%80%9D-truer-now-than-ever/: "Walmart's one of those companies laying people off, but according to the website Business Insider, the megachain's CEO Michael Duke gets paid 1,034 times more than his average worker." As a matter of fact, "In the past 30 years, compensation for chief executives in America has increased 127 times faster than the average worker's salary."

85. Adam Mordecai, "9 out of 10 Americans Are Completely Wrong about This Mind-Blowing Fact," http://www.upworthy.com/9-out-of-10-americans-are-completely-wrong-about-this-mind-blowing-fact-2?g=3&c=upw1.

86. Barton Gellman, *Angler: The Cheney Vice Presidency* (New York: Penguin Press, 2008), 299–326 (2004); David S. Cloud, Eric Schmitt, and Thom Shanker, "Rumsfeld Faces Growing Revolt by Retired Generals, *New York Times*, April 13, 2006, http://www.nytimes.com/2006/04/13/washington/13cnd-military.html?_r=0.

87. *Young India*, December 15, 1921; in Mahatma Gandhi, *The Essential Gandhi: His Life, Work, and Ideas: an Anthology* (New York: Vintage, 1963), 150.

88. Mahatma Gandhi, "Towards Realization," in *Works* (Delhi: Publications Division, Ministry of Information and Broadcasting, Govt. of India, [1958]–1994), Vol. 88, 185.

13. WHY AMERICANS MUST END AMERICA'S SELF-GENERATING WARS

1. E.g., Jonathan S. Landay, "Do U.S. drones kill Pakistani extremists or recruit them?" McClatchy Newspapers, April 7, 2009, http://truth-out.org/archive/component/k2/item/83464:do-us-drones-kill-pakistani-extremists-or-recruit-them.

2. Oliver Villar and Drew Cottle, *Cocaine, Death Squads, and the War on Terror: U.S. Imperialism and Class Struggle in Colombia* (New York: Monthly Review Press, 2011); Peter Watt and Roberto Zepeda, *Drug War Mexico: Politics, Neoliberalism and Violence in the New Narcoeconomy* (London: Zed Books, 2012); Mark Karlin, "How the Militarized War on Drugs in Latin America Benefits Transnational Corporations and Undermines Democracy," Truthout, August 5, 2012, http://truth-out.org/news/item/10676-how-the-war-on-drugs-in-latin-america-benefits-transnational-corporations-and-undermines-democracy.

3. Peter Dale Scott, *American War Machine: Deep Politics, the CIA Global Drug Connection, and the Road to Afghanistan* (Lanham, MD: Rowman & Littlefield, 2010), 217–37.

4. Patrick Cockburn, "Opium: Iraq's Deadly New Export," *Independent* (London), May 23, 2007, http://www.independent.co.uk/news/world/middle-east/opium-iraqs-deadly-new-export-449962.html.

5. Scott, *American War Machine*, 134–40.

6. See Karlin, "How the Militarized War on Drugs in Latin America Benefits Transnational Corporations and Undermines Democracy."

7. Sekhar Bandyopadhyay, *From Plassey to Partition: A History of Modern India* (New Delhi: Orient Longman, 2004), 231.

8. Kevin Phillips, *Wealth and Democracy: A Political History of the American Rich* (New York: Broadway Books, 2002), 185.

9. "The seed of imperial ruin and national decay—the unnatural gap between the rich and the poor. . . . the swift increase of vulgar, jobless luxury—are the enemies of Britain" (Winston Churchill, quoted in Phillips, *Wealth and Democracy*, 171).

10. John A. Hobson, *Imperialism* (London: Allen and Unwin, 1902; reprint, 1948), 6. The book's chief impact in Britain at the time was to permanently stunt Hobson's career as an economist.

11. Hobson, *Imperialism*, 12. Cf. Arthur M. Eckstein, "Is There a 'Hobson–Lenin Thesis' on Late Nineteenth-Century Colonial Expansion?" *Economic History Review*, May 1991, 297–318, especially 298–300.

12. Cf. Robert Hall, *Plato (Political Thinkers)* (New York: HarperCollins, 1981), 4.

13. Some in the establishment share this anxiety: see Loren Thompson, "Four Ways the Ukraine Crisis Could Escalate to Use of Nuclear Weapons," *Forbes*, April 24, 2014, http://www.forbes.com/sites/lorenthompson/2014/04/24/four-ways-the-ukraine-crisis-could-escalate-to-use-of-nuclear-weapons/.

14. See Ralph Raico, "Introduction," *Great Wars and Great Leaders: A Libertarian Rebuttal* (Auburn, AL: Ludwig von Mises Institute, 2010), http://mises.org/daily/5088/Neither-the-Wars-Nor-the-Leaders-Were-Great.

15. Carroll Quigley, *Tragedy and Hope: A History of the World in Our Time* (San Pedro, CA: GSG & Associates, 1975); Carroll Quigley, *The Anglo-American Establishment* (GSG & Associates Publishers, 1981), http://www.thirdworldtraveler

.com/New_World_Order/Anglo_American_Estab.html. Discussion in Laurence H. Shoup and William Minter, *The Imperial Brain Trust: The Council on Foreign Relations & United States Foreign Policy* (New York: Monthly Review Press, 1977), 12–14; Michael Parenti, *Contrary Notions: The Michael Parenti Reader* (San Francisco: City Lights Books, 2007), 332.

16. For the little-noticed interest of oil companies in Cambodian offshore oilfields, see Peter Dale Scott, *The War Conspiracy: JFK, 9/11, and the Deep Politics of War* (New York: Skyhorse Publishing, 2013), 216–37.

17. Thomas Pakenham, *Scramble for Africa: The White Man's Conquest of the Dark Continent from 1876–1912* (New York: Random House, 1991).

18. See books by Barbara Tuchman, notably *The Guns of August* (New York, Macmillan, 1962), and *The March of Folly: From Troy to Vietnam* (New York: Alfred A. Knopf, 1984).

19. Pakenham, *Scramble for Africa*.

20. E. Oncken, *Panzersprung nach Agadir: Die deutsche Politik wehrend der zweiten Marokkokrise 1911* (Düsseldorf, 1981). *Panzersprung* in German has come to be a metaphor for any gratuitous exhibition of gunboat diplomacy.

21. Thom Shanker, "Global Arms Sales Dropped Sharply in 2010, Study Finds," *New York Times,* September 23, 2011.

22. Thom Shanker, "U.S. Arms Sales Make Up Most of Global Market," *New York Times*, August 27, 2012 .

23. Stephen Ambrose, *Eisenhower: Soldier and President* (New York: Simon and Schuster, 1990), 325.

24. Robert Dallek, *An Unfinished Life: John F. Kennedy, 1917–1963* (Boston: Little, Brown and Co., 2003), 50.

25. William Arkin: *American Coup: How a Terrified Government Is Destroying the Constitution* (Boston: Little Brown, 2013), 14.

26. Jane Mayer, *The Dark Side: The Inside Story of How the War on Terror Turned into a War on American Ideals* (New York: Doubleday, 2008), 114.

27. Richard J. Aldrich, "America Used Islamists to Arm the Bosnian Muslims," *Guardian* (London), April 21, 2002; summarizing Cees Wiebes, *Intelligence and the War in Bosnia* (Münster, DE: LIT Verlag, 2003).

28. Shanker, "U.S. Arms Sales Make Up Most of Global Market," *New York Times*, August 27, 2012.

29. David E. Spiro, *The Hidden Hand of American Hegemony: Petrodollar Recycling and International Markets* (Ithaca, NY: Cornell University Press), 1999, x; Peter Dale Scott, *The Road to 9/11: Wealth, Empire, and the Future of America* (Berkeley: University of California Press, 2007), 41–42.

30. Scott Shane and Andrew W. Lehren, "Leaked Cables Offer Raw Look at U.S. Diplomacy," *New York Times*, November 29, 2010. Cf. Nick Fielding and Sarah Baxter, "Saudi Arabia is Hub of World Terror: The Desert Kingdom Supplies the Cash and the Killers," *Times* (London), 2007, hhttp://www.thesundaytimes.co.uk/sto/news/world_news/article74750.ece.

31. The United Nations has listed the branch offices in Indonesia and the Philippines of the Rabita's affiliate, the International Islamic Relief Organization, as belonging to or associated with al-Qaeda.

32. "A former head of intelligence for the Transitional National Council in Libya . . . said that extremist militia in Libya were financing militant groups in Mali and al Qaeda in the Islamic Maghreb as well as providing them with logistical support" (Paul Cruickshank and Tim Lister, "Algeria Attack May Have Link to Libya Camps," CNN, January 23, 2013, http://www.cnn.com/2013/01/18/world/africa/algeria-attackers/).

33. Mayer, *The Dark Side*, 114.

34. See Mark Curtis, *Secret Affairs: Britain's Collusion with Radical Islam* (London: Profile, 2011), 237–47; also Peter Dale Scott, "Bosnia, Kosovo, and Now Libya: The Human Costs of Washington's On-Going Collusion with Terrorists," Asian-Pacific Journal: Japan Focus, July 29, 2011, http://japanfocus.org/-Peter_Dale-Scott/3578; Paul L. Williams, *The Al Qaeda Connection: International Terrorism, Organized Crime, and the Coming Apocalypse* (Amherst, NY: Prometheus Books, 2005), 68–89; William Blum, "The United States and Its Comrade-in-Arms, Al Qaeda," Counterpunch, August 13, 2012, http://www.counterpunch.org/2012/08/13/tales-of-an-empire-gone-mad/.

35. Christopher Boucek, "Yemen: Avoiding a Downward Spiral," Carnegie Endowment for International Peace, 2009, 12. President Saleh was using al-Qaedists to combat dissident remnants from the former socialist republic of South Yemen, with which North Yemen had nominally merged in 1990.

36. "In Yemen, 'Too Many Guns and Too Many Grievances' as President Clings to Power," PBS Newshour, March 21, 2011, http://www.pbs.org/newshour/bb/world/jan-june11/yemen_03-21.html.

37. Robert Lacey, *The Kingdom: Arabia and the House of Sa'ud* (New York: Avon, 1981), 346–47, 361.

38. John Kerry, *Al Qaeda in Yemen and Somalia: A Ticking Time Bomb: A Report to the Committee on Foreign Relations* (Washington, DC: U.S. Government Printing Office, 2010), 10.

39. Scott, *The Road to 9/11*, 152–56.

40. Curtin Winsor, "Saudi Arabia, Wahhabism and the Spread of Sunni Theofascism," *Islam Daily*, August 3, 2007, http://www.islamdaily.org/en/wahabism/5807.saudi-arabia-wahhabism-and-the-spread-of-sunni-the.htm.

41. Shane and Lehren, "Leaked Cables Offer Raw Look at U.S. Diplomacy."

42. Nick Fielding and Sarah Baxter, "Saudi Arabia is Hub of World Terror," *Sunday Times* (London), November 4, 2007: "Extremist clerics provide a stream of recruits to some of the world's nastiest trouble spots. An analysis by NBC News suggested that the Saudis make up 55% of foreign fighters in Iraq. They are also among the most uncompromising and militant."

43. Rachel Ehrenfeld, "Al-Qaeda's Source of Funding from Drugs and Extortion Little Affected by bin Laden's Death," Cutting Edge, May 9, 2011, http://www.thecuttingedgenews.com/index.php?article=51969&pageid=20&pagename=Security.

44. *Sunday Times* (London), November 4, 2007.

45. BBC, July 17, 2012, http://www.bbc.co.uk/news/world-africa-18870130.

46. Al Jazeera, July 19, 2012, http://m.aljazeera.com/SE/201271012301347496.

47. "Newsweek, Richard Cohen, and More," *The Weekly Standard*, May 30, 2005, http://www.weeklystandard.com/Content/Public/Articles/000/000/005/642eforh.asp. Cf. *Newsweek*, May 30, 2005.

48. David Ottaway, "The King and Us: U.S.-Saudi Relations in the Wake of 9/11," *Foreign Affairs*, May-June 2009. Cf. David B. Ottaway, *King's Messenger: Prince Bandar bin Sultan and America's Tangled Relationship with Saudi Arabia* (New York: Walker, 2008), 236–38, 262–63.

49. Barak Ravid, "U.S. Envoy: Arab Peace Initiative Will Be Part of Obama Policy," *Haaretz*, April 5, 2009; Ottaway, "The King and Us."

50. Charles Krauthammer, "At Last, Zion: Israel and the Fate of the Jews," *Weekly Standard*, May 11, 1998.

51. The term "War on Terror" is no longer officially used by the Obama administration (which instead uses the term Overseas Contingency Operation). But it is still commonly used by politicians, in the media and by some aspects of government officially, such as the United States's Global War on Terrorism Service Medal. The continuity with past policies of the global war on terrorism is unmistakable.

52. "We have no idea how such a war would end," [Brzezinski] said. "Iran has military capabilities, it could retaliate by destabilizing Iraq" (Salon, March 14, 2012, http://www.salon.com/2012/03/14/former_bush_official_warns_against_iran_attack/).

53. See Jennifer Daskal and Stephen I. Vladek, "After the AUMF," *Harvard National Security Journal*, 2014, 115–46, http://harvardnsj.org/wp-content/uploads/2014/01/Daskal-Vladeck-Final1.pdf.

54. See Scott, *The Road to 9/11*, 183–242; also chapter 3 of this book.

55. Peter Dale Scott, *Drugs, Oil, and War: The United States in Afghanistan, Colombia, and Indochina* (Lanham, MD: Rowman & Littlefield, 2003), 40, 100; Scott, *The War Conspiracy*, 324, 377.

56. Scott, *The Road to 9/11*, 183–87.

Selected Bibliography

Note: A more complete bibliography can be found at http://www.peterdalescott.net/ADSbib.html.

BOOKS

Arkin, William. *American Coup: How a Terrified Government Is Destroying the Constitution.* New York: Little Brown, 2013.

Bacevich, Andrew. *American Empire: The Realities and Consequences of U.S. Diplomacy.* Cambridge, MA: Harvard University Press, 2002.

Baer, Robert. *See No Evil: The True Story of a Ground Soldier in the CIA's War on Terrorism.* New York: Crown, 2002.

Baer, Robert. *Sleeping with the Devil.* New York: Crown, 2003.

Balko, Radley. *Rise of the Warrior Cop: The Militarization of America's Police Forces.* New York: PublicAffairs, 2013.

Bamford, James. *A Pretext for War: 9/11, Iraq, and the Abuse of America's Intelligence Agencies.* New York: Doubleday, 2004.

Berger, J. M. *Jihad Joe: Americans Who Go to War in the Name of Islam.* Washington, DC: Potomac Books, 2011.

Bird, Kai. *The Chairman: John J. McCloy—The Making of the American Establishment.* New York: Simon & Schuster, 1992.

Bronson, Rachel. *Thicker than Oil: America's Uneasy Partnership with Saudi Arabia.* Oxford: Oxford University Press, 2006.

Carroll, James. *House of War: The Pentagon and the Disastrous Rise of American Power.* Boston: Houghton Mifflin, 2006.

Castronovo, Russ, and Susan Gillman, eds. *States of Emergency: The Object of American Studies.* Chapel Hill: University of North Carolina Press, 2009.

Chomsky, Noam. *The Essential Chomsky.* Edited by Anthony Arnove. New York: New Press, 2008.

Clarke, Richard. *Against All Enemies: Inside America's War on Terror.* New York: Free Press, 2004.

Cockburn, Andrew. *Rumsfeld: His Rise, Fall, and Catastrophic Legacy.* New York: Scribner, 2007.

Coll, Steve. *The Bin Ladens: An Arabian Family in the American Century*. New York: Penguin Press, 2008.

Coll, Steve. *Ghost Wars: The Secret History of the CIA, Afghanistan, and bin Laden, from the Soviet Invasion to September 10, 2001*. New York: Penguin Press, 2004.

Colodny, Len, and Tom Shachtman. *The Forty Years War: The Rise and Fall of the Neocons, from Nixon to Obama* (New York: HarperCollins, 2009).

Cooley, John. *Unholy Wars: Afghanistan, America, and International Terrorism*. London: Pluto Press, 1999.

Cooper, Andrew Scott. *The Oil Kings: How the U.S., Iran, and Saudi Arabia Changed the Balance of Power in the Middle East*. New York: Simon & Schuster, 2011.

Curtis, Mark. *Secret Affairs: Britain's Collusion with Radical Islam*. London: Profile, 2011.

Donner, Frank J. *The Age of Surveillance: The Aims and Methods of America's Political Intelligence System*. New York: Vintage Books, 1981.

Dorrien, Gary. *Imperial Designs: Neoconservatism and the New Pax Americana*. New York: Routledge, 2004.

Dorril, Stephen. *MI6: Inside the Covert World of Her Majesty's Secret Intelligence Service*. New York: Free Press, 2000.

Dreyfuss, Robert. *Devil's Game: How the United States Helped Unleash Fundamentalist Islam*. New York: Metropolitan Books, 2005.

Dubose, Lou, and Jake Bernstein. *Vice: Dick Cheney and the Hijacking of the American Presidency*. New York: Random House, 2006.

Ellsberg, Daniel. *Secrets: A Memoir of Vietnam and the Pentagon Papers*. New York: Viking, 2002.

Feinstein, Andrew. *The Shadow World: Inside the Global Arms Trade*. New York: Farrar, Straus and Giroux, 2011.

Fenton, Kevin. *Disconnecting the Dots*. Walterville, OR: TrineDay, 2011.

Gentry, Curt. *J. Edgar Hoover: The Man and the Secrets*. New York: W. W. Norton, 1991.

Greenwald, Glenn. *No Place to Hide: Edward Snowden, the NSA, and the U.S. Surveillance State*. New York: Metropolitan Books/Henry Holt, 2014.

Griffin, David Ray. *The New Pearl Harbor Revisited: 9/11, the Cover-Up, and the Exposé*. Northampton, MA: Olive Branch Press, 2008.

Hancock, Larry, and Stuart Wexler. *Shadow Warfare: The History of America's Undeclared Wars*. Berkeley, CA: Counterpoint Press, 2014.

Herman, Edward S. *The Terrorism Industry: The Experts and Institutions that Shape Our View of Terror*. New York: Pantheon Books, 1990.

Hersh, Burton. *Bobby and J. Edgar: The Historic Face-Off between the Kennedys and J. Edgar Hoover that Transformed America*. New York: Carroll & Graf, 2007.

Hogan, Michael J. *A Cross of Iron: Harry S. Truman and the Origins of the National Security State, 1945–1954*. Cambridge: Cambridge University Press, 1998.

Johnson, Chalmers. *The Sorrows of Empire: Militarism, Secrecy and the End of the Republic*. New York: Metropolitan/Henry Holt, 2004.

Juhasz, Antonia. *The Tyranny of Oil: The World's Most Powerful Industry—and What We Must Do to Stop It*. New York: HarperCollins/William Morrow, 2008.

Kohlmann, Evan. *Al-Qaida's Jihad in Europe.* New York: Berg, 2004.

Lacey, Robert. *Inside the Kingdom: Kings, Clerics, Modernists, Terrorists, and the Struggle for Saudi Arabia.* New York: Penguin Books, 2009.

Lance, Peter. *Triple Cross: How bin Laden's Master Spy Penetrated the CIA, the Green Berets, and the FBI—and Why Patrick Fitzgerald Failed to Stop Him.* New York: Regan, 2006.

Levine, Steve. *The Oil and the Glory: The Pursuit of Empire and Fortune on the Caspian Sea.* New York: Random House, 2007.

MacQueen, Graeme. *The 2001 Anthrax Deception: The Case for a Domestic Conspiracy.* Atlanta, GA: Clarity Press, 2014.

Mann, James. *The Rise of the Vulcans: The History of Bush's War Cabinet.* New York: Viking, 2004.

Mayer, Jane. *The Dark Side: The Inside Story of How the War on Terror Turned into a War on American Ideals.* New York: Doubleday, 2008.

Mazzetti, Mark. *The Way of the Knife: The CIA, a Secret Army, and a War at the Ends of the Earth.* New York: Penguin Press, 2013.

Noah, Timothy. *The Great Divergence: America's Growing Inequality Crisis and What We Can Do about It.* New York: Bloomsbury Press, 2012.

Olmstead, Kathryn. *Challenging the Secret Government: The Post-Watergate Investigations of the CIA and FBI.* Chapel Hill: University of North Carolina Press, 1996.

Ottaway, David B. *The King's Messenger: Prince Bandar bin Sultan and America's Tangled Relationship with Saudi Arabia.* New York: Walker, 2008.

Parenti, Michael. *Contrary Notions: The Michael Parenti Reader.* San Francisco: City Lights Books, 2007.

Parmar, Inderjeet. *Foundations of the American Century: The Ford, Carnegie, and Rockefeller Foundations in the Rise of American Power.* New York: Columbia University Press, 2012.

Parry, Robert. *Secrecy and Privilege: Rise of the Bush Dynasty from Watergate to Iraq.* Arlington, VA: Media Consortium, 2004.

Parry, Robert. *Trick or Treason: The October Surprise Mystery.* New York: Sheridan Square Press, 1993.

Peters, Gretchen. *Seeds of Terror: How Heroin Is Bankrolling the Taliban and Al Qaeda.* New York: Thomas Dunne Books, 2009.

Phillips, Kevin. *The Politics of Rich and Poor: Wealth and the American Electorate in the Reagan Aftermath.* New York: HarperCollins, 1991.

Phillips, Kevin. *Wealth and Democracy: A Political History of the American Rich.* New York: Broadway Books, 2002.

Prados, John. *Safe for Democracy: The Secret Wars of the CIA.* Chicago: Ivan R. Dee, 2006.

Priest, Dana, and William Arkin. *Top Secret America: The Rise of the New American Security State.* New York: Little Brown, 2011.

Risen, James. *State of War: The Secret History of the CIA and the Bush Administration.* New York: Free Press, 2006.

Rothkopf, David J. *Superclass: The Global Power Elite and the World They Are Making.* New York: Farrar, Straus and Giroux, 2008.

Ryan, Kevin Robert. *Another Nineteen: Investigating Legitimate 9/11 Suspects*. Microbloom, 2013.

Sanders, Jerry. *Peddlers of Crisis: The Committee on the Present Danger and the Politics of Containment*. Boston: South End Press, 1983.

Scahill, Jeremy. *Dirty Wars: The World Is a Battlefield*. New York: Nation Books, 2013.

Schell, Jonathan. *The Unconquerable World: Power, Nonviolence, and the Will of the People*. New York: Metropolitan Books, 2003.

Scott, Peter Dale. *American War Machine: Deep Politics, the CIA Global Drug Connection, and the Road to Afghanistan*. Lanham, MD: Rowman & Littlefield, 2010.

Scott, Peter Dale. *Deep Politics and the Death of JFK*. Berkeley: University of California Press, 1998.

Scott, Peter Dale. *Drugs, Oil, and War: The United States in Afghanistan, Colombia, and Indochina*. Lanham, MD: Rowman & Littlefield, 2003.

Scott, Peter Dale. *The Road to 9/11: Wealth, Empire, and the Future of America*. Berkeley: University of California Press, 2007.

Scott, Peter Dale. *The War Conspiracy: JFK, 9/11, and the Deep Politics of War*. New York: Skyhorse Publishing, 2013.

Sherrill, Robert. *The Oil Follies of 1970–1980: How the Petroleum Industry Stole the Show (and Much More Besides)*. Garden City, NY: Anchor Press/Doubleday, 1983.

Shorrock, Tim. *Spies for Hire: The Secret World of Intelligence Outsourcing*. New York: Simon & Schuster, 2008.

Soufan, Ali H. *The Black Banners: The Inside Story of 9/11 and the War against al-Qaeda*. New York: W. W. Norton, 2011.

Srodes, James. *Allen Dulles: Master of Spies*. Washington, DC: Henry Regnery, 1999.

Stein, Judith. *Pivotal Decade: How the United States Traded Factories for Finance in the Seventies*. New Haven, CT: Yale University Press, 2010.

Summers, Anthony. *Official and Confidential: The Secret Life of J. Edgar Hoover*. New York: G. P. Putnam's Sons, 1993.

Summers, Anthony, with Robbyn Swan, *The Arrogance of Power: The Secret World of Richard Nixon*. New York: Viking Penguin, 2000.

Summers, Anthony, and Robbyn Swan. *The Eleventh Day: The Full Story of 9/11 and Osama bin Laden*. New York: Ballantine Books, 2011.

Theoharis, Athan, ed. *The FBI: A Comprehensive Reference Guide*. Phoenix, AZ: Oryx Press, 1999.

Theoharis, Athan G. *The FBI & American Democracy: A Brief Critical History*. Lawrence: University Press of Kansas, 2004.

Trapp, Kimberley N. *State Responsibility for International Terrorism*. New York: Oxford University Press, 2011.

Trento, Joseph J. *Prelude to Terror: The Rogue CIA and the Legacy of America's Private Intelligence Network*. New York: Carroll and Graf, 2005.

Warde, Ibrahim. *The Price of Fear: The Truth behind the Financial War on Terror*. Berkeley: University of California Press, 2007.

Wawro, Geoffrey. *Quicksand: America's Pursuit of Power in the Middle East*. New York: Penguin Press, 2010.

Weiner, Tim. *Enemies: A History of the FBI*. New York: Random House, 2012.

Weiner, Tim. *Legacy of Ashes: The History of the CIA*. New York: Doubleday, 2007.

Wilford, Hugh. *America's Great Game: The CIA's Secret Arabists and the Shaping of the Modern Middle East*. New York: Basic Books, 2013.

Wilson, Eric, ed. *The Dual State: Parapolitics, Carl Schmitt and the National Security Complex*. Farnham, UK: Ashgate, 2012.

Wilson, Eric, and Tim Lindsey, eds. *Government of the Shadows: Parapolitics and Criminal Sovereignty*. London: Pluto Press, 2008.

Wright, Lawrence. *The Looming Tower: Al-Qaeda and the Road to 9/11*. New York: Alfred A. Knopf, 2006.

Yetiv, Steven A. *The Petroleum Triangle: Oil, Globalization, and Terror*. Ithaca, NY: Cornell University Press, 2011.

Zegart, Amy B. *Flawed by Design: The Evolution of the CIA, JCS, and NSC*. Stanford, CA: Stanford University Press, 1999.

REPORTS

Joint Congressional Inquiry into Intelligence Community Activities before and after the Terrorist Attacks of September 11, 2001, *Report*, 107th Congress, 2nd Session, S. Rept. 107-351 and H. Rept. 107-792, 173–77, http:// www.gpo.gov/fdsys/search/pagedetails.action?browsePath=107/HRPT/ [700%3b799]&granuleId=CRPT-107hrpt792&packageId=CRPT-107hrpt792.

National Commission on Terrorist Attacks upon the United States. *The 9/11 Commission Report*. New York: W. W. Norton, 2004. http://www.9-11commission.gov/report/911Report.pdf.

President's Commission on the Assassination of President Kennedy [Warren Commission], *Hearings*, https://www.maryferrell.org/mffweb/archive/docset/getList.do?docSetId=1006.

Senate Select Committee to Study Governmental Operations with Respect to Intelligence Activities [Church Committee], *Final Report; Book I—Foreign and Military Intelligence; Book II—Intelligence Activities and the Rights of Americans; Book III—Supplementary Detailed Staff Reports on Intelligence Activities and the Rights of Americans*. Washington, DC: U.S. Government Printing Office, 1976. https://www.maryferrell.org/mffweb/archive/docset/getList.do?docSetId=1014.

ARTICLES

Karlin, Mark. "How the Militarized War on Drugs in Latin America Benefits Transnational Corporations and Undermines Democracy." Truthout, August 5, 2012. http://truth-out.org/news/item/10676-how-the-war-on-drugs-in-latin-america-benefits-transnational-corporations-and-undermines-democracy.

Krugman, Paul. "Why We're in a New Gilded Age" [a review of *Capital in the Twenty-First Century* by Thomas Piketty]. *New York Review of Books*, May 8, 2014. http://www.nybooks.com/articles/archives/2014/may/08/thomas-piketty-new-gilded-age/.

Lofgren, Mike. "A Shadow Government Controls America." Reader Supported News, February 22, 2014. http://readersupportednews.org/opinion2/277-75/22216-a-shadow-government-controls.

Tunander, Ola. "Democratic State vs. Deep State: Approaching the Dual State of the West." In *Government of the Shadows: Parapolitics and Criminal Sovereignty*, edited by Eric Wilson and Tim Lindsey. London: Pluto Press, 2008, 56–72.

Permissions

Earlier versions of these chapters originally appeared as follows:

Chapter 1: "The Doomsday Project, Deep Events, and the Shrinking of American Democracy," Asia-Pacific Journal: Japan Focus, January 24, 2011, http://japanfocus.org/-Peter_Dale-Scott/3476.

Chapter 2: "The Deep State and the Wall Street Overworld," Asia-Pacific Journal: Japan Focus, March 10, 2014, http://japanfocus.org/-Peter_Dale-Scott/4090.

Chapter 3: "Is the State of Emergency Superseding our Constitution? Continuity of Government Planning, War and American Society," Asia-Pacific Journal: Japan Focus, November 28, 2010, http://japanfocus.org/-Peter_Dale-Scott/3448.

Chapters 4, 5, and 6: "The Falsified War on Terror: How the US Has Protected Some of Its Enemies," Japan Focus: Asia-Pacific Journal, October 7, 2013, http://japanfocus.org/-Peter_Dale-Scott/4005.

Chapter 7: "Launching the U.S. Terror War: The CIA, 9/11, Afghanistan, and Central Asia," The Asia-Pacific Journal: Japan Focus, March 15, 2012, http://japanfocus.org/-Peter_Dale-Scott/3723.

Chapter 9: "The Doomsday Project and Deep Events: JFK, Watergate, Iran-Contra, and 9/11," The Asia-Pacific Journal: Japan Focus, November 21, 2011, http://japanfocus.org/-Peter_Dale-Scott/3650.

Chapter 10: "The American Deep State, Deep Events, and Off-the-Books Financing," The Asia-Pacific Journal: Japan Focus, April 7, 2014, http://japanfocus.org//-Peter_Dale-Scott/4104.

Chapter 11: "The Unchecked Security State: Part I: The Toxic Legacy of Hoover's Illicit Powers," The Asia-Pacific Journal: Japan Focus, April 29, 2013, http://japanfocus.org/-Peter_Dale-Scott/3932.

Chapter 12: "The Unchecked Security State: Part II: The Continuity of COG Detention Planning, 1948–2001," The Asia-Pacific Journal: Japan Focus, April 29, 2013, http://japanfocus.org/-Peter_Dale-Scott/3933.

Chapter 13: "Why Americans Must End America's Self-Generating Wars," Asia-Pacific Journal: Japan Focus, August 26, 2012, http://japanfocus.org/-Peter_Dale-Scott/3819.

Index

About the Author

Peter Dale Scott, a former Canadian diplomat and professor of English at the University of California, Berkeley, is a poet, writer, and researcher. His diplomatic service included two years of work at the U.N. General Assembly and U.N. conferences and two years in Poland. An antiwar speaker and nonviolent activist during the Vietnam and Gulf Wars, he was a cofounder of the Peace and Conflict Studies Program at UC Berkeley.

Scott's books have been translated into seven languages, including Russian and Bahasa Indonesia. His articles and poetry have been translated into twenty languages, including Turkish, Arabic, Farsi, Chinese, and Japanese. His most recent political books are *The Road to 9/11: Wealth, Empire, and the Future of America* (2007), *American War Machine: Deep Politics, the CIA Global Drug Connection, and the Road to Afghanistan* (2010), and *The War Conspiracy: JFK, 9/11 and the Deep Politics of War* (2008, 2013).

Other political books have focused on war, covert operations, the politics of crime, and the international drug traffic. They include *The Politics of Escalation in Vietnam* (in collaboration, 1966); *Deep Politics and the Death of JFK* (1993, 1998); *The United States and the Overthrow of Sukarno, 1965–1967* (published four times in Indonesian); *The Iran-Contra Connection* (in collaboration, 1987); *Cocaine Politics: Drugs, Armies, and the CIA in Central America* (in collaboration, 1991); and *Drugs, Oil, and War: The United States in Afghanistan, Colombia, and Indochina* (2003).

Further books on the John F. Kennedy assassination include *Crime and Cover-Up: The CIA, the Mafia, and the Dallas-Watergate Connection* (1977); *Oswald, Mexico, and Deep Politics* (1995, 2013); and *The Assassinations: Dallas and Beyond* (in collaboration, 1976).

Peter Dale Scott is also a poet and in 2002 received the Lannan Poetry Award. His poetry volumes include *Coming to Jakarta: A Poem about Terror* (1989), *Listening to the Candle: A Poem on Impulse* (1992), *Crossing Borders:*

Selected Shorter Poems (1994), *Minding the Darkness: A Poem for the Year 2000* (October 2000), *Mosaic Orpheus* (2009), and *Tilting Point* (2012). With Czeslaw Milosz, he translated and published the first translations into English of the Polish poet Zbigniew Herbert.

The former U.S. poet laureate Robert Hass has written (*Agni*, 31/32 [1990], 335) that "*Coming to Jakarta* is the most important political poem to appear in the English language in a very long time."

WAR AND PEACE LIBRARY

Series Editor: Mark Selden